The Peasants' Revolt of 1381

History in Depth

GENERAL EDITOR: G. A. Williams

Henry S. Wilson: Origins of West African Nationalism
R. B. Dobson: The Peasants' Revolt of 1381
J. R. Pole: The Revolution in America 1754–1788
D. S. Chambers: Patrons and Artists in the Italian Renaissance

IN PREPARATION
R. Martin: The General Strike
R. C. Mettam: State and Society of Louis XIV
B. Harrison: Robert Lowery: Portraits of a Radical
Hans Koch: Das Volk
Raphael Samuel: The Victorian Underworld
H. C. Porter: Puritanism in Tudor England
Dorothy Thompson: The Early Chartists
Lionel Butler: The Fourth Crusade
W. H. Hargreaves-Mawdsley: Spain under the Bourbons 1700–1833

The Peasants' Revolt of 1381

R. B. DOBSON

Senior Lecturer in History, University of York

MACMILLAN
ST MARTIN'S PRESS

Selection and editorial matter © R. B. Dobson 1970

First published 1970 by
MACMILLAN AND CO LTD
Little Essex Street London WC2
and also at Bombay Calcutta and Madras
Macmillan South Africa (Publishers) Pty Ltd Johannesburg
The Macmillan Company of Australia Pty Ltd Melbourne
The Macmillan Company of Canada Ltd Toronto
St Martin's Press Inc New York
Gill and Macmillan Ltd Dublin

Library of Congress catalog card no. 78-118571

SBN (boards) 333 09139 6
(paper) 333 10285 1

Printed in Great Britain by
THE PITMAN PRESS
Bath

To my mother and in memory of my father

Contents

Acknowledgements

I am grateful to the copyright owners and publishers of the following volumes, who have kindly given permission to reproduce excerpts in the original or translation:

Columbia University Press, New York, *Chaucer's World*, compiled by E. Rickert; *Historical Poems of the XIVth and XVth Centuries*, ed. R. H. Robbins.

Longmans, Green & Co., *England under the Lancastrians*, ed. J. H. Flemming.

Manchester University Press, *The Anonimalle Chronicle, 1333–1381*, ed. V. H. Galbraith.

Oxford University Press, *Fourteenth Century Verse and Prose*, ed. K. Sisam; *The Great Revolt of 1381*, by C. Oman.

Translations from Crown-copyright records in the Public Record Office, London, are printed by permission of the Controller of H.M. Stationery Office.

General Editor's Preface

Historical perception demands immediacy and depth. These qualities are lost in attempts at broad general survey; for the reader of history depth is the only true breadth. Each volume in this series, therefore, explores an important historical problem in depth. There is no artificial uniformity; each volume is shaped by the problem it tackles. The past bears its own witness; the core of each volume is a major collection of original material (translated into English where necessary) as alive, as direct and as full as possible. The reader should feel the texture of the past. The volume editor provides interpretative notes and introduction and a full working bibliography. The volume will stand in its own right as a 'relived experience' and will also serve as a point of entry into a wider area of historical discourse. In taking possession of a particular historical world, the reader will move more freely in a wider universe of historical experience.

*

In this volume Dr R. B. Dobson examines in depth one of the most dramatic and celebrated episodes in English and European history, the Peasants' Revolt of 1381. Here, for the first time, are made available sequences of evidence in depth which enable the reader to reconstruct the crisis for himself. The volume stands as a vital contribution to the history of medieval society and to the history of 'pre-industrial' revolt in general.

The core of the volume is the Revolt itself. The social and economic experience of the fourteenth-century peasantry, too complex to lend itself to full documentation, finds expression in a number of significant documents – statutes, petitions, chronicles, poems – which give the reader a grip on realities and then the documentation bodies out into a vivid, rich, complex and contradictory narrative, a re-living of experience, almost a symphony of discord.

The structure of the book is narrative; the reader can 'read the story' for himself. The most striking feature of this narrative is the wealth of sources employed. Four or five chroniclers, often contradictory, are brought to bear on every important incident; significant and often colourful evidence is presented from government and judicial records. The first outbreaks over the Poll Taxes, the risings in Kent and Essex, the celebrated entry into London and the death of Wat Tyler are covered in all their fullness and complexity. The great bulk of the material has been newly translated, and often for the first time, from the original Latin and Norman-French. The scope of the collection extends to detailed coverage of the risings in the Eastern counties and to areas which have in the past escaped the historian. Perhaps most striking of all is the reconstruction of the repression, not only from chronicles but from commissions and individual trials, and the recovery of a tradition of peasant struggle, with a suggestion of comparison with the German revolt in the sixteenth century.

For while Dr Dobson eschews any crude sociology of revolt, he is not content with narrative, however remarkable in its totality. A final section on interpretations of the revolt ranges from contemporary comment, through Gower, Burke and Paine, to William Morris and Friedrich Engels and adds a whole dimension to the reader's perception. The student of history, it has been said, should read documents until he hears their authors speaking; here, on the Peasants' Revolt, and for the first time, he can do just that; and directly, for the literature of protest, the dark and enigmatic songs of rebels are given him. 'We are the People of England', said Chesterton, 'That never have spoken yet.' Here, some of them, in a hurling time of our history, find voice.

GWYN A. WILLIAMS

Preface

My first and greatest debt is to Professor Gwyn Williams of the University of York, the general editor and founding-father of this series. This book owes its genesis to his original conception of a collection of documents which might enable students to analyse precise historical problems in depth and hence avoid the dangers of 'that wilderness of general surveys from which we are all trying to escape'. In this respect at least I have observed the spirit as well as the letter of Professor Williams's original commission; for, as the reader will soon be aware, there is little that is 'general' about this book. The great revolt of 1381 – as I try to show in my short introduction to the documents – might serve as an excellent representative instance of the popular rebellion in pre-industrial Western Europe. But the primary purpose of this volume is to reveal the distinctive rather than symbolic significance of what was, after all, a unique and unparalleled catastrophe in English history.

The Peasants' Revolt of 1381 is a subject for which it is genuinely possible to 'let the documents tell the story' – hence its appearance in this series. I have accordingly adopted as a general principle the translation of as many documents as possible in their entirety rather than the inclusion of a long series of fragmentary extracts from many sources. As the course of events in 1381 is related in all its complexity by contemporary participants and observers themselves, I have made no attempt to re-tell the story in my introduction, which is confined to a quite brief consideration of the problems raised by the rebellion and its original authorities. The more technical issues are discussed in short introductions to each document, in which I assess the reliability of a particular source and its implications for the study of the great revolt. Footnotes have been used as sparingly as possible but are introduced where further elucidation of the text appeared helpful. It seemed important not to allow the theories and interpretations of recent historians to intervene between the original sources and the reader. Therefore the last document in the book is an extract from William Morris's *Dream of John Ball*, published in 1888, that is just before the intensive modern academic study of the Peasants' Revolt began. For the most important secondary works written since that date the reader is referred to the books and articles listed in Sections 4 and 6 of the bibliography. These provide a detailed guide to the issues raised in the following pages, especially if read in the light of Professor Postan's very recent warning 'against too naïve or too economic a sociology of rebellion – a sociology which considers every rebellion as a direct reaction to intensified oppression or deepening poverty'.

The obligations incurred by me during the compilation of this book are too numerous to be acknowledged in full. But I would like to mention the name of Professor Williams once again, this time for his continued support and interest, without which the collection of documents would never have been completed. His own enthusiasm for revolutionary activity has at times had a greater influence on my choice of documents than either of us expected. I also owe much to my other colleagues in the History Department at York, particularly to Professor G. E. Aylmer, Professor G. Leff, Dr M. C. Cross, Dr M. J. Angold and Mr P. Rycraft. Dr G. A. Holmes was kind enough to look at my typescript at short notice and suggest various additions. My thanks also go to Professor L. H. Butler and his fellow members of the Medieval History Department at the University of St Andrews where I gave my first lecture on the Peasants' Revolt.

I have profited greatly from the advice of Professor G. R. Potter, who read all the proofs of this book with his usual salutary vigilance. Mrs V. Liversidge typed most of a sometimes untidy manuscript with her customary efficiency and willingness; and I am also grateful to Miss A. Hewitt and Miss J. Hallett for their helpful secretarial assistance. Mr Bernard Barr of the York Minster Library added to his many services to the study of history at York by placing his expertise in medieval Latin at my disposal. I am only too conscious that my translations from Latin and

Norman-French have at times been less than elegant; and there may even be occasions when, as Henry Knighton wrote of the rebels of 1381, I 'have leapt before I looked'. Without Mr Barr's assistance I would have fallen from grace more often and more heavily: without my wife's encouragement and forbearance I might not have leapt at all.

Introduction

Any study of the great revolt of 1381 is inevitably bound to raise issues of wide-ranging social, political and cultural significance; but the documents collected and translated in this volume are first and foremost selected to tell a story rather than adorn a thesis. The events of June 1381, how they happened and why they took the form they did, are the major themes of this book. For this reason as well as because of considerations of space, I have deliberately, if reluctantly, refrained from including texts illustrative of analogous popular rebellions either in England or Western Europe – with the two exceptions of Jack Cade's revolt in 1450 (see no. 62) and the German Peasants' War of the early 1520s (no. 64). I have been similarly frugal in my choice of documents to elucidate the social and economic condition of the English peasantry in the later middle ages. Intensive research upon this subject in recent years has begun to reveal the extraordinary complexity of social relationships in late fourteenth-century England. It would be absolutely impossible to do justice to such complexity in a volume devoted to the Peasants' Revolt itself; and the condition of the medieval English peasantry is a subject which now urgently needs its own source-books.[1] There is perhaps no area in the whole field of English history in which it is more true that a little learning is likely to mislead and prove a dangerous guide. For almost a hundred years historians have been in the habit of drawing on the evidence for the 1381 revolt in order to make wide and controversial generalisations about agrarian society in the preceding and subsequent centuries. This practice usually begs the important questions: and the Peasants' Revolt has too often been allowed to become all things to all men. A possible justification of this book is that it attempts to restore the uprising of 1381 to its participants and victims, the men who rebelled and the men who suffered by

[1] But now see J. Z. Titow, *English Rural Society, 1200–1350* (London, 1969).

rebellion. Only then is one fully able to appreciate that although the great revolt has lessons, they are – like the lessons of all genuine 'history in depth' – curiously ambiguous and ambivalent.

The extracts which follow are therefore certain to raise more problems than they solve. The time is not yet ripe for a new 'interpretation' of the Peasants' Revolt; and no such interpretation is advanced here either explicitly or by means of a partial selection of documents. It is indeed one of the attractions of the rebellion as a subject for historical study that the great majority of the original chronicle authorities and a representative range of the surviving legal and other records can be presented within the covers of one book. It goes without saying, so voluminous are the sources, that I have been unable to include all the significant documents bearing on the great revolt; and it is equally obvious that a compilation of translated documents is never a satisfactory substitute for the original authorities themselves. This collection would lose much of its point if it deterred rather than encouraged the would-be student of the Peasants' Revolt to consult the sources in their original form and language. But even those with a working knowledge of medieval Latin and Norman-French may find it of some use as a practical handbook to the mysteries of 1381. The story of the year has been told many times and in almost every possible way. But the sources on which that story depends have hitherto never been presented in a uniform manner even to a specialist audience. With the single exception of Froissart's famous but often fanciful description of the revolt (which has appeared in several popular translations and editions), the primary authorities for the rebellion have been allowed to lie in unnecessary obscurity, often in danger of being completely hidden under the massive layers of subsequent interpretation and comment. I can only hope that the reader of the following pages will sometimes share my own greatest pleasure while compiling this book – direct contact with the thoughts and emotions of the contemporary observers of the uprising. It seems almost inconceivable – to take the most extreme example – that there should still exist no systematic translation of the works of Thomas

Walsingham of St Albans, that greatest and most interesting of
late medieval English historians. It has been said that 'the *Chronicon
Angliae* for this period indeed reads like the "Annals" of the reign
of Nero'.[1] The tale Walsingham has to tell is certainly as exciting
as anything in Tacitus and – for the modern English reader at
least – deserves to be as well known.

On the other hand nearly everything written by contemporaries
about the rebels of 1381 was written by their enemies. Consequently no collection of original sources for the revolt can hope
to provide a fully impartial view. At first sight the records are
surprisingly voluminous and informative. The Peasants' Revolt
was violent and dramatic enough to elicit at least some description
and comment from almost all of the not inconsiderable number
of contemporary chroniclers. At the same time the survival of
long series of official administrative and legal records at the
Public Record Office makes it possible to study various aspects of
the rising in great detail. Nevertheless the historian's gratitude for
what records survive is soon tempered by a sense of frustration
at a body of evidence which 'gives with such supple confusions
that the giving famishes the craving'. Certain themes of limited
significance, like the procedure by which the poll taxes of 1377
to 1381 were collected, can be explored in literally enormous
detail. But the problems likely to interest the reader first and
most – the motives of the rebels, the attitudes of the king and
magnates, the character of Wat Tyler – remain almost if not
quite hidden from us for ever.

More precisely, our knowledge of the Peasants' Revolt is
irrevocably controlled and restricted by the interests and thought-
sequences of its contemporary historians. The limitations of the
medieval chronicler in general and the late medieval English
chronicler in particular are too well known to require stating at
length. Ever since the early sixteenth century when Polydore
Vergil arrived at the court of Henry VII as an apostle of the new
Italian 'renaissance' approach to the composition of history, the
reputation of his medieval predecessors has tended to be low

[1] S. Armitage-Smith, *John of Gaunt* (London, 1904), p. 135.

rather than high. At times the chroniclers of 1381 deserve their contemptuous dismissal at the hands of Vergil, as 'nudi, rudes, indigesti ac mendosi', and even Buckle's still unkinder criticism that they compensated for the absence of truth by the invention of falsehood. Not one of the historians cited in this book was particularly scrupulous in checking the reliability of his information. All were capable of embroidering freely and imaginatively around their subject matter. With the probable exception of the author of the description of the rebellion preserved in the *Anonimalle Chronicle*, who seems to have been an eye-witness of events in London (no. 25), the chroniclers of the revolt depended very largely on hearsay rather than documentary evidence. Consequently they were more successful in communicating the atmosphere of crisis and rumour that characterised the summer of 1381 than the precise sequence of events. As so often in the political history of fourteenth- and fifteenth-century England the absence of a reliable court chronicler is particularly regrettable. No detailed account survives of the attitudes adopted by the young Richard and his counsellors when confronted with the rebellion. Froissart's and the *Anonimalle Chronicle*'s occasional attempts to outline royal policy seem to be based on surmise rather than definite information; while Walsingham and Henry Knighton are inevitably better guides to the risings in St Albans and Leicester than to happenings in London. Admittedly these two chroniclers were prepared to incorporate transcripts of relevant documents into the course of their narratives; but except for an occasional letter or charter (see nos. 43, 53, 71) the great revolt of 1381 rarely provided its contemporary chroniclers with much in the way of quotable record evidence.

In a more general sense still his treatment of the Peasants' Revolt can be looked upon as a touchstone of the emotional prejudices of the medieval chronicler. Walsingham and Froissart, unlike each other in almost every other respect, were at least united in their contemptuous dismissal of the great mass of the English population. 'We search the chroniclers' narratives in vain at the time of the Peasants' Rising for any trace of sympathy with the aspirations of townsmen and peasants.'[1] In their different ways the historians of 1381 all reflected a hierarchical social viewpoint so well-established and accepted that they scarcely needed to justify their hostility towards the rebels. By rebelling against their lords it seemed self-evident that Wat Tyler and his fellows had sinned against God as well as against man. Even the greatest radical of the period, John Wycliffe, shared this social conservatism: as he argued (with dubious logic) 'all things not to the will of the Lord must end miserably'. This is partly revealed to us Englishmen by that lamentable popular conflict in which the archbishop first and many others were cruelly put to death. As all suffering results from sin, it cannot be denied that in this case the sin of the people was the cause.'[2] Despite a prevalent view to the contrary, the medieval chronicler was deeply interested in problems of historical causation. But unfortunately his intellectual curiosity rarely freed itself from the *a priori* belief that the fundamental cause of the rebellion was the moral shortcomings of the rebels themselves. To his credit Thomas Walsingham was at times capable of taking a broader view. At the end of his long discussion of the causes of the rebellion he interpreted the revolt as a manifestation of the sickness of society as a whole: 'let us acknowledge that we are all to blame' (no. 68). But this too is to beg the question; and only when the Peasants' Revolt of 1381 ceased to be regarded as a culpable act of treason was a sensitive approach to its causation possible. The assumption that

'No subiect ought for any kind of cause,
    To force the lord, but yeeld him to the lawes'[3]

was, and is, unlikely to promote a genuine understanding of the nature of revolutionary activity in the past.

Despite such prejudices and preconceptions, the chroniclers of the Peasants' Revolt compare extremely favourably with those who related the story of other popular risings in the middle ages. In this respect the modern historian of the 1381 rebellion is a

[1] J. Taylor, *The Use of Medieval Chronicles* (Hist. Ass. Pamphlet, 1965), p. 17.
[2] Wycliffe, *Tractatus de Blasphemia* (Wyclif Society, 1893), pp. 189–90.
[3] *The Mirror for Magistrates*, ed. L. B. Campbell (Cambridge, 1938), p. 177.

good deal more fortunate than the student of, for instance, the French *Jacquerie* of 1358 or Cade's revolt of 1450. Admittedly few of the Latin chronicles translated in this collection exist in satisfactory modern editions: the only printed version of the important *Vita Ricardi Secundi* (no. 11) was published by Thomas Hearne as long ago as 1729. On the other hand the detailed investigation of fourteenth-century chronicles by modern scholars, and particularly by Professor V. H. Galbraith, makes it possible to evaluate their writing with much more confidence and sensitivity than was the case a generation ago. Thomas Walsingham, for example, now stands revealed as a much more ambitious, voluminous and self-conscious writer of history than was appreciated by the Victorian editors of his works in the Rolls Series.[1] Similarly Henry Knighton's account of events in 1381 deserves to be treated with considerably more respect since the establishment of the view that this canon of Leicester himself – and not an anonymous continuator – wrote the relevant part of the chronicle.[2] Many intricate textual problems remain unresolved. Although the anonymous continuator of the *Eulogium Historiarum* and the 'monk of Westminster' preserve interesting and unique information as to the course of events in London (nos. 29, 30), their narratives survive in single manuscripts. It has consequently proved impossible as yet to establish the exact authorship of these accounts of the revolt or the sources of their information.

The *Chroniques* of Jean Froissart present a different and even more baffling problem. All contemporary historians of the revolt were apparently prepared to present rumours as facts; but Froissart often seems to have elaborated highly circumstantial descriptions of episodes in the revolt without benefit even of rumour. As the reader will soon discover, some of Froissart's stories are so implausible and so unsupported by any other type of evidence that he probably fabricated them in the privacy of

---

[1] V. H. Galbraith, *The St Albans Chronicle, 1406–1420*; 'Thomas Walsingham and the St Albans Chronicle', *Eng. Hist. Rev.*, XLVII (1932) 12–29.

[2] V. H. Galbraith, 'The Chronicle of Henry Knighton', *Fritz Saxl Memorial Essays*, pp. 136–45.

his chamber. The late Professor Huizinga's remark that Froissart wrote with 'the mechanical exactitude of a cinematograph'[1] pays indirect tribute to his skill in presenting battle-scenes but is otherwise almost ludicrously misleading. Froissart did not himself witness the English rising of 1381 and his account of the rebellion is highly influenced and coloured by his greater knowledge and experience of predominantly urban popular disturbances in contemporary Flanders. More generally, the Peasants' Revolt attracted Froissart's interest and enthusiasm because it illustrated almost to perfection one of his and his audience's favourite themes – the vicissitudes of fortune. The violent death on subsequent days of both an archbishop of Canterbury and a rebellious demagogue provided the most extreme example possible of the operations of Froissart's favourite text: 'How wonderful and strange are the fortunes of this world'. For Froissart, even more than for the English chroniclers, the historical fact was not intrinsically valuable unless it could fulfil an exemplary role.[2] The medieval historian's self-imposed duty was not to understand the Peasants' Revolt in its own terms but to show how it revealed the eternal truths of human life on earth.

Much the most important supplement to the chroniclers' narratives of the revolt is the evidence of trial proceedings directed against the rebels during subsequent months. The greatest discoveries in this field were almost all made by the young French scholar, André Réville, shortly before his death in 1894. Réville's intensive research among the governmental and legal records of Richard II's reign and, in particular, his close examination of the *Coram Rege* Rolls transformed the study of the

---

[1] J. Huizinga, *The Waning of the Middle Ages* (Penguin Books edition), p. 282. Huizinga's violent attack on Froissart here betrays a complete incomprehension of his aims.

[2] This conclusion emerges very clearly from S. G. Nichols's discussion of 'Discourse in Froissart's *Chroniques*', *Speculum*, XXXIX (1964) 279–87. For the most detailed, but now sometimes dated, discussion of Froissart and the English chroniclers as authorities for the 1381 rising, see G. Kriehn, 'Studies in the Sources of the Social Revolt in 1381', *American Historical Review*, VII (1901–2) 254–85, 458–84.

Peasants' Revolt. The inclusion of Réville's transcripts from such sources in the bulky appendix of *Le Soulèvement des Travailleurs d'Angleterre* (published under the capable care of Professor Petit-Dutaillis in 1898) immediately made this volume what it still remains – the indispensable guide to the history of the rebellion. Detailed legal charges, almost invariably taking the form of jurors' indictments presented before sheriffs or specially appointed royal justices, survive in the case of twenty-two London rebels as well as more than two hundred insurgents elsewhere in the country. Of similar value, although normally less informative, are the details of treasonable activity recorded in the copies of royal letters of pardon to individual rebels enrolled on the Patent Rolls. These too survive in great numbers: for as Charles Oman asserted, with slight if pardonable exaggeration, during the three years after 1381 'the King was pardoning a few rebels almost every week'.[1] Several of the more important and representative legal presentments and letters of pardon are translated (often from the original record) in this collection of documents (nos. 23, 24, 32–4, 39, 40, 45–7, 57–9): they provide a wealth of circumstantial detail unobtainable from any other source.

Unfortunately, the evidence of indictments and pardons confronts the modern student of the revolt with problems of interpretation almost as difficult as those presented by the chroniclers. Several early twentieth-century historians prejudiced rather than enhanced their understanding of the Peasants' Revolt because of an almost mystical belief in the inherent superiority of 'record evidence' to that of contemporary narratives. But, as so often, a crude antithesis of record and chronicle is likely to do more harm than good.[2] The legal records of the Peasants' Revolt need to be approached with quite as much caution and circumspection as the histories of Froissart and Walsingham. The terminology of the inquisitions is itself often likely to mislead.

[1] C. Oman, *Great Revolt of 1381*, p. 152.
[2] See the remarks of Professor Holt on another famous problem, *King John* (Hist. Association Pamphlet, G53, 1963), pp. 3–16.

What exactly did a presenting jury mean when it accused a
rebel of belonging to the *magna societas*, or 'great society' (no. 40)?
And how seriously should one take the extremely common
allegation that a particular culprit was 'the first commencer'
of the rising or 'the principal causer' of the death of Sudbury or
Hales? More generally, and as Walsingham suggests, several
jurors were only too ready to exploit their position in order to
score off personal enemies and revenge private injuries. It seems
even more certain (though by the nature of the case direct
evidence is nearly always lacking) that many juries acted purely
as spokesmen for a detailed series of allegations which had been
meticulously prepared long before the trial took place. The
classic example is the longest and most famous of all the jurors'
presentments, the two inquisitions taken before the sheriffs of
London as late as November 1382 (no. 32). Recent analysis of
these documents has cast serious doubts on their veracity; and
the very fact that two different versions were completed makes it
less likely that either was completed in good faith. It now seems
virtually certain that the five London aldermen accused of
complicity in the rebellion were in fact being 'framed' by their
political opponents within the city, the supporters of John of
Northampton, mayor of London during the two years after
October 1381. By a curious irony, the inquisitions of November
1382 throw more light on the vicious factionalism within the
city after the rebellion than on the exact role played by the
Londoners themselves in the Peasants' Revolt. The English
government was often aware of the inequities and corruption
which characterised the working of the local courts: the number
of rebel trial cases evoked to the central *Coram Rege* court was
very considerable indeed. But it would be a grave mistake to
believe that even the king and his immediate counsellors were
noted for their dispensation of impartial justice. The concession
of pardons to erstwile rebels followed no intelligible principle;
and it is startling to realise that such notorious and murderous
captains as Sir Roger Bacon of Norfolk, Thomas Sampson, the
leader of the Ipswich rebels, Thomas Engilby of Bridgwater

(no. 45) and the viciously insolent Thomas Farndon of London
(no. 32) were all eventually restored to royal favour. Royal
letters of pardon, like the jurors' inquisitions themselves, were
procured by means of a complicated series of personal pressures
about which very little can now be known. It is essential to
remember that the operation of the English legal machinery in
the fourteenth century was a good deal less impressive in practice
than it was in theory.[1] Nor, in the light of what happened *after*
1381, is it difficult to understand why the rebels of that year may
have believed 'that the land could not be fully free until the
lawyers had been killed' (no. 20).

   In a situation where so much of the original evidence, 'deceives
with whispering ambitions, Guides us by vanities', it is hardly
surprising that the definitive book on the Peasants' Revolt has
not been written. The great revolt has hitherto defeated the
attempts of historians who have tried to solve all its problems,
proving too mysterious in its motivation and too complex in its
ramifications for entirely satisfactory analysis. Several excellent
short and predominantly narrative accounts of the rebellion do
exist, notably that by Professor McKisack in her volume in the
Oxford 'History of England' series.[2] But a satisfactorily large-
scale and detailed history of the revolt is still lacking. The author
who came nearest to achieving this aim was the young André
Réville – from whose death at the age of twenty-seven the study
of the Peasants' Revolt seems at times never to have recovered.
Réville's posthumous *Le Soulèvement des Travailleurs* contains
his own analysis of the revolt in Hertfordshire and the eastern
counties (considerably more sophisticated than Edgar Powell's
Rising in East Anglia in 1381 published two years previously) as
well as a lengthy introduction by Professor Petit-Dutaillis. The
latter is still the most searching general survey of the Peasants'
Revolt in existence. Charles Oman's *Great Revolt of 1381*

----

[1] See, for example, Professor E. L. G. Stones's study of 'The Folvilles of Ashby-
Folville, Leicestershire, and their associates in crime, 1326–1347', *Trans. Royal
Hist. Soc.*, 5th series, VII (1957), 117–36.

[2] M. McKisack, *The Fourteenth Century*, pp. 406–23.

(published in 1906) added relatively little to the work of Réville
and Petit-Dutaillis and has at times the unfortunate effect of
making an exciting and controversial subject seem dull and
simple. But Oman's book is still the best and indeed the only
detailed commentary in English on the revolt: a new edition,
revised by Dr E. B. Fryde, appeared in 1969.

Remarkably little research upon the problems of the Peasants'
Revolt has been attempted during the last sixty years. George
Kriehn's 'Studies in the Sources of the Social Revolt of 1381'
produced an ingenious and influential re-interpretation of the
confrontation between Richard and Tyler at Smithfield;[1] but
the author never lived to complete the large-scale analysis of the
revolt for which these 'studies' seemed to prepare the way.
Much the most interesting book published on the revolt in more
recent years is *The English Rising of 1381* (1950), a co-operative
venture in which R. H. Hilton's neo-Marxist analysis of 'feudal
society' (misleadingly entitled 'The Preparation for the Rising')
proved considerably more cogent than H. Fagan's narrative of the
rising itself. Meanwhile Professor Wilkinson and Miss Ruth
Bird had independently re-investigated the part played by
Londoners during the rebellion.[2] But with one or two minor
exceptions what the former wrote in 1940 – 'It cannot be said
that of recent years English historians have given much attention
to the Revolt of 1381' – applies even more forcefully a generation
later. It may be, as Professor Wilkinson then asserted,
that few 'sources of outstanding importance remain to be
discovered'. But some new discoveries have been made – including
that of a letter written by a German merchant resident in
London who experienced the revolt at first hand;[3] and much
of the more familiar evidence cries out for a thorough
reassessment.

[1] *American Historical Review*, VII (1901–2) 254–85, 458–84.
[2] B. Wilkinson, 'The Peasants' Revolt of 1381', *Speculum*, XV (1940) 12–35;
R. Bird, *The Turbulent London of Richard II*, pp. 52–62.
[3] A facsimile of the letter, dated 17 June 1381, is reproduced by Professor G.
Barraclough (to whom I am grateful for the reference) in 'The Historian and his
Archives', *History Today*, IV (1954) 413.

In retrospect it is possibly not too difficult to appreciate the reasons why interest in the Peasants' Revolt, among both historians and the general public, has tended to wane since the years immediately before and after 1900. At that time the rising was often thought to have a clear relevance to contemporary social issues in a way which can now seem almost hilariously maladroit. According to E. Lipson, 'It was the first great struggle between capital and labour', while for G. M. Trevelyan, 'the general tone of the rising was that of Christian Democracy'.[1] Sixty years ago the late fourteenth century was commonly viewed as a decisive watershed in the social, political and religious history of England. The Black Death, the Peasants' Revolt, the emergence of Wycliffe and Chaucer seemed to mark the dawn of a genuinely new era. Trevelyan's own prolific career as a historian began with *England in the Age of Wycliffe*, a subject specifically chosen because it represented 'the meeting place of the medieval and modern'. Few present-day historians would dare to claim as much. According to the modern orthodoxy, the catastrophic onslaught of bubonic plague (no. 4) merely accelerated social and economic forces already fully evident in early fourteenth-century England.[2] And while Wycliffe and Chaucer were undoubtedly figures of the utmost importance it is by no means clear that they achieved any permanent revolution in the religious and literary life of their county. Much of the promise that historians once detected in the early years of Richard II remained unfulfilled: the dawn of a new age proves on examination to be a false one.

The same arguments inevitably seem to apply to the great revolt itself. It is possible to accept the validity of Stubbs's comment that 'the rising of the commons is one of the most portentous phenomena to be found in the whole of our history'[3] without reaching any agreement about exactly what it portends.

---

[1] E. Lipson, *Economic History of England*, I (9th edn) 121; G. M. Trevelyan, *England in the Age of Wycliffe* (1904 edn), p. 202.

[2] But see B. F. Harvey, 'The Population Trend in England between 1300 and 1348', *Trans. Royal Hist. Soc.*, 5th series, XVI (1966) 23–42.

[3] W. Stubbs, *Constitutional History of England* (Oxford, 1875), II 449.

Is the outbreak of a general insurrection in the early summer of 1381 less significant than the fact that it was a unique episode with no very close analogies? Is it more important for the history of medieval England that the lower orders produced a major rebellion so seldom rather than that they rebelled at all? The confidence with which historians of an earlier generation generalised about the causes of the great revolt is sadly lacking today. In 1913 Professor Petit-Dutaillis' general survey of the Peasants' Revolt devoted considerably more space to the 'causes of the rising' than to its 'general characteristics and results'. But for Professor Postan in 1966 this 'passing episode in the social history of the late middle ages' is almost inexplicable: 'Why, then, the Peasant Revolt? Why indeed!'[1] In the long term it seems very likely that our understanding of the great revolt will be enhanced by the current historical reaction against undue emphasis on problems of causation, human motives and 'the idol of origins'.[2] But meanwhile previous interpretations of the Peasants' Revolt all need to be approached in a critical, not to say sceptical, spirit.

In the first place the traditional description of the 1381 rising as a 'Peasants' Revolt' (although retained in this book because of its familiarity) is itself deceptive. In no part of England for which documentary evidence survives in quantity do peasants appear to have risen in complete isolation from members of other social classes. At Canterbury, Norwich, Yarmouth, Bury St Edmunds, Ipswich, St Albans, Winchester and Bridgwater as well as London the riots of the year were the product of an alliance, at times uneasy, between townsmen and villagers from the surrounding regions. In England's largest county the disturbances took the exclusive form of urban risings and riots. Although disorder in York, Beverley and Scarborough was precipitated by news of events in London, the issues at stake in these three towns were essentially self-generated and not at all

---

[1] *Cambridge Economic History of Europe*, 1 (Cambridge, 1966) 609–10.
[2] Cf. G. Barraclough, 'History and the Common Man', a Presidential Address to the Historical Association, 1966.

conditional on the intervention of the local peasantry (nos. 46–8).
At Scarborough, a borough with relatively little constitutional
autonomy, the revolt was characterised by a series of stormy
protests against the oppression of royal bailiffs and officials within
the town. In York and Beverley dissident civic factions seized
the opportunity to adopt terrorist tactics in an attempt to force
their way into offices of power and patronage. But in neither
town, nor indeed anywhere in England, is there evidence of a
concerted plan to carry through a 'democratic' or even radical
urban revolution. The violent episodes of 1381 failed to have any
sustained effect on the balance of power within the existing
constitutional framework of the provincial English town.

The same general conclusion emerges from a study of the
otherwise very different and much more explosive situation
within London itself. The exact role played by the Londoners
during June 1381 remains as controversial an issue now as it was
at the time; but their intervention was certainly important and
probably decisive. Without some London support the peasants
from Kent and Essex could never have enjoyed their brief
moment of exhilarating and exhausting power. It has been seen
that the five London aldermen indicted in November 1382
were probably innocent of capital treason: they can no longer be
regarded as the arch villains of the revolt. On *a priori* grounds
alone there are obvious difficulties in believing that well-established London citizens would regard Wat Tyler and his men as
natural allies. But nearly all the chroniclers agree that there was
a good deal of sympathy for the peasants' cause among the lower
classes within the city. Even the official city account of the revolt
admits that the insurgents were assisted by London's 'perfidious
commoners of their own condition' (no. 31). Surviving but
incomplete lists of the names of Londoners involved in acts of
rebellion (154 in the Rolls of Parliament and 238 in the London
Plea and Memoranda Rolls) point to a massive participation by
Londoners in the revolt. The great majority of those accused or
pardoned were obscure characters, usually 'foreigns' or non-
citizens, whose only aims seem to have been plunder and revenge

on personal enemies within the city. Although Mayor William Walworth was by all accounts an astute, capable and even ruthless ruler in his city, he had the misfortune to preside over London's fortunes at a time when the normally unshakeable control exercised by the late medieval merchant oligarchy had already been weakened by civic faction. In the face of the unexpected crisis of June 1381 the usual self-confidence of the London aldermanic class temporarily collapsed. It can be no coincidence that four months later, on 13 October, John of Northampton, the most radical force in current city politics, secured election as mayor. But within a few years Northampton's great rival, Nicholas Brembre, carried through a successful constitutional counter-revolution; and before long the Peasants' Revolt could be remembered as a source of city pride rather than humiliation. The heroism of William Walworth at Smithfield was the feature of the revolt most frequently publicised by fifteenth-century London chronicles. In London, as in other English towns, the memory of the upheavals of 1381 helped to persuade men of substance and property to be content with the stolidly conservative and unexciting government they received throughout the next century.

But the great revolt of 1381 does more than illustrate the dangers of presenting medieval English society in terms of a sharp dichotomy between town and country. Even if we confine our attention to the rural elements within the rebellion it proves impossible to analyse the movement as one of exclusively peasant grievances. The prominent role played by 'poor priests' as sowers of discord and as rebel leaders is one of the best-known features of the revolt. John Wrawe and John Ball (nos. 38, 39, 70), to take the two most famous examples, were members of the large ecclesiastical proletariat of late medieval England, a class whose clerical status was too rarely rewarded by a sufficiently responsible religious function. How far these priests accurately reflected the genuine social grievances of their age rather than (as the chroniclers preferred to believe) injecting their own note of

2

personal hysteria into the rebellion is difficult to decide. But in many cases, notably that of John Wrawe, criminal depravation in 1381 was probably the result of economic deprivation in previous years. More remarkable are those instances in which members of the county gentry actively contributed towards the disorders of the year. It is just possible that the participation of knights like Sir Roger Bacon and Sir Thomas Cornuerd in the East Anglian risings testifies to the economic difficulties of the smaller English landlords at a time of acute labour shortage. According to this interpretation, the crisis of 1381 may have promoted (if only temporarily and in restricted areas of eastern England) a political alliance between the richer peasantry and lesser squirarchy of the type that made the Hussite movement so formidable a threat to the established order in early fifteenth-century Bohemia. But Sir Roger Bacon was hardly the John Zizka of the Peasants' Revolt. The great majority of English gentlemen who took part in the rebellion did so for personal and usually discreditable reasons. The collapse of order in the summer of 1381 encouraged existing 'gentry gangs' to extend the range of their blackmailing and 'protection racket' activities. Other knights and esquires were unable to resist the pressures towards involvement in the risings which emanated from their friends, affinities and 'cousinage': the charges made in parliament against Sir William Coggan suggest that he might have lost his position as local 'good lord' if he had refused to lend his weight to the conspiracies hatched by the vicar and other rebels of his native Bridgwater (no. 45b). It is abundantly clear that most rebel bands actively desired gentry support and went to considerable lengths to secure it whenever possible. Personal attacks on secular landlords were indeed extremely infrequent throughout the course of the rebellion. The execution of Sir Robert Salle on Mousehold Heath outside Norwich (no. 42) is attributable to the Norfolk rebels' fury at Salle's unwillingness to accept the avuncular role they offered him. Despite the words of John Ball's famous text, the 'gentleman' as such was never the prime target of peasant hostility in 1381.

There are other reasons for refusing to interpret the great revolt in terms of a crude class struggle. The late fourteenth-century English peasantry was itself too variegated a body to allow concise definition. The stratification of peasant society and the existence within it of both a kulak and a proletarian element from a very early date is now one of the commonplaces of medieval English agrarian history. At times the argument is carried to excess; and it may be as well to remember that the majority of the rebels of 1381 lived in villages where (as in the West Midlands a century earlier), 'although wealthier peasant families might employ one or two hired men, the essential labour force was derived from within the family'.[1] But certainly most of the villages involved in the Peasants' Revolt must have included within their ranks families which had prospered as well as others which had suffered from such economic trends as the rise in labour costs during the preceding generation. The great unsolved problem of the Revolt, and indeed of medieval rural society in general, is the extent to which these economic differences were reflected in social attitudes. How far had the economic and social polarisation of the English peasant destroyed the traditional cohesion of his village community? Was the Peasants' Revolt a protest of individual rebels or of entire villages? Were the chroniclers correct in suggesting that the first serious riots in the three Essex villages of Fobbing, Corringham and Stanford-le-Hope took the form of mass risings of entire village communities (no. 19)? No firm answers to these questions can yet be offered – except in so far as the evidence points towards a situation in which a very great number of the rebels were not simply peasants but village craftsmen and tradesmen. Of the thirteen Somersetshire rebels excluded from the general amnesty proclaimed at the end of 1381, seven were described as scrivener, hosier, servant, waller, webber, shethier and soothsayer respectively.[2] It seems appropriate that the first identifiable rebel of 1381, Thomas Baker of Fobbing, was (at least according to

[1] R. H. Hilton, *A Medieval Society* (London, 1966), p. 89.
[2] *Rot. Parl.*, III, 113.

Henry Knighton; no. 21) a baker by profession; and that even
Wat Tyler himself was rumoured to have worked as an Essex
tiler (no. 30). Several rebel grievances – most obviously their
hostility towards the statutes and justices of labourers – are
more readily explicable if the rebellion can be seen as less of a
peasants' and more of an artisans' protest movement. In some
ways the great revolt marks the first significant intervention
of the English *sans-culottes* in national politics.

Although the rebels of 1381 cannot be forced into any one
archetypal pattern, they were stirred to protest by a series of
common as well as individual grievances. Apparently these
grievances, unlike those of Cade's 'poor commons of Kent'
in 1450 (no. 62), were never committed to writing. The rebels'
'programme' has to be inferred from the distorted comments of
the chronicles (see especially no. 25) as well as their own actions.
Certain general themes emerge quite clearly. By medieval
standards this was a revolt of reasonably self-possessed subjects
of the crown, aware of their rights as well as obligations. With
minor exceptions (nos. 49–50), the insurrection lost its impetus
once it crossed the shadowy line which divided the more
politically conscious areas of south-eastern England from the
more remote and seignorially 'oppressive' midlands and the
north. For this reason alone it is difficult to resist Froissart's
famous theory that the rebellion owed its genesis to 'the ease and
riches that the common people were of'. Such an interpretation
still seems more convincing than any hypothesis which ascribes
the revolt to a social movement *de profundis*, a protest rooted in
despair at the intolerable oppression of a reactionary landlord
class. This is not to deny the existence of a limited 'feudal' or
seignorial reaction during the generation which preceded the
rebellion. Certain reactionary measures, most obviously the
attempt to restrict mobility of labour and hold down wages,
provoked a wave of hostility towards the justices of the peace
in and before 1381 (nos. 5–8). Tenant and landlord (particularly
ecclesiastical landlord) certainly often did look upon one another
as bitter antagonists. The rising at St Albans – perhaps the only

locality in England where it is possible to set the events of 1381 within a detailed context of existing manorial relationships – was only one particularly vicious round in a continuous boxing-match: for both the abbot and his tenants a voluntary concession was inconceivable and an extorted concession something to be retracted as soon as possible (no. 43).

Each English village could no doubt have told its own and different story: and in most of these one suspects that the inert rather than 'reactionary' landlord was the central figure. Both landlord and tenant were of course the prey of economic forces even more incomprehensible to themselves than to us. Of these possibly the most critical and certainly the most neglected was the movement of agricultural prices and consequently of real wages during the years immediately before 1381. In the light of our present knowledge that so many pre-industrial popular disturbances took the form of 'grain riots', an intensive study of regional harvest conditions between the Black Death and the Peasants' Revolt would seem an urgent desideratum. Only then can the current assumption that this period was one of sustained economic improvement for the mass of English peasants, labourers and artisans be put to some form of statistical test. Nevertheless, as Ireland in the 1840s will always remind us, the range of emotional response to conditions of food scarcity or abundance can never be economically predetermined. Even more mysterious than the economic pressures of the last quarter of the fourteenth century is the social context within which they operated and which gave them human substance. The complete abolition of villein status, to cite the most extreme and intriguing of all the rebel demands at Mile End and Smithfield, clearly held a significance within the popular imagination out of all proportion to its known economic implications (nos. 8, 63).[1] Moreover, the insurrection was accompanied by genuinely irrational elements

[1] An important preliminary guide to the exceptionally difficult problem of differentiating between villeinage as a social stigma and villein services as an economic liability is R. H. Hilton's 'Freedom and Villeinage in England', *Past and Present*, no. 31 (1965), pp. 3–19. See the same author's *The Decline of Serfdom in Medieval England* (London, 1969).

as well as mild millenarian tendencies – hinted at, rather than expressly stated, in a cluster of obscure vernacular letters (no. 71). themselves echo the words of William Langland which *Piers the Plowman*, like the Peasants' Revolt itself, opens up an extraordinary and sensational world, for which nothing else in the fourteenth century has quite prepared us.

Granted the difficulties of ever understanding the economic condition and social aspirations of the medieval peasant and townsman, it is hardly surprising that nearly all the most recent discussions of the great revolt have tended to stress its political causes. To some extent an admission of defeat, this change of emphasis is nevertheless absolutely justifiable. It remains to be proved that England was passing through a genuinely revolutionary situation in the early 1380s and that 'All conditions for an uprising were ripe.'[1] What is clear is that the early years of Richard II's reign were ones of acute political *malaise*, illustrated at some length in the first part of this book (nos. 9–14). During the ten years before 1381 England experienced almost all the evils that could befall a polity ruled by a system of hereditary monarchy. In 1377 an exceptionally old king, Edward III, had been succeeded by his young grandson, Richard II: neither was physically capable of relieving the tension created by faction within the higher nobility and disillusion among the county knights and provincial burgesses. Above all, the outbreak of a new phase of Anglo-French war in the summer of 1369 had inaugurated a period of military stalemate and disaster. In the 1370s the Hundred Years War brought not plunder and glory but weariness and frustration in its train. More specifically, it brought danger too. At no time since the Capetian attempt to seize King John's crown in the years after Magna Carta had England been in greater fear of a French invasion (no. 11). Many inhabitants of south-eastern England experienced the horrors of war at first hand, horrors which lost nothing in the telling as rumours spread with remarkable speed through the country.[2]

[1] Hilton and Fagan, *English Rising of 1381*, p. 49.
[2] F. R. H. Du Boulay, *The Lordship of Canterbury*, p. 115.

In 1381, as in 1450, the men of Kent rebelled as a protest against the government's inability to defend them from the dangers of French attack. According to the *Anonimalle Chronicle* (no. 19), the very first concerted action of the Kentish rebels was to provide that 'the sea-coasts be kept free from enemies'. Fears of sinister French influence provoked a series of incredible conspiracy theories and atrocity stories (no. 58); and the great revolt of 1381 can never be satisfactorily understood unless it is placed within the context of a rumour-infested '*grande peur*'.

But rumours were endemic to medieval rural society; and it was of course the familiar combination of military disaster and excessive war taxation which converted anxiety into action. The most reliable (the *Anonimalle Chronicle* and Henry Knighton) as opposed to the most imaginative (Froissart and Walsingham) chronicles were in no doubt that the rebellion in Kent and Essex was the direct consequence of official attempts to enforce payment of the third poll tax in the spring of 1381. All allowances made for the intense suspicion with which medieval subjects regarded any novelty in the sphere of taxation, the three poll taxes of 1377 to 1381 provide a classic example of a rewarding financial experiment doomed to extinction by excessive and insensitive early use. The original decision to introduce the first 'tallage of groats' in 1377 is understandable enough (no. 15). By the closing months of Edward III's reign, the French wars were already ruinously expensive and the government could hardly be blamed for seeking some alternative to the traditional and now stereotyped parliamentary tenths and fifteenths. In financial terms the 1377 poll tax, which probably raised about £22,000, was a qualified success and not surprisingly established a precedent. In May 1379 the commons in Richard II's third parliament, alarmed by the failure of John of Gaunt's attack on St Malo in the previous summer, agreed to the imposition of a second poll tax (no. 16). A new graduated scale of assessment was probably introduced in the interests of increasing revenue (only the less substantial married man was to pay less than he had done two years previously) as much as of social justice. Nor is

the other conventional view – that the poll taxes represent the
selfish class interests of parliamentary knights and burgesses who
wished to spread the burden of taxation lower down the social
scale – beyond question. There is no evidence that the concept
of the poll tax originated with the parliamentary commons.

At the critical Northampton parliament of November 1380, a
very heavy tallage of three groats was recommended to an
indecisive commons by lords, prelates and royal counsellors
obsessed with the need to pay English troops quartered in France
before they deserted *en masse* (no. 17). On 7 December 1380, the
day after the commons had consented to the imposition of the
third poll tax and left Northampton, the collectors set to work
under the authority of royal letters patent. Despite inevitable
difficulties and delays, this first attempt to collect the poll tax
does not seem to have met with any organised local resistance.
If the government had been prepared to accept the original
collectors' first returns at their face value, it seems highly likely
that there would have been no general insurrection at that time.
But early in 1381, the king's council, conscious of massive tax
evasion, inaugurated a series of complicated attempts to compel
full payment of the levy.[1] The most efficient and consequently
the most hated of these measures was the appointment on
16 March and later of bodies of commissioners charged with
reassessing and enforcing payment of the tax in various English
counties (no. 18). It was in these counties – notably Essex, Kent,
Norfolk, Suffolk and Hertfordshire – that tax risings began
during May and early June. The great revolt of 1381 accordingly
takes its place within that category of popular insurrections
(Yorkshire in 1489, Cornwall in 1497 and even Bohemia in the
1410s are obvious analogies) which owed their outbreak to an
almost instinctive and Poujadist protest against personal taxation.

But it would probably be a mistake to believe that the first
riots against tax collectors took the form of a single, simultaneous
series of outbreaks. The evidence of the *Anonimalle Chronicle*

---

[1] Tout, *Chapters*, III 359–65, provides much the best guide. See also E. B.
Fryde's comments on pp. xviii–xxii of Oman, *Great Revolt* (1969 edn).

(no. 19) makes it reasonably clear that the Peasants' Revolt had a precise geographical point of origin: – three marshland villages near Brentwood in southern Essex. The failure of Chief Justice Bealknap to crush the first stirrings of organised resistance to the tax collectors was probably decisive. From that moment onwards the revolt followed the classic pattern of pre-industrial popular movements.[1] The first outbreaks of disaffection sparked off a series of explosions which progressed from village to village according to an intelligible (although still imperfectly documented) geographical and chronological sequence. During the early days of June the movement owed most of what little cohesion it possessed to the rebels' determination to hunt out and revenge themselves upon the royal officials responsible for their oppression. As horizons widened, John of Gaunt, Archbishop Sudbury and Treasurer Hales rapidly replaced local justices and jurors as the predestined scapegoats of the year. But hostility towards the king's ministers was combined, as so often in the history of popular disturbances, with an intense and genuine devotion to the person of the king himself. Inevitably regarded by the insurgents as the source and symbol of all justice, Richard II had the additional advantage of being too young to incur personal blame for the recent misconduct of the French wars. It is just possible that one or two of the more audacious rebel leaders may have contemplated the abduction and even the assassination of their king (no. 68); but for the great majority of the rebels the criticism that 'there were more kings than one and they would neither suffer nor have any king except King Richard' was not only well-founded but heart-felt. Their desire to seek redress from the person of the king as well as to destroy the 'traitors' in his entourage was sufficient motive to induce the insurgents to march on London. By 1381, moreover, that city had already completed its slow evolution 'from commune to capital' and was beginning to exert a genuine metropolitan attraction on rebels as well as courtiers. The long walk from eastern Kent via Blackheath to

[1] E. J. Hobsbawm, *Primitive Rebels* (1959) and Georges Rudé, *The Crowd in History* (1964) are now essential reading for the Peasants' Revolt.

London on 11 and 12 June not only fostered a much-needed solidarity among the rebel companies themselves: it established a precedent to be followed, with varying degrees of success, by Jack Cade in 1450, the Bastard Fauconberge in 1471 and Sir Thomas Wyatt in 1554.

Above all, the march from Canterbury to London promoted the rise to power of a more than local rebel leader, 'a king of the ruffians and idol of the rustics'. Virtually every aspect of Wat Tyler's career is controversial – his exact identity, his social and geographical origins and his relationship with his even more mysterious fellow captain, Jack Straw or Rackstraw. But it is beyond question that Tyler was able to exercise a very real if temporary authority over a most heterogeneous collection of rebel bands. On 13 June, when Tyler was in London, a small company in Thanet issued proclamations under his authority and that of Jack Rackstraw (no. 23); and Walsingham's vivid picture of Tyler's interview with a party of St Albans tenants leaves no doubt of his appeal to the imagination of the would-be rebel (no. 43). Every insurrectionary movement of the type experienced by England in 1381 is fated to throw up popular leaders at short notice; and it follows that the qualities and abilities of such leaders tend to be the single most important derminant of the course of the rebellion. Even their admirers would have to admit that most of the rebel captains of 1381 fall into the well-known category of 'social bandits'. Others acted as more articulate and well-intentioned spokesmen, but for purely local interests: William Grindcobbe's moving quest for 'a little liberty' was firmly based on the specific situation at St Albans (no. 43). Some leaders thought in more grandiose terms of a popular revival of the local English country or provincial unit: Geaffrey Litster's role as 'King of the Commons' and *idolus Northfolkorum* in Norwich castle bears striking testimony to the persistence of archaic tribal sentiment as well as loyalty to the ideal of the shire community (no. 41).[1] Against this background of strong

---

[1] These features of the revolt are interestingly discussed in McKisack, *Fourteenth Century*, pp. 420–1.

centrifugal tendencies on the part of the rebels, Wat Tyler's ability to play a part on a larger stage seems especially impressive. No doubt he owned his initial authority to his overlordship of the Kentish rebels, whose country 'king' he planned to be; but by all accounts he aimed, during his brief days of power within London itself, at extracting general concessions from the king and his courtiers. Whether or not he was present (as the author of the *Anonimalle Chronicle* asserts) at the important Mile End conference with Richard II on Friday 14 June, on the following day Tyler's readiness to act and negotiate as undisputed leader cost him his life. The differing accounts of Tyler's death at Smithfield can probably never be satisfactorily reconciled. All the evidence has undergone some distortion and it is impossible to substantiate in full either of the two most ingenious interpretations: – that Tyler was the innocent victim of a pre-conceived royalist plot, or that he truculently provoked a violent reaction from the royal party in order to restore his waning authority over his men.

The complete collapse of the rebels' confidence at Smithfield after Tyler's assassination brutally exposed – even without benefit of Richard's spirited ride to claim their loyalty – the inherent and inevitable fragility of the movement. After the first orgies of plunder, destruction and killing it is remarkable that the insurrectionary bands retained any cohesion at all. Internal weaknesses rather than the counter-measures of the govern-ment –which revealed itself, both in London and the provinces, as curiously vulnerable to popular onslaught – doomed the rebellion to eventual failure. The rebels' cause was almost inevitably bound to be discredited by the rapid transformation of a relatively peaceful demonstration into a series of violent attacks on property. The number of acts of physical violence committed by the rioters can easily be exaggerated; but like other rural and city mobs 'they liked the sound of breaking glass'. The destruction of such famous buildings as the Savoy and Temple together with the emergence on the scene of criminals and religious fanatics like John Sterlyng of Essex (no. 53) alienated men of substance as well as many of the insurgents themselves. There were more practical problems too. Quite apart from the medieval rebel's natural disinclination to abandon his wife, family and homestead for more than a few days, he was faced with the ever-present possibility of starvation. Froissart commented on the lack of victuals at Blackheath, 'wherewith they were sore displeased', but seems to have assumed that once in London the rebels were suitably and even lavishly entertained by the citizens there. But late medieval London was itself only provisioned with considerable difficulty (no. 56); and by the morning of Saturday 15 June many of those rebels who still remained in London must have been hungry as well as exhausted after the experience of sleeping in the open for successive nights 'like slaughtered pigs' (nos. 26, 27). The severity of the food shortage naturally depended on the size of the rebel companies, a subject about which no certainty is possible. Although the chronicles of the revolt include many references to the total numbers of rebels, they continually contradict themselves as well as one another. Walsingham estimated John Wrawe's company in west Suffolk at more than 50,000, the *Anonimalle Chronicle* at 10,000 (nos. 35, 38): it is hard to believe that Wrawe can ever have led more than a few hundred men. Most chroniclers wrote in terms of 40,000, 50,000, or even 60,000 rebels in all. A more realistic guess (though no more than that) might restrict the total number of insurgents who entered London to less than 10,000, of whom only a minority were still in or near the city at the time of Smithfield. The rebel cause was, in any case, more likely to be prejudiced than enhanced by sheer weight of numbers.

By the evening of 15 June in London, and by the end of the month in eastern England (nos. 41, 52–6), the insurrection had therefore proved as abortive as it had previously seemed dangerous. In Engels's words, 'this sally beyond both the present and even the future could be nothing but violent and fantastic, and of necessity fell back into the narrow limits set by the contemporary situation' (no. 78). Like the English Chartists of the 1840s, the rebels of 1381 pursued a series of confused aims

capable of achievement only under different circumstances and
as a result of different pressures. No doubt the turbulent scenes
in the summer of that year had some effect on contemporary
attitudes and opinions; but it is difficult to measure these in
concrete terms. In general the results of the great revolt appear
to have been negative where they were not negligible. The view
that the rebels, even in their failure, 'struck a vital blow at
villeinage' and were responsible for the legal enfranchisement of
the English peasant has long been discredited. The extinction of
villeinage and the emancipation of the peasant was a slow and
tortuous process, within which the early 1380s seem to have no
particular significance (nos. 8, 63). If, to take the example of one
phenomenon for which there is now overwhelming documentary
evidence, the late fourteenth century saw a marked acceleration
in demesne leasing by the English landlord, this too was largely
the result of long-term economic and social forces. Throughout
the fifteenth century such forces – rising wages, a relatively
stagnant population and depressed prices – are usually assumed
to have operated in the interests of the English peasant, agricultural
labourer and village craftsman. Due allowance made for the
series of minor social disturbances which succeeded the great
revolt (no. 61), a general peasant revolt in fifteenth-century
England had little economic justification or *rationale*. The truth
of the famous dictum that 'la révolte agraire apparaît aussi
inséparable du régime seigneurial que, par exemple, de la grande
entreprise capitaliste, la grève', is a little less self-evident than
Marc Bloch assumed. In fifteenth-century English conditions,
tenants apparently did not find it impossible to resist pressures
from their landlords by more peaceful methods – refusal to take
up holdings, collective bargaining and even on occasion the
'rent-strike'.[1] With the historian's unfair benefit of hindsight, it
might well seem that the Peasants' Revolt of 1381 was – in both

---

[1] See, e.g., C. Dyer, 'A Redistribution of Incomes in Fifteenth-century
England?', *Past and Present*, no. 39 (1968), pp. 11–33. This is not of course to deny
the evidence for intermittent seignorial reaction immediately after the failure of
the 1381 revolt: see Oman, *Great Revolt* (1969 edn), pp. xli, 153–4.

the Marxist and more general sense – a historically unnecessary
catastrophe.

As the revolt had little measurable effect on the social and
economic condition of the English peasant and labourer, it seems
tempting to argue that its greatest impact was in the field of
politics. But here again its results were largely negative. The
rebels of 1381 effectively killed the poll tax as an instrument
of taxation: there was henceforward less possibility that the
English Exchequer might develop a lucrative form of direct
per capita taxation of the type evolving in contemporary France.
It has sometimes been argued that their experiences in June 1381
had traumatic effects on the characters of two of the greatest
personalities of the age. But Stubbs's view that 'John of Gaunt
was changed almost as by miracle'[1] and ceased to play an
aggressive part in English political warfare after that year seems
inherently implausible: it certainly under-estimates the extent
to which the duke of Lancaster had been a force for compromise
before the outbreak of the rebellion. More famous and persistent
is the belief that the young Richard II's exposure to the dramatic
confrontations at Mile End and Smithfield encouraged him to
over-estimate his political power and fatally fostered his 'absolut-
ist' tendencies. It is barely possible that the fourteen-year old
monarch's daring after Tyler's death taught a would-be lion
to know his own strength; but there is little contemporary
evidence for such an interpretation. 'At fourteen he had learned
that miracles might be worked by one who wore a crown.'[2]
Indeed they might: but this was a lesson Richard could derive
from more reliable and respectable tutors than the rebels at
Smithfield.

For the young Richard, as for all the other protagonists on the
scene, the events of 1381 presented little cause for self-congratulation. In the last resort the great revolt has no readily discernible
effect on the nature of the late medieval English government.
The style and methods of Richard II's kingship remain

---

[1] Stubbs, *Constitutional History*, II 463.
[2] R. H. Jones, *The Royal Policy of Richard II* (Oxford, 1968), p. 19.

controversial. But at no time in a crisis-ridden reign is there any suggestion that he contemplated a readjustment of the social order in the interests of those who had thought of him as their saviour in 1381.[1] One of the most remarkable features of the revolt was the speed with which it became irrelevant to the traditional themes and preoccupations of political life. As early as August 1381 the greatest threat to the stability of the realm was no longer the renewed danger of a peasant uprising but the bitter personal feud between two of the king's greatest magnates, John of Gaunt and his former ally, Henry Percy, earl of Northumberland (no. 60). In the light of this quarrel, which at times brought the kingdom to the edge of civil war, it is not even easy to believe that the Peasants' Revolt led to a closing of the ranks on the part of the English nobility. The bloodily dramatic political struggles of Richard II's reign were fought within a small aristocratic society which needed to pay little attention to the great issues of 1381. For the purposes of practical politics, the great revolt could be allowed to disappear into oblivion.

Of course the memory of the stormy scenes in London between 13 and 15 June 1381 was preserved in later years – but for many centuries by the conservative rather than radical elements in English society (nos. 73-5). William Courtenay, the unfortunate Sudbury's successor as archbishop of Canterbury and, according to his recent biographer, the 'strong man' of 1381, lost no time in pointing out that only by the extirpation of religious heresy could the threat of another social upheaval be averted.[2] The Peasants' Revolt continued to provide, after the Reformation as before, an admirably suitable lesson for the many who wished to exploit the obsessive English dread that 'the centre might not

---

[1] But see B. F. Harvey, 'Draft Letters Patent of Manumission and Pardon for the men of Somerset in 1381', *Eng. Hist. Rev.*, LXXX (1965) 89–91, for a restatement of the view that Richard may have adopted a more tolerant attitude towards the question of villein enfranchisement than the parliamentary commons of 1381.

[2] J. Dahmus, *William Courtenay, Archbishop of Canterbury* (Pennsylvania U.P., 1966), p. 297; and, more generally, see M. E. Aston, 'Lollardy and Sedition, 1381–1431', *Past and Present*, no. 17 (1960), pp. 1–44.

hold' and 'perpetual conflict' (to use Sir Thomas Elyot's phrase) drag the English polity into chaos. In Queen Elizabeth I's own famous words, spoken within a not dissimilar context: 'I am Richard II: know ye not that.'[1] But whether the earl of Essex thought of himself as Wat Tyler, with whom he was compared by contemporary publicists at the time of his abortive rising, is another matter entirely. Many civil rebellions in late medieval, Tudor and Stuart England certainly reflected several of the aspirations and grievances previously expressed in 1381 (no. 62); but these sometimes striking similarities were ones of which it seems certain that the later rebels were themselves largely unaware. When, as late as the summer of 1549, Robert Kett's Norfolk rebels demanded 'thatt all bonde men may be ffre for god made all ffre with his precious blode sheddyng', they presumably had no conception that they were re-echoing the sentiments of John Ball's sermon.[2] Post-medieval England experienced an important, and unjustly neglected, history of revolutionary movements, but not – as far as we can tell – an articulate revolutionary tradition. Only in the late eighteenth century, with the emergence of a genuinely new radical movement, were the rebels of 1381 rescued from their stock role of 'presumptuous rebels' and accorded a modest place in the pantheon of English working-class heroes. In the event Wat Tyler did have at least one, and self-appointed, political descendant:– the Bradford Chartist, Isaac Jefferson, a blacksmith 'alias Wat Tyler' whose 'Herculean strength', 'velveteen smoking jacket' and 'cap of the knight templar form' aroused some consternation in May 1848.[3]

But none of the revolutionary or left-wing parties of more recent times have ever taken the rebels of 1381 very warmly to their hearts. As the documents in this collection make clear,

---

[1] L. B. Campbell, *Shakespeare's Histories* (London, 1964), p. 191.

[2] A. Fletcher, *Tudor Rebellions*, pp. 74, 143.

[3] *Northern Star*, 3 June 1848. I owe this reference to the generosity of Mr A. J. Peacock. Cf. the lines of a Chartist song, 'For Tyler of old, a heart-chorus bold/Let Labour's children sing!' (*Poetical Works of Thomas Cooper*, London, 1877, p. 285).

their legacy to the present is both ambiguous and disconcerting
(nos. 78, 79). Even Tom Paine's powerful advocacy (no. 76)
has failed – nearly two centuries later – to secure for Tyler a
public monument. The modern visitor to West Smithfield will
encounter commemorative plaques to Protestant martyrs and a
Scottish 'nationalist' but no visible memorial to the greatest
rebel of them all. To the more persistent enquirer the custodians of
Fishmongers' Hall may reveal a wooden effigy of Mayor William
Walworth and the dagger with which he is reputed to have
stabbed Wat Tyler. But the Peasants' Revolt offers the historian
virtually nothing in the way either of relics or of iconography.
Even the home-made banners upon which the Sheffield Chartists
of the 1840s painted the portraits of their heroes, 'ranging from
Wat Tyler to Byron and Shelley' have long since disappeared
into oblivion.[1] But it may be symbolically appropriate that an
obscure and evanescent rising has left so little in the way of
tangible memorial.[2] Although the Peasants' Revolt is slightly less
mysterious to us today than it was to many of its participants, the
final judgment of the very first historian of the rising can still
afford to stand: 'The Laurel of success crowned not the Rebels,
they crumble to their first dust again, are ruined by their own
weight and confusion. They had risen like those Sons of the
Dragon's teeth, in tempests, without policy or advice. Their
leaders were meerly fantastical, but goblins and shadows, men
willing to embroyl, and daring, whose courage was better than
their cause.'[3]

---

[1] B. Simon, *Studies in the History of Education, 1780–1870* (London, 1960) p. 249.

[2] A possible exception is the stone cross beside the road from North Walsham
to Norwich, 'said, and not improbably, to mark the field of battle in 1381' (*A
General History of the County of Norfolk*, printed by and for John Stacey, Norwich,
1829, II 964).

[3] John Cleveland, *The Rustick Rampant, or Rurall Anarchy affronting Monarchy*
(London, 1658), Introduction.

Note on the Translations

The Peasants' Revolt took place at a time immediately preceding the general adoption of the English language as a normal and familiar means of written communication. With one or two minor exceptions the primary sources of the great revolt of 1381 were written in Latin or Norman-French; and only from the years immediately before and after 1400 does there begin to survive a copious supply of historical documents written by Englishmen in English. The very first of the extracts in this collection is itself symptomatic of the gradual movement towards the use of the native language: in the late 1380s John Trevisa translated Ranulf Higden's famous world history or *Polychronicon* into English (no. 1) at the request of Lord Berkeley. However, Trevisa's translation was by no means as immediately popular as the original Latin editions – and it was during the first two decades of the fifteenth century that the progression towards the vernacular became unmistakably apparent. At the end of the reign of Henry IV (1399–1413), the first English king to have his will written in English, the trend had become irreversible. By the time of Cade's revolt in 1450 (no. 62) the majority of the important narrative sources are in English; and the Peasants' Revolt is the last great popular disturbance in English history to be almost exclusively recorded in languages other than English itself.

There are consequently very few English documents in the following pages and nearly all of these are in verse rather than prose. One poem describing the course of the revolt, 'Tax has tenet us Alle' (no. 66), was written in a mixture of Latin and English – thus symbolising the transition from the use of one language to the other. Several pieces of vernacular verse are also included either because they reflect contemporary attitudes (nos. 10 and 72), comment upon the revolt as such (nos. 51 and 65) or illustrate popular grievances (no. 71). As these extracts are few in number, short in length and of no great linguistic complexity, it has seemed most sensible to retain their original

format and spelling. Accordingly no attempt has been made to
'translate' these poems into modern English, and alterations have
normally been confined to matters of punctuation and the use of
capital letters. Unfamiliar words have been explained in a short
glossary appended to the extracts themselves.

French or Norman-French was still the most fashionable means
of expression at the English court in the 1380s and our knowledge
of the great revolt is heavily reliant on three primary authorities
all written in that language. Extracts from the Rolls of Parliament,
the *Anonimalle Chronicle* and Froissart's chronicles inevitably
figure prominently in this collection. My translations from the
official Rolls of Parliament have been made directly from the only
complete edition, published by the Record Commission in
1783: they preserve that volume's numbering of the different
paragraphs. By general agreement the long description of the
Peasants' Revolt to be found in the *Anonimalle Chronicle* is
the single most important narrative source for the history of the
rebellion. I have translated the whole of this account despite
the fact that an English version of most of the text already exists,
printed by Charles Oman as Appendix V of his *Great Revolt of
1381*. Although Oman's work proved extremely helpful, his
translation was based on a copy of the original manuscript
made by Francis Thynne in the 1590s. I have thought it advisable
to produce an extensively revised translation from the only
complete and definitive edition of the *Anonimalle Chronicle*
published by Professor Galbraith in 1927.

The whole of Froissart's famous description of the 1381 revolt
clearly has to be included in any source-book of the great revolt;
but in this case alone it seemed unnecessary, and indeed positively
unwise, to make a new translation. The English version of
Froissart published by John Bourchier, second Lord Berners,
in 1523-5 is in itself so celebrated and impressive a work of early
Tudor literature that it appeared most sensible to retain it and pay
the slight price of minor inaccuracies. I have of course compared
Berners's translation with Froissart's own text as published in
various French editions: – a comparison which leaves one with a

very great respect for the former's standards of accuracy and skills as a translator. Berners captured the spirit as well as most of the letter of Froissart's prose with an almost uncanny fidelity, curiously comparable to Scott Moncrieff's translation of Proust's *A la Recherche du temps perdu.* Berners naturally made some mistakes, though less serious ones than is often assumed. Where he omits factual information completely or seriously misrepresents the meaning of Froissart's sentences, I have added the appropriate emendation either in a foot-note or inserted within square brackets during the course of the narrative. Those who would prefer to read a very recent and readily available translation of Froissart can in any case safely rely on the selections (which include much of the chronicler's account of the Peasants' Revolt) edited by Geoffrey Brereton for Penguin books in 1968.

All the other important chronicle authorities for the great revolt of 1381 as well as the voluminous series of relevant legal and governmental records were written in medieval Latin. The various representative accounts of trial proceedings against the rebels dispersed throughout this collection are obviously indispensable to any detailed analysis of the Peasants' Revolt; but they present a serious problem to both translator and reader. Given the general principle of translating as many documents as possible in their entirety, it has been necessary to include a good deal in the way of conventional legal formulae and stereotyped phraseology. Official verbiage has, I hope, been reduced to a tolerable minimum; but I have sometimes preferred the risk of inducing boredom to the opposite danger of presenting short extracts out of their proper context. Those who find a few of the following documents tediously verbose may derive some consolation from the knowledge that the original Latin was not less so.

The translation of extracts from late fourteenth-century Latin chroniclers presents one with the opposite difficulty. With one or two exceptions the chroniclers of the early years of Richard II were not at all given to prolixity. They wrote in short, staccato sentences to convey as much factual information as possible without any wastage of words. Henry Knighton, the 'monk of Westminster' (whose accounts of the great revolt are translated *in extenso*) and their contemporaries had few pretensions to literary skill. They used similes and metaphors very rarely and generally make their meaning clear by means of short, clipped and unemotional sentences and phrases. These characteristics are deliberately reflected in my translations – as is the fact that it was most unusual for such chroniclers to construct a consecutive argument running over more than two or three sentences. To all these generalisations the one major exception is the inimitable Thomas Walsingham of St Albans, by any standards the most distinctive as well as the most idiosyncratic historian of late medieval England. When reading Walsingham, and perhaps only when reading Walsingham, is it possible to recapture in personal terms the emotional shock experienced by English rulers and landlords in the summer of 1381. Walsingham, who often tends to communicate by means of suggestion and insinuation rather than explicit statement, is not an easy chronicler to translate. His sentences are sometimes as tortuous as his meaning is opaque. How successfully Walsingham's characteristic tone of bitter and convoluted despondency is conveyed by my translations from his *Historia Anglicana* and *Chronicon Angliae* is not for me to say. I can only hope that my efforts may deserve no more severe a verdict than Professor Galbraith's tribute to Walsingham's own Latin prose style: 'even if unspeakable, it is at least unmistakable'. Walsingham's spelling of place and personal names is often, like that of all his contemporaries, erratic: throughout the book I have aimed for consistency except in the case of those names (e.g. Wat Tyler) where variations of spelling seemed worth preserving.

Walsingham himself remarked upon his description of the Peasants' Revolt that 'we have written – but not without labour': a comment which might be applied to parts of this book. The translations which follow inevitably represent a compromise between the need to be faithful to the meaning of the original text and a desire to produce a reasonably readable version in English. No such compromise can ever be ideal; but to such a compromise there was no real alternative.

The Chronology of the Revolt

Readers of the following documents will soon appreciate that the detailed chronology of the English Peasants' Revolt presents several intricate and indeed insoluble problems. It is, for example, impossible to give exact dates for such important episodes as the first outbreak of violence in Essex or the rout of the Norfolk rebels at North Walsham. But there is reliable direct or circumstantial evidence for all the dates mentioned in the following lists, and I have included references to several European as well as English provincial risings in order to supplement those documented at length in the course of this collection.

1. THE FOURTEENTH-CENTURY BACKGROUND

1302, May–July:	the 'Matins of Bruges' and the Flemish victory against French at Courtrai.
1323–8:	the peasant rising in western Flanders.
1337, Oct.:	the conventional 'beginning' of the Hundred Years War.
1337–45:	Jacques van Artevelde popular leader in Ghent.
1347–54:	the Cola di Rienzo risings and revolts in Rome.
1348–9:	the first appearance of the 'Black Death' in England.
1349, June:	the English Ordinance of Labourers.
1351, Feb.:	the first Statute of Labourers.
1356, Sept.:	English victory at Poitiers and capture of John II of France.
1358, May–June:	the *Jacquerie* in northern France.
1360, May:	Treaty of Bretigny between French and English monarchs.

1362, Nov.:	John of Gaunt created duke of Lancaster.
1369, June:	Edward III resumes title of king of France and war re-commences.
1375, May:	Simon of Sudbury translated from London to archbishopric of Canterbury.
1375, June:	Truce of Bruges leaves Edward III in possession of few French lands.
1376, April–June:	the 'Good Parliament' at Westminster attacks royal officials.
1376, 8 June:	death of Edward, the 'Black Prince'.
1376, Aug.–Sept.:	radical and anti-oligarchical reforms to constitution of city of London.
1377, Jan.–Feb.:	Edward III's last parliament grants the first poll tax.
1377, 19 Feb.:	riots in London after Wycliffe's trial before Convocation in St Paul's.
1377, 21 June:	death of Edward III and succession of Richard II.
1378, July–Aug.:	the rising of the *Ciompi* in Florence.
1379, April–May:	Richard II's third parliament grants the second poll tax.
1380, 30 Jan.:	Archbishop Sudbury appointed Chancellor of England.
1380, 13 Oct.:	William Walworth elected mayor of London for the ensuing year.
1380, Nov.–Dec.:	Richard II's fifth parliament grants the third poll tax.
1381, 1 Feb.:	Robert Hales appointed Treasurer of England.
1381, 13 Oct.:	John of Northampton elected mayor of London (served until October 1383).
1382, 20 Jan.:	Marriage of Richard II and Anne of Bohemia.
1382, Feb.:	the 'Harelle' or urban rising in Rouen.
1382, March:	the rising of the *Maillotins* in Paris.
1382, May:	the 'Earthquake' synod at Blackfriars, London, condemns Wycliffe's teaching.

1383, 27 Nov.:	the battle of Roosebeke and the death of Philip van Artevelde, captain-general of Ghent.
1384, Jan.–Aug.:	successful counter-revolution in London and restoration of old constitution.
1384, 31 Dec.:	death of John Wycliffe at Lutterworth.
1399, 30 Sept.:	Richard II displaced by Henry Bolingbroke as king of England.
1410:	Pope Alexander V's condemnation of John Huss's teaching followed by serious risings in Prague.

2. THE OUTBREAK AND COURSE OF REBELLION IN LONDON AND S.E. ENGLAND

1380

6 Dec.:	NORTHAMPTON, end of parliament after grant of third poll tax.

1381

16 March:	appointment of commissioners to enforce poll tax in 9 counties.
3 May:	appointment of commissioners to enforce poll tax in 6 other counties.
12 May:	John of Gaunt leaves Savoy Palace for the Scottish Marches.
mid-May:	ESSEX, rumours and reports of tax resistance in the county.
Thur. 30 May? (or earlier)	ESSEX, violent attack on John de Bampton's party at Brentwood by villagers of Fobbing, Corringham and Stanford
Sat. 1 June:	ESSEX, local and London rebels reported to be conspiring in county.
Sun. 2 June (or earlier)	ESSEX, armed attack on Robert Bealknap and his commission near Brentwood.

Sun. 2 June:	KENT, Abel Ker and rebels from Erith attack abbey of Lesnes.
Mon. 3 June:	ESSEX, Abel Ker's band crosses Thames and recruits men in the county.
	ESSEX, Thomas Farndon of London reported to be plotting Hales's death with rebels of the county.
	KENT, dispute at Gravesend after arrest of villein of Simon Burley.
Tue. 4 June:	KENT, Abel Ker's reinforced band returns over Thames from Essex.
Wed. 5 June:	KENT, Ker's band enters Dartford and incites town to rebellion.
Wed. 5 June?:	KENT, royal commission of trailbaston (with John Legge) repulsed on way to Canterbury.
Thur. 6 June:	KENT, rebels enter Rochester and force capitulation of royal castle.
Fri. 7 June:	KENT, rebels enter Maidstone: probable rise to command of Wat Tyler.
8-9 June:	KENT, widespread violence, looting and gaol-breaking in north Kent.
Mon. 10 June:	KENT, Tyler and rebels enter Canterbury in morning and control city.
	ESSEX, sack of Treasurer Hales's manor of Cressing Temple.
Tue. 11 June:	KENT, Tyler and rebels leave Canterbury in morning and march to London – via Maidstone?
Wed. 12 June:	LONDON, rebel company probably assembles on Blackheath in late evening: contingents reach Lambeth and break open Marshalsea?
	LONDON, Richard II and his court moves from Westminster to Tower: Sudbury relinquishes the Great Seal.

Thur. 13 June: LONDON, Richard II's abortive voyage to Rotherhithe (in the morning) is followed by the entry of both Kent and Essex rebels into the city. The attack on the Savoy takes place at about 4.0 P.M. and the burning of St John's, Clerkenwell, later in the evening.

Fri. 14 June: LONDON, Jack Straw and his rebels burn Hales's manor of Highbury. Richard II present at Mile End conference in morning. Executions of Sudbury, Hales, etc. outside Tower: morning?

ST ALBANS, arrival of rebel deputation: townsmen march to London.

MIDDLESEX, rebels enter monastery of Grace and coerce monks.

Sat. 15 June: LONDON, Richard II's morning visit to Westminster Abbey is followed by his confrontation with Wat Tyler at Smithfield.

ST ALBANS, townsmen destroy folds and hold first meeting with abbot.

Sun. 16 June: LONDON, Richard II, at the Wardrobe, makes Hugh Segrave temporary keeper of Great Seal.

SURREY, a group of Essex rebels extorting ransoms at Clandon.

ST ALBANS, abbey agrees to concede moderate charter to town.

Tue. 18 June: LONDON, Richard II's commission to sheriffs etc. to resist rebels.

Sat. 22 June: LONDON, Richard II leaves the city and stays at Waltham.

27–30 June?: ESSEX, Richard II and court directing repression from Havering atte Bower.

28 June: ESSEX, rout of Essex rebels at Billericay.

1 July:	KENT, attempt by rebels to resist royal commissioners of peace at Canterbury.
2 July:	ESSEX, Richard II, at Chelmsford, formally revokes his previous charters of manumission.
12 July:	ST ALBANS, Richard II arrives amid the suppression of revolt there.
15 July:	ST ALBANS, execution of John Ball.
20 July:	ST ALBANS, Richard II leaves for Berkhamsted after receiving fealty of men of Hertfordshire.
10 Aug.:	READING, Richard II and John of Gaunt present at Council where William Courtenay appointed Chancellor, Hugh Segrave Treasurer.
13 Nov.:	WESTMINSTER, opening assembly of first parliament after the revolt.

3. REBELLION IN EAST ANGLIA

1381

Sun. 9 June:	CAMBRIDGESHIRE, attack on Cottenham house of Roger of Harleston, burgess of Cambridge.
Wed. 12 June:	N. ESSEX, sack of Richard Lyons's manor of Overhall at Liston on Stour.
Thur. 13 June:	W. SUFFOLK, John Wrawe's band loots Cavendish church and enters Bury.
Fri. 14 June:	W. SUFFOLK, Sir John Cavendish beheaded at Lakenheath.
	W. NORFOLK, Geoffrey Parfeye's band extorts 20 marks from Thetford.
	E. SUFFOLK, two rebel bands appear south of Ipswich.

Sat. 15 June: W. SUFFOLK, Prior Cambridge of Bury
                     St Edmunds beheaded at Mildenhall.
                     ——, rebels assault abbey of Bury and
                     behead John Lakenheath.
                     ELY, outbreak of revolt in city led by
                     Richard de Leycester.
                     CAMBRIDGE, burgesses' alliance with
                     county rebels leads to a night of violence.

Sun. 16 June: CAMBRIDGE, widespread looting and
                     bonfire of university records.
                     E. SUFFOLK, rebel bands enter Ipswich
                     and destroy property there.

Mon. 17 June: CAMBRIDGE, mayor and rebels assault
                     Barnwell priory.
                     ELY, Leycester and his band execute Sir
                     Edmund Walsingham, a Cambridgeshire
                     justice.
                     PETERBOROUGH, outbreak of brief
                     rebellion against the abbot.
                     E. NORFOLK, rebel assembly on Mouse-
                     hold Heath and Litster's entry into
                     Norwich.

Tue. 18 June: E. NORFOLK, Sir Roger Bacon and his
                     company enter Great Yarmouth.
                     ——, riots at Lowestoft, led by Richard
                     Resch of Holland.
                     N.E. SUFFOLK, John Wrawe leads assault
                     on Mettingham castle.
                     RAMSEY, abbot and Bishop Despenser
                     disperse rebel band from Ely.

19–20 June: CAMBRIDGE, Bishop Despenser crushes
                     rebels and beheads John Hanchach.

20–21 June: E. NORFOLK, Sir Roger Bacon still
                     inciting risings N. of Yarmouth.

Sat. 22 June?:   W. SUFFOLK, Litster's envoys to Richard
                     II intercepted at Icklingham.

Sun. 23 June:	W. SUFFOLK, the earl of Suffolk arrives in Bury to pacify the town.
Mon. 24 June:	E. NORFOLK, Bishop Despenser enters and pacifies Norwich.
	——, Litster still recognised as 'chief leader' in the county.
25 or 26 June?:	E. NORFOLK, Bishop Despenser routs Litster and rebels at N. Walsham.

1382

late Sept.:	E. NORFOLK, abortive conspiracy to recapture Norwich and kill Bishop Despenser.

4. REBELLION ELSEWHERE IN ENGLAND

1380

Sept.:	SALISBURY, armed insurrection by commons of the town.
26 Nov.:	YORK, armed attack on Guildhall and expulsion of Mayor John de Gisburne.

1381

Tue. 7 May:	BEVERLEY, members of the commons assault the Guildhall.
Sat. 15 June:	BEDFORDSHIRE, tenants demand charter of privileges from prior of Dunstable.
Sun. 16 June:	BUCKINGHAMSHIRE, rebels from Berkhamsted attack Ashridge and King's Langley.
mid-June?:	——, tenants of royal manor of Langley Marish withdraw services.
Mon. 17 June:	YORK, partial destruction of walls, gates, property within the city.
17–18 June?:	LEICESTER, citizens await an assault by rebels from London.
mid-June?:	LEICESTERSHIRE, refusal of Hospitallers' tenants at Rothley to pay tithes.

Wed. 19 June: SOMERSET, attack on Hospital of St John at Bridgwater.

Fri. 21 June: SOMERSET, execution of Hugh Lavenham at Ilchester.

Sun. 23 June: SCARBOROUGH, riots led by Robert Galoun and others – until 30 June.

late June?:   WINCHESTER, urban rising, apparently led by cloth-workers.

late June?:   S.W. SUSSEX, withdrawal of services by tenants of earl of Arundel.

late June?:   NORTHAMPTON, William Napton leads a rising of 'community' against mayor.

1 July: YORK, armed attack on Bootham Bar.

5 July: WORCESTER, rumours of a peasant rising by tenants of priory.

6 July: BEVERLEY, murder of William Haldane by John Erghom and others.

early July: WARWICKSHIRE, news of risings persuades earl of Warwick to return there.

10 July: LINCOLN, earl of Nottingham and others appointed to resist rebellion in the county.

29 July: WIRRAL, rising of the abbot of Chester's villeins.

11 Aug.:   YORK, archbishop and John of Gaunt commissioned to terminate disputes.

12 Oct.:   BEVERLEY, John of Gaunt and others commissioned to restore peace.

1382

18 Oct.:   YORK, SCARBOROUGH, BEVERLEY, royal letters of pardon to these three boroughs.

List of Authorities

The extracts in this volume have been translated, copied or collated from various narrative or record sources to which the following list provides an alphabetical guide as well as (where necessary) an index of abbreviations. Further details are provided in the bibliography. The list should also be of use to those who would prefer to read the narrative of a particular chronicler consecutively rather than according to the chronological and regional pattern adopted by the plan of this book.

No. of Document

Powell, E. and Trevelyan, G. M., *The Peasants'*
Rising and the Lollards (London, 1899)   24, 49

PUBLIC RCORD OFFICE: description and references of
documents:

C.54	— Close Rolls	12
C.60	— Fine Rolls	18
C.66	— Patent Rolls	34, 45a, 56
KB.9	— King's Bench, Ancient Indictments	40
KB.27	— King's Bench, *Coram Rege* Rolls	24, 32, 33, 39, 46c, 47, 57 58, 59
SC.8	— Ancient Petitions	48
Chester 25	— Chester Indictment Rolls	49

Putnam, B. H., *Enforcement of Statute of Lab-*
ourers, 1349–59 (1908)   6c

Registrum Edmundi Lacy (Canterbury and York
Society, 1918)   63b

Réville, A., *Le Soulèvement des Travailleurs*   12, 32a, 33,
d'Angleterre en 1381 (Paris, 1898)   34, 39, 46c,
          47, 56, 57, 58

Robbins, R. H., ed., *Historical Poems of the*   10, 51, 65, 66,
XIVth and XVth Centuries (New York, 1959)   71 b–f

Rotuli Parliamentorum (*Rot. Parl.*), vols II and III   7, 8a, 9, 15b,
          17, 37, 45b,
          46a, 60, 63d,
          67

Russell, J. C., *British Medieval Population* (Albuquerque, 1948)   3

Rymer's *Foedera* (The Hague, 1739–45)   63a

Sisam, K., ed., *Fourteenth Century Verse and Prose*
(Oxford, 1921)   10, 51, 71a

Southey, Robert, *Wat Tyler*   77

No. of Document

Sparvil-Bayly, J. A., 'Essex in Insurrection,
　　1381', *Trans. Essex Arch. Soc.*, 1878　　　　24
Statutes of the Realm, vol. 1 (1810)　　　　　5
Stow, John, *Annales* (London, 1631)　　　　62
Strawe, *The Life and Death of Jacke* (London,
　　1593)　　　　　　　　　　　　　　　74
Vale Royal, *The Ledger Book of* (Lancs. and
　　Cheshire Record Society, 1914)　　　　8c
Vita Ricardi Secundi, ed. T. Hearne (Oxford,
　　1729)　　　　　　　　　　　　　　　11
Walsingham, Thomas, *Chronicon Angliae* (Rolls　20, 26, 38, 41,
　　Series, 1874)　　　　　　　　　　43, 53, 61a
Walsingham, Thomas, *Historia Anglicana* (2 vols;　15a, 20, 26,
　　Rolls Series, 1863–4)　　　　　　38, 41, 43, 53,
　　　　　　　　　　　　　　　　　61, 68, 70a,
　　　　　　　　　　　　　　　　　71a

Wilkinson, B., 'The Peasants' Revolt of 1381',
　　Speculum, 1940　　　　　　　　　　32b
Wright, T., ed., *Political Poems and Songs* (2 vols;
　　Rolls Series, 1859–61)　　　　　　10, 51, 66
York Memorandum Book (2 vols; Surtees Society,
　　1912–15)　　　　　　　　　　　　46b

PART I

The Background to the Peasants' Revolt

The following extracts are intended not to explain the great revolt but to set the English political and social scene for the violent events of May and June 1381. They cannot provide a comprehensive guide to the causes of the Peasants' Revolt for the simple reason that the rising was so complex a series of episodes and incidents that it continues to defy simple analysis. Our knowledge of the social forces present in late fourteenth-century England is still less than adequate to explain the surprising developments of 1381. Two themes can however be distinguished relatively clearly within the changing political and economic activities of Englishmen in the generation before the great revolt. The first appearance of bubonic plague, the Black Death of 1348–9, ushered in a period of falling population and rising wages. The response of the government and of the county landlords represented in the English parliamentary commons was an attempt to control competition for a dwindling supply of labour by means of stringent labour laws (nos. 5–6).

But the rising of 1381 was as much a reaction against excessive war taxation as against the statutes of labourers. The grievances of the rebels can never be properly understood unless they are placed within the context of an expensive and increasingly dangerous dynastic war between the kingdoms of England and France (nos. 11–13). The problems created by labour shortage at home and military failure abroad were the subject of much contemporary comment and are illustrated at some length and from many points of view in the pages which follow. But despite gloomy prognostications such as those of John Gower (no. 14), the great revolt of 1381 obviously startled, not to say stunned, contemporaries. Isolated acts of peasant rebellion were not unknown to fourteenth-century England (no. 8); but the widespread uprising of 1381 had no precedent. The rebels of that year no doubt voiced some of the abiding truths of the human condition in medieval society; but their ability to do so depended, as will be seen, on a precise series of historical relationships which made a unique explosion possible and likely.

1 The Character of the English

Higden's *Polychronicon*, Rolls Series, 1865–86, II 167–71

John Trevisa, a Cornish clerk and scholar educated at Oxford, translated Higden's *Polychronicon* in the late 1380s. In his well-known description of the English character, Trevisa points to a paradox noted by many other late medieval commentators: the aggressiveness of Englishmen led to exceptional success in military adventure abroad at the price of extreme social and political instability at home.

Notheless men of the south beeth esier and more mylde; and men of the north be more unstable, more cruel, and more unesy; the myddel men beeth somdele partyners with bothe. Also they woneth hem to glotonye more than other men, and beeth more costlewe in mete and in drynke and in clothyng. . . . These men been speedful bothe on hors and on foote, able and redy to alle manere dedes of armes, and beeth i-woned to have the victorie and the maistrie in everich fight wher no treson is walkynge; and beeth curious, and kunneth wel i-now telle dedes and wondres that thei haveth i-seie. Also they gooth in dyvers londes, unnethe beeth eny men richere in her owne lond othere more gracious [fortunate] in fer and in straunge londe. They konneth betre wynne and gete new than kepe her owne heritage; therfore it is that they beeth i-spred so wyde and weneth that everich londe is hir owne heritage. The men beeth able to al manere sleithe and witte, but to fore the dede blondrynge and hasty, and more wys after the dede; and leveth ofte lightliche what they haveth bygonne. Therfore Eugenius the pope seide that Englisshe men were able to do what evere they wolde, and to be sette and putte to fore all othere, nere that light wytte letteth [if only inconstancy did not prevent them]. And as Hannibal saide that the Romayns myghte nought be overcome but in hir owne cuntray; so Englische men mowe not be overcome in straunge londes, but in hir own cuntray they beeth lightliche overcome. These men despiseth hir owne and preiseth other menis, and unnethe beeth apaide [content] with hir owne estate; what byfalleth and semeth other men, they wolleth gladlyche take to hem self. Therfor hit is that a yeman arraieth hym as a squyer, a squyer as a knight, a knight as a duke, and a duke as a king.

2 The Lay Population of English Counties and Towns according to the Poll Tax Returns of 1377 and 1381

Powell, *Rising in East Anglia*, pp. 121–3

The following table, compiled by Edgar Powell from the 'great enrollments' of the 1377 and 1381 poll taxes, is undoubtedly a more accurate guide to the distribution of the lay population of England than to its size. The poll tax returns do not provide a full census, for they omit all beggars and children (see below, nos. 15–17) as well as the many inhabitants of the country who successfully evaded the tax. A simple comparison of the figures for 1377 with those of 1381 printed below leaves no doubt that tax-evasion was a serious problem in the latter year. By general agreement only the 1377 poll tax returns are likely to provide a reasonably reliable indication of the size of population. Professor Russell calculated the total population (clerical and lay) of England in 1377 at 2,232,373 on the assumptions that there ought to be added to the figures provided by the returns 50 per cent for children and another 5 per cent for beggars and those who evaded assessment.[1] Most later critics have argued that Professor Russell underestimated this total figure. What now seems fairly well-established is that the population of England had been well over four millions before

[1] J. C. Russell, *British Medieval Population* (Albuquerque, 1948), p. 146.

the Black Death of 1348–9, but had probably dropped considerably below that total by the time of the Peasants' Revolt. The two counties of Durham and Cheshire, excluded from the returns, are not likely to have been densely populated.

Counties and Towns	1377	1381
Bedfordshire	20339	14895
Berkshire	22723	15696
Buckinghamshire	24672	17997
Cambridgeshire	27350	24324
Cambridge	1902	1739
Cornwall	34274	12056
Cumberland	11841	4748
Penrith	no separate return	75
Carlisle	678	no separate return
Derbyshire	23243	15637
Derby	1046	no separate return
Devonshire	45635	20656
Exeter	1560	1420
Plymouth	not given	no separate return
Dartmouth	506	no separate return
Dorsetshire	34241	19507
Essex	47962	30748
Colchester	2955	1609
Gloucestershire	36760	27857
Gloucester	2239	1446
Bristol	6345	5662
Hampshire	33241	22018
Southampton	1152	1051
Isle of Wight	4733	3625
Winchester	not given	no separate return
Herefordshire	15318	12659
Hereford	1903	no separate return
Ludlow	1172	no separate return
Hertfordshire	19975	13296

Counties and Towns	1377	1381
Huntingdonshire	14169	11299
Kent	56557	43838
Canterbury	2574	2123
Rochester	570	no separate return
Lancashire	23880	8371
Leicestershire	31730	21914
Leicester	2101	1708
Lincolnshire		
Lincoln	3412	2196
Close of Lincoln	157	no separate return
Boston	2871	no separate return
Grimsby	no separate return	562
Kesteven	21566	15734
Holland	18592	13795
Stamford	1218	no separate return
Lindsey	47303	30235
Middlesex	11243	9937
London	23314	20397
Norfolk	88797	66719
Norwich	3952	3833
Lynn	3127	1824
Yarmouth	1941	no separate return
Northamptonshire	40225	27997
Northampton	1477	1518
Northumberland	14162	not given
Newcastle	2647	1819
Nottinghamshire	26260	17442
Nottingham	1447	1266
Newark	1178	no separate return
Oxfordshire	24982	20588
Oxford	2357	2005
Rutland	5994	5593
Shropshire	23574	13041
Shrewsbury	2082	1618

Counties and Towns	1377	1381
Somerset	54604	30384
Bath	570	297
Wells	901	487
Staffordshire	21465	15993
Lichfield	1024	no separate return
Suffolk	58610	44635
Ipswich	1507	963
Bury St Edmunds	2445	1334
Surrey	18039	12684
Southwark	no separate return	1059
Sussex	35326	26616
Chichester	869	787
Warwickshire	25447	20481
Coventry	4817	3947
Westmorland	7389	3859
Wiltshire	42599	30627
Salisbury	3226	2708
Worcestershire	14542	12043
Worcester	1557	932
Yorkshire		
York	7248	4015
Hull	1557	1124
Scarborough	no separate return	1480
Beverley	2663	no separate return
North Riding	33185	15690
East Riding	38238	25184
West Riding	48149	23029
Total	1355201	896451

[These figures may now be compared with those – identical for 1377 but slightly variant in 1381 – prepared by Dr E. B. Fryde from alternative accounts of the final returns of the poll taxes and printed in Oman, *Great Revolt* (1969 edn), appendix II, pp. 162–6.]

3 The Clerical Population of English Dioceses according to the Poll Tax Returns of 1377 and 1381

J. C. Russell, *British Medieval Population*, pp. 134–7. Cf. Oman, *Great Revolt* (1969 edn), pp. 163–4, for a more detailed and accurate table of the clerical population in 1381, derived from the same Enrolled Accounts [E.359/4] at the Public Record Office

The procedure by which direct taxation was levied on the English clergy during the later middle ages was sharply differentiated from that used for the laity. Not only was clerical taxation granted in the convocations of Canterbury and York rather than in parliament but the machinery of collection and payment into the Exchequer was quite distinct from its lay counterpart. The following table is a simplified version of that printed by Professor Russell: although not absolutely reliable, it provides useful comparative figures. It must be remembered that the mendicant friars were specifically excluded from the tax and that these figures (like those for the laity) are likely to conceal a good deal of tax-evasion. It is, once again, difficult to reconcile the figures for the two years with one another, and it seems certain that those for 1377 are the more reliable. Professor Russell calculated that the total number of the English clergy in this year was 33,231, or approximately 1·5 per cent of the total population. This is probably an underestimate and in any case rests on elements of what Professor Russell himself describes as 'pure conjecture'.

Diocese	1377	1381
Canterbury	1094	787
Bath and Wells	1083	1120
Chichester	641	723
Ely	1006	757
Exeter	2001	1360
Hereford	824	820
Lichfield	2122	1744

Lincoln	6496	6594
London	2329	1995
Norwich	3692	3711
Rochester	224	?275
Salisbury	1908	2064
Winchester	1291	1287
Worcester	1673	1381
York	3271	2858
Carlisle	232	—
Durham	—	598

4 The Black Death of 1348–9

Chronicon Henrici Knighton, Rolls Series, 1889–95, II 58–65

Of all descriptions of the catastrophic effects of the first visitation of bubonic plague in England, that written by Henry Knighton, a canon of St Mary's Abbey, Leicester, is the most informative and interesting. On the basis of what is admittedly extremely inconclusive evidence, most historians now content themselves with the assumption that approximately a third of the English population died under the onslaught of the 'prima pestilentia' in 1348–9.[1] As Knighton points out, the resulting dislocation inevitably led to a short-term fall in the prices of agricultural goods as well as to a more permanent shortage of labour.

In this and the following year (1348–9) there was a general mortality among men throughout the whole world. It began first in India, and spread thence into Tharsis, thence to the Saracens, and at last to the Christians and Jews; so that in the space of a single year, namely from Easter to Easter, as it was rumoured at the court of Rome, 8000 legions of men perished in those distant regions, besides Christians. . . .

[1] For the most recent discussion of this problem see P. Ziegler, *The Black Death* (London, 1969), pp. 224–31.

Then the dreadful pestilence made its way along the coast by Southampton and reached Bristol, where almost the whole strength of the town perished, as it were surprised by sudden death; for few kept their beds more than two or three days, or even half a day. Then this cruel death spread on all sides, following the course of the sun. And there died at Leicester, in the small parish of St Leonard's, more than 380 persons, in the parish of Holy Cross, 400, in the parish of St Margaret's, Leicester, 700; and so in every parish, in a great multitude. Then the bishop of Lincoln sent notice throughout his whole diocese giving general power to all priests, both regulars and seculars, to hear confessions and give absolution with full episcopal authority to all persons, except only in case of debt. In such a case, the debtor was to pay the debt, if he were able, while he lived, or others were to be appointed to do so from his goods after his death. In the same way the Pope gave plenary remission of all sins (once only) to all receiving absolution at the point of death, and granted that this power should last until Easter next following, and that every one might choose his own confessor at will.

In the same year there was a great plague among sheep everywhere in the kingdom, so that in one place more than 5000 sheep died in a single pasture; and they rotted so much that neither bird nor beast would touch them. There was great cheapness of all things, owing to the general fear of death; for there were very few people who took any account of riches or property of any kind. A horse that was formerly worth 40s could be had for half a mark [6s 8d], a fat ox for 4s, a cow for 12d, a heifer for 6d, a fat wether for 4d, a sheep for 3d, a lamb for 2d, a large pig for 5d; a stone of wool was worth 9d. Sheep and oxen strayed at large through the fields and among the crops, and there were none to drive them off or herd them; but for lack of keepers they perished in remote by-ways and hedges in inestimable numbers throughout all districts, because there was such a great scarcity of servants that no one knew what he ought to do. For there was no recollection of so great and terrible a mortality since the time of Vortigern, king of the Britons, in whose day, as Bede testifies, in his book concerning the deeds of the English, the living did not suffice to bury the dead.[1]

In the following autumn a reaper was not to be had for less than 8*d*, with his food, a mower for less than 12*d*, with food. Therefore many crops rotted in the fields for lack of men to gather them. But in the year of the pestilence, as has been said above of other things, there was so great an abundance of all kinds of corn that virtually no one cared for it.

The Scots, hearing of the dreadful pestilence in England, surmised that it had come about at the hand of an avenging God, and it became an oath among them, so that, according to the common rumours that reached England, they were accustomed to swear 'be the foul deth of Engelond'. So the Scots, believing that a terrible vengeance of God had overtaken the English, came together in Selkirk forest with the intention of invading the realm of England, when the fierce mortality overtook them and their ranks were thinned by sudden and terrible death. About 5000 died in a short time. And as the rest, the strong and the feeble, were making ready to return to their own homes, they were pursued and intercepted by the English, who killed a very great number of them.

Master Thomas Bradwardine was consecrated by the Pope as archbishop of Canterbury, and when he returned to England, he came to London, and was dead within two days.[2] He was renowned above all other clerks in Christendom, especially in theology and other liberal sciences. At this time there was everywhere so great a scarcity of priests that many churches were left destitute, without divine service, masses, matins, vespers or sacraments. A chaplain was scarcely to be had to serve any church for less than £10 or 10 marks; and whereas when there was an abundance of priests before the pestilence a chaplain could be had for 4, 5 or even 2 marks with his board, at this time there was scarcely one willing to accept any vicarage at £20 or 20 marks.

[1] See *Venerabilis Baedae Opera Historica*, ed. C. Plummer (Oxford, 1896), I 32.
[2] Bradwardine, a noted scholar of theology and medicine, was consecrated archbishop on 19 July and died on 25 August 1349.

Within a little time, however, vast numbers of men whose wives had died in the pestilence flocked to take orders, many of whom were illiterate, and as it were mere laymen, save in so far as they could read a little, although without understanding. Ox hides rose to the outrageous price of 12*d*, a pair of shoes to 10, 12 or 14*d*, and a pair of leather thigh-boots to 3*s* or 4*s*.

Meanwhile the king sent notice into all counties of the realm that reapers and other labourers should not receive more than they used to take, under a penalty defined by statute; and he introduced a statute for this reason. But the labourers were so arrogant and hostile that they took no notice of the king's mandate; and if anyone wanted to employ them he was obliged to give them whatever they asked, and either to lose his fruits and crops, or satisfy at will the labourers' greed and arrogance. When it became known to him that they did not observe his ordinance and gave higher stipends to their labourers, the king levied heavy amercements upon abbots, priors, knights of greater and lesser degree, and others great and small throughout the countryside, taking 100*s* from some, 40*s* or 20*s* from others, according as they were able to pay. Moreover he took 20*s* from each carucate throughout the kingdom, and notwithstanding this, he also took a fifteenth.

Then the king caused many labourers to be arrested, and sent them to prison, numbers of whom escaped and went away to the forests and woods for a time, and those who were taken were heavily amerced. Most swore that they would not take daily stipends at a higher rate than had formerly been the custom, and so were set free from prison. The same thing was done in the case of other craftsmen in the boroughs and vills. . . .

After the pestilence many buildings both great and small in all cities, boroughs and vills fell into ruins for lack of inhabitants, and in the same way many villages and hamlets were depopulated, and there were no houses left in them, all who had lived therein being dead; and it seemed likely that many such hamlets would never again be inhabited. In the following winter there was such a shortage of servants for all sorts of labour as it was believed had never been before. For the sheep and cattle strayed in all

directions without herdsmen, and all things were left with
no one to care for them. Thus necessaries became so dear that
what had previously been worth 1*d* was now worth 4*d* or 5*d*.
Moreover the great men of the land and other lesser lords who had
tenants, remitted the payment of their rents, lest their tenants
should go away, on account of the scarcity of servants and the
high price of all things – some half their rents, some more, some
less, some for one, two, or three years according as they could
come to an agreement with them. Similarly, those who had let
lands on yearly labour-services to tenants as is the custom in the
case of villeins, were obliged to relieve and remit these services,
either excusing them entirely, or taking them on easier terms, in
the form of a small rent, lest their houses should be irreparably
ruined and the land should remain completely uncultivated. And
all sorts of food and necessities became excessively dear.

5   The Statute of Labourers, 1351

Statutes of Realm, I 311–13 : 25 Edward III, Stat. 2, cc. 1–7

As the preceding passage from the chronicle of Henry Knighton has
shown, Edward III and his council took drastic steps to restrain the
dramatic rise in wages while plague was still devastating the country.
The royal ordinance of 18 June 1349 (recapitulated below in the
preamble to the later statute) was designed to compel the able-bodied
to work and to maintain wage-rates at their level in 1346. In February
1351, during the first parliament held after the Black Death, the
notorious Statute of Labourers made the labour laws more precise and
elaborated in detail upon the methods by which they were to be
enforced. During the thirty years which followed, the statute, later
revised and re-issued, came to be (in Trevelyan's phrase) 'the favourite
child' of the parliamentary Commons. At a time of acute labour

shortage, a policy of wage restraint served the interests of the comparatively small county landlord at the expense of the great magnate with
reserves of capital and, more obviously, of the agricultural worker.

Against the malice of servants who were idle and unwilling to
serve after the pestilence without taking outrageous wages it
was recently ordained by our lord the king, with the assent of the
prelates, nobles and others of his council, that such servants, both
men and women, should be obliged to serve in return for the
salaries and wages which were customary (in those places where
they ought to serve) during the twentieth year of the present
king's reign (1346–7) or five or six years previously. It was also
ordained that such servants who refused to serve in this way
should be punished by imprisonment, as is more fully stated in
the said ordinance. Accordingly commissions were made out to
various people in every county to investigate and punish all those
who offended against the ordinance. But now our lord king has
been informed in this present parliament, by the petition of the
commons, that such servants completely disregard the said
ordinance in the interests of their own ease and greed and that
they withhold their service to great men and others unless they
have liveries and wages twice or three times as great as those they
used to take in the said twentieth year of Edward III and earlier,
to the serious damage of the great men and impoverishment of
all members of the said commons. Therefore the commons ask
for a remedy. Wherefore, in the said parliament and by the assent
of the prelates, earls, barons and other magnates as well as that
of the commons there assembled, the following things were
ordained and established to prevent the malice of the said servants.
1. First, that carters, ploughmen, leaders of the plough, shepherds,
swineherds, domestic and all other servants shall receive the
liveries and wages accustomed in the said twentieth year and
four years previously; so that in areas where wheat used to be
given, they shall take 10d for the bushel, or wheat at the will of
the giver, until it is ordained otherwise. These servants shall be
hired to serve by the entire year, or by the other usual terms,

and not by the day. No one is to receive more than 1*d* a day at the time of weeding or hay-making. Mowers of meadows are not to be paid more than 5*d* an acre or 5*d* a day; and reapers of corn are to be limited to 2*d* in the first week of August, 3*d* in the second week and so on to the end of August. Less is to be given in those areas where less used to be given and neither food nor any other favour is to be demanded, given or taken. All such workers are to bring their tools openly in their hands to the market towns; and there they are to be hired in a public and not in a secret place.

2. Item, that no one is to receive more than $2\frac{1}{2}d$ for threshing a quarter of wheat or rye, and more than $1\frac{1}{2}d$ for threshing a quarter of barley, beans, peas or oats, if so much used to be given. In those areas where reaping was paid by means of certain sheaves and threshing by certain bushels, the servants shall take no more and in no other way than was usual in the said twentieth year and previously. These same servants are to be sworn twice every year before the lords, stewards, bailiffs and constables of every vill to keep and observe these ordinances. These servants are not to depart from the vills in which they live during the winter to serve elsewhere in the summer if they can find work in their own vills at the wages mentioned above; saving that the people of the counties of Stafford, Lancaster and Derby and those of Craven, the Marches of Wales and Scotland and elsewhere may come and work in other counties during August and then return safely, as they have been accustomed to do before this time. Those who refuse to take such an oath, or to fulfil what they have sworn or undertaken shall be put in the stocks for three days or more by the said lords, stewards, bailiffs and constables of the vills or sent to the nearest gaol, there to remain until they are willing to submit to justice. For this purpose stocks are to be constructed in every vill between now and Whitsunday.

3. Item, that carpenters, masons, tilers and other roofers of houses shall not take more for their day's work than the accustomed amount; that is to say, a master carpenter 3*d* and other [carpenters] 2*d*; a master mason of free-stone 4*d* and other masons 3*d*; and

their servants $1\frac{1}{2}d$. Tilers are to receive $3d$ and their boys $1\frac{1}{2}d$; thatchers of roofs in fern and straw $3d$ and their boys $1\frac{1}{2}d$. Plasterers and other workers on mud walls, as well as their boys, are to receive payment in the same manner, without food or drink. These rates are to apply from Easter to Michaelmas: outside that period less should be paid according to the assessment and discretion of the justices assigned for the purpose. Those who perform carriage by land or water shall receive no more for such carriage than they used to do in the said twentieth year and four years before.

4. Item, that cordwainers and shoemakers shall not sell boots, shoes or anything else connected with their mystery otherwise than they did in the said twentieth year. Goldsmiths, saddlers, horse-smiths, spurriers, tanners, curriers, pelterers, tailors and all other workmen, artificers and labourers, as well as all other servants not specified here, shall be sworn before the said justices to conduct and employ their crafts and offices in the way they did in the said twentieth year and earlier, without refusing because of this ordinance. If any of the said servants, labourers, workmen or artificers infringe this ordinance after taking such an oath, they shall be punished by fine, ransom or imprisonment, according to the discretion of the said justices.

5. Item, that the said stewards, bailiffs and constables of the vills shall be sworn before the same justices to inquire diligently, by all the good ways they can, concerning all those who infringe this ordinance. They are to certify the names of all these offenders to the justices whenever they arrive in a district to hold their sessions. And so the justices, having been notified of the names of such rebels by the stewards, bailiffs and constables, shall have them arrested, to appear before themselves to answer for such contempts; so that the offenders shall pay fine and ransom to the king if they are convicted. Moreover, the offenders shall be ordered to prison, where they shall remain until they have found surety to serve, receive their payments, perform their work and sell their saleable goods in the manner prescribed above. And if any of the offenders breaks his oath, and is convicted of it, he

shall be imprisoned for forty days. And if he is convicted another time, he shall be imprisoned for a quarter of a year, so that each time he offends and is convicted, he shall receive a double penalty. Each time the justices come to a certain district, they shall enquire of the said stewards, bailiffs and constables if they have made a good and lawful certificate, or have concealed anything because of gifts, procurement or affinity; and the justices shall punish them by fine and ransom if they be found blameworthy. And the same justices shall have power to enquire and make due punishment of the said officials, workmen, labourers and other servants whatsoever; and also of hostelers, harbergers and those who sell victuals by retail or other things not specified here. This may be done either at the suit of a party or by presentment. The justices may hear, determine and execute the case (by means of an *Exigend* after the first *Capias*, if need be[1]); and they may depute others, as many and of the sort they think best, to see to the keeping of the same ordinance. And those who wish to sue such servants, workmen and labourers for any excess from which they suffer, shall have this excess returned to them if the servants are attainted of the offence as a result of their suit. And if it happens that some men will not sue to recover their excess, then it shall be levied from the said servants, labourers, workmen and artificers and delivered to the collectors of the fifteenth, in alleviation of the vills where such excesses have been taken.

6. Item, that no sheriffs, constables, bailiffs, gaolers, clerks of justices or sheriffs or any other officials whatsoever shall receive anything for the sake of their offices from the said servants, either for fees, suit of prison or anything else. If they have taken anything from this source, they shall deliver it (for the past and the future) to the collectors of tenths and fifteenths to help the commons when these subsidies are being levied. The justices shall enquire in their sessions if these officials have taken anything from the said servants; and the justices shall cause to be levied

[1] A writ of *Capias* instructed the royal official to 'take' the body of the defendant, i.e. to arrest him; while the *Exigend* ordered the sheriff to 'exact' the presence of the culprit in court upon pain of outlawry.

from such officials what they find (by means of such inquests) they have received; and these sums, together with the excesses, fines, ransoms and amercements of all those amerced before the justices, shall be delivered to the said collectors in alleviation of the vills. And in a case when the excess fund in a vill exceeds the amount of the fifteenth for that vill, the remainder shall be levied and paid by the collectors to the nearest poor vills, on the advice of the justices, to relieve their fifteenths. Fines, ransoms, excesses and amercements from the said labourers and servants at the time when future fifteenths are being levied shall be delivered to the collectors by means of indentures completed between the collectors and the justices. In this way, the collectors can be charged on their account by means of the indentures, in the event that the said fines, ransoms, amercements and excesses are not paid in aid of the said fifteenth. When the fifteenth ceases, this income shall be levied to the king's use and answered for to him by the sheriff of the county.

7. Item, that the said justices should hold their sessions in all the counties of England at least four times a year, namely at the feasts of the Annunciation [25 March], of St Margaret [20 July], St Michael [29 September] and St Nicholas [6 December]; and also at all times that the justices shall think necessary. Those who speak in the presence of the justices, or do anything else in their presence or absence to encourage or maintain the said servants and labourers against this ordinance, shall be severely punished according to the discretion of the justices. If any of the said labourers, servants or artificers flee from one county to another because of this ordinance, the sheriffs of the county where such fugitives are found shall have them apprehended, at the order of the justices of the counties from which they have fled, and bring them to the chief gaol of the said counties. There they are to remain until the next session of the justices; and the sheriffs are to return the orders they have received before the justices at their next sessions. And this ordinance is to be held and kept within the city of London as in other cities, boroughs and elsewhere throughout the land, both within franchises and without.

6 The Enforcement of the Statute of Labourers

According to nearly all contemporary comments, the statutes of labourers failed completely in their purpose of safeguarding the supply of labour and restricting wages to their pre-Black Death level. In the definitive work on the subject, *The Enforcement of the Statute of Labourers, 1349–1359*, Miss Bertha Putnam did however make out a strong case for the view that in the 1350s at least prosecutions under the terms of the statutes were undertaken with considerable efficiency and some success. It therefore seems only just to set Knighton's contemptuous dismissal of the statute by the side of some actual presentments which resulted from its operation. The third extract illustrates the dangers inherent in over-simplifying a very complex social situation: some English peasants of the late fourteenth century might find it to their positive advantage to plead villein status. It should be emphasised that the justices of the peace who tried cases of trespass on the statutes of labourers were usually county gentlemen with a strong personal interest in the policy of wage-restraint. Many such justices were the target of attack in 1381; and it can be no coincidence that the risings of that year tended to be most violent in those counties where it is known the hated labour laws were strictly enforced.

A. THE STATUTE OF LABOURERS ACCORDING TO HENRY KNIGHTON

Chronicon Henrici Knighton II 74

In the same year the statute concerning servants was published, and from that time they served their masters worse from day to day than they had done previously. But through the agency of the justices and other officials the profits of the king always went on increasing, as did his power over the people.

B. TRESPASSES ON THE STATUTE OF LABOURERS, 1373-5

Some Sessions of the Peace in Lincolnshire, 1360-75, Lincoln Record Society, XXX (1937) 24, 25, 57, 63

Item they present that John of Redemyld, late servant of John West of Carleton and retained in his service at Carleton, departed from that service without reasonable cause and the licence of the said John West before the end of the term agreed between them; he left on the feast of the Translation of St Thomas [7 July] in the forty-seventh year [1373], whereas he should have remained until the following feast of St Martin [11 November].

Item it is presented that John Julian of Neunton, William Smyth of Laughton and Robert Joy of the same received from Hugh of Clifton and others at Neuton on Trent in the forty-seventh year [1373] 8*d* an acre for every acre mowed by them; whereas by the statute they should have taken 5*d* and no more. And so each of them received 3*s* 4*d* in excess [wages] that year, against the form of the ordinance.

Item they present that Alice, wife of John Redhed of East Ravendale, was retained to serve Robert of Bokenale during the autumn of the forty-eighth year [1374] in return for receiving wages and salary according to the form of the ordinance of labourers; but she renounced this service and worked outside the town in order to get higher wages – to the harm of the said Robert and against the form of the said ordinance.

The jurors of the said wapentake declare that John Gale, dwelling with Thomas of Talous, on the Thursday after Whitsuntide in the forty-eighth year [25 May 1374] enticed John Donney, servant of Walter Hardegray of Edlyngton away from Walter's service; and he admitted and retained him in his own service at Edlyngton, giving him for his yearly wage one mark and his food as well as other goods, against the form of the ordinance of labourers, etc.

C. A PREFERENCE FOR BOND SERVICE, 1350

Translated in E. Rickert, *Chaucer's World* (New York, 1948), pp. 358–9, from Putnam, *Enforcement of Statute of Labourers, 1349–1359*, pp. 249*–50*

Surrey. William atte Merre of Merrow was attached to answer Peter Semere of a plea why he refused to serve – whereas it is ordained that any man and woman of the lord King's realm of England, being able of body and below the age of sixty years, not living by trade or practising any specific mystery or having his own land about the tilling of which he can occupy himself, not being a servant to another, if he should be required to serve in a service considered fitting to his estate, shall be bound to serve him who so requests and shall take only the wages, liveries, rewards, or salaries which were in force, in the place where he should serve, in the twentieth year of the lord King or the average in the five or six preceding years. The same Peter says that he, on Monday after the Purification of the Blessed Mary in the 24th year aforesaid [8 February 1350], at Merrow in the presence of John atte Dene and William Hereward, offered the said William fitting service to serve the said Peter in the town of Merrow, William to receive from the said Peter as is declared in the statute aforesaid, and the said William refused absolutely to serve the said Peter in form aforesaid, and still refuses, in contempt of the lord King and against the ordinance of the said statute and to the damage of the said Peter in 100s. . . .

And the said William . . . says that he cannot serve the said Peter, because, he says, he is a villein (*nativus*) of the prior and convent of the Blessed Mary of Boxgrave, of their manor of Merrow, and that the prior of the church aforesaid who now is was seised of him as of his villein and of his services as villein in right of his church . . . and that the said prior and all his predecessors from time immemorial have been seised of him and of all his ancestors as of their villein, to tallage them high and low, and to take from them redemptions for the marriage of their daughters as in right of their said church; and he says that the prior and convent let the said manor with the appurtenances to John Chene . . . for his life, and that the said John Chene has the said William in his necessary service in the said manor . . .

And because the judges had their suspicions as to the admissions of the said William, they offered him a book to swear that he was speaking truth concerning the above matters; and he took his oath as above. Wherefore it was adjudged that the said Peter should take nothing by his complaint, and that the said William should serve the said John Chene as his lord. Thereupon he is delivered to Walter de Wernham, the bailiff of the said John Chene, to serve him according to statute and the custom of the said manor.

7   Commons' Petition against Vagrants, 1376

Rot. Parl., II 340-1

Complaints about the ineffectiveness of the Statute of Labourers showed no signs of decreasing in the years immediately before the Peasants' Revolt. The following petition of the commons, presented in the Good Parliament of 1376, presents an alarming picture of widespread vagrancy and disorder. To the gentry and burgesses of late fourteenth-century England, as to those of Elizabeth's reign, the lawless vagabond was something of an *idée fixe*. Whether their diagnosis of the social evils of their age was an accurate one is more open to question. If so, it is not a little paradoxical that the dramatic decline of the country's total population in the period that followed the Black Death should have been accompanied by an apparent increase in the number of landless vagrants. Much more certainly the following petition reflects the shortage and high cost of agricultural labour in the 1370s.

To our lord the king and his wise parliament, the commons show and request that, although various ordinances and statutes have been made in several parliaments to punish labourers, artificers and other servants, yet these have continued subtly and by great malice aforethought, to escape the penalty of the said ordinances and statutes. As soon as their masters accuse them of bad service, or wish to pay them for their labour according to the form of the statutes, they take flight and suddenly leave their employment and district, going from county to county, hundred to hundred and vill to vill, in places strange and unknown to their masters. So the said masters do not know where to find them to have remedy or suit against them by virtue of the said statutes. If such vagrant servants be outlawed at the suit of any party, the suitor receives no profit and the fugitives no penalty or punishment because they cannot be found, and never consider returning to the district where they had served previously. Above all and a greater mischief is the receiving of such vagrant labourers and servants when they have fled from their masters' service; for they are taken into service immediately in new places, at such dear wages that example and encouragement is afforded to all servants to depart into fresh places, and go from master to master as soon as they are displeased about any matter. For fear of such flights, the commons now dare not challenge or offend their servants, but give them whatever they wish to ask, in spite of the statutes and ordinances to the contrary – and this chiefly through fear that they will be received elsewhere, as is said above. But if all such fugitive servants were taken throughout the kingdom when they came to offer their services, and then placed in the stocks or sent to the nearest gaol, to stay there until they confessed from where they had come and from whose service, and made surety to return to their old service; and if it were known in all areas that such vagrants were to be arrested and imprisoned in this way and not received, as they now are, into service, they would have no desire to flee from their districts as they do – to the great impoverishment, destruction and ruin of the commons, if remedy is not applied as quickly as possible.

And let it be known to the king and his parliament that many of the said wandering labourers have become mendicant beggars in order to lead an idle life; and they usually go away from their own districts into cities, boroughs and other good towns to beg, although they are able-bodied and might well ease the commons by living on their labour and services, if they were willing to serve. Many of them become 'staff strikers' and lead an idle life, commonly robbing poor people in simple villages, by two, three or four together, so that their malice is very hard to bear. The majority of the said servants generally become strong thieves, increasing their robberies and felonies every day on all sides, to the destruction of the kingdom. Therefore let it please our said lord king and his parliament, for the common profit of the said commons, the safe-keeping of the peace and the destruction of such felons and felonies, to forbid (under certain penalties and both within and without franchises) any sustenance and alms to be given to such false mendicants and beggars who are able to serve and work, to the great profit and ease of the said commons. Alms should be given only to those who cannot help themselves or purchase food. And let it be established by statute that all such false beggars as well as the said 'staff strikers' shall be apprehended throughout the realm, within and without franchises, wherever they shall be found; and their bodies should be placed in stocks or led to the nearest gaol, until they show themselves willing to submit and return to their own areas and serve their neighbours according to the form of the said ordinances and statutes. . . . [the procedure by which these proposals are to be enforced is then specified at length].

8   Peasant Discontents and Resistance before 1381

Although difficult to measure in quantitative terms, there is little doubt that the 1370s were a decade which coincided with a growing tide of peasant discontent against the landlord. Several petitions presented to Richard II's first parliament in the autumn of 1377 reflect serious concern at the political dangers of this prevailing trend. Of these perhaps the first of the following documents is the best known as it is certainly the most revealing. The innumerable previous complaints that agricultural workers had evaded the operations of the statutes of labourers are now followed by the more general allegation that villeins are withholding their services completely from their lords and are engaged in widespread conspiracies. The open reference to the possibilities of a popular rebellion like that in France makes explicit an analogy, the *Jacquerie* of 1358, which must often have presented itself to English observers during the years before and after 1381.

But peasant discontent and peasant protest was already a familiar element in the English rural scene; and it has often been argued, most forcefully by Professor R. H. Hilton,[1] that the great revolt of 1381 was a logical if extreme extension of social movements clearly evident long before the first arrival of the Black Death. Although they are impossible to quantify in any meaningful way, numerous examples survive of peasant agitation against the oppression of landlords before 1381. Of these, the two illustrated here are especially revealing without being necessarily representative. The early fourteenth-century petition of the tenants of Bocking Hall in Essex against the injustices of an over-zealous steward was the work of a group of peasants fully conscious of their common interests and remarkably skilled in presenting their grievances in an articulate legal form. The villeins at Darnall and Over in Cheshire who rose against the abbot and convent of Vale Royal in 1336 proved to be more violent and less successful. Like so many of the rebels of 1381 they combined a deep-rooted objection to their villein status with the belief that the king might prove to be their saviour.

[1] 'Peasant Movements in England before 1381', *Essays in Economic History*, vol. II, ed. E. M. Carus-Wilson, pp. 73–90.

A. COMMONS' PETITION AGAINST
REBELLIOUS VILLEINS, 1377

Rot. Parl., III 21-2

To our lord the king and the council of parliament, the commons
of the realm show that in many parts of the kingdom of England
the villeins and tenants of land in villeinage, who owe services
and customs to the lords for various reasons and within various
lordships, both ecclesiastical and secular, have (through the advice,
procurement, maintenance and abetting of certain persons)
purchased in the king's court for their own profit exemplifications from the Book of Domesday – concerning those manors and
vills where these villeins and tenants live.[1] By colour of these
exemplifications, and through misunderstanding them as well
as the malicious interpretation made of them by the said counsellors, procurers, maintainers and abettors, they have withdrawn
and still withdraw the customs and services due to their lords,
holding that they are completely discharged of all manner of
service due both from their persons and their holdings. These
men have refused to allow the officials of the lords to distrain
them for the said customs and services; and have made confederation and alliance together to resist the lords and their
officials by force, so that each will aid the other whenever they
are distrained for any reason. And they threaten to kill their
lords' servants if these make distraint upon them for their customs
and services; the consequence is that, for fear of the deaths that
might result from the rebellion and resistance of these men,
the lords and their officials do not make distraint for their customs
and services. Accordingly the said lords lose and have lost

---

[1] The contemporary patent rolls confirm that exemplifications of Domesday
Book were in considerable demand for at least a century before 1381. Their
relevance to the facts of late fourteenth-century law and society seems doubtful:
conceivably several petitioners for exemption from seignorial services relied,
very naïvely, on the lack of reference to such services in Domesday itself. More
specifically, exemplifications from Domesday Book enabled many tenants to
claim the legal privileges of ancient demesne and so royal protection against an
increase in services to their lords.

much profit from their lordships, to the great prejudice and destruction of their inheritances and estates. Moreover in many parts of the realm the corn lies unharvested for this reason and is lost for all time, to the serious damage of all the commons. Therefore it is feared that, unless a speedy remedy is applied, either war might easily break out within the realm because of the said acts of rebellion, or the villeins and tenants will, to avenge themselves on their lords, adhere to foreign enemies in the event of a sudden invasion. To sustain their errors and rebellions they have collected large sums of money among themselves to meet their costs and expenses; and many of them have now come to court to secure assistance in their designs. Therefore let it please our lord king and his council to ordain a due and speedy remedy, directed against the said councillors, procurers, maintainers and abettors as well as the said villeins and tenants and especially those who have now come to court. Action should be taken so that those who stay in lodgings (*à l'hostel*) should know of their punishment and in order to avoid a danger of the sort that recently occurred in the realm of France because of a similar rebellion and confederation of villeins against their lords.

The Reply. As regards the exemplifications made and granted in Chancery, it is declared in parliament that these neither can nor ought to have any value or relevance to the question of personal freedom; nor can they be used to change the traditional terms of tenure and its customs or to the prejudice of the lords' rights to have their services and customs as they used to be in the past. If they wish, the lords may have letters patent under the Great Seal recording this declaration. As for the rest of this article, the lords who feel themselves aggrieved shall have special commissions of inquiry appointed under the Great Seal and directed either to the Justices of the Peace or to other suitable persons. These commissions shall investigate all such rebels, their counsellors, procurers, maintainers and abettors. Those indicted before the commissioners, for either past or future offences, shall be imprisoned; and they shall not be released from prison either by mainprise, bail or any other method without the assent of their lords until they are attainted or acquitted. And if such rebellious tenants are attainted of the offences mentioned above, they shall not be released until they have made a fine with the king and have the consent of their lords. Such fines shall not prejudice the franchises and liberties of lords who have a right to fines and amercements from their tenants. As for the counsellors, procurers, maintainers and abettors, let there be a similar procedure; if the lords proceed against them by writ or by bill they shall not be released until they have (according to their estate and the seriousness of their offences) made a fine with the king and have the permission of the aggrieved lords. Saving the franchises and liberties of the lords, as is said above.

B. THE BOCKING PETITION, *c*. 1300-30

Translated in J. F. Nichols, 'An Early Fourteenth Century Petition from the Tenants of Bocking to their Manorial Lord', *Economic History Review*, II (1929-30) 300-7, which provides a full discussion. Clauses 4, 5 and 6 are omitted.

1. To their very dear, honourable and rightful lord, the poor tenants of Bocking pray to your lordship for grace and remedy, that, whereas you have your Leet in your Manor of Bocking aforesaid on Saint Matthew's Day [September 21st] and the custom of the said manor is such that the tenants for the time being ought to make full presentment through thirty-six 'capital pledges', duly sworn, on that same day, of matters touching the Crown, as of indictments and of purprestures which may be redressed on that day, and for other matters of which they may be in doubt, they ought to have, and always have had, an opportunity of adjourning for further consideration until [the next meeting of the court] three weeks later to make full presentment, now comes John le Doo, your bailiff, and, on the first day of the leet, of his own conceit, without [making] inquest, [proceeds against] the presenters and against reason amerces them on a charge of

concealment before presentment has been made, and by such amercement has caused them to be grievously distrained, on which account they pray for remedy.

(This petition was made in the time of Prior Henry of Eastry.[1]) Reply was made that the deed had not been done by him nor by his wish, and that in future he would not suffer such evil to be done to any tenant of the vill but that they should be maintained in their customs in all matters.

2. And that whereas each free tenant had full liberty to sell his land in such wise that the purchaser should be enfeoffed to hold of the capital lord by the services and customs due therefrom, the said John le Doo came and caused the aforesaid tenants to be distrained when they had thus made purchase of your fief, so that they were not able to enjoy their purchase or hold [the tenement] in peace until they had paid a fine for their holding at his will, and for this cause they seek remedy.

Reply as before.

3. Furthermore, Sire, that whereas the aforesaid tenants who were liable to be amerced in your court ought, when so amerced, to be 'affeered' by their peers according to the extent of their trespass, then came the said John le Doo and refused to accept such affeerement, but has, of his own conceit, increased their burdens twofold or even threefold and by such means has vexed the tenants and brought them to destruction, against all reason and the Great Charter that Holy Church ought to uphold.[2] And for this they pray remedy.

Reply as before. . . .

7. And that whereas the aforesaid tenants ought to render certain services such as ploughings and other specified services according as the custom of the manor requires, the aforesaid John le Doo comes and demands other services and customs that they are not bound to render, and on this account causes them to be distrained

---

[1] Prior of Christ Church, Canterbury, from 1284 to 1331.

[2] A rare example of an appeal by manorial tenants to the protection of Magna Carta, in this case the famous Clause 39. 'Affeerment' was the assessment of an amercement.

4

by the bedels of the Manor suffering no manner of delivery to be made for such distraint by warranty nor pledge, nor in any other manner by warrantors (*mainpernours*) in your own court, without naming the Prior in our plea, against whom we are not able to allege any charge concerning tort done. And for this they pray remedy.

Reply as before.

8. Moreover, whereas they ought by reason of their tenure to mow your meadows in your Manor aforesaid, and spread the grass and turn and load the hay, and afterwards carry it to your granges, by which service they ought to be and have been accustomed since whereof memory runs not to the contrary, to be quit of suit of court and of all other services from the day that they commence to mow for the three whole weeks next ensuing, your bailiff John le Doo comes and demands that they shall do suit at your court during the aforesaid three weeks, which demand is evidently against reason and contrary to their customs, and by this pretext he has grievously amerced them and caused them to be distrained, and for this they pray for remedy.

Reply as before.

C. REVOLT OF THE VILLEINS OF DARNALL AND OVER, 1336

Translated by G. G. Coulton, *The Medieval Village*, pp. 132–5, from *The Ledger Book of Vale Royal Abbey*, Lancs. and Cheshire Record Society, LXVIII (1914) 37 ff.

Be it remembered that in the year 1336, . . . the villeins of Dernehale and Over conspired against their lords, the abbot and convent . . . Sir Hugh de Fren, then justiciar of Chester, came to a place which is called Harebache Crose, at which a great number of villeins had taken refuge together, and they laid a serious complaint against the said abbot, [declaring] that, whereas they were free and held their lands and tenements from aforetime by charter of the Lord the King, the aforesaid abbot, contrary to his customs hitherto observed in his manor of Dernehale, had put them in close confinement in shackles, as though they were villeins, and forced them to serve him in all villein services. And when these men returned home to their houses, by the abbot's command they were put in fetters in the house of John Badekoc at Over, on account of their complaints aforesaid, until they should come and acknowledge their bondage, and submit themselves to the abbot's grace. . . . After the said countrymen had made a fine at the will of the abbot, and sworn upon the holy Gospels of God that they would never again contrive any such thing against the abbot and convent, and confessed that they were villeins, they and their sons after them to all eternity, according to the customs always observed in the manor of Dernehale, as you have them more in detail set forth in this same book under the heading of Dernehale, then those wretched men, seeing themselves thus frustrated, called together all their neighbours of their own condition, and plotted by night to get their liberty by rebelling against the aforesaid abbot. And they sent some of their number on behalf of them all on a pilgrimage to St Thomas of Hereford; and these men, contrary to their oath, came to the King in the northern parts, and for many days were begging his favour, which they did not deserve to find; and afterwards they came to unforeseen misadventure, for they robbed certain people of their goods, and were all to their great chagrin carried off to Nottingham gaol, being wholly stripped of all their own goods that they had with them. Afterwards, before the justices of the Lord the King in that place, they were condemned to be hanged; but because it was not customary by the law of the kingdom to inflict death for theft to the amount of which they were guilty, they were set at liberty after some time by the grace of the King, not without great expense to the other country people of Over. . . . But they did not desist from the matter they had undertaken, but forthwith repaired to the Lord the King in his parliament held at Westminster, and presented a petition to parliament setting forth that the abbot oppressed them so greatly with injuries and contumelies and villein services, that they did not dare to return to their homes, their wives and their children. . . .

Now when these things had been accomplished, the abbot was on his return to the monastery, and a great crowd of the country people of Dernehale came to meet him in the high way on the feast of the Nativity of St John the Baptist, about the ninth hour, at Exton in the county of Rutland; and they attacked and slew his groom, William Fynche, with an arrow . . . Now Walter Walsh, the cellarer, and John Coton, and others of the abbot's servants were about half a league behind the abbot, having tarried for certain business; and when they saw the fight from afar they came up at full speed, and the said armed bondmen came up against them to assault them; but the aforesaid cellarer (blessed be his memory) like a champion sent from God to protect his house and father, though he was all unarmed, not without enormous bloodshed felled those sacrilegious men to the earth, and left all those whom he found in that place half-dead, according to the law of the Lord. But certain of them fled, and the said John Coton followed after them and took them. Meanwhile the sound of people running up on all sides was heard, and after all the abbot was ignominiously taken, with all his people, by those bestial men of Rutland, and was brought to the city of Stamford, where the king then was, together with his bondmen; but on the morrow, through the aid of the Mother of Mercy, in whose cause he was acting, the abbot, with all his followers, obtained his rights, and the bondmen were left there in chains and in the greatest misery, while the abbot returned in safety to his monastery. . . . And when they [the bondmen] came before Geoffrey de Scop and his colleagues, for the death of the above said William, they were set at liberty, and obtained a writ to the abbot to deliver up forthwith their lands and goods and chattels, if they had been seized by reason of the death of the aforenamed William, and not otherwise. But since the abbot had other just causes against them, they derived no advantage from that writ. And at length the bondmen, finding no other place in which they might be longer concealed, returned to the abbot their lord, submitting themselves and their goods to his grace, and the abbot put them all in fetters as his bondmen. And so it came to pass that, touching the holy gospels, they all swore they were truly the bondmen of the abbot and convent, and that they would never claim their freedom against them and their successors. And for many Sundays they stood in the choir, in the face of the convent, with bare heads and feet, and they offered wax candles in token of subjection. . . .

9   Political Protest in the Good Parliament of 1376

Rot. Parl., II 322–4

Of all the medieval English kings after the Conquest only Edward III lived long enough to show signs of unmistakable senility. The chief responsibility for the disastrous decade of the 1370s was inevitably laid at the feet of a once glorious but now incapable monarch. 'The weakness of an aged king', in Walsingham's phrase, led to a general and well-founded collapse of public morale. The return to England of the ailing Black Prince in 1371, the naval defeat at La Rochelle in 1372 and John of Gaunt's magnificent but misguided *chevauchée* from Calais to Bordeaux during the last months of 1373 all served to reveal the inherent weaknesses of Edward III's control over his great French domain. Between the truce of Bruges in 1375 and the great revolt of 1381 English influence across the channel dwindled to a precarious grasp of Calais and the coast-line from Bordeaux to Bayonne. At home the 1370s were characterised by a series of constitutionally intriguing but politically vicious attempts to unearth and discredit those royal ministers and favourites who could be held responsible for the military disasters of the decade. The classic instance is the famous Good Parliament of the early summer of 1376 in which the belligerent commons were surprisingly effective in adopting the new-fangled procedure of impeachment to prosecute charges against those whom they considered to be the war profiteers of the day. By their exposure of governmental inadequacy the county knights and burgesses undoubtedly encouraged the rebels to react even more violently five years later.

10. Also, the commons, considering the mischiefs in the land, showed to the king and to the lords of parliament what would be to the honour of the king and to the profit of the entire country, now seriously distressed in various ways by several misfortunes such as the wars of France, Spain, Ireland, Guienne, Brittany and elsewhere, as well as other adversities, so that the officers who are customarily at the king's charge are no longer sufficient for such great governance without additional help. Wherefore they begged that our lord king's council should be enforced by lords of the land, prelates and others so that it should remain continually at the number of ten or twelve, as the king wished; in such a manner that no major business should be put through or accomplished without the assent and advice of all, while lesser business would need the advice and assent of six or four at least, as the case required. Moreover, at least six or four of these counsellors should reside continually at the royal council. And our lord the king, considering the said request to be both honourable and very profitable to himself and all his kingdom, gave it his assent; always provided that the Chancellor, Treasurer, Keeper of the privy seal and all other royal ministers should be able to manage and conduct the business appertaining to their offices without the presence of the said counsellors, whom the king has appointed or will appoint at intervals in the future at his pleasure. And it is ordained and agreed that these same counsellors, whether appointed now or serving in the future, shall take an oath to keep this ordinance and to do right to everyone, according to their powers. And it is similarly ordained that they shall take nothing (except small gifts of food and drink or other presents easily distinguishable from bribes) from any

party in return for a promise or other transaction related to business which is about to be brought or laid before them; under penalty of restoring to the party concerned double what they have taken, as well as the costs and damages suffered by him, and of rendering to our lord the king six times the amount they have taken. . . .

15. Afterwards the said commons came into parliament and there made open protestation that they were as willing and firm in purpose to help their noble liege lord with their bodies and goods, and with whatever they had, as ever any others were in the past; and so they would always be, as far as they were able. But they said that it seemed certain to them that if their said liege lord had always had around him loyal officers and good counsellors, the same our lord the king would have been very rich in treasure and so would have had no great need to charge his commune by way of subsidy or tallage or otherwise; considering the great sums of gold which had been brought inside the realm through the ransoms of the kings of France and Scotland[1] and those of other princes and lords, which amounted to a very large sum. And they further said that they believed it was for the individual profit and advantage of several men in the king's entourage, and of others in collusion with them, that the king and kingdom of England were so seriously impoverished and many of its merchants ruined and brought to nothing. Therefore, it appeared to them that it would be to the profit of our said lord king and of all his kingdom if due amendment were made with all possible speed. And the commons themselves promised our said lord the king that if he would quickly bring the guilty to justice and take from them what law and reason demanded, they would undertake that, besides what they had given him in this parliament, he would be rich enough to long maintain his wars and other affairs without greatly charging his said commune in any way in the future. Moreover, they maintained that by this action our lord the king would perform a most meritorious deed, of great pleasure to God and of much

[1] i.e. John II and David II, captured respectively at the battles of Poitiers (1356) and Neville's Cross (1346).

profit and relief to the whole of his commune of England, who would consequently be more forward and well disposed in helping their said liege lord with all their power in the event of his needing their favourable support. In connection with this proposal, the said commons then made a declaration on three points in particular. . . .

17. Firstly, Richard Lyons, merchant of London, was impeached and accused by the said commons of several deceits, extortions and other evils, committed by him against our lord king and his people, both at the time when he was present at the house and council of the king as also at the time when he was farmer of royal subsidies and customs. Especially had the said Richard, by a secret agreement made between himself and others of our lord king's privy council to their private profit and advantage, procured the issue of several patents and writs of licence to carry large amounts of wool, wool-fells and other merchandise elsewhere than to the Staple of Calais – against the ordinances and prohibitions previously made in parliament, to the ruin of the said Calais Staple and the Mint there and to the great injury of the king and kingdom of England as well as the destruction of the said town of Calais. Moreover, he had imposed, and caused to be imposed, certain new taxes on wool, wool-fells and other merchandise, without assent of parliament; and, once raised and collected, a large proportion of these taxes were converted to his own use and that of his said party in the king's entourage, without the view or testimony of any controller and without being charged by record or otherwise than by his own will; but he alone was treasurer and receiver of this money and the high Treasurer of the kingdom had nothing to do with it at all. And it is commonly said that at times he took ten shillings in one lot and twelve pence in another on each sack etc., which amounts to a very large sum for all the time that he was receiver or treasurer, as is said above. And similarly [the commons complained] of another new tax of four pence charged by him on each pound of money sent abroad by Lombards and other merchants in way of exchange, imposed on his own authority

and without warrant or assent of parliament or otherwise. And although this tax of four pence on the pound was largely collected and kept to the king's use, our lord the king paid nothing from this source. And they also complained of various loans made for the king's purposes without real cause. . . .

18. To which the said Richard, present in parliament, replied that as for the said loan of twenty thousand marks made to the king, he was completely blameless. He said further that he had had neither profit nor gain, nor received anything at all, from the aforesaid loan, either in money or otherwise; and he could disprove these charges by all reasonable means when asked to do so. And as for the said taxes of ten shillings, and twelve pence on a sack of wool etc., and the four pence on a pound of money, he could clearly not deny that he had raised and collected these and had had part of the proceeds brought before him; i.e. twelve pence on each sack of wool etc. But he maintained that this was done at the express command of our lord the king, and at the request and with the assent of those merchants who had asked for such licences. . . .

19. On account of which, the said Richard was adjudged to be imprisoned at the king's will; and to suffer fine and ransom according to the gravity and horror of his trespass: and to lose his freedom of the city of London and was never again to hold royal office nor come near the council or household of the king. And on a second occasion the said Richard was summoned before the lords of parliament and informed that they believed his misdeeds to be so serious and dreadful that it was beyond his means to give satisfaction for them. And so the said Richard submitted himself to the king's grace, in body, lands, tenements, goods and chattels; and he willed and conceded that his body, lands, goods and chattels should be at the king's disposal, to ordain and deal with as he pleased; asking the king to grant him his life if it pleased him, but if not, to do with him and whatever he possessed entirely as he wished. Consequently it was awarded that all his lands, tenements, goods and chattels should be seized into the king's hands and his body retained in prison at the

king's will. And as for the extortions made by the said Richard or his deputies during the period when he was farmer of the said subsidies or customs, as described above, it was ordained in parliament that a proper inquiry should be made by qualified men in all the ports of England.

21. Item, William, Lord Latimer, was impeached and accused by clamour of the said commons of various deceits, extortions, grievances and other evils, committed by him and others of his following from the time he stayed with the king our lord, both in Brittany when he held office under the king, and also in England when he was chamberlain and a member of the royal privy council.

10　Poem on the Death of Edward III

Robbins, *Historical Poems*, pp. 102–6; Wright, *Political Poems*, I 215–18; Sisam, *Fourteenth Century Verse and Prose*, pp. 157–60

The following English poem on the death of King Edward III in 1377 has, in Wright's words, 'for its burthen the transitory character of human greatness and the want of durability in popular gratitude'. Both themes were of course medieval and later commonplaces but it is tempting to argue that these verses owe most of their interest to the accuracy with which they reflect the contemporary *malaise* of England in the late 1370s. The author's melancholy seems genuine and his literary skill is unquestionable, resembling that of the also anonymous author of the poem on the catastrophes of 1381–2 (see below, no. 65). Both poems are to be found in the Vernon Manuscript at the Bodleian Library, Oxford. The following stanzas seem to have been written very soon indeed after Edward III's death and before the Peasants' Revolt: and it is noticeable that their writer, like the rebels of 1381, rests all his hopes for the future on 'this ympe', the young Richard II. The poem contains fourteen stanzas of which eight are printed here.

A, dere God, what mai this be,
 That alle thing weres and wastes awai?
Frendschip is but a vanyte,
 Unnethe hit dures al a day.
Thai beo so sliper at assai,
 So leof to han, and loth to lete,
And so fikel in heore fai,
 That selden I-seise is sone forgete.

I sei hit not withouten a cause,
 Ande therfore takes riht good hede,
For if ye construwe wel this clause
 I puit you holly out of drede,
That for puire schame yor hertes wol blede,
 And ye this matere wysli trete;
He that was ur moste spede
 Is selden I-seye and sone forgete.

Sum tyme an Englisch schip we had,
 Nobel hit was, and heih of tour;
Thorw al Cristendam hit was drad;
 And stif wolde stande in uch a stour,
And best dorst byde a scharp schour
 And other stormes, smale and grete;
Now is that schip, that bar the flour,
 Selden seise and sone forgete.

This goode schip I may remene
 To the chivalrye of this londe;
Sum tyme thei counted nought a bene
 Beo al Fraunce, Ich understonde.

Thei tok and slough hem with heore honde,
 The power of Fraunce, both smal and grete;
And brought the king hider to byde her bonde,
 And nou riht sone hit is forgete.

The rother was nouther ok ne elm;
 Hit was Edward the thridde, the noble kniht;
The prince his sone bar up his helm,
 That never scoumfited was in fiht.
The kyng him rod and rouwed ariht,
 The prince dredde nouther stok nor strete.
Nou of him we lete ful liht,
 That selde is seise is sone forgete.

This gode comunes, bi the rode,
 I likne hem to the schipes mast;
That with heore catel and heore goode
 Mayntened the werre both furst and last.
The wynd that bleus the schip with blast,
 Hit was gode preyers, I sei hit strete,
Nou is devotnes out I-cast,
 And mony gode dedes ben clen forgete.

Thus ben this lordes ileid ful lowe;
 The stok is of the same rote;
An ympe biginnes for to growe,
 And yit I hope schal ben ur bote,
To holde his fomen under fote,
 And as a lord be set in sete.
Crist leve that he so mote,
 That selden i-seise be not forgete.

And therfore, gode sires, taketh reward
Of yor douhti kyng, that deyede in age,
And to his son Prince Edward,
That welle was of alle corage.
Suche two lordes of heigh parage
Is not in eorthe whom we schal gete.
And nou heore los beginneth to swage,
That seld i-seise is sone forgete.

Glossary

at assai, *when put to the test*; leof, *eager*; han, *have*; lete, *give up*; spede, *cause of success*; And brought the king hider, *John II of France after his capture at Poitiers in 1356*; him rod, *sailed*; bote, *remedy*; mote, *may*.

11 A Disastrous Start to a New Reign, 1377

Vita Ricardi II, ed. Hearne (1729), pp. 1–4

Richard II inherited the crown of England from his grandfather under the worst of circumstances. It can be argued that the Anglo-French war of 1369–89 presented the English government with its most serious military challenge between the French invasion of 1216 and the war against Spain in the latter part of Elizabeth's reign. The following extract reveals the humiliation of the English at the hands of the French during the first few months after Richard's coronation. The chronicler, usually known as 'the monk of Evesham', is not an important independent authority for the early years of Richard, but his account of the situation in 1377, based on Walsingham's longer work, is sufficiently concise to serve as a short and accurate introduction to the troubles of Richard's minority.

Richard of Bordeaux, a boy not yet fully eleven years of age, son of Edward Prince of Wales, himself the first-born of Edward King of England, was solemnly crowned King by Simon archbishop of Canterbury at Westminster on 15 July 1377.[1] The coronation was celebrated with great ceremony of a sort never seen anywhere before, in the presence of the archbishops, bishops, other prelates of the church and all the magnates of his realm. At this time the King raised four men to the rank of earl, namely his uncle lord Thomas of Woodstock to Buckingham; the lord Percy to Northumberland; the lord Mowbray to Nottingham; and a certain knight from Gascony, Guichard d'Angle, the king's tutor, to Huntingdon.

In this year, at about the feast of the birth of John the Baptist [24 June], there was a complete collapse of peace negotiations; for the French refused to keep the peace unless an agreement highly favourable to themselves could be reached. Such an agreement would have been to the serious prejudice of the English kingdom. During this same period, the Scots burnt the town of Roxburgh at the instigation of the earl of Dunbar. As a result lord Henry Percy, the new earl of Northumberland, entered the earl of Dunbar's land with ten thousand soldiers; he then burnt the towns subject to Dunbar and plundered the area for three days.

Afterwards the French landed in the Isle of Wight on 21 August: when they had looted and set fire to several places, they took a thousand marks as ransom for the island. Then they returned to the sea and sailed along the English coastline continuously until Michaelmas. They burnt many places and killed, especially in the southern areas, all the people they could find. As they met with little resistance they carried off animals and other goods as well as several prisoners. It is believed that at this time more evils were perpetrated than had been caused by enemy attacks on England during the previous forty years.

In this same year, the French assaulted the town of Winchelsea but the abbot of Battle came out in force to prevent them from entering the town. While this battle was being fought, the

[1] Rightly 16 July 1377.

French sent a group of their ships to burn the town of Hastings. In this same year, the French invaded England near the town of Rottingdean close to Lewes in Sussex. There they were opposed by the prior of Lewes, a Frenchman by birth but an Englishman by benefice, together with a small band of armed men of the country. Soon after the battle began, the prior was captured and led to the French ships together with two knights, lords John Fallesley and Thomas Cheyne, as well as an esquire called John Brokas. Another esquire, a Frenchman who had been in the service of the prior of Lewes for many years, fought so stoutly, fiercely and persistently against his fellow Frenchmen that his stomach was pierced by their swords and his bowels dropped to his feet. Disregarding this injury, he pursued the enemy, trailing his intestines far behind him. Almost a hundred Englishmen were killed in this battle together with many more Frenchmen. The latter carried off their dead or burnt their bodies to deprive the English of the consolation of burying Frenchmen. One Frenchman was captured there who, on the point of death and shortly before he was fatally wounded, declared, 'If the English had made the duke of Lancaster their king, they would not now be invaded by Frenchmen as they are'.

In the same year the Frenchmen took the town of Ardres by means of treason: its keeper was a certain lord Gunny, a German by birth, who escaped the penalties he deserved for his treason thanks to the prince's indulgence.

In the same year, after the king's coronation, two bishops, two earls, two barons, two bannerets, two knights bachelor and a civil lawyer were chosen by common assent to govern the king and the kingdom while Richard remained a minor. And it was ordained that these persons should be elected anew every year. During the term of Michaelmas in this year, a parliament was summoned at London which lasted almost until Christmas. In this parliament the clergy granted the king two tenths, to be paid together at the beginning of March. The laity granted the king two fifteenths, to be paid together on 2 February for the defence of the realm and the destruction of its enemies.

In the same year, immediately after the feast of All Saints [1 November 1377], lord Thomas of Woodstock, earl of Buckingham, together with the duke of Brittany, lord Latimer and the prior of the hospital of St John in England set sail with a large number of armed men but without horses. However on the night of 11 November there occurred a violent storm which destroyed all the armaments of the ships and so compelled them to return to land. After the ships had been repaired, they put out to sea; but they returned after Christmas, having achieved little or nothing.

12 Desertion from the English Army, 1380

Close Roll, 4 Richard II, memb. 36 [C. 54/220]; cf. C.Cl.R., 1377–81, p. 403; Réville, p. LXXIII

Many of the English expeditionary armies to France during the course of the Hundred Years War had to face the problem of desertion before the journey across the Channel removed most of the temptation to abscond. But reluctance to serve abroad seems to have increased dramatically in the late 1370s; and the following writ is of particular interest in that its recipients included the bailiffs of Maidstone and Rochester, storm-centres of revolt less than a year later.

CONCERNING THE ARREST OF THOSE WHO WITHDREW FROM THE KING'S EXPEDITION

The king to the bailiffs of Maidstone, greeting. We have learnt that many men-at-arms and archers were retained to set forth in our service on the present expedition across the sea and for that reason reached the coast and received wages from us; but, disregarding their service to us on this expedition, they then returned from the said coast to the town of Maidstone, in contempt of ourselves and to the manifest postponement of this expedition. Therefore we, completely refusing to tolerate such contempt, command you as strictly as we can to arrest without delay all and each of the said men-at-arms and archers retained for this expedition who have entered or shall enter the said town in the future. You are to have them securely guarded in our prison until we decide to take measures for their delivery; and you are to certify clearly and openly in our chancery the names of all and each of the men so arrested. And if you fail to observe this command you will completely forfeit our grace. Witnessed by the king at Westminster, 13 July [1380].

Similar writs were sent on the same day to:
> the constable of the town of Aylesford.
> the bailiffs of the town of Rochester.
> the bailiffs of the town of Newenton.

13 Proposals to protect Shipping at London, 1380

Translated by H. T. Riley from *London Letter Book H*, fo. cxxv in *Memorials of London and London Life*, pp. 444-5

The dangers of a French invasion continued to concern the inhabitants of south-eastern England during the last months before the outbreak of the Peasants' Revolt. The scheme proposed below was apparently never carried out; but it testifies to a general belief in the inability of Richard II's government to defend even the capital city of the realm from French and Castilian galleys. John Philipot, an enterprising London merchant, had cleared the seas of a notorious Scottish pirate in 1378 and was to be knighted by Richard II after Smithfield (see below, no. 31).

Be it remembered that on Tuesday, 2 October [1380] in full congregation of the mayor, aldermen and commoners, as well by each trade as by wards chosen from the more reputable and more substantial men of the said city, as a Common Council for the same, it was granted in general that upon every pound of clear rental, over and above reprises, within the liberty of the said city, there should be levied 6d so soon as conveniently might be; for the building of a stone tower, that was to be made on one side of the water of Thames, opposite to another like stone tower, which John Phelipott, by reason of the grant aforesaid, and on condition that the same should be carried out, had promised and granted that he himself would build on the other side of the Thames: 60 king's feet in height, and 20 feet wide within the walls of the tower, and that at his own costs and charges.

For which undertaking on his part, the whole congregation, as well for themselves as for the whole of the City, acknowledged that they were bound to return to the said John Phelipott boundless thanks. It was also agreed on the same day that by counsel and supervision of skilful men the said towers should be so placed and situated in the water of Thames, that within an iron chain extended from the one to the other, the whole fleet of the English shipping, lying on this side of it, as well as the said city, would be secure from hostile attacks and protected, without any ground for alarm.

14 John Gower foresees the Peasants' Revolt

Gower, *Mirour de l'omme* or *Speculum Meditantis*, ed. in vol. 1 of G. C. Macaulay, *The Complete Works of John Gower* (Oxford, 1899–1902), lines 26482–26506.

After 1381 a large number of English writers were prepared to generalise, with benefit of hindsight, about the causes of the Peasants' Revolt. The poet John Gower is apparently unique in actually foreseeing the probability of a major social cataclysm several years before it occurred. Only one manuscript of Gower's *Mirour de l'omme* survives, discovered in the University Library, Cambridge, by G. C. Macaulay in 1895. This lengthy poem, written in French, was (in Gower's own words) designed to 'treat of the vices and virtues and the various classes of the world, and to teach by what right path the sinner who has erred should return to a recognition of his creator'.[1] Like nearly all Gower's works its composition is difficult to date exactly; but the many allusions to contemporary events within the text indicate that Gower wrote the poem, under strong French influence, between about 1376 and 1378.[2] Later in his life, Gower was to have an opportunity to develop, at almost obsessive length, his attitude to the rebelliousness of the poor.[3]

> But it is certainly a great error
> to see the higher estate
> in danger from the villein class.
> It seems to me that lethargy
> has put the lords to sleep
> so that they do not guard against
> the folly of the common people,
> but they allow that nettle to grow
> which is too violent in its nature.

[1] This description is to be found in the famous colophon attached to numerous manuscripts of Gower's later poems, the Latin *Vox Clamantis* and the French *Confessio Amantis*.

[2] See J. H. Fisher, *John Gower* (New York, 1964), pp. 95, 99.

[3] See below, no. 73.

He who observes the present time
is likely to fear that soon,
if God does not provide his help,
this impatient nettle
will very suddenly sting us,
before it can be brought to justice.

There are three things of such a sort
that they produce merciless destruction
when they get the upper hand:
One is a flood of water,
another is a raging fire
and the third is the lesser people,
the common multitude;
for they will not be stopped
by either reason or by discipline.

PART II

The Three Poll Taxes and the Outbreak of Revolt

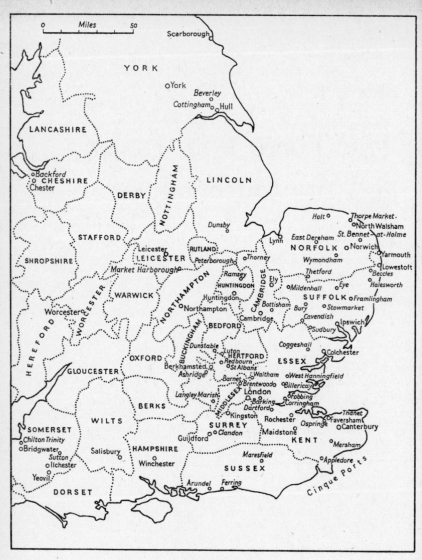

England in 1381

According to the unknown author of an English poem on the rising of 1381, 'Tax has tenet us alle'. Certainly no account of the Peasants' Revolt which fails to give due emphasis to the three poll taxes of 1377 to 1381 can hope to be at all convincing. There is no serious doubt that the English government's desperate attempts to break out of a position of extreme financial insolvency precipitated the riots which led to a general revolt. As the following extracts show, the means by which the parliamentary commons were induced to grant these taxes can be studied in considerable detail, as can the complicated procedure used to assess and collect the levies.[1] By comparison the location and dating of the first outbreaks of active discontent are problematical to a degree. It seems probable that isolated acts of resistance to the activities of the poll tax commissioners occurred early in May. Certainly by the end of that month there is evidence of armed opposition at a more than local level. At first sight the accounts of the early disturbances written by contemporary chroniclers appear to conflict seriously with one another; but the main outlines of their narratives can be reconciled with that of the best informed source, the Anonimalle Chronicle. Open defiance of the tax commissioners apparently first led to outright rebellion in three marshland villages near Brentwood, from which it soon spread to the rest of the county of Essex. The men of Essex rapidly developed considerable cohesion and esprit de corps; but contemporaries were

---

[1] See the valuable new introduction by E. B. Fryde to Oman, *Great Revolt* (new edn, 1969), pp. xii–xxii. Besides the three poll taxes of 1377, 1379 and 1381 (respectively assessed at £22,586, £19,304 and £44,843), the parliament of October–November 1378 granted two tenths and fifteenths and that of January–March 1380 one and a half tenths and fifteenths (assessments estimated at £75,629 and £56,721 respectively). Dr Fryde's figures therefore provide the first detailed demonstration of how 'inordinately heavy' the taxation of 1377–81 was.

much more alarmed by the greater initiative, determination and co-ordination soon displayed by the rebels of Kent. Although it is impossible to know exactly when and where it was taken, the decision to march on London was crucial and brought a startled government into a state of near panic. Under the guidance of Wat Tyler, John Ball and other leaders, the Kentishmen were never again quite so united or successful as during their long walk from Canterbury to Blackheath on 11 and 12 June.

15 The Grant of the First Poll Tax, 1377

The closing months of Edward III's life were dominated by the attempt of his son, John of Gaunt, to restore confidence in the monarchy and prevent a revival of the dangerous criticism voiced in the Good Parliament of 1376 (see above, no. 9). The last parliament of the reign, which met at Westminster between 27 January and 23 February 1377, was accordingly a 'reactionary' assembly in the strict sense of the word – devoted to the undoing of the measures of the previous year. Exactly how this conservative parliament came to concede the first poll tax in English history remains an unsolved mystery. Walsingham's description of the 'tallage of groats' as a 'hitherto unheard-of event' is certainly justified. Like the ill-fated parish tax of 1371, the poll tax of 1377 no doubt testified to a desire to find an alternative to the stereotyped subsidies on movable property (the parliamentary tenths and fifteenths) and also to spread the burden of taxation more widely. The belief that John of Gaunt was personally responsible for the introduction of this new tax may help to account for the hatred in which he was held by the rebels of 1381.

A. ACCORDING TO THOMAS WALSINGHAM
Historia Anglicana, I 323–4

About the feast of the Purification [2 February 1377] a parliament met in London assembled by the duke [of Lancaster] who was acting as the king's deputy at the time the latter was hopelessly ill. In this parliament a subsidy was demanded on behalf of the king from the clergy and lay people.[1] A hitherto unheard-of tax was granted to him, namely that he should take a groat, or four pence, from each lay person of either sex older than fourteen years – except for notorious paupers who begged publicly. The king was also granted from all members, male or female, of the

[1] The spiritual peers were successful in their claim that the poll tax on the clergy should be granted in convocations and not parliament. See 'Clerical Poll-taxes in the diocese of Salisbury', ed. J. L. Kirby, *Collectanea of Wiltshire Archaeological and Natural History Society, Records Branch*, xii (1956), p. 157.

religious orders and all ecclesiastics promoted to a benefice, twelve pence; and from all ecclesiastics not so promoted, one groat. The friars of the four orders of mendicants were excepted: they were not scourged because they do not take part in human labour like other men.

B. ACCORDING TO THE ROLLS OF PARLIAMENT

Rot. Parl., II 363–4

18. Item, after the said prelates, lords and commons had re-assembled in parliament, the commons were instructed by the king to withdraw by themselves to their accustomed place in the chapter-house of Westminster abbey. There they should first and chiefly discuss and take counsel amongst themselves as to the ways by which the malice of the said enemies could be properly resisted – to the salvation of the king, the kingdom, the navy and themselves. The commons were also asked to discuss how the expenses so urgently needed for defence purposes could be most quickly met with the least annoyance and discomfort to the people. Meanwhile the prelates and lords would, for their part, have a similar discussion on the question. The commons were told that a full report of what each of the two groups had decided would then be conveyed to the other. And so the commons departed to the chapter-house. The following prelates and lords were however appointed within parliament to go with the commons so as to help and commune with them and provide them with greater information on the issues to be discussed: – namely, the bishops of Lincoln, Chichester, Hereford and Salisbury; the earls of Arundel, Warwick, Salisbury and Stafford; and the Lords Percy, Roos, FitzWalter and Basset.

19. The noble lords and commons assembled in this parliament fully appreciate the great charges and almost insupportable expenditure to be met by our lord king, increasing as it does from day to day in order to maintain the war and the defence of the realm as well as for other purposes. Therefore they, with their

common assent and free will, have granted to our lord the king in order to maintain his said wars, four pence to be taken from the goods of each person of the kingdom, both male and female, over the age of fourteen years. The only exceptions are to be genuine beggars. The lords and commons beg their said liege lord to excuse them from granting a greater subsidy on this occasion: they would have been well-disposed to do so if they had not already been incapacitated by the poverty resulting from the great losses at sea and other misfortunes of the preceding bad years. 20. The said commons then requested that it would please our lord the king to name, as he thought best, two earls and two barons to serve as keepers and treasurers of this subsidy just conceded, the subsidy yet to be granted by the clergy of England and the subsidies on wools, hides and wool-fells granted in the last parliament. The commons requested that these earls and barons should take an oath in their presence that whatsoever they received from all these subsidies should be completely spent on the wars and not otherwise; and that the lord high treasurer of England should not take any of these subsidies or intervene in any manner. [The commons were later persuaded to withdraw this petition on the grounds of the cost involved in maintaining a separate group of four war-treasurers.]

16 The Grant of the Second Poll Tax, 1379

Anonimalle Chronicle, pp. 126–9; cf. *Rot. Parl.*, III 57–8; Wilkins, *Concilia*, III 141–2

Edward III died on 21 June 1377 at a time when 'litill and litill al tho Jofull and blyssed thynges, good fortune and prosperite decresed and myshapped, And Infortunat thynges, and unprofytable harmes, with many evele, bygan for to sprynge, and, the more harm is, conteyned longe tyme after'.[1] Despite contemporary hopes to the contrary, the replacement of the elderly king by his eleven-year old grandson, Richard II, failed to check the rising tide of discontent at governmental corruption and military mismanagement. The surviving records of the first two parliaments of the new king's reign reflect a general mood of querulous criticism as well as the almost frenzied attempts by the royal ministers to raise money for war and defence. Their lack of success led directly to the summoning of a third parliament, which assembled at Westminster in late April 1379. Under considerable pressure and alarmed by the failure of John of Gaunt's siege of St Malo in the previous summer and the growing rumours of an imminent French invasion of England, the commons agreed to the imposition of a second poll tax. The introduction of an elaborately graded scale of assessment gave the 1379 poll tax a form radically different from that of two years previously. Modern historians have usually interpreted the adoption of a graduated tax in terms of the commons' recognition of the principle of social justice: according to Tout, 'it would have won the hearts of modern radical reformers'.[2] The new sliding-scale clearly favoured married couples (who, like single men and women, paid at a minimum rate of 4d) but must have been very difficult to operate.

The following detailed description of the 1379 poll tax is to be found in the *Anonimalle Chronicle*. It has of course less authority than the official records of the 1379 parliament and convocations. But the chronicler has transcribed the terms of the official lists then circulated throughout England almost word for word; and his own introductory comment deserves to be noticed. In a tabulated form, the details of the assessment may help to provide a rough guide to the social status of various classes in late fourteenth-century England; and it is noticeable that lawyers were assessed at an apparently excessive rate.

In the year 1379, King Richard II held his parliament at London. It began on Wednesday after Easter [27 April], and in this parliament there was granted a subsidy so wonderful that no one had ever seen or heard of the like. This was the way it was to be paid:

---

[1] *The Brut, or The Chronicles of England*, ed. F. W. D. Brie (Early English Text Soc., 1908), p. 334; a translation of Walsingham, *Historia Anglicana*, I 328.

[2] Tout, *Chapters in Mediaeval Administrative History*, III 348.

(i) The dukes of Lancaster and Brittany, 10 marks
each [i.e. £6 13s 4d]
Each earl of England £4
Each widowed countess, like an earl £4
Each baron and banneret or knight
who is able to spend as much as a
baron 40s
Each widowed baroness 40s
Each banneress, like a banneret 40s
Each bachelor and each squire who
ought, by statute, to be a knight 20s
Each widowed lady, whether wife of
a knight or a squire, by assessment 20s
Each squire of lesser estate 6s 8d
Each lady, widow of such a squire or
of a sufficient merchant 6s 8d
Each squire not in possession of lands,
rents or castles, who is in service or
in arms 40d

(ii) The chief Prior of the Hospital of St
John in England will pay like a baron 40s
Each Commander of this order in
England will pay like a bachelor 20s
Each other brother knight of the order 13s 4d
All other brothers of the order, each
like a squire without possessions 40d

(iii) Each Justice, of either of the two
Benches; and those who have been
Justices of the Benches; and the
chief Baron of the Exchequer, each 100s
Each sergeant and great apprentice of
the law 40s
Other apprentices who follow the law,
each 20s
All other apprentices of lesser estate,
and attorneys, each 6s 8d

(iv) The mayor of London is to pay, like
   an earl   £4

   Each alderman of London is to pay,
   like a baron   40s

   All other mayors of the great towns
   of England are to pay, each like a
   baron   40s

   All other mayors of the remaining
   small towns, according to the extent
   of their estate   20s, 10s or 6s 8d

   All the municipal officers (*iurates*) of
   large towns and the great merchants of the kingdom are to pay,
   like a knight   20s

   All other sufficient merchants are to
   pay   3s 4d[1]

   All lesser merchants, and artificers
   who have profit from the land,
   according to the extent of their
   estate   2s, 12d or 6d[2]

   Each sergeant and franklin of the
   country according to his estate   6s 8d or 40d

   Farmers of manors and parsonages,
   and great merchants dealing in stock
   and other lesser trade, according to   6s 8d, or 40d,
   their estate   2s or 12d

(v) All advocates, notaries and procura-
   tors who are married are to pay like
   a sergeant of the law   40s

   Apprentices of the law and attorneys,
   each according to their estate   40s, 20s or 6s 8d

   Pardoners and summoners who are
   married, according to their estate   40d, 2s, or 12d

---

[1] 13s 4d in *Rot. Parl.*, III 58
[2] 6s 8d, 3s 4d, added in ibid., p. 58.

All hostlers who do not belong to the
estate of merchants, each according
to his estate   40d, 2s, or 12d

Each married man, for himself and
his wife if they do not belong to the
estates above-mentioned and are
over the age of 16 years, genuine
beggars excepted, is to pay   4d

Each single man and woman of this
last estate and of the same age   4d

(vi) Each foreign merchant of whatever
condition is to pay according to his
estate like the others above   20s, 6s 8d, 40d,
                                                       2s, or 12d

Each pleader (*pleder*)   6d

(vii) As for the clergy and the men of Holy Church, it was
granted that they should pay according to their estate in the
following manner:

Each archbishop ought to pay   10 marks
                                                       [i.e. £6 13s 4d]

Each bishop, abbot and prior with the
dignity of the mitre as well as abbots
and priors who are peers of the
realm and parliament, as well as
priors of cathedral churches   6 marks [i.e. £4]

All other abbots, priors, prioresses,
deans, archdeacons, provosts,
chanters [i.e. precentors], chancel-
lors, treasurers, and prebendaries,
both of cathedral churches and
colleges, and parsons with the cure
of any benefice or ecclesiastical
office which is worth more than
500 marks per annum   60s

All other abbots, priors, prioresses, deans, etc. (as above) holding a benefice or office worth between £200 and 500 marks per annum   40s

All other abbots, priors, prioresses, deans and others holding a benefice or office worth between £100 and £200 per annum   30s

Item, abbots, priors, prioresses, etc. who hold to the value of between 100 marks and £100 per annum   20s

Item, abbots, priors, prioresses and deans who hold to the value of between £40 and 100 marks per annum   13s 4d

Item, abbots, priors, prioresses, etc. who hold to the value of between £20 and £40 per annum   10s

Item, each abbot, prior, dean and others, except prioresses, who hold to the value of between £10 and £20 per annum   5s

(viii) Item all other curates having church benefices as well as parish and annual chaplains, each   2s

Item, monks, canons and other religious from houses valued at £200 (and more) per annum, each   40d

Item, monks, canons and other religious from houses valued at between 100 and 300 marks, each   20d

Item, monks, canons and other religious from houses valued at between £40 and 100 marks per annum, each   12d

Item, all other monks, canons and religious of houses valued at less

than £40 per annum; and all other
clerks without advancement, of
whatever order and condition, if
they are of more than 16 years, the
mendicant clergy excepted, each   4d
Item, ladies of religion of houses
worth more than £40 per annum,
recluse nuns of the Order of
Sempringham alone excepted, each   4d

17 The Northampton Parliament of 1380 and the Grant of the Third Poll Tax: according to the Rolls of Parliament

Rot. Parl., III 88–90

The graduated poll tax conceded by the commons in the spring
parliament of 1379 did little to ameliorate the government's financial
position. Because of corrupt administration the amount collected
proved completely inadequate. In a parliament held at Westminster in
January 1380 Lord Richard Scrope, the Chancellor, declared that the
proceeds of the poll tax 'together with a similar subsidy granted to
the king by the clergy of his realm' amounted to less than £22,000
at a time when the half-year's wages of English troops on an ill-fated
Breton expedition exceeded £50,000 (*Rot. Parl.*, III 73). Scrope's
admission of failure was followed by his own replacement as Chancellor – on 30 January 1380 – by the archbishop of Canterbury, Simon
Sudbury, and a heavy tax on movables. But, as Tout noted, 'the
political history of 1380 almost repeated that of 1379'. The earl of
Buckingham's costly *chevauchée* through northern and central France
failed to influence a position of complete military stalemate. In a state

of near desperation, the government called another parliament to assemble at Northampton on 5 November 1380. The royal officials deliberately avoided Westminster because of their known unpopularity in London. Chancellor Sudbury proceeded to give an accurate and depressing picture of the emergency. The following extracts from the parliamentary roll describe various stages of the subsequent debate and the commons' final and fateful decision to concede a third poll tax, on this occasion at the exceptionally high rate of a shilling per person.

1. On Monday after All Saints Day, 5 November 1380, the first day of this present parliament, several of the prelates and lords of the realm who had come to the town of Northampton assembled together with the king's great officers in a chamber set aside within St Andrew's priory[1] by the royal council. There, in the hearing of all, the archbishop of Canterbury, then Chancellor of England, had the Great Charter of the liberties of England read aloud. Afterwards those present waited a long time for the arrival of other prelates, lords and commons of the realm who, as was well known, had not yet reached Northampton because of the dangerous roads throughout much of the kingdom due to the outrageous floods of water following excessive and continuous rain and storms. Therefore, and because the sheriffs had not yet been able to return the parliamentary writs, parliament was adjourned until the following Thursday by our lord the king, who had managed with great difficulty to reach the manor of Moulton near Northampton. Accordingly the lords and prelates were ordered and the commons outside informed that they should retire to their lodgings to take their ease. And all were instructed to return early in the morning of the said Thursday to hear the declaration of the causes for which the lord king had summoned this parliament.

2. On the said Thursday, 8 November, our lord the king himself came into parliament at the place assigned for its meeting within the said priory; and he was accompanied by the prelates, the

---

[1] The monastery of St Andrew's, Northampton, was a large Cluniac alien priory.

Chancellor and Treasurer as well as other prelates and temporal lords who had arrived. But the number of temporal lords was very small because My Lord of Spain [John of Gaunt] together with a large number of the earls and barons of the kingdom had been for various reasons sent by the king to the march of Scotland, where they still were. Then were called within parliament the justices and royal sergeants, others of the king's council, the proctors of absent prelates, the knights of the counties, the barons of the Cinque Ports, citizens of cities and burgesses of boroughs who had been summoned to parliament. Then the Chancellor speaking on behalf of and at the command of the king introduced the matters on which he was to speak by a good sermon.

3. Then the Chancellor rehearsed how the king was desirous above all things of preserving and maintaining the inviolable liberties of Holy Church and the peace of the realm as well as of punishing evildoers. Then he moved on to the matters with which he was entrusted by the king and said in particular: 'Sirs, it neither is nor ought to be unknown to you how the noble lord, the earl of Buckingham, with a large number of other great lords, knights, esquires, archers and other good men of the realm (whom God save in his mercy) set forth in the service of our lord the king and his kingdom to the parts of France; on which expedition the king has spent what you gave him at the last parliament as well as much of his own money. What is more, because of the debts he has incurred for the expedition to Scotland and the defence of his liege subjects in Guienne, the money due to the earl of March for Ireland and other matters, he has placed the largest part of his great jewels in pledge and these are on the point of being lost.

4. And let it be known that nothing has actually been received from the subsidy of wools because of the present riot in Flanders.[1] Moreover, the wages of the soldiers of the Calais march, of Brest and Cherbourg, are more than a quarter and a half [of a

---

[1] An allusion to the rising of Bruges, Ghent and other Flemish towns against Count Louis de Male between 1379 and 1382.

year] in arrears, for which reason the castles and fortresses of the king are in great danger as the said soldiers are on the point of leaving because of the arrears. Let it be well known that neither our lord king nor any Christian king can endure such burdens without the aid of his commons. Therefore consider the outrageous indebtedness of the king and how, as is said above, his jewels are on the point of being lost: consider too that the king is obliged by convenant and indentures to pay the earl of Buckingham and the other members of his company for the half-year to come, as well as to send them reinforcements of men and horses – which will amount to a very large sum. Moreover, one must add the outrageous expenses necessary for the safe-keeping of the sea coasts against galleys this coming season so that the enemy's malice and misdeeds can be better resisted than they were last season: – when, as you know, they caused great damage and evil to the kingdom. Therefore, will you advise our lord the king and show him, as best you can, how it seems to you these expenses can be best met, to the least discomfort to yourselves and the commons of the realm and the best defence of the kingdom against all its enemies both on land and sea. On these matters, let it please you to take counsel as quickly as you can so that a good and effective arrangement is made as speedily as possible to the assistance of our king, the lords and all yourselves. . . .'

9. Afterwards, the said Chancellor instructed the commons on the king's behalf to leave for their lodgings to take their ease for the rest of that day but to return in good time on the following morning. They were to hold their assembly in the new dorter of the priory [of St Andrew], assigned to them for their common assembly. And for God's sake they were to leave off all other matters which might provoke rancour or conflict; and discuss sensibly the business entrusted to them and other issues necessary and profitable to the king and his kingdom. Moreover the Chancellor declared to all the prelates, lords and commons then present with the king that this parliament would continue day after day until the king's business was completed; and he forbade anyone

summoned to this parliament to leave until parliament was finished and they had licence to depart.

10. Afterwards, when the commons had inter-communed and discussed for a day the business entrusted to them, they returned to parliament in the presence of our lord the king, the prelates and the lords. Then Sir John Gildesburgh, knight, who was spokesman for the commons, asked on their behalf to have a clearer statement of their business and especially of the total sum demanded from them to support the said charges. He asked that this sum should be modified and that no more should be demanded than was necessary and practicable; for they knew that the commons were of too poor and feeble a condition to bear any heavier charge. Nevertheless they had high hopes for a good issue from the war and the bringing of it to a profitable and honourable end for the king and his kingdom – through the aid of God and the good rule of our host at present in French parts; and [they had confidence] of the greater success to be achieved, if it pleased God, if the said host was reinforced in good time by men and money. . . .

11. Accordingly a schedule was made before the great officers and the king's council, containing the various sums necessary for the attention of the commons: which sums amounted to £160,000 sterling. And this schedule was delivered to the commons for their information and so that they should give a good reply as soon as possible.

12. After this, the commons returned again into parliament, informing the king and the lords of parliament that it seemed to them that the sum demanded from them was very outrageous and completely insupportable by them. Therefore let it please them to reduce the sum in order to demand only what the commons could bear and was necessary for the reasons described above. Moreover, they requested that the prelates and lords would commune by themselves on the matter and indicate the means by which it seemed to them that such a tolerable sum could be levied and collected to the least discomfort of the people.

13. Afterwards, when the prelates and lords had considered and

discussed the matter at length, they called the commons before them yet again and gave them their advice as to what it seemed they could do. Their first suggestion was that the commons should grant a certain sum in the form of groats from each male and female throughout the kingdom, the strong helping the weak. If this did not please the commons, then their advice was to levy for a term a certain imposition throughout the kingdom and to take a tax on the pound of every kind of merchandise bought and sold in the kingdom, as often as such commodities were sold. And thirdly their advice was to raise a sum by means of tenths and fifteenths. However, tenths and fifteenths are seriously burdensome to the poor commons in various ways; and the impositions [of poundage] suggested have not yet been assessed in order to know what sum they will raise – besides which, it will be a long time before they produce any notable amount. Therefore it seems to the lords that if four or five groats are granted from each person, this would produce a good and substantial sum. By this means, the king would be properly assisted and each person in the realm could support the burden, provided that the strong were constrained to help the weak. And so it seems to the lords that this kind of levy of groats would be best and the least burdensome, as is said.

Item, when the commons had discussed the matter again and considered at length the type of levy required, they came into parliament, making a protestation that they had not come on that occasion to make a grant; but they had thought over what to say – that if the clergy agreed to support a third part (denier) of the burden, they would grant £100,000 to be raised from a certain number of groats drawn from each person, male and female, throughout the kingdom: provided that the laity was assessed at 100,000 marks and the clergy, who occupied a third part of the realm, at 50,000 marks. The commons went on to request the lord king and the temporal lords to ask the clergy to hasten the time of their council and assembly and to impose on them the said charge of 50,000 marks at this time. To which the clergy replied that they never made their grant within parliament, nor ought they to do so: laymen neither ought nor could constrain the clergy, nor could the laymen be constrained in this way. It seemed to them that if either party ought to be free, it ought to be rather the clergy than the laity.

14. [The clergy went on] to request the king that the complete liberty of Holy Church should be maintained as it had stood previously; and that the commons should be charged with the duty of doing what was incumbent upon them. For their part, the clergy would certainly do (as they had in the past) what they ought and were obliged to do – considering the present great necessity. Afterwards, when the commons had discussed this matter at length in the presence of the temporal lords, they came into parliament in the presence of our lord the king and there made their grant to him, delivering it to him in a written schedule, of which the form is as follows:

The Declaration to our lord the king and to his council by the commons of England concerning the matters with which the commons are charged in this present parliament; with regard to various necessities shown to them relative to the salvation of the kingdom and the safe-keeping of the sea.

15. First, the lords and commons are agreed that to meet the necessities above mentioned three groats should be given from each lay person of the realm, within franchise or without, both male and female and of whatsoever estate or condition, who have reached the age of fifteen – except for genuine beggars who will be charged nothing. This is on condition that at all times the levy shall be made in due order and form and that each lay person shall be charged equally according to his means in the following manner: that is to say, that for the sum total reckoned for each township, the sufficient shall (according to their means) aid the lesser, provided that the most wealthy do not pay more than sixty groats for themselves and their wives and no one at all should pay less than one groat for himself and his wife.[1] No one shall be charged to pay elsewhere than in the place of his, his wife's and

---

[1] An arrangement which obviously penalised the inhabitants of poor villages and towns: Oman, *Great Revolt*, pp. 26–7.

his children's home, or where he lives in service. All artificers, labourers, servants and other laymen, including servants dwelling with any prelate or temporal lord, abbots, collegiate priors, clerks of Chancery and the Common and King's Bench, the Exchequer, office of Receipt as well as those living with all other officers, knights, esquires, merchants, citizens, burgesses and all other persons, shall be assessed and taxed according to the amount of their estate and in the form described above. And commissions shall be directed to suitable persons, in the counties as well as the cities and boroughs, making them collectors and controllers of the said sum; and they shall be sworn to perform their offices well and loyally. It is not the intention of the commons to make this present grant except for the support of the earl of Buckingham and the other lords and men of his company in Brittany as well as the defence of the realm and safe-keeping of the sea. And this present grant should not be taken in the form or way that any previous levy of groats was taken, but should be charged only on persons who are now alive. Two-thirds of the payment should by made in the quinzaine of the next feast of St Hilary [27 January 1381]; and the remaining third by the following Whitsuntide [2 June 1381]. It is to be absolutely understood that no knight, citizen or burgess present at this parliament should be made either a collector or controller of the said sums. And let it please our lord king and his council to ordain that the servants of the king's household as well as those of other lords throughout the realm should be fully charged according to the intention of this grant.

And the commons request that for the duration of the war, neither judgment of eyre nor of trailbaston should take place among the poor commons; but that justices of peace should continue their activities according to the terms of their commission.

And the commons grant to our lord the king the subsidy of wools, to last until next Martinmas [11 November].

16. And let it be remembered that this grant of subsidies was made on 6 December in this present year. . . .

18 Appointment of Commissioners to enforce payment of the Third Poll Tax, March 1381

Fine Roll, 4 Richard II [C. 60/183], memb. 9; cf. *C.F.R.*, *1377–83*, pp. 248–9; printed in Oman, *Great Revolt*, pp. 183–5, from L.T.R. Originalia Roll [E. 371/140]

Immediately after the commons at the Northampton parliament had conceded the third poll tax and departed (on 6 December 1380) the work of collection began. According to the evidence of the collectors' first returns, the full levy of three groats per head was being exacted throughout most of England during the winter months of 1380–1. But from a very early date the royal council was aware of the existence of widespread tax evasion. In order to enforce full payment of the tax the government took various measures, of which the appointment of commissions of the type outlined below was at once the most drastic and the most misguided. According to Henry Knighton (see below, no. 21), it was one of the king's serjeants-at-arms, John Legge, who suggested such commissions of inquiry; and the popular belief that he had done so certainly cost him his life (see below, p. 162). The new commissioners appointed on and after 16 March were unable to complete their work before the revolts began. Nevertheless the government's vigilant methods proved remarkably successful: over £37,000, approximately four-fifths of the total assessment, had reached the Exchequer by the end of May. Such efficiency was hardly likely to endear the new commissioners to the people at large; and they were widely held to be collecting a new tax rather than making good the deficiencies of the subsidy granted in the previous parliament. Their activities were undoubtedly responsible for the wave of tax-resistance which led directly to outbreaks of violence and disorder throughout south-eastern England; and there is a close correlation between those shires where the rebellion raged most fiercely and those to which such commissions were dispatched. The terms of the following commission for Norfolk were closely followed in the case of the other counties: in nearly all cases the duty of enforcing the collection of the poll tax was entrusted to the sheriff, a royal serjeant-at-arms, a clerk and a handful of county knights and notables. Of these, the serjeant-at-arms appointed

from the royal household seems usually to have been the most active
as well as the most unpopular member.

Concerning an enquiry into the names of all lay persons exceeding
the age of fifteen years who have not paid the subsidy granted to
the king.

The king to the sheriff of Norfolk, Stephen de Hales, knight,
Hugh Fastolf, Nicholas de Massyngham, William Wenlok, clerk,
and John de Ellerton, his serjeant-at-arms, greetings. As is fully
revealed by trustworthy and notable evidence, the men commissioned by us as taxers and collectors of the subsidy of three
groats to be levied from each lay person of the kingdom (granted
to us by the lords, magnates and communities of our kingdom
in our last parliament at Northampton for the safety and defence
of our kingdom) have spared many persons of the county:
they have omitted some deliberately, some through negligence
and others through favour. The result is that a large part of the
said subsidy in the county of Norfolk is concealed and withheld
from us by the negligence and failings of the said taxers and
collectors although it ought to have been raised for our needs if
the taxation and assessment had been well and honestly carried
out. Unless amends are soon made, these failings will obviously
redound to serious prejudice of ourselves and our kingdom as
well as delaying and disturbing the ordinances made and
negotiated by ourselves and our council for the health and
honour of our kingdom and its subjects. As we wish to avoid
these dangers as effectively as we can and to have an accurate
account of the said subsidy as it was granted in parliament,
with the advice of our council we ordain and appoint you (or
four, three or two of you) to investigate and inspect all the
indentures concerning the assessment and collection of the
said subsidy made between the said collectors and the constables
and other people of all the vills and boroughs of the county.
Alternatively you are to inspect true copies of the said assessments
containing the number and names of all persons assessed to the
said subsidy by the said taxers and their sub-taxers. You are to

examine and inquire into the number of all lay persons, both men and women, of the said county, whether within or without franchises, provided they are more than fifteen years of age – excepting only genuine beggars and those who survive solely by alms. When necessary, you are to inform yourselves by means of the oaths of the constables and bailiffs of each vill and borough and of other sound and law-worthy men from any place in the county, within or without the franchises (or by other methods when these seem more expedient to you) of each lay person of whatever vill of the said county who ought to pay the said subsidy but was omitted or concealed by the said taxers or collectors. You are to draw up a written statement of the numbers and names of such persons and deliver it to the said taxers and collectors by means of a properly made written indenture between you and them, so that they can make a faithful levy and collection of the said subsidy according to the form of its original grant. Moreover, you are to have made indentures between yourselves and the constables and two other men of every vill in the county, containing the total numbers of all the persons who can be found in the vill and who are obliged or ought to pay the subsidy according to the form of its grant. In this way no lay person in the county shall be omitted at all against the form of the said grant.

You are to certify to the Treasurer and Barons of the Exchequer with all possible speed the number and names of all persons whom you find in each vill and parish; and you shall bring to the Exchequer your parts of the said indentures. You are to seize and arrest all those whom you find acting in opposition or rebellion to the above commands; such men are to be held in our prisons where they are to stay until we make provision for their punishment. And so we enjoin and command you – or four, three or two of you – that (on the faith and loyalty which you owe us and under penalty of forfeiting all you can forfeit to us) you put aside all other things and possible excuses; and travel personally from vill to vill and place to place in the said county, within and without liberties, to make the said scrutiny and examination. You are to collect the required information by the means which seem best to you, and to do all the other things mentioned above. For we have commanded the said collectors to deliver to you – or four, three or two of you – their said indentures or true copies thereof; and also that they should cause to be collected and levied with all speed the said subsidy from those persons whom you will certify to them by your indentures; and the collectors will account to us for these sums at our Exchequer. By these letters we also firmly command (on the faith and loyalty they owe us) all dukes, earls, barons, knights, bailiffs, mayors, bailiffs and officials as well as our other loyal and faithful men in the county (within and without liberties) to assist, counsel, advise and obey you – or four, three or two of you – in the execution of your duties. And you, the said sheriff, are to seize all those who act in opposition or rebellion to the payment of the said subsidy and the other matters specified above; and you are to keep them safely in our prison, as previously stated. And you – or four, three or two of you – will cause to come before you, at the time and place which you assign for this, both the constables and bailiffs and other worthy and lawful men of each vill or parish of the county so that you can make due enquiry. Witnessed by the king at Westminster on 16 March (by the council).

Similar commissions were assigned to other counties as follows:
16 March: Suffolk, Cambridge, Huntingdon, Essex,
           Hertford, Somerset, Northampton, Gloucester
 3 May: Nottingham and Derby, Devon and Cornwall,
           Kent, West Riding of Yorkshire
20 May: city of Canterbury

19 The Outbreak of the Revolt according to the 'Anonimalle Chronicle'

Anonimalle Chronicle, pp. 133–40; previously translated from Thynne's transcript in Oman, *Great Revolt*, pp. 186–93

Since it was first printed from a sixteenth-century copy in 1898 the *Anonimalle Chronicle*'s account of the Peasants' Revolt has been generally accepted as the single most important source for the history of the rising. The author, of the following pages was evidently exceptionally well-informed as to the origins and early course of the revolt; and the general accuracy of his narrative is confirmed by the evidence of later inquisitions and indictments. He makes intelligible a good deal that would otherwise be a matter for surmise and conjecture.

At this time[1] the commons of southern England suddenly rose in two groups, one in Essex and the other in Kent. They directed their evil actions against the duke of Lancaster and the other lords of the realm because of the exceptionally severe tenths and fifteenths and other subsidies lightly conceded in parliaments and extortionately levied from the poor people. These subsidies did nothing for the profit of the kingdom but were spent badly and deceitfully to the great impoverishment of the commons – and it was for this reason, as you will now hear, that the commons rose.

Because in the year 1380[2] subsidies had been granted lightly at the parliament of Northampton and because it seemed to various lords and the commons that these subsidies had not been properly or honestly collected but had been raised from the poor people and not the rich, to the great profit and advantage of the

[1] While John of Gaunt was on the Marches negotiating with the Scots.

[2] The clumsy repetition of material from the previous paragraph suggests that at this point the author of the *Anonimalle Chronicle* started to copy, probably verbatim, his account of the Peasants' Revolt from another chronicle. It is also at this point that Francis Thynne began his sixteenth-century transcript, first published by G. M. Trevelyan in 1898 (*Anonimalle Chronicle*, pp. xxii, xxxiii, 193).

collectors and the deception of the king and commons, the royal council appointed certain commissions to make inquiry in every township how they had been levied.[1] Among these commissions, one for Essex was sent to one Thomas [recte John] de Bamptoun, a lord's steward, who was considered a king or great lord in that country because of his great state. One day before Whitsuntide[2] he sat in the town of Brentwood in Essex in order to make an inquisition; and he displayed the commission sent to him to raise all the money in default and to inquire how the collectors had raised the aforesaid subsidy. He had summoned before him the townships of a neighbouring hundred and wished to levy from them a new subsidy, commanding the people of those townships to make a diligent inquiry, give their reply and pay their money. Among these townships was Fobbing, where all the people replied that they would pay nothing at all because they had an acquittance from himself for the said subsidy. On which the said Thomas threatened them violently; and he had with him two of the king's serjeants-at-arms. For fear of his malice, the people of Fobbing took counsel with those of Corringham; and the people of both townships rose and assembled, instructing those of Saniforth [Stanford-le-Hope] to rise with them for their common profit. Then the people of these three townships gathered to the number of a hundred or more and with one assent went to the said Thomas de Bamptoun and told him outright that they would not deal with him nor give him any money. On which the said Thomas commanded the serjeants-at-arms to arrest these people and put them in prison. But these commons rose against the royal officers, would not be arrested and were ready to kill the said Thomas and the two serjeants. Accordingly Thomas fled towards London and the king's council while the commons went into the woods for fear of his malice. They hid there for some time and until they were almost famished; and afterwards went from town to town inciting other people to rise against the great lords and the good men of the country.

[1] The Essex commission was dated from Westminster on 16 March: see above, p. 122.   [2] Whit Sunday fell on 2 June in 1381.

Because of what happened to the said Thomas, Sir Robert Bealknap, Chief Justice of the Common Bench, was sent into the country on a commission of trailbaston. Indictments against various persons were laid before him, and the people of the area were so fearful that they proposed to abandon their holdings. Wherefore the commons rose against him and came before him to tell him that he was a traitor to the king and kingdom and was maliciously proposing to undo them by the use of false inquests taken before him. Accordingly they made him swear on the Bible that never again would he hold such sessions nor act as a justice in such inquests. And they forced him to tell them the names of all the jurors. They captured all of these jurors that they could, beheaded them and threw their houses to the ground. And Sir Robert travelled home as quickly as possible. Afterwards, and before Whitsunday, fifty thousand of the commons gathered, going to the various manors and townships of those who would not rise with them, throwing their buildings to the ground and setting them ablaze. At this time they captured three of Thomas de Bamptoun's clerks, cut off their heads and carried them about with them on poles for days as an example to others. They proposed to kill all the lawyers, jurors and royal servants they could find. Meanwhile all the great lords and other notable people of that country fled towards London or to other counties where they might be safe.

Now the high master of the Hospital of St John of Clerkenwell in London [Sir Robert Hales, the Treasurer] had a very fine and pleasant manor in Essex[1] which he had ordered to be filled with victuals and other necessities for the holding of his general chapter: so it was well supplied with wines and suitably stocked for such an important lord and his brothers. And at this time the commons arrived at this manor, ate the food, drank three casks of good wine and threw the building to the ground, then burning it to the serious damage and loss of the said master. Then the commons sent several letters to those in Kent, Suffolk and Norfolk,

[1] The Hospitallers' commandery of Cressing Temple, not sacked until 10 June (Réville, p. 204).

asking them to rise with them; and when they were assembled they left in various companies, doing great mischief in the surrounding countryside.

Afterwards, on Whit Monday [3 June] Sir Simon de Burley, a knight of the king's household, came to Gravesend in the company of two of the king's serjeants-at-arms and there he charged a man with being his own serf.[1] The good men of the town came to Burley to arrange a settlement because of their respect for the king, but Sir Simon would not take less than £300 in silver, a sum which would have ruined the said man. On which the good men of Gravesend requested Burley to mitigate his demand, but they could not come to terms nor reduce the amount, although they told Sir Simon that the man was a Christian and of good repute and so ought not to be ruined for ever. Wherefore the said Sir Simon grew angry and irritable, much despising these good townsfolk; and out of the haughtiness of his heart, he made the serjeants bind the said man and lead him to Rochester castle for safe-keeping. Great evil and mischief derived from this action; and after his departure, the commons began to rise, welcoming within their ranks the men of many Kentish townships. And at this moment a justice was assigned by the king and his council to go into Kent on a commission of trailbaston as had happened in Essex. With the justice went a serjeant-at-arms of our lord the king called Master John Legge who carried with him a great number of indictments against the people of that area, to make the king rich. They intended to hold their sessions at Canterbury but were turned back by the commons.

After this the commons of Kent, although without a chief or leader, gathered together in great numbers from day to day. On the Friday before [*sic:* presumably a mistake for *after*] Whit Sunday [31 May or 7 June][2] they came to Dartford and took counsel together. They ordained that no one who lived at any

---

[1] The name of this serf was Robert Belling (Réville, p. 187). But Burley himself had left London for the continent on 15 May to help negotiate Richard II's marriage with Anne of Bohemia (Tout, *Chapters*, III 368).

[2] The true date of the rebels' arrival at Dartford seems to have been 5 June.

place within twelve leagues of the sea should come with them but should keep the sea-coasts free from enemies. They said among themselves that they [*sic*: read *there*] were more kings than one and that they would neither suffer nor have any king except King Richard. At this same time the commons of Kent came to Maidstone, cut off the head of one of the best men of the town and cast to the ground various houses and tenements of people who would not rise with them, as had happened in Essex. On the following Friday [7 June][1] they arrived in Rochester and there met a great number of the Essex commons. And because of the case of the man of Gravesend, they laid siege to Rochester castle to free their companion from Gravesend whom Sir Simon had imprisoned. They laid strong siege to the castle and although the constable defended it vigorously for half a day he at last handed the castle over for fear of the great multitude of people who had come without reason from Essex and Kent. The commons entered the castle and delivered their companion and all the other prisoners from it. The men of Gravesend returned home with their companion in great joy and without doing anything more; but the people from Maidstone took their way with the rest of the commons through the surrounding countryside. And they made their chief one Watt Teghler of Maidstone, to maintain and advise them.

On the Monday after Trinity Sunday [10 June] they came to Canterbury before the hour of noon. Four thousand of them entered St Thomas's mother-church at the time of High Mass and, after kneeling, all cried to the monks with one voice asking them to elect a monk to be archbishop of Canterbury, 'for he who is archbishop now is a traitor and will be beheaded for his iniquity'. And so he was within the following five days. And when they had done this, they went into the town to their fellows and with one assent they summoned the mayor, bailiffs and commons of the town and examined them as to whether they would swear in good will to be faithful and loyal to King Richard and the loyal commons of England or not. The mayor

---

[1] The siege of Rochester took place on 6 June.

replied that they would willingly do this, and so they swore their oaths. The rebels then demanded if there were any traitors among the townsfolk of Canterbury. Three were mentioned and their names revealed, to be immediately dragged out of their houses by the commons and beheaded. Afterwards the commons took five hundred men of the town with them towards London, but left the others to guard the city.

At this time the commons had as their counsellor a chaplain of evil disposition named Sir John Balle, who advised them to get rid of all the lords, archbishops, bishops, abbots and priors as well as most of the monks and canons so that there should be no bishop in England except for one archbishop, namely himself; no religious house should hold more than two monks or canons, and their possessions should be divided among the laity. For which advice he was regarded as a prophet by the commons, and laboured with them day by day to strengthen them in their malice. He was well rewarded later by being drawn, disembowelled, hanged and beheaded as a traitor.

After this the commons went to many towns and raised the people there, some willingly and some not, until a good sixty thousand were gathered together. On their journey towards London they met several men of law and twelve of the king's knights, whom they captured and forced to swear that they would support the commons under threat of execution. They did much damage in Kent, notably to Thomas de Heseldene, servant of the duke of Lancaster,[1] because of their hatred for the said duke. For this reason they cast his manors and houses to the ground and sold his live-stock – horses, oxen, cows, sheep and pigs – and all sorts of corn at a cheap price. Every day the commons were eager to have his head along with that of Sir Thomas Orgrave, clerk of the Receipt and sub-Treasurer of England.

When the king heard of their doings he sent messengers to them on Tuesday after Trinity Sunday [11 June] asking why they were acting in this way and for what reason they had risen in his

[1] Thomas Haselden was controller of John of Gaunt's household. Cf. p. 240 below.

land. And they sent replies by the said messengers that they had risen to save him and to destroy traitors to him and the kingdom. The king sent messengers to them again asking them to stop their activity out of reverence to him until he could speak with them, when he would make reasonable amends, according to their will, for the injustices done to them. The commons requested through his messengers that he would meet and speak with them at Blackheath. The king sent messengers for a third time saying that he would willingly meet them on the next day, at the hour of Prime, to hear their intentions. Then the king, who was staying at Windsor, moved with all possible speed to London. The mayor and the good men of the city came to meet him and lead him safely to the Tower of London. At this place assembled all the council as well as all the lords of the surrounding area, namely the archbishop of Canterbury and Chancellor of England, the bishop of London, the master of the Hospital of St John of Clerkenwell (then Treasurer of England), the earls of Buckingham, Kent, Arundel, Warwick, Suffolk, Oxford and Salisbury and others to the number of six hundred.

And on the eve of Corpus Christi Day[1] the commons of Kent came to Blackheath, three leagues from London, to the number of fifty thousand, to await the king; and they displayed two banners of St George and sixty pennons. And the commons of Essex, to the number of sixty thousand, arrived on the other side of the water to help them and have the king's reply. On this Wednesday,[2] being in the Tower of London and deciding to deal with the matter, the king had his barges got ready and took with him

[1] i.e. on 12 June. As the peasants of Kent seem to have left Canterbury (70 miles away) on the morning of Tuesday, 11 June, they can hardly have arrived at Blackheath before the evening of the following day.

[2] It is reasonably clear, from the author's own earlier and later references as well as other sources, that Richard's voyage to Greenwich took place on the morning of Thursday, 13 June. But the chroniclers disagree and it is just possible to argue (like Professor Wilkinson in 'The Peasants' Revolt', pp. 16-17) that Richard's excursion by barge took place late on 12 June and the rebels left Blackheath for London before the end of that day. However in his latest work, *The Later Middle Ages in England, 1216-1485* (London, 1969), p. 160, Professor Wilkinson seems to have abandoned his earlier theories.

in his own barge the archbishop, Treasurer and certain others of his council. Accompanied by four other barges for his men, he travelled to Greenwich, three leagues from London. But there the said Chancellor and Treasurer informed the king that it would be too great folly to go to the commons for they were unreasonable men and did not know how to behave. As the king, on the persuasion of the Chancellor and Treasurer, would not come to them, the commons of Kent sent him a petition asking him to grant them the heads of the duke of Lancaster and fifteen other lords, of whom fourteen [sic] were bishops present with him in the Tower of London. These were their names: Master Simon of Sudbury, archbishop of Canterbury and Chancellor of England; Sir Robert Hales, prior of the Hospital of St John, Treasurer of England; Sir John Fordham, Clerk of the Privy Seal and bishop-elect of Durham; Sir Robert Bealknap, Chief Justice of the Common Bench; Sir Ralph Ferreres; Sir Robert Plesyngtoun, Chief Baron of the Exchequer; John Legge, serjeant-at-arms of our lord the king; Thomas de Bamptoun already mentioned, and others. To this proposal the king would not assent, whereupon the commons sent to him again a yeoman, praying that he would come and speak with them. The king replied that he would do so willingly; but the said Chancellor and Treasurer advised him to do the opposite and to tell the commons that if they wished to come to Windsor on the following Monday they would receive a reasonable reply there. And the said commons had a watch-word (*wache word*) in English among themselves, 'With whom haldes yow?', to which the reply was, 'Wyth kynge Richarde and wyth the trew communes'; and those who did not know how to reply or would not do so were beheaded and put to death.

And at this time there came a knight[1] as quickly as he could, crying to the king to wait; on which the king was startled and waited for his arrival and to hear what he wished to say. The said knight came to the king and told him that he had heard from a servant who had been held by the rebels during the day

---

[1] Compare Froissart's long account of the role played by Sir John Newton, below, no. 22.

that if the king went to them, all the land would be lost; for the rebels would never let him leave them in any way but would lead him round the whole of England with them, and they would force him to grant them all their desires, their purpose being to kill all the lords and ladies of great renown as well as all the archbishops, bishops, abbots and priors, monks and canons, parsons and vicars on the advice and counsel of the aforementioned Sir John Ball. Therefore the king returned to London as quickly as he could and arrived in the Tower at the hour of Tierce. Meanwhile the man we have described as a yeoman hastened to Blackheath, crying out to his companions that the king had left and that it would be good for them to go on to London to carry out their designs. [*Continued by no. 25 below, p. 155.*]

20 The Outbreak of the Revolt according to Thomas Walsingham

Walsingham, *Historia Anglicana*, I 453–6; cf. *Chronicon Angliae*, pp. 285–8

Walsingham's account of the early stages of the Peasants' Revolt provides surprisingly little in the way of circumstantial detail but a good deal of inimitable moral comment. He does however confirm that the origins of the rebellion could be traced back to a couple of Essex villages – unnamed by him but presumably Fobbing and Corringham. From there it spread to the rest of the county and across the Thames to Kent. For Walsingham the revolt was above all a mass peasant rising, at first alarmingly successful because it met with no organised opposition from the landlords of south-eastern England.

Concerning the misery which afflicted England by the tumult of the rustics and other commons

At about this time the kingdom of England suffered – as a chastisement for its sins – a great and unexpected calamity not experienced by previous ages; and if God, the lord of all mercies, had not suppressed it quickly out of his accustomed goodness, the government of the realm would have been completely destroyed and the episode a source of shame and derision to all peoples.

For the rustics, whom we call 'nativi' or 'bondsmen', together with other country-dwellers living in Essex sought to better themselves by force and hoped to subject all things to their own stupidity. Crowds of them assembled and began to clamour for liberty, planning to become the equals of their lords and no longer to be bound by servitude to any master. In order to put their desires into effect, men from those two villages which were the originators and first causers of these evils sent messages to every village however small. No man was to be excused and all, both old and vigorous, were to assemble with weapons as they could; all men who failed, neglected or scorned to come knew that their goods would be scattered, their homes burnt or destroyed and their heads cut from their necks. So terrible a threat compelled all to assemble and abandon the business of ploughing and sowing as well as their wives and estates. In a short time so large a body was forced to assemble that it could be reckoned at five thousand of the most mean commons and rustics. Of those who gathered to conquer the kingdom, some carried only sticks, some swords covered with rust, some merely axes and others bows more reddened with age and smoke than old ivory: many of their arrows had only one plume. Among a thousand of these men it was difficult to find one who was properly armed; but, because they formed so large a number, they believed the whole kingdom would be unable to resist them. To gain greater support, they sent messengers to Kent to inform the people there of their plans, inviting them to meet them in order to acquire their liberty, concert further action and change the evil customs for and of the kingdom.

Therefore the Kentishmen, hearing of things most of them already desired, without delay assembled a large band of commons and rustics in the same manner as the men of Essex: in a short time they stirred up almost the whole province [of Kent] to a similar state of tumult. Soon they blocked all the pilgrimage routes to Canterbury, stopped all pilgrims of whatever condition and forced them to swear: first, that they would be faithful to King Richard and the commons and that they would accept no king who was called John: – on account of their hatred of John, duke of Lancaster who called himself 'King of Castile' because of his marriage to the daughter and heiress of Peter, King of Castile. The pilgrims also had to swear that they would come and join the rebels whenever they were sent for, and that they would induce their fellow citizens or villagers to join them; and that they would neither acquiesce nor consent to any tax levied in the kingdom henceforth except only for the fifteenths which their fathers and ancestors had known and accepted.

Soon afterwards the news of these deeds passed rapidly through the counties of Sussex, Hertford, Cambridge, Suffolk and Norfolk; and all the people expected great happenings. They wished to have everything themselves and would pursue their enterprise (however audaciously) wherever it should lead – many hoping for a better future but others fearing that all would end to the ruin of the kingdom. The latter predicted the division of the kingdom as a result of such activities and its consequent desolation and destruction. The rebels however received so many crowds of reinforcements from these people and were such an enormous number that they feared resistance from no one. The insurgents then began to reveal their designs and to execute all the lawyers in the land whom they could capture – not only apprentices but also old justices and all the kingdom's jurors, without respect for piety; for the rebels declared that the land could not be fully free until the lawyers had been killed. This sentiment so excited the rustics that they went to further extremes and declared that all court rolls and old muniments should be burnt so that once the memory of ancient customs had been wiped out their lords would be completely unable to vindicate their rights over them; and so it was done. As yet the lords were not alert to the need for opposing these iniquities; but they remained inert, staying quiet and motionless in their homes until the men of Kent and Essex had attracted an army of about one hundred thousand commons and rustics. They were joined by men from all parts who were oppressed by debt or feared the censure of the law because of their misdeeds, and they formed so large a conglomeration of plebeians that no one could remember seeing or hearing of the like. And so the mob came to the place called 'le Blakheth' where they decided to view their numbers and count the multitude of their fellows. While they were at this place knights came to them on behalf of the king asking the reason for their disorder and the assembly of such a mob. The king's messengers were told that the insurgents had assembled to talk with the king on certain issues and affairs and that they should return to the king and ask him to come to them and hear the desires of their hearts.

This message was therefore conveyed to the king, who was advised by some that he should hurry to meet the rebels. But Master Simon of Sudbury, archbishop of Canterbury and then Chancellor of the realm as well as Lord Robert de Hales, master of the Hospital of St John and then Treasurer of England, steadfastly opposed this advice declaring that the king ought not to approach such bare-legged ruffians but rather to take measures to abase the pride of the rascals. When they had heard this reply the common people were furious and swore they would seek out those traitors to the king, namely the said archbishop and Robert, and carry off their heads, by which action they believed they would be safer themselves. They immediately took the road to London and reached Southwark, filling up all the places there and in the surrounding area. [*Continued by no. 26 below, p. 168.*]

Dir. reaction to poll-tax collectors — Anon
Knighton

Froissart
& Walsingham.
Sen. alarming
mass rising.

21 The Outbreak of the Revolt according to Henry Knighton

Chronicon Henrici Knighton, II 129–32

Although very brief, Henry Knighton's description of the outbreak of the rebellion is that of an independent authority. He preserves for posterity the name of the first leader of sedition, Thomas Baker of Fobbing in Essex, and agrees with the *Anonimalle Chronicle*, as against Walsingham and Froissart, in seeing the revolt as a direct reaction to the unscrupulous activities of the poll tax commissioners.

(A.D. 1380) There was granted to the lord king from the bishops, abbots and merchants a certain tax of two shillings from each married man. The unmarried paid twelve pence; members of religious orders holding possessions paid six shillings and eight pence; clerks holding one benefice paid six shillings and eight pence. Yet this tax did not bring into the king's exchequer as large a sum as the tax of four pence in the previous year. Accordingly the king's ministers were surprised and complained that the collection of the tax had been badly and dishonestly managed.

Therefore a certain John Leg with three colleagues asked the king to give him a commission to investigate the collectors of this tax in Kent, Norfolk and other parts of the country.[1] They contracted to give the lord king a large sum of money for his assent; and most unfortunately for the king his council agreed. One of these commissioners came to a certain village to investigate the said tax and called together the men and women; he then, horrible to relate, shamelessly lifted the young girls to test whether they had enjoyed intercourse with men. In this way he compelled the friends and parents of these girls to pay the tax for them: many would rather pay for their daughters than see them touched in such a disgraceful way. These and similar actions by the said inquisitors much provoked the people. And when the commons of Kent and the neighbouring areas suffered such evils

[1] See above, no. 18.

and the imposition of new and almost unbearable burdens which appeared to be endless and without remedy, they refused to bear such injuries any longer. They conferred together as to what remedial action or assistance could be found. And after each man had pondered on these problems but no one had dared to make the first move for fear that he would suffer irrevocable harm, at last a certain Thomas Baker of Fobbing (so called because of his trade) took courage and began to exhort and ally himself with the men of his village.[1] Then these men leagued themselves with others and in turn they contacted their friends and relations so that their message passed from village to village and area to area. They asked their friends to advise them and to bring assistance for those serious and urgent matters which affected them all. The people gathered together most eagerly in great troops, delighted that the day had come when they could help each other in the face of so urgent a necessity.

In the following year on – May [13 June seems to be meant] this wicked mob of people from Kent and Sothereye [*Southwark*] and many other neighbouring places began to assemble. Apprentices left their masters and ran to join the people. And so they gathered on the Blackheath and displayed their great numbers. No longer restricting themselves to their original grievance and not satisfied by minor crimes, they now planned much more radical and merciless evils: they determined not to give way until all the nobles and magnates of the realm had been completely destroyed. They directed the first of their wicked assaults on the archbishop of Canterbury's town of Maidstone. In the archbishop's prison there was a certain chaplain, John Balle, held a most famous preacher to the laity. For many years he had sowed the word of God in a foolish manner, mixing tares with the wheat, and pleasing laymen beyond measure. He excessively attacked the position, law and liberties of the church

---

[1] A Thomas Baker was listed as one of the rebels from Fobbing, less than two miles from the Thames estuary in southern Essex, in an inquest of 3 July 1381 (Réville, p. LXXI). Men from Fobbing joined in the successful attack on John de Bampton and his fellow-justices at Brentwood in late May: see above, p. 124.

and shamefully introduced many errors into the relations of clerks and laymen within the church of Christ. He had darkened the province for many years in this way and was accordingly tried and lawfully convicted by the clergy who committed him to perpetual imprisonment in the said gaol. But the people broke into the prison, brought him out and made him go with them, for they proposed to promote him as archbishop. [*Continued by no. 27 below, p. 181.*]

22 The Outbreak of the Revolt according to Froissart

Froissart, trans. Berners, ed. G. C. Macaulay, pp. 251–5; cf. Froissart, *Chroniques*, X 97–107

Jean Froissart was an ambitious as well as a famous writer, explicitly conscious of the distinction between the ordinary chronicler and the historian like himself whose self-imposed duty it was to enlarge upon and explain events. For that reason alone, Froissart's description of the early stages of the Peasants' Revolt, first written before the autumn of 1388, was bound to be more entertaining and imaginative than those of other chroniclers. But as nearly always, it is difficult to know quite how much of Froissart's confident narrative one should consider seriously. Conditioned by his experiences of popular movements in Flanders, he makes little of the poll tax and blames the London burgesses for inciting the English peasants to rebel before beginning his meandering and discursive story of the revolt.

Of his [John Ball's: see below, no. 69 for the passage which immediately precedes this] words and deeds there were much people in London informed, such as had great envy at them that were rich and such as were noble; and then they began to speak among them and said how the realm of England was right evil governed, and how that gold and silver was taken from them by them that were named noblemen: so thus these unhappy men of London began to rebel and assembled them together, and sent word to the foresaid countries that they should come to London and bring their people with them, promising them how they should find London open to receive them and the commons of the city to be of the same accord, saying how they would do so much to the king that there should not be one bondman (*serf*) in all England.

This promise moved so them of Kent, of Essex, of Sussex, of Bedford and of the countries about, that they rose and came towards London to the number of sixty thousand. And they had a captain called Water Tyler, and with him in company was Jack Straw and John Ball: these three were chief sovereign captains, but the head of all was Water Tyler, and he was indeed a tiler of houses, an ungracious patron.

When these unhappy men began thus to stir, they of London, except such as were of their band, were greatly affrayed. Then the mayor of London and the rich men of the city took counsel together, and when they saw the people thus coming on every side, they caused the gates of the city to be closed and would suffer no man to enter into the city. But when they had well imagined, they advised not so to do, for they thought they should thereby put their suburbs in great peril to be brent; and so they opened again the city, and there entered in at the gates in some place a hundred, two hundred, by twenty and by thirty, and so when they came to London, they entered and lodged: and yet of truth the third part of these people could not tell what to ask or demand, but followed each other like beasts, as the shepherds did of old time, saying how they would go conquer the Holy Land, and at last all came to nothing.[1] In like wise these villains and poor people came to London, a hundred mile off, sixty mile, fifty mile, forty mile and twenty mile [leagues] off, and from all countries about London, but the most part came from the

[1] A reference to the French peasants or *Pastoureaux* of 1250 who planned to rescue their king Louis IX from captivity in Egypt.

countries before named, and as they came they demanded ever for the king. The gentlemen of the countries, knights and squires, began to doubt, when they saw the people began to rebel; and though they were in doubt, it was good reason; for a less occasion they might have been affrayed. So the gentlemen drew together as well as they might.

The same day that these unhappy people of Kent were coming to London, there returned from Canterbury the king's mother, princess of Wales,[1] coming from her pilgrimage. She was in great jeopardy to have been lost, for these people came to her chare [*char*] and dealt rudely with her, whereof the good lady was in great doubt lest they would have done some villany to her or to her damosels. Howbeit, God kept her, and she came in one day from Canterbury to London, for she never durst tarry by the way. The same time king Richard her son was at the Tower of London: there his mother found him, and with him there was the earl of Salisbury, the archbishop of Canterbury, sir Robert of Namur, the lord of Gommegnies and divers other, who were in doubt of these people that thus gathered together, and wist not what they demanded. This rebellion was well known in the king's court, or any of these people began to stir out of their houses; but the king nor his council did provide no remedy therefor, which was great marvel. And to the intent that all lords and good people and such as would nothing but good should take ensample to correct them that be evil and rebellious, I shall shew you plainly all the matter, as it was.

The Monday before the feast of Corpus Christi [10 June] the year of our Lord God a thousand three hundred and eighty-one these people issued out of their houses to come to London to speak with the king to be made free, for they would have had no bondman [*serf*] in England. And so first they came to Saint Thomas of Canterbury, and there John Ball had thought to have found the bishop[*sic*] of Canterbury, but he was at London with the king. When Wat Tyler and Jack Straw entered into Canterbury, all the common people made great feast, for all the town was

---

[1] Joan of Kent, widow of the Black Prince.

of their assent; and there they took counsel to go to London to
the king, and to send some of their company over the river of
Thames into Essex, into Sussex and into the counties of Stafford
[*Stanfort*] and Bedford, to speak to the people that they should all
come to the farther side of London and thereby to close London
round about, so that the king should not stop their passages, and
that they should all meet together on Corpus Christi day [or the
day after]. They that were at Canterbury entered into Saint
Thomas' church and did there much hurt, and robbed and brake
up the bishop's chamber, and in robbing and bearing out their
pillage they said: 'Ah, this chancellor of England hath had a good
market to get together all this riches: he shall give us now account
of the revenues of England and of the great profits that he hath
gathered sith the king's coronation.' When they had this Monday
thus broken the abbeys of [Saint Thomas and] Saint Vincent,[1]
they departed in the morning and all the people of Canterbury
with them, and so took the way to Rochester and sent their
people to the villages about. And in their going they beat down
and robbed houses of advocates and procurers of the king's
court and of the archbishop, and had mercy of none.

And when they were come to Rochester, they had there good
cheer; for the people of that town tarried for them, for they were
of the same sect, and then they went to the castle there and took
the knight that had the rule thereof, he was called sir John
Newton, and they said to him: 'Sir, it behoveth you to go with
us and you shall be our sovereign captain and to do that we will
have you.' The knight excused himself honestly and shewed them
divers considerations and excuses, but all availed him nothing,
for they said unto him: 'Sir John, if ye do not as we will have
you, ye are but dead.' The knight, seeing these people in that
fury and ready to slay him, he then doubted death and agreed
to them, and so they took him with them against his inward
will; and in like wise did they of other countries in England,
as Essex, Sussex, Stafford, Bedford and Warwick, even to

---

[1] Froissart is presumably referring to St Augustine's Abbey, Canterbury. Saint
Thomas's Church was of course Christ Church Cathedral, Canterbury.

Lincoln;[1] for they brought the knights and gentlemen into such obeisance, that they caused them to go with them, whether they would or not, as the lord Moylays, a great baron, sir Stephen of Hales[2] and sir Thomas [Stephen] of Cosington and other.

Now behold the great fortune. If they might have come to their intents, they would have destroyed all the noblemen of England, and thereafter all other nations would have followed the same and have taken foot and ensample by them and by them of Gaunt [Ghent] and Flanders, who rebelled against their lord. The same year the Parisians rebelled in like wise and found out the mallets of iron, of whom there were more than twenty thousand, as ye shall hear after in this history; but first we will speak of them of England.

When these people thus lodged at Rochester departed, and passed the river and came to Brentford,[3] alway keeping still their opinions, beating down before them and all about the places and houses of advocates and procurers, and striking off the heads of divers persons. And so long they went forward till they came within a four mile [leagues] of London, and there lodged on a hill called Blackheath; and as they went, they said ever they were the king's men and the noble commons of England: and when they of London knew that they were come so near to them, the mayor, as ye have heard before, closed the gates and kept straitly all the passages. This order caused the mayor, who was called Nicholas [recte, William] Walworth, and divers other rich burgesses of the city, who were not of their sect; but there were in London of their unhappy opinions more than thirty thousand.

Then these people thus being lodged on Blackheath determined to send their knight to speak with the king [to ask him to come and talk to them] and to shew him how all that they have done or will do is for him and his honour, and how the realm of England hath not been well governed a great space for

---

[1] The French text reads, 'Essex, Sussex, Kent, Stanfort, Bedford and the diocese of Norwich to Yarmouth and Lynn'.

[2] For Walsingham's reference to Sir William Morley and Sir Stephen Hales, see below, p. 258.

[3] Presumably a mistake for Dartford on the Darent. Froissart's previous allusion was to the 1382 rising of the *Maillotins* in Paris.

the honour of the realm nor for the common profit by his
uncles and by the clergy, and specially by the archbishop of
Canterbury his chancellor; whereof they would have account.
This knight durst do none otherwise, but so came by the river
of Thames to the Tower.[1] The king and they that were with
him in the Tower, desiring to hear tidings, seeing this knight
coming made him way, and was brought before the king into a
chamber; and with the king was the princess his mother and his
two brethren, [Thomas] the earl of Kent and the lord John
Holland, the earl of Salisbury, the earl of Warwick, the earl of
Oxford, the archbishop of Canterbury, the lord [prior] of
Saint John's [Hospital], sir Robert of Namur, the lord of Vertaing,
the lord of Gommegnies, sir Henry of Senzeille, the mayor of
London and divers other notable burgesses. This knight, sir
John Newton, who was well known among them, for he was
one of the king's officers, he kneeled down before the king and
said: 'My right redoubted lord, let it not displease your grace
the message that I must needs shew you, for, dear sir, it is by
force and against my will.' 'Sir John,' said the king, 'say what ye
will: I hold you excused.' 'Sir, the commons of this your realm
hath sent me to you to desire you to come and speak with them on
Blackheath; for they desire to have none but you: and, sir, ye
need not have any doubt of your person for they will do you
no hurt; for they hold and will hold you for their king. But, sir,
they say they will shew you divers things, the which shall be right
necessary for you to take heed of, when they speak with you; of
the which things, sir, I have no charge to shew you: but, sir, an it
may please you to give me an answer such as may appease them
and that they may know for truth that I have spoken with you;
for they have my children in hostage till I return again to them,
and without I return again, they will slay my children incontinent.'
    Then the king made him an answer and said: 'Sir, ye shall
have an answer shortly.' Then the king took counsel what was
best for him to do, and it was anon determined that the next

----

[1] Berners severely condenses the French text here: Newton is said to have
arrived by boat.

morning [a Thursday] the king should go down the river by water and without fail to speak with them. And when sir John Newton heard that answer, he desired nothing else and so took his leave of the king and of the lords and returned again into his vessel, and passed the Thames and went to Blackheath, where he had left more than threescore thousand men. And there he answered them that the next morning they should send some of their council to the Thames, and there the king would come and speak with them. This answer greatly pleased them, and so passed that night as well as they might, and the fourth part of them fasted for lack of victual, for they had none, wherewith they were sore displeased, which was good reason.

All this season the earl of Buckingham was in Wales, for there he had fair heritages by reason of his wife, who was daughter to the earl of Northumberland and Hereford;[1] but the voice was all through London how he was among these people. And some said certainly how they had seen him there among them; and all was because there was one Thomas in their company, a man of the county of Cambridge [Kent in French text], that was very like the earl. Also [the earl of Cambridge and] the lords that lay at Plymouth to go into Portugal were well informed of this rebellion and of the people that thus began to rise; wherefore they doubted lest their viage should have been broken, or else they feared lest the commons about Hampton, Winchester and Arundel would have come on them: wherefore they weighed up their anchors and issued out of the haven with great pain, for the wind was sore against them, and so took the sea and there cast anchor abiding for the wind. And the duke of Lancaster, who was in the marches of Scotland between Moorlane and Roxburgh entreating with the Scots, where it was shewed him of the rebellion, whereof he was in doubt, for he knew well he was but little beloved with the commons of England; howbeit, for all those tidings, yet he did sagely demean himself as touching the

---

[1] Eleanor de Bohun married Buckingham in 1374. Her father, Humphrey de Bohun, earl of Hereford and Northampton (*not* Northumberland) had died in 1373 without male issue.

6

treaty with the Scots. The earl Douglas, the earl of Moray, the earl of Sutherland and the earl Thomas Versy [Sir Thomas Erskine], and the Scots that were there for the treaty knew right well the rebellion in England, how the common people in every part began to rebel against the noblemen; wherefore the Scots thought that England was in great danger to be lost, and therefore in their treaties they were the more stiffer again the duke of Lancaster and his council.

Now let us speak of the commons of England and how they persevered.

In the morning on Corpus Christi day [13 June] king Richard heard mass in the Tower of London, and all his lords, and then he took his barge with the earl of Salisbury, the earl of Warwick, the earl of Oxford and certain knights, and so rowed down along the Thames to Rotherhithe [a royal manor], whereas was descended down the hill a ten thousand men to see the king and to speak with him. And when they saw the king's barge coming, they began to shout, and made such a cry, as though all the devils of hell had been among them. And they had brought with them sir John Newton to the intent that, if the king had not come, they would have stricken him all to pieces, and so they had promised him. And when the king and his lords saw the demeanour of the people, the best assured of them were in dread; and so the king was counselled by his barons not to take any landing there, but so rowed up and down the river. And the king demanded of them what they would, and said how he was come thither to speak with them, and they said all with one voice: 'We would that ye should come aland, and then we shall shew you what we lack.' Then the earl of Salisbury answered for the king and said: 'Sirs, ye be not in such order nor array that the king ought to speak with you.'[1] And so with those words no more said: and then the king was counselled to return again to the Tower of London, and so he did. [Continued by no. 28 below, p. 187.]

---

[1] According to the *Anonimalle Chronicle* (above, p. 130) it was Sudbury and Hales rather than the earl of Salisbury who persuaded Richard not to disembark at Greenwich.

23 The Rebels in Canterbury according to Jurors' Presentments

Translated from the original jurors' presentments by W. E. Flaherty, 'The Great Rebellion in Kent', *Archaeologia Cantiana*, III (1860) 73–7

The following extracts from the inquisitions held before Thomas Holland, earl of Kent, at Canterbury on 8 July 1381 reveal (in Flaherty's words) 'the insurgents in full fury'. These and similar presentments prove that violent acts of lawlessness were widespread throughout the whole of Kent during the month of June and even later. At Canterbury itself the rebels were most active on Monday 10 June, the day on which the city was entered in force by the Kentish commons. According to the jurors, John Hales of Malling rather than Wat Tyler led the attack on royal and civic officials that day. But on 13 June, three days later, rebels in Thanet were alleged to have made a proclamation under a commission from John Rakestraw (presumably the Jack Straw of the chronicles) and Watte Tegheler – an interesting, because rare, reference to the practical authority of the leaders of the revolt.

On Monday, on the morrow of the Translation of St Thomas the Martyr [8 July 1381] at Canterbury, before Thomas Holland, earl of Kent and his associates . . . in the foresaid county, by the oath of [twelve named jurors] who say upon their oath that Henry Whyte, tayllor, of Westgate, Henry Foghel of Lyde in Romney Marsh, John Reade of Thanet and William Munde, weaver, came with force and arms, with others unknown, to the house of William Medmenham in Canterbury, viz. on Monday on the morrow of Trinity [10 June 1381] and feloniously broke into the said house, and the goods and chattels of the said William Medmenham, to the value of ten pounds, feloniously trampled upon and carried away.

Also they say that on Monday on the morrow of the Holy Trinity aforesaid [10 June 1381], the foresaid Henry Whyte and Nicholas Cherchegate and John Barbour of Newenton, with others unknown, came to the house of Thomas Holte in Westgate next Canterbury, and feloniously broke into the said house, and feloniously took and carried away the goods and chattels of the said Thomas, to the value of forty pounds.

Also they say that on the Monday aforesaid, Richard Baker of Lenham, together with others, came with force and arms to the house of Thomas Oteryngton . . . there took the said Thomas feloniously and carried him out, and threatened him with loss of life, and so compelled him to the said. . . .

William Sporier of Canterbury, with many others unknown, came to the house of the said Thomas Oteryngton and there feloniously broke open his doors and upon him did make an assault . . . the said Thomas despaired of his life.

Also they say that on the Monday aforesaid, John London of Otehell near Canterbury and Henry Whyte of Canterbury feloniously killed John Tebbe at Canterbury, and that William Cymekyn feloniously procured and abetted the death of the said John Tebbe.

Also they say that on the same day, Thomas Olever, John Lukke, carpenter, and John Hunte of Canterbury came to the house of the said John Tebbe and feloniously broke into the said house, and took and feloniously carried away his goods and chattels, to the value of twenty pounds.

Also they say that on Tuesday next after the feast of Holy Trinity [11 June 1381], Henry Twysdenn, John Twysdenn [and others] of Canterbury went to the gaol of Maidstone and feloniously broke into the same, and took out and feloniously set at liberty all the prisoners there imprisoned. . . .

Also they say that John Sales [recte, Hales] of Malling on the Monday aforesaid came to Canterbury with a great multitude of the enemies of our lord the king, by him raised and assembled, and feloniously broke open the houses of Thomas Holte, William de Medmenham, John Tebbe, the castle of Canterbury, the town hall (praetorium) of Canterbury. . . Sir Richard de Hoo, knight, Thomas de Garwenton and Sir Thomas Fog, knight, and stole and carried away goods, chattels and muniments, to the value of a thousand pounds, and feloniously set free the prisoners that were in the said castle and town hall; and they say that he was the first and principal originator of the insurrection and levying of all the enemies of our Lord the King.

Also, they say that John Cook, sawyer (*saghier*), of Canterbury, on the day that the said John Tece was slain, dragged the said John from his horse down to the ground, and was then the abettor of his death.

Also, they say that John Besyngbi, of Canterbury, was ... of Thomas Holbeein, together with others unknown, on the day of the foresaid death, feloniously broke open the houses, chambers, and chests, and burnt the books and other muniments, touching our Lord the King's crown, and other muniments ... burnt.

Also, they say that, on Thursday, on the feast of Corpus Christi [13 June 1381], Stephen Samuel, John Wenelok, John Daniels, Thomas Soles, John Tayllor, Sacristan of the Church of St John in Thanet, and John Bocher, Clerk of the said church of Thanet, by commission of John Rakestraw and Watte Tegheler, made proclamation in the foresaid church, and compelled a levy of the country there, to the number of two hundred men, and made them go to the house of William de Medmenham, and they feloniously broke open the gates, doors, chambers, and chests of the said William, and carried away his goods and chattels to the value of twenty marks, and took and feloniously burnt the rolls touching the Crown of our Lord the King, and the rolls of the office of Receiver of Green Wax for the county of Kent.

Also, they say that, on Monday next after the feast of Peter and Paul, in the fifth year of the King's reign [1 July 1381], John Gybonn, of Maidstone, came to the town hall (*praetorium*), before the bailiffs of the city of Canterbury, and required the said bailiffs to make levy of the whole community of the said city, to resist the lords and justices assigned to keep the peace of our Lord the King in the county of Kent.

24 The Indictment of two Essex rebels

Coram Rege Roll, Hilary 5 Richard II [KB. 27/483], Rex, memb. 26; cf. Powell and Trevelyan, *Peasants' Rising and the Lollards*, p. 17; Sparvil-Bayly, 'Essex in Insurrection, 1381', *Trans. Essex Arch. Soc.*, new series, 1 [1878] 215

The trial of John Hermare and Nicholas Gromond raises in an acute form the question of the reliability of the legal records for the events of 1381. After producing royal letters of pardon of 20 December 1381, both men eventually went free and it is a good deal less than certain that they were genuinely guilty of all the offences listed below. If the accusations were well-founded, we are presented with the interesting case-history of two Essex rebels who were among the first to rise in their own county, joined the attack on the Savoy on 13 June and were later engaged (on the day after Smithfield) in violent extortion at Clandon in the middle of Surrey. One supposes that few of the rebels of 1381 can have enjoyed so adventurous a month.

(*Margin:* Essex) Richard, by the grace of God king of England and of France, lord of Ireland, to his beloved Robert de Newton, recently deputy of Alan de Buxhull, late constable of our Tower of London, greeting. For various reasons we wish to be informed of the reason why John Hermare and Nicholas Gromond of Havering were detained in our prison at the said Tower under your custody, and how and in what way they were sent there to be guarded. Therefore we order you to return the information to our chancery clearly and openly under your seal and without delay, in the company of this writ. Witnessed by myself at Westminster, 15 February [1382].

The cause of the seizure of John Hermare and Nicholas Gromond appears in the schedule attached to this writ: –

John Hermare and Nicholas Gromond of Havering-atte-Bower were taken at Guildford because on the Sunday after Corpus Christi Day [16 June 1381] they rose with a great multitude of people of the county of Essex and came to the house of William West at Clandon; and there they made the said William – for fear of themselves and of their fellows whom they alleged were at Kingston – enter into a bond of twenty pounds sterling to the said John with the condition that he should pay John ten pounds on 1 August. The two rebels were also taken because it was testified in the country that they had acknowledged, in the presence of many both at Clandon and Guildford, that they were the first who rebelled in the county of Essex; and that they were the first who came to the Savoy where they broke doles of wine and did other evil actions; and for this reason they were detained in Guildford gaol. And they did many other evils. . . .

PART III

The Rebels in London,
13–15 June 1381

London in 1381

On the Thursday, Friday and Saturday of Corpus Christi week (13–15 June) 1381, Londoners experienced what was probably the most exciting and certainly the most disorderly crisis in the history of the medieval city. For all the chroniclers of the Peasants' Revolt these three days marked the climax of the insurrection, the period when (in the words of Froissart attributed to the young Richard II) 'the heritage and realm of England were near lost'. In retrospect, it seems obvious that no band of medieval English rebels was likely to be able to retain its cohesion for more than a few days; but the very fact that Wat Tyler and his fellows were foredoomed to failure has endowed their story with a tragic and almost epic quality. Contemporaries were in general agreement as to the most striking incidents in the drama – the sack of the Savoy on Thursday afternoon, the Mile End conference and the execution of Archbishop Sudbury and his fellow 'traitors' on the following day, the young Richard's visit to Westminster abbey on the Saturday morning shortly before the final celebrated confrontation between king and rebel captain at Smithfield. But, as the reader of the following extracts will soon discover, the detailed chronology of events in London between 13 and 15 June bristles with many controversial and unsolved problems. Exactly when did the rebels cross London Bridge? How many men did Wat Tyler and Jack Straw have in their companies? Where did they sleep during the nights of 13 and 14 June? How far did the rebel bands from the counties of Kent and Essex retain their separate identities after obtaining access to the city? Who was the spokesman for the rebels at the Mile End conference? Why were Sudbury and Hales extracted from the Tower with so little opposition? Did the execution of the archbishop and treasurer occur at the same time or later than the Mile End meeting? How many rebels still remained in London on the morning of Saturday, 15 June? For what purpose was the assembly at Smithfield arranged? Who killed Wat Tyler? And why was his death the turning-point of the entire rebellion? These are famous questions – and ones to which our sources give either vague or discordant answers. Most crucial of all perhaps is the problem of the participation of Londoners themselves in the tumultuous scenes of the week. How many Londoners and what kind of Londoners were willing accomplices of the rebels from Kent and Essex? This is the question which the trial records quoted below, and above all the famous inquisitions held before the London sheriffs, fail to resolve as completely as was once believed. The great revolt still withholds many of its more intriguing secrets.

25 The Rebels in London according to the 'Anonimalle Chronicle'

Anonimalle Chronicle, pp. 140–50; previously translated from Thynne's transcript in Oman, *Great Revolt*, pp. 193–203: continued from no. 19 above

In any attempt to collect evidence for the course of events in London between 13 and 15 June pride of place must inevitably be given to the account of the author of the *Anonimalle Chronicle*. As the foot-notes will suggest, the latter is not invariably accurate; but the range and depth of his knowledge is unrivalled and it seems virtually certain that he was an eye-witness, probably in the king's entourage, of many of the episodes he describes.

On this same Wednesday and before the hour of Vespers,[1] the commons of Kent, to the number of sixty thousand, arrived in Southwark where the Marshalsea was. They broke up and cast to the ground all the houses of the Marshalsea and removed all the prisoners imprisoned there for debt or felony. They then beat to the ground a fine place belonging to John de Imworth, then Marshal of the Marshalsea of the King's Bench and warden of the prisoners therein. All the houses of the jurors and professional informers (*questmongers*) belonging to the Marshalsea were also thrown to the ground during that night. At the same time the commons of Essex came to Lambeth, near London, a manor of the archbishop of Canterbury, entered into its buildings, destroyed a great number of the archbishop's goods and burnt all the register books and chancery remembrancers' rolls they found there.[2]

On the next day, Thursday 13 June, which was the feast of

[1] The author has been relating events which apparently occured on the Thursday, although Wednesday does seem the most likely date for the attack on the Marshalsea; but the question remains partly open. Imworth's Christian name was Richard not John.

[2] But is it likely that the Essex men would have crossed the Thames to Lambeth? The 'monk of Westminster' (see below, no. 29) provides more reliable testimony to the fact that Lambeth was sacked by Kentishmen on 12 June.

Corpus Christi with the Dominical Letter F, the said commons of Essex went in the morning to Highbury, two leagues north of London and a very fine manor of the Master of the Hospital of St John of Clerkenwell.[1] They set it on fire to the great damage and loss of the Hospitallers of St John. Some of these commons returned to London, but others stayed out in the open fields all night.

And on this same day of Corpus Christi, in the morning, the commons of Kent broke down a brothel (*une measone destwes*) near London Bridge, occupied by Flemish women who had farmed it from the mayor of London. And then they went on to the bridge so as to cross towards the city, but the mayor was ready before them and had the chain drawn up and the bridge lifted to prevent their passage. And the commons of Southwark rose with the others and cried to the keepers of the said bridge to lower it and let them enter, or otherwise they would be undone. And for fear of their lives, the keepers let them enter, greatly against their will.[2] At this time all the religious as well as the parsons and vicars devoutly went in procession to pray to God for peace.

At this same time the said commons took their way through London, doing no harm or injury until they came to Fleet Street. Meanwhile, so it was said, the commons of London had set fire to and burnt the fine manor of the Savoy, before the commons of the country arrived. In Fleet Street, the said commons of Kent broke open the Fleet prison, removed all the prisoners and let them go where they would. Then they stopped and cast to the ground and burnt a shop belonging to a chandler and another belonging to a marshal which stood in the middle of the said street. Men now suppose that there will never be another house there – to the destruction of the beauty of that street. Afterwards they went to the Temple to destroy the tenants of the said

---

[1] Walsingham's detailed and circumstantial account (below, no. 26) makes it clear that Highbury was burnt early on Friday, 14 June. See also below, p. 219.

[2] The author ignores the allegations of treachery which surrounded the episode of the opening of London Bridge to the rebels.

Temple; and they threw the houses to the ground and cast down the tiles so that the houses were left roofless and in a poor state. They also went into the church, seized all the books, rolls and remembrances kept in the cupboards of the apprentices of the law within the Temple, carried them into the high road and burnt them there.

And on their way to the Savoy they destroyed all the houses which belonged to the Master of the Hospital of St John. And then they went to the place of the bishop of Chester, near the church of St Mary-le-Strand, where lord John Forham, bishop-elect of Durham and clerk of the Privy Seal, was staying;[1] they rolled tuns of wine out of his cellar, drank their fill, and departed without doing further damage. Then they went towards the Savoy, and set fire to several houses belonging to various questmongers and others on the western side of the city; and at last they came before the Savoy, broke open the gates, entered the place and came to the wardrobe. They took all the torches they could find, and lighted them, and burnt all the cloths, coverlets and beds, as well as all the very valuable head-boards (of which one, decorated with heraldic shields, was said to be worth a thousand marks). All the napery and other goods they could discover they carried into the hall and set on fire with their torches. They burnt the hall and the chambers as well as all the apartments within the gates of the said palace or manor, which the commons of London had left unguarded. It is said that they found three barrels of gunpowder, and thinking it was gold or silver, they threw them into the fire so that the powder exploded and set the hall in a greater blaze than before, to the great loss and damage of the duke of Lancaster. And the commons of Kent received the blame for this arson, but some said that the Londoners were really guilty of the deed, because of their hatred for the said duke.

Then one party of the rebels went towards Westminster and set on fire a place belonging to John of Butterwick, under-sheriff

---

[1] Bishop Thomas Hatfield of Durham had died on 8 May 1381; Fordham (Keeper of the Privy Seal 1377–81) was provided to the see on 9 September 1381.

of Middlesex, and other houses of various people.[1] They broke open Westminster prison, and let out all the prisoners condemned by the law. Afterwards they returned to London by way of Holborn, and in front of St Sepulchre's church they set on fire the houses of Simon Hosteler, and several others, and they broke open Newgate prison, and released all the prisoners, regardless of the reason for which they had been imprisoned. This same Thursday the said commons came to St Martin-le-Grand, and dragged out of the church from the high altar a certain Roger Legett, an important assizer (cisour); they took him into the Cheap where his head was cut off.[2] On that same day eighteen persons were beheaded in various places of the town.

At this time a great body of the commons went to the Tower of London to speak with the king. As they could not get a hearing from him, they laid siege to the Tower from the side of St Katherine's, towards the south.[3] Another group of the commons, who were within the city, went to the Hospital of St John, Clerkenwell, and on their way they burnt the place and houses of Roger Legett, questmonger, who had been beheaded in Cheapside, as well as all the rented property and tenements of the Hospital of St John they could find. Afterwards they came to the beautiful priory of the said hospital, and set on fire several fine and pleasant buildings within it – a great and horrible piece of damage to the priory for all time to come. They then returned to London to rest or to do more mischief.

At this time the king was in a turret of the great Tower of London, and saw the manor of the Savoy and the Hospital of Clerkenwell, and the houses of Simon Hosteler near Newgate, and John Butterwick's place, all in flames. He called all the lords

[1] Sir John Butterwick's house was actually burnt on Friday 14 June (Réville, p. 210).

[2] One of the reasons for Legett's unpopularity is revealed by the accusation made against him in 1375 that he had hidden iron man-traps on a dike newly raised by him in Fiketts Field to the peril of the royal chancery clerks (C.Cl.R., 1374–77, 210). As a questmonger (see below) he evidently made a business of conducting inquests or assizes.

[3] St Katherine's hill, hospital and church lay immediately to the east of the Tower, outside the city walls.

about him into a chamber, and asked their counsel as to what should be done in such a crisis. But none of them could or would give him any counsel; and so the young king said that he would order the mayor of the city to command the sheriffs and aldermen to have it cried within their wards that everyone between the age of fifteen and sixty, on pain of life and limb, should go next morning (which was Friday) to Mile End, and meet him there at seven of the bell.[1] He did this in order that all the commons who were stationed around the Tower would be persuaded to abandon the siege, and come to Mile End to see him and hear him, so that those who were in the Tower could leave safely at their will and save themselves as they wished. But it came to nothing, for some of them did not have the good fortune to be saved.

Later that Thursday, the said feast of Corpus Christi, the king, remaining anxiously and sadly in the Tower, climbed on to a little turret facing St Katherine's, where a large number of the commons were lying. He had it proclaimed to them that they should all go peaceably to their homes, and he would pardon them all their different offences. But all cried with one voice that they would not go before they had captured the traitors within the Tower, and obtained charters to free them from all manner of serfdom, and certain other points which they wished to demand. The king benevolently granted their requests and made a clerk write a bill in their presence in these terms: 'Richard, king of England and France, gives great thanks to his good commons, for that they have so great a desire to see and maintain their king; and he grants them pardon for all manner of trespasses and misprisions and felonies done up to this hour, and wills and commands that every one should now quickly return to his own home: He wills and commands that everyone should put his

[1] According to Froissart (see below p. 190) the decision to hold a meeting at Mile End was taken on Friday 14 June. Professor B. Wilkinson ('Peasants' Revolt of 1381', p. 21) rejects the evidence of the *Anonimalle Chronicle* at this point because of 'the inherent improbability of its account, which makes a boy of fourteen suddenly announce the momentous decision to go to Mile End'. Nor is it clear that Mayor William Walworth was then in a position to command the Londoners to go to Mile End.

grievances in writing, and have them sent to him; and he will provide, with the aid of his loyal lords and his good council, such remedy as shall be profitable both to him and to them, and to the kingdom.' He put his signet seal to this document in their presence and then sent the said bill by the hands of two of his knights to the people around St Katherine's. And he caused it to be read to them, the man who read it standing up on an old chair above the others so that all could hear. All this time the king remained in the Tower in great distress of mind. And when the commons had heard the bill, they said that it was nothing but a trifle and mockery. Therefore they returned to London and had it cried around the city that all lawyers, all the men of the Chancery and the Exchequer and everyone who could write a writ or a letter should be beheaded, wherever they could be found. At this time they burnt several more houses within the city. The king himself ascended to a high garret of the Tower to watch the fires; then he came down again, and sent for the lords to have their counsel. But they did not know how to advise him, and were surprisingly abashed.

On the next day, Friday,[1] the commons of the country and the commons of London assembled in fearful strength, to the number of a hundred thousand or more, besides some four score who remained on Tower Hill to watch those who were within the Tower. Some went to Mile End, on the way to Brentwood, to wait for the king's arrival, because of the proclamation that he had made. But others came to Tower Hill, and when the king knew that they were there, he sent them orders by a messenger to join their companions at Mile End, saying that he would come to them very soon. And at this time of the morning he advised the archbishop of Canterbury and the others who were in the Tower, to go down to the little water-gate, and take a boat and save themselves. And the archbishop proceeded to do this; but a wicked woman raised a cry against him, and he had to turn back to the Tower, to his own confusion.

And by seven of the bell the king himself came to Mile End,

[1] Friday, 14 June.

and with him his mother in a carriage (*whirlicole*), and also the earls of Buckingham, Kent, Warwick and Oxford, as well as Sir Thomas Percy, Sir Robert Knolles, the mayor of London and many knights and squires; and Sir Aubrey de Vere carried the royal sword. And when the king arrived and the commons saw him, they knelt down to him, saying 'Welcome our Lord King Richard, if it pleases you, and we will not have any other king but you.' And Wat Teghler,[1] their master and leader, prayed on behalf of the commons that the king would suffer them to take and deal with all the traitors against him and the law. The king granted that they should freely seize all who were traitors and could be proved to be such by process of law. The said Walter and the commons were carrying two banners as well as pennons and pennoncels while they made their petition to the king. And they required that henceforward no man should be a serf nor make homage or any type of service to any lord, but should give four pence for an acre of land. They asked also that no one should serve any man except at his own will and by means of regular covenant. And at this time the king had the commons arrayed in two lines, and had it proclaimed before them that he would confirm and grant that they should be free, and generally should have their will; and that they could go through all the realm of England and catch all traitors and bring them to him in safety, and then he would deal with them as the law demanded.

Because of this grant Wat Tyghler and the commons took their way to the Tower, to seize the archbishop and the others while the king remained at Mile End. Meanwhile the archbishop had sung his mass devoutly in the Tower, and confessed the prior of the Hospital of Clerkenwell and others; and then he heard two or three masses and chanted the *Commendatio*, and the *Placebo* and *Dirige*, and the Seven Psalms, and the Litany; and when he was at the words 'Omnes sancti orate pro nobis', the commons entered and dragged him out of the chapel of the Tower, and

[1] No other chronicler mentions Wat Tyler's presence at the Mile End meeting; and it has usually been supposed by modern historians that neither he nor the queen mother nor the earl of Buckingham can have attended this assembly.

struck and hustled him roughly, as they did also the others who were with him, and led them to Tower Hill. There they cut off the heads of Master Simon of Sudbury, archbishop of Canterbury, of Sir Robert Hales, High Prior of the Hospital of St John's of Clerkenwell, Treasurer of England, of Brother William of Appleton, a great physician and surgeon, and one who had much influence with the king and the duke of Lancaster. And some time after they beheaded John Legge, the king's serjeant-at-arms, and with him a certain juror. At the same time the commons had it proclaimed that whoever could catch any Fleming or other aliens of any nation, might cut off their heads; and so they did accordingly. Then they took the heads of the archbishop and of the others and put them on wooden poles, and carried them before them in procession through all the city as far as the shrine of Westminster Abbey, to the contempt of themselves, of God and of Holy Church: for which reason vengeance descended on them shortly afterwards. Then they returned to London Bridge and set the head of the archbishop above the gate, with the heads of eight others they had executed, so that all who passed over the bridge could see them. This done, they went to the church of St Martin's in the Vintry, and found therein thirty-five Flemings, whom they dragged outside and beheaded in the street.[1] On that day there were beheaded 140 or 160 persons. Then they took their way to the places of Lombards and other aliens, and broke into their houses, and robbed them of all their goods that they could discover. So it went on for all that day and the night following, with hideous cries and horrible tumult.

At this time, because the Chancellor had been beheaded, the king made the earl of Arundel Chancellor for the day, and entrusted him with the Great Seal;[2] and all that day he caused

---

[1] St Martin Vintry, at the corner of Royal and Thames streets, survived until the Great Fire. The surrounding area was a favourite resort for alien merchants in late medieval London.

[2] Sudbury resigned the Great Seal to Richard II at the Tower on Wednesday, 12 June. The king entrusted it temporarily to Arundel at the Great Wardrobe on Friday 14 June after his return from Mile End. On Sunday 16 June the king,

various clerks to write out charters, patents, and letters of protection, granted to the commons in consequence of the matters before mentioned, without taking any fines for the sealing or transcription.

On the next day, Saturday, great numbers of the commons came into Westminster Abbey at the hour of Tierce, and there they found John Imworth, Marshal of the Marshalsea and warden of the prisoners, a tormentor without pity; he was near the shrine of St Edward, embracing a marble pillar, hoping for aid and succour from the saint to preserve him from his enemies. But the commons wrenched his arms away from the pillar of the shrine, and dragged him into Cheap, and there beheaded him.[1] And at the same time they took from Bread Street a valet named John of Greenfield, merely because he had spoken well of Brother William Appleton and the other murdered persons; and they brought him into Cheap and beheaded him. All this time the king was having it cried through the city that every one should go peaceably to his own country and his own house, without doing more mischief; but to this the commons would not agree.

And on this same day, at three hours after noon, the king came to Westminster Abbey and about 200 persons with him. The abbot and convent of the said abbey, and the canons and vicars of St Stephen's Chapel, came to meet him in procession, clothed in their copes and their feet bare, half-way to Charing Cross; and they brought him to the abbey, and then to the high altar of the church. The king made his prayers devoutly, and left an offering for the altar and the relics. Afterwards he spoke with the anchorite, and confessed to him, and remained with him some time. Then the king caused a proclamation to be made that all the commons of the country who were still within the city should come to Smithfield to meet him there; and so they did.

And when the king with his retinue arrived there, he turned

---

again at the Great Wardrobe, transferred it to the steward of his household, Hugh Segrave.

[1] Imworth's name (see p. 155) was Richard, not John. He seems to have been dragged from Westminster Abbey in the king's own presence (Réville, p. 212).

to the east, in a place before St Bartholomew's a house of canons: and the commons arrayed themselves in bands of great size on the west side. At this moment the mayor of London, William of Walworth, came up, and the king ordered him to approach the commons, and make their chieftain come to him.[1] And when he was called by the mayor, this chieftain, Wat Tyghler of Maidstone by name, approached the king with great confidence, mounted on a little horse so that the commons might see him. And he dismounted, holding in his hand a dagger which he had taken from another man; and when he had dismounted he half bent his knee and took the king by the hand, shaking his arm forcefully and roughly, saying to him, 'Brother, be of good comfort and joyful, for you shall have, in the fortnight that is to come, forty thousand more commons than you have at present, and we shall be good companions'. And the king said to Walter, 'Why will you not go back to your own country?' But the other answered, with a great oath, that neither he nor his fellows would leave until they had got their charter as they wished to have it with the inclusion of certain points which they wished to demand. Tyghler threatened that the lords of the realm would rue it bitterly if these points were not settled at the commons' will. Then the king asked him what were the points which he wished to have considered, and he should have them freely and without contradiction, written out and sealed. Thereupon the said Wat rehearsed the points which were to be demanded; and he asked that there should be no law except for the law of Winchester[2] and that henceforward there should be no outlawry (ughtelarie) in any process of law, and that no lord should have lordship in future, but it should be divided among all men, except for the king's own lordship. He also asked that the goods of Holy Church should not remain in the hands of the religious, nor of parsons and vicars,

---

[1] According to Walsingham's less reliable account (below, p. 177), Sir John Newton, constable of Rochester Castle, was sent to summon Tyler to the king.

[2] Tyler's reference here is somewhat cryptic: but the 'law of Winchester' may have been coveted because it substituted mutilation and blinding for common hanging as punishment for serious felonies. More probably it refers to a claim by the peasants of 1381 to the same rights as sokemen of the ancient royal demesne.

and other churchmen; but that clergy already in possession should
have a sufficient sustenance and the rest of their goods should be
divided among the people of the parish. And he demanded that
there should be only one bishop in England and only one prelate,
and all the lands and tenements of the possessioners should be
taken from them and divided among the commons, only reserving for them a reasonable sustenance. And he demanded that
there should be no more villeins in England, and no serfdom nor
villeinage (*ne nulle servage ne nayfte*) but that all men should be
free and of one condition. To this the king gave an easy answer,
and said that Wat should have all that he could fairly grant,
reserving only for himself the regality of his crown. And then
he ordered him to go back to his own home, without causing
further delay.

During all the time that the king was speaking, no lord or
counsellor dared or wished to give answer to the commons in any
place except for the king himself. Presently Wat Tyghler, in the
presence of the king, sent for a jug of water to rinse his mouth,
because of the great heat that he felt; and as soon as the water
was brought he rinsed out his mouth in a very rude and villainous
manner before the king. And then he made them bring him a jug
of ale, and drank a great draught, and then, in the presence of the
king, climbed on his horse again. At that time a certain valet from
Kent, who was among the king's retinue, asked to see the said
Wat, chieftain of the commons. And when he saw him, he said
aloud that he was the greatest thief and robber in all Kent. Wat
heard these words, and commanded the valet to come out to him,
shaking his head at him as a sign of malice; but Wat himself
refused to go to him for fear that he had of the others there. But
at last the lords made the valet go out to Wat, to see what the
latter would do before the king. And when Wat saw him he
ordered one of his followers, who was mounted on horseback
and carrying a banner displayed, to dismount and behead the said
valet. But the valet answered that he had done nothing worthy
of death, for what he had said was true, and he would not deny it,
although he could not lawfully debate the issue in the presence of

his liege lord, without leave, except in his own defence: but that
he could do without reproof, for whoever struck him would be
struck in return. For these words Wat wanted to strike the valet
with his dagger, and would have slain him in the king's presence;
but because he tried to do so, the mayor of London, William of
Walworth, reasoned with the said Wat for his violent behaviour
and contempt, done in the king's presence, and arrested him. And
because he arrested him, the said Wat stabbed the mayor with his
dagger in the body in great anger. But, as it pleased God, the
mayor was wearing armour and took no harm, but like a hardy
and vigorous man drew his dagger (*baselarde*) and struck back at
the said Wat, giving him a deep cut in the neck, and then a great
blow on the head. And during this scuffle a valet of the king's
household drew his sword, and ran Wat two or three times
through the body, mortally wounding him. Wat spurred his
horse, crying to the commons to avenge him, and the horse
carried him some four score paces, and then he fell to the ground
half dead. And when the commons saw him fall, and did not know
for certain how it happened, they began to bend their bows and
to shoot. Therefore the king himself spurred his horse, and rode
out to them, commanding them that they should all come to him
at the field of St John of Clerkenwell.[1]

Meanwhile the mayor of London rode as hastily as he could
back to the city, and commanded those who were in charge of
the twenty-four wards to have it cried round their wards, that
every man should arm himself as quickly as he could, and come
to the king's aid in St John's Fields, where the commons were,
for he was in great trouble and necessity. But at this time almost
all of the knights and squires of the king's household, and many
others, were so frightened of the affray that they left their liege
lord and went each his own way.

Afterwards, when the king had reached the open fields, he
made the commons array themselves on the west side. And presently the aldermen came to him in a body, bringing with them
the keepers of the wards arrayed in several bands, a fine company

---

[1] Clerkenwell Fields lay a few hundred yards almost exactly north of Smithfield.

of well-armed men in great strength. And they enveloped the
commons like sheep within a pen. Meanwhile, after the mayor
had sent the keepers of the town on their way to the king, he
returned with a good company of lances to Smithfield in order to
make an end of the captain of the commons. And when he came to
Smithfield he failed to find there the said captain Wat Tyghler, at
which he marvelled much, and asked what had become of the
traitor. And he was told that Wat had been carried by a group of
the commons to the hospital for the poor near St Bartholomew's,
and put to bed in the chamber of the master of the hospital. The
mayor went there and found him, and had him carried out to the
middle of Smithfield, in the presence of his companions, and had
him beheaded. And so ended his wretched life. But the mayor
had his head set on a pole and carried before him to the king, who
still remained in the field. And when the king saw the head he
had it brought near him to subdue the commons, and thanked
the mayor greatly for what he had done. And when the commons
saw that their chieftain, Wat Tyghler, was dead in such a manner,
they fell to the ground there among the corn, like beaten men,
imploring the king for mercy for their misdeeds. And the king
benevolently granted them mercy, and most of them took to
flight. But the king appointed two knights to lead the other men
from Kent through London, and over London Bridge, without
doing them harm, so that each of them could go peacefully to his
own home. Then the king ordered Mayor Walworth to put a
bascinet on his head because of what was to happen, and the
mayor asked for what reason he was to do so; and the king told
him that he was much beholden to him, and that for this reason
he was to receive the order of knighthood. The mayor answered
that he was not worthy nor able to have or maintain a knight's
estate, for he was only a merchant and had to live by trade; but
finally the king made him put on the bascinet, and took a sword
in both his hands and strongly dubbed him knight with great
good will. The same day he made three other citizens of London
knights for the same reason and on that same spot: and these are
their names – John Philipot, Nichol Brymber and (blank in the

MS.):[1] and the king gave Sir William Walworth £100 in land, and each of the others £40 in land, for them and their heirs. And after this the king took his way to London to his Wardrobe[2] to ease him of his great toils. [*Continued by no. 35 below, p. 235.*]

26 The Rebels in London according to Thomas Walsingham

Walsingham, *Historia Anglicana*, 1 456–67: continued from no. 20 above. Cf. *Chronicon Angliae*, pp. 288–99

In his account of the rebels' activities in London, Walsingham largely confines himself to two long set-pieces: – a lengthy description of the martyrdom of Archbishop Sudbury, recited with great gusto, and an impressively detailed narrative of the death of Wat Tyler at Smithfield. Otherwise the St Albans chronicler tends to speculate rather more wildly than most of his colleagues as to the final aims of Tyler and his men. There is no confirmation for many of his allegations nor for his belief that the insurgents planned to kill Richard on the night of Saturday 15 June. But on the other hand most recent historians have shared Walsingham's obviously genuine perplexity as to the reasons for the royalist party's curious lack of nerve and failure to put up any defence against the rebels until their leader had been assassinated.

The mayor and aldermen of London, fearing for the city, ordered the gates to be closed immediately; but the common people of the city and especially the poor favoured the rustics and stopped the mayor from closing the gates by using force

---

[1] For the missing name, that of Robert Launde, see below, no. 31.

[2] The royal Wardrobe was adjacent to Baynard's Castle in the south-west of the city: see below, p. 210. According to Froissart (p. 198) Richard went to the Queen's Wardrobe in La Reol.

and threatening to kill him if he tried to do so. And so throughout the following night (the eve of Corpus Christi) the rascals enjoyed free access to and exit from the city. They had persuaded the community of Londoners and the rest of the kingdom to favour them by asserting that their intention was merely to discover the traitors of the kingdom, after which they would disband. And they gained greater credence by saying that they would not plunder at all but buy everything at a fair price: and that if they discovered anyone guilty of theft, they would execute him because they detested robbers.

On the next day (Corpus Christi) the rebels went in and out of London and talked with the simple commons of the city about the acquiring of liberty and the seizure of the traitors, especially the duke of Lancaster whom they hated most of all; and in a short time easily persuaded all the poorer citizens to support them in their conspiracy. And when, later that day, the sun had climbed higher and grown warm and the rebels had tasted various wines and expensive drinks at will and so had become less drunk than mad (for the great men and common people of London had left all their cellars open to the rebels), they began to debate at length about the traitors with the more simple men of the city. Among other things they assembled and set out for the Savoy, the residence of the duke of Lancaster, unrivalled in splendour and nobility within England, which they then set to the flames. This was done in defiance of the duke whom they called a traitor and to inspire fear among the other traitors. This news so delighted the common people of London that, thinking it particularly shameful for others to harm and injure the duke before themselves, they immediately ran there like madmen, set fire to the place on all sides and so destroyed it. In order that the whole community of the realm should know that they were not motivated by avarice, they made a proclamation that no one should retain for his own use any object found there under penalty of execution. Instead they broke the gold and silver vessels, of which there were many at the Savoy, into pieces with their axes and threw them into the Thames or the sewers. They tore the golden cloths and silk hangings to pieces and crushed them underfoot; they ground up rings and other jewels inlaid with precious stones in small mortars, so that they could never be used again. And so it was done. Finally, and in order not to pass by any opportunity of shaming the duke completely, they seized one of his most precious vestments, which we call a 'jakke', and placed it on a lance to be used as a target for their arrows. And since they were unable to damage it sufficiently with their arrows, they took it down and tore it apart with their axes and swords.

The Burning of Temple Bar and the House of St John's Hospital

After these malicious deeds, the rebels destroyed the place called 'Temple Bar' (in which the more noble apprentices of the law lived) because of their anger towards Robert de Hales, Master of the Hospital of St John, as mentioned above; and there many muniments which the lawyers were keeping in custody were consumed by fire. Even more insanely they set fire to the noble house of the Hospital of St John at Clerkenwell so that it burnt continuously for the next seven days.

On the morning of Friday [14 June], a day of tribulation, anguish, calamity and misery, before Matins had finished at St Albans there arrived men marching rapidly from the town of Barnet. These announced that the commons had commanded them to collect the commons of Barnet and Saint Albans – who were to arm themselves with the weapons which they could best handle and proceed immediately to London. If not, twenty thousand of the commons would come together to burn down these two towns and lead them off under duress. On receiving this news the abbot, fearing the arrival of the commons and the damage that would follow, immediately summoned all the servants and villeins of his court and asked them to hurry to London in order to assuage the rebels' malice and prevent their arrival at St Albans. Without delay the villeins as well as the abbot's esquires went to meet the others and enthusiastically took the road to London. But whereas our men from the abbey went to do good, the villeins from the town of St Albans were ready to serve the other commons. When this party was approaching London and near a certain estate of the Master of St John's Hospital called Highbury they saw there a multitude of twenty thousand rustics and common people who had set fire to its buildings, already burning inextinguishably, and were striving to pull down with their tools all that the fire could not destroy. I myself saw men summoned and forced before one of the leaders of the rebels, called 'John Strawe', who made them promise that they would adhere to King Richard and the commons.

At that time the crowd of rustics was divided into three separate sections, of which one (as we have seen) was busy destroying the manor of Highbury. A second band waited in London in the place called 'le Mile End', while a third occupied Tower Hill.[1] The last group near the Tower was so disrespectful and insolent that it intercepted the king's victuals which were being conveyed to the Tower. Moreover they were so insanely foolish as to compel the king to hand over to them the archbishop and the Master of the Hospital of St John and all the others hidden in the Tower whom they called traitors; otherwise he knew he would have been killed himself. And so the king, being in a quandary, allowed the rebels to enter the Tower and to search the most secret places there at their wicked will, like someone who could deny them nothing with safety. At that time there were in the Tower six hundred soldiers, skilled in arms, strong and most expert, as well as six hundred archers, all of whom (marvellously enough) were inclined to appear more like the dead than the living. For they were certainly dead to all memories of valiant military deeds and to the remembrance of previous strife and glory – in short, when faced with the rustics, they lacked almost all the military audacity of Loegria.[2]

For who would ever have believed that such rustics, and most inferior ones at that, would dare (not in crowds but individually)

[1] See above, p. 161, for the view that the Tower was invaded *after* the Mile End meeting.

[2] i.e. England: according to Geoffrey of Monmouth Loegria was that part of Britain assigned to King Locrine.

to enter the chamber of the king and of his mother with their filthy sticks; and, undeterred by any of the soldiers, to stroke and lay their uncouth and sordid hands on the beards of several most noble knights. Moreover, they conversed familiarly with the soldiers asking them to be faithful to the ribalds and friendly in the future. The rebels suggested that the soldiers might swear to help seek the traitors of the kingdom, although they themselves could not avoid the obvious mark of treachery in that they had raised flags and pennants and had not hesitated to make the armed entry mentioned above. After the rebels had done all these things and had gained access singly and in groups to the rooms in the Tower, they arrogantly lay and sat on the king's bed while joking; and several asked the king's mother to kiss them. But (marvellous to relate), the many knights and squires present dared not resist any of these unseemly deeds, nor raise their hands in opposition nor keep the rebels quiet by means of secret words. The rebels, who had formerly belonged to the most lowly condition of serf, went in and out like lords; and swineherds set themselves above soldiers although not knights but rustics. This happened, we believe, because God wished to show the English that a man's strength does not rest in his own bravery nor ought he to rely on arrow or sword, but rather on Him who saves us from our afflictions and is accustomed to confound our gaolers with His mercy and pity. But enough of these remarks: now we will direct our pen to the matter of the archbishop.

Concerning what happened to the Archbishop
When therefore the fatal hour had come when it was manifest that divine vengeance lay in wait for the kingdom of England, the rustics, those doomed ribalds and whores of the devil, sought the common father of the whole people, the archbishop and primate. As has been said, they entered the gates of the Tower on a devilish instinct and in a great throng with an enormous cry. Finding there one of the archbishop's servants they furiously asked him to lead them to the place in which the pious father, whom they called a traitor, was hiding. This servant, not daring to disobey

the order, led the rebels to the Chapel – where, after celebrating Mass and receiving Holy Communion, the archbishop was busy at his prayers. The archbishop, conscious of the rebels' imminent arrival and intentions, had spent the whole of the previous night in confession and devout prayers; and so in great confidence he bravely awaited the rebels, frequently reproaching them, both while saying Mass and afterwards, for their delay: 'When will they arrive? Good God, why are they waiting? For already the time has come, if it pleases God, that they should come.'

When the archbishop finally heard the rebels coming, he said to his men with great fortitude: 'Let us go with confidence, for it is better to die when it can no longer help to live. At no previous time of my life could I have died in such security of conscience.' A little later the executioners entered crying, 'Where is that traitor to the kingdom? Where the despoiler of the common people?' The archbishop was not at all disturbed and replied to their shouts: 'Good, my sons, you have come; behold, I am the archbishop whom you seek, but not a traitor or despoiler.' On seeing him, those limbs of Satan laid their impious hands on him and tore him from the Chapel, paying no respect to the sanctity of the place or its holy altars nor to the image of the Cross at the top of his crozier, nor even to the sacrament which a priest held before him. Worse than those demons who fear Christ's sacraments and flee from them, they disregarded the presence of the Saviour and dragged the archbishop along the passages by his arms and hood to their fellows outside the gates on Tower Hill. When he arrived there, a most horrible shouting broke out, not like the clamour normally produced by men, but of a sort which enormously exceeded all human noise and which could only be compared to the wailings of the inhabitants of hell. Such shouts used to be heard whenever the rebels beheaded anyone or destroyed houses, for as long as God permitted their iniquity to be unpunished. Words could not be heard among their horrible shrieks but rather their throats sounded with the bleating of sheep, or, to be more accurate, with the devilish voices of peacocks. The archbishop, as we have said, stood among the crowd, surrounded

by thousands of ruffians and saw many of their swords drawn
about his head to threaten him with death. But he said to those
standing near: 'What is it, dearest sons, what is it that you propose
to do? What sin have I committed towards you for which you
wish to kill me? Beware lest, if you kill me, who am your pastor,
prelate and archbishop, the fury of a just vengeance should fall
on you; certainly for such a deed all England will be laid under an
interdict.'

Scarcely could the archbishop finish this speech before the
rebels broke out with the horrible shout that they feared neither
an interdict nor the Pope; all that remained for him, as a man
false to the community and treasonable to the realm was to submit his neck to the executioners' swords. The archbishop now
realised that his death was imminent and inevitable; after many
proofs of his pious exhortation and the above-mentioned salutary
words (for he was a most eloquent man and incomparably the
wisest in the kingdom), he finally forgave, as far as he could,
the sin of his executioner (following the Saviour who prayed to the
Father on behalf of his persecutors) and knelt to offer his neck to
the sword. He was first struck severely but not fatally in the neck.
He put his hand to the wound and said: 'Ah! Ah! this is the hand
of God.' As he did not move his hand from the place of sorrow
the second blow cut off the top of his fingers as well as severing
part of the arteries. But the archbishop still did not die, and only
on the eighth blow, wretchedly wounded in the neck and on the
head, did he complete what we believe is worthy to be called his
martyrdom. His body lay there unburied throughout the whole
of that Friday, the festival of St Basil, and the next day too: no
one dared to bury it for fear of the insane mob raging everywhere.
The executioner himself soon experienced divine vengeance and
was driven mad and struck blind. Some members of the crowd
of rustics, driven by greed, secretly approached the archbishop's
body on the night after his execution in order to steal the ring
which was on his finger.

Now a certain man, blind for many years and long sustained
by the alms of the archbishop, heard of his death and the reason

for it. In all faith he prayed to God to restore his vision through the archbishop's merits and so recovered his sight. When the archbishop was being buried, a man from Dover who had been blind for two years was advised in a dream to approach the body and that night sight was also restored to him. A certain woman, pregnant but unable to give birth, besought the archbishop's help and on that very day was delivered of male triplets, all of whom were baptised. Many other miracles were manifest after the archbishop's death as well as many signs of the judgment of God's vengeance on those who caused his death or willingly consented to it; but we will mention these when the proper opportunity arises.

With the archbishop there were killed not only Robert Hales, a most strenuous knight and Treasurer of the kingdom, but also John Leg, one of the king's attendants, and a Franciscan friar, because he was said to be a familiar of John of Gaunt, duke of Lancaster, whom the rebels held in hatred and rancour. On that same day many other men, both Flemings and Englishmen, were executed for no real cause but only to satisfy the cruelty of the domineering rustics. For to them it was a solemn game, if they could seize anyone who did not make fealty to them or failed to co-operate with them or who was especially hated by an individual rebel, to drag off his hood immediately and to rush into the streets with their usual clamour to kill him. Nor did they show any reverence to holy places but killed those whom they hated even if they were within churches and in sanctuary. I have heard from a trustworthy witness that thirty Flemings were violently dragged out of the church of the Austin Friars in London and executed in the open street. Seventeen others were taken from another parish church in London. All these, to the contempt of holy sanctuary and by a cursed mob who at that time feared neither God nor man, paid the like penalty of losing their heads.

When the king and those who were of his council saw such crimes being committed, they held urgent discussions immediately. The situation did not allow a longer time for deliberation, especially as everyone was confounded by the killing of the

7

archbishop of Canterbury and the Treasurer of the realm, the two most powerful men in the kingdom; and they feared that if the great could be murdered then the ordinary men would not be spared. The lord king with the advice of the council who were then with him, offered the rebels peace in order to settle the fury which was then in full spate – on the condition that they would desist from burning and overthrowing houses and from killing and would return to their own homes without delay. There they would be given charters confirming the said peace. The men of Essex received this promise willingly for they were already weary of their long labours and longed to see their homes, wives and children once again. However they appointed several representatives to stay behind in order to obtain the king's charter. So it was done, and there remained the men from Kent throughout the following night.

How the rustics planned to burn down London
On the next day, Saturday 15 June (the feast of Saints Vitus and Modestus), behold, the men of Kent showed themselves no less persistent in their wicked actions than on the previous day: they continued to kill men and to burn and destroy houses. The king sent messengers to the Kentishmen telling them that their fellows had left to live in peace henceforward and promising that he would give them too a similar form of peace if they would accept it. The rebels' greatest leader was called 'Walter Helier' or 'Tylere' (for such names had been given to him because of his trade), a cunning man endowed with much sense if he had decided to apply his intelligence to good purposes. He said that he would willingly embrace the king's peace but only if its conditions were determined according to his own judgment. As it seemed to him that he was stronger than the king and the king's council, he had decided to keep them waiting by quibbling objections until the next day; on the following night he could then pursue his evil schemes more easily. For he had planned, because all the poor commons of London favoured him, to despoil the city that very night; first he would kill the king and all

his important supporters and then he would light fires at four
places in the city and burn it down. But God who opposes the
proud and shows favour to the humble did not allow Tyler's
wicked plans and aims to come to fruition. He graciously and
suddenly brought this iniquitous design to nothing. For when
charters (according to the form we will describe later) had been
written for Tyler three times and none of them would please
him, the king finally sent one of his knights called John Newton
to ask rather than order (for Tyler's arrogance was already
well known) him to come to the king; thus Tyler might discuss
the articles which he insisted should be included in the charter
with the king himself. I have inserted one of these in our chronicles so that the reader can see clearly how unreasonable were the
others.

Of the arrogance of Walter Tyler

Now, above all things, Tyler desired to obtain a commission for
himself and his men to execute all lawyers, escheators and others
who had been trained in the law or dealt in the law because of
their office. He believed that once all those learned in the law
had been killed, all things would henceforward be regulated by
the decrees of the common people; there would be no more law
at all, or, if so, it would be determined by his own judgment.
Indeed he is said to have arrogantly declared on the day before
these events, and with his hands placed on his lips, that within four
days all the laws of England would emanate from his own mouth.
And so, when lord John Newton asked him to hurry (as we have
said), Tyler indignantly replied, 'If you wish to make haste, go
back yourself to your lord, the king; I will come when it pleases
me to do so'. After the departure of this knight Tyler followed a
little later on horse-back; and he arrived near the place called
'Smythfeld' where the king was stationed and where the said
knight came again to hear and carry back his wishes. So Sir
John Newton came up to him on a war horse to hear what he
proposed to say. Tyler grew indignant because the knight had
approached him on horseback and not on foot, and furiously

declared that it was more fitting to approach his presence on foot than by riding on a horse. Newton, still not completely forgetful of his old knightly honour, replied, 'As you are sitting on a horse it is not insulting for me to approach you on a horse'. At this the ruffian grew indignant, brought out his knife (which we commonly call a 'daggere') and threatened to strike the knight and called him a traitor. But the latter, hating that name, angrily called Tyler a liar and drew his knife too. The rascal could not bear to be so insulted before his rustics and prepared to rush on the knight.

As the king saw the knight to be in danger and as he wished to calm the rascal's temper for the time being, he ordered Newton to descend from his horse and to hand over the knife he had drawn to the scoundrel. But since Tyler's angry temper could not be placated and as he still furiously sought to rush at the knight in whatever way he could, the mayor of London, William Walworth, and many royal knights and squires who were standing near came up to the king; for they believed it would have been shameful, unprecedented and intolerable if, in their presence, the king had allowed a noble knight to fall before him to so shameful a death. Therefore they came quickly to the aid of the knight and to arrest the rascally Tyler.

On this the king, although a boy and of tender age, took courage and ordered the mayor of London to arrest Tyler. The mayor, a man of incomparable spirit and bravery, arrested Tyler without question and struck him a blow on the head which hurt him badly. Tyler was soon surrounded by the other servants of the king and pierced by sword thrusts in several parts of his body. His death, as he fell from his horse to the ground, was the first incident to restore to the English knighthood their almost extinct hope that they could resist the commons. Immediately the commons saw Tyler's downfall they cried with sorrow for his death: 'Our captain is dead; our leader has been treacherously killed. Let us stay together and die with him; let us fire our arrows and staunchly avenge his death.' And so they drew their bows and prepared to shoot.

But the king, with marvellous presence of mind and courage for so young a man, spurred his horse towards the commons and rode around them, saying, 'What is this, my men? What are you doing? Surely you do not wish to fire on your own king? Do not attack me and do not regret the death of that traitor and ruffian. For I will be your king, your captain and your leader. Follow me into that field where you can have all the things you would like to ask for.'

Now the king had acted thus lest in their bitter state of mind the rustics should set fire to the houses at Smithfield where they were when their leader, the said traitor, was killed. Accordingly the commons followed the king and his accompanying knights to an open field before they had fully decided whether they ought to kill the king or be quiet and return home with the royal charters.

Meanwhile the mayor of London, riding quickly with a single servant, entered the city and began to shout: 'Most noble, gracious and pious citizens, go to help your king without delay for he is threatened with death; assist me too, your own mayor, for I am in the same danger. Even if you decide not to help me because of my failings, at least do not abandon your own king.' When they heard this speech the notables of London together with others who loved the king, immediately armed themselves to the number of a thousand men. Soon they were assembled in the streets waiting for a knight who could lead them to the king. As it happened, Robert Knolles appeared, whom they all asked to be their leader in case an unorganised and irregular approach might end in their rout. Knolles graciously agreed to lead a section of the citizens while other knights led the rest, splendidly armed, to the presence of the king. The king as well as the knights and esquires who were with him rejoiced at the unexpected arrival and assistance of so many armed men. They immediately surrounded the entire band of rustics with armed men, just as sheep are enclosed within a fold until it pleases the labourer to choose which he wants to send out to pasture and which he wants to kill.

What a wonderful change God had brought about. Throwing down their staffs, their single and double-headed axes, their swords, bows and arrows, the rustics humbly sank to the ground; those who had just previously gloried in holding the king's life not only at their mercy but in their power, now sought for mercy themselves. The wretches took refuge in corn fields and caves, dykes and ditches, hoping to save their lives by flight or concealment; yet in their hands a little while before had lain the life and death of almost all of Loegria.[1] The knights who were with the king desired to avenge not so much their injuries as their shame on the rustics; they asked the king to allow them to remove the heads of at least one or two hundred of the criminals as a warning to posterity that the knightly order was of some worth against the rustics. But the king refused to agree to their requests, saying that many of the commons had followed the mob out of fear; if he assented to the proposal, it might well be that the innocent would be punished and the guilty escape unharmed. But he ordered that a proclamation should be made immediately to the Londoners: the citizens were to have no further communication with the rebels nor were any of them to be admitted into the city that night. The commons were allowed to spend the night under the open sky. However the king ordered that the written and sealed charter which they had requested should be handed to them in order to avoid more trouble at that time. He knew that Essex was not yet pacified nor Kent settled; and the commons and rustics of both counties were ready to rebel if he failed to satisfy them quickly. The tenor of the charter extracted by force from the lord king was as follows, the names of the communities being changed to suit the counties to which copies were sent.

Royal Charter concerning the manumission of the rustics
'Richard, by the grace of God, king of England and France, and lord of Ireland, to all his bailiffs and faithful men to whom these present letters come, greetings. Know that by our special grace we have manumitted all our liegemen, subjects and others of the county of Hertford; and we have freed and quitted each of them from bondage by the present letters. We also pardon our said

---

[1] See above, p. 171 n.

liege men and subjects for all felonies, acts of treason, transgressions and extortions performed by them or any one of them in whatsoever way. We also withdraw sentences of outlawry declared against them or any of them because of these offences. And we hereby grant our complete peace to them and each of them. In testimony of which we order these letters of ours to be made patent. Witnessed by myself at London on 15 June in the fourth year of my reign.'

Once they had this charter, the commons returned to their homes. But still the earlier evils by no means ceased, as we will now show by describing the actions of the villeins of St Albans after their return. In order to understand this properly, we will repeat what we have said, and begin again on the day when they left St Albans, namely the previous Friday. [*Continued by no. 43 below, p. 269.*]

27 The Rebels in London according to Henry Knighton

Chronicon Henrici Knighton, II 132–8: continued from no. 21 above

Henry Knighton's short but factually detailed account of incidents in London stands in straightforward contrast to Walsingham's more embellished narrative. In general, Knighton's information carries conviction and his Lancastrian connections give his description of the sack of the Savoy particular authority. But he makes several mistakes of fact, the most influential of these being his erroneous identification of Wat Tyler with Jack Straw. More seriously, Knighton apparently made little attempt to establish the correct chronology of events and, for instance, relates the story of the murders on Tower Hill before that of the destruction of the Savoy.

On Wednesday before the feast of the Consecration [12 June] the people arrived in Southwark and came to the king's prison of the Marshalsea which they immediately broke open. They compelled all the prisoners to join and help them; and also forced all those they met, whether pilgrims or men of whatever condition, to go with them.

On the Friday immediately following the feast of the Consecration [14 June][1] the people passed over the bridge into the city of London. No one opposed them although it is said that the citizens knew of their approach long beforehand. The people then went to the Tower where resided the king surrounded with a large company of knights, esquires, valets and other men. For it is said that there were about 150 knights in the Tower (180 according to some) as well as the king's mother and the duchess of Brittany and many other ladies. Henry, earl of Derby, son of John, duke of Lancaster, was also there although still a young boy.[2] Also within the Tower was Simon of Sudbury, archbishop of Canterbury and Chancellor of England, as well as brother Robert de Hales, prior of the Hospital of England and royal Treasurer. John Leg and another John from the order of Friars Minors, a vigorous soldier, an expert physician and a favourite servant of John, duke of Lancaster, ran into the Tower with three others to seek shelter under the king's wings. Now the commons had decided to kill the archbishop and the other persons named above with him; it was for this that they had come to the Tower and later they were to carry out their intentions. But the king, desiring to free the archbishop and the others from the mouths of the wolves, sent a message to the commons asking them to meet him at a place outside the city called Myltros [Mylcros, i.e. Mile End] and talk to him there about their proposals. But the knights who should have gone with the king completely lost their courage and showed, sad to say, no spirit whatsoever; they seemed to be struck by womanly fears and dared not leave but stayed within the Tower. The king went to the place he had assigned, followed

[1] Presumably an error for Thursday, 13 June.
[2] The future Henry IV (1399–1413) was born in 1366, the year before Richard II.

by many members of the criminal mob. Many others, however, stayed where they were. When they had arrived at the rendezvous the commons complained to the king about their intolerable servitude and heavy oppressions which they neither could nor would sustain any longer. The king, for the sake of peace and because of the circumstances at the time, granted the commons, at their petition, a charter under his great seal – declaring that all men in the realm of England should be free and of free condition; they and their heirs should be forever released from the yoke of servitude and villeinage. This charter was quashed, annulled and adjudged worthless by the king and magnates of the realm in the parliament held at Westminster after Michaelmas that year.[1]

While this charter was being granted, behold the wretched sons who remained near the Tower drew forth the archbishop and his said companions and summoned them to their deaths – all without the use of any aggression or force, sword or arrow but only by means of threatening words and disorderly shouts. The victims, voluntarily and without protesting, offered themselves like lambs to the shearer: barefooted, with their heads uncovered and their belts laid aside, they went freely to their deaths as if they were murderers or thieves and deserved this fate. And so – alas and for sorrow! – the two morning-stars of the kingdom, the worthy with the unworthy and seven in all, were executed on Tower Hill before the king returned. For, as has been said, John Leg and his three colleagues were responsible for this irreparable loss.[2] The executioners transfixed the heads of the murdered men on spears and sticks so that they could be recognised by the other commons. They then marched onwards in ever-increasing malice to the manor of the duke of Lancaster called 'Sawey'. This was a splendidly designed building, completed not long before and constructed from the foundations by the most noble Henry, first duke of Lancaster: John of Gaunt married his daughter, the lady Blanche, and so succeeded to the inheritance. It was believed that the Savoy had no rival in England. These servants of the devil destroyed this manor, burnt it and reduced it to ashes together

[1] See below, pp. 329–30.   [2] See above, p. 135.

with all its contents except for a bed and a few other things which were taken away by the keeper just before the commons arrived. In that manor were all the treasures of the said Duke John, his bed-hangings and other adornments, innumerable riches, all the metal goods which could be wanted for daily use as well as his charters and records: all these, sad to say, perished together in the fury of the mob. And let it be known that the keeper of the said wardrobe asserted and swore that he believed no Christian king nor anyone else had a better wardrobe: he said that it was so full of silver vessels and jewels, not counting others gilded or made of pure gold, that five carts could hardly have held them. One of the criminals chose a fine piece of silver and hid it in his lap; when his fellows saw him carrying it, they threw him, together with his prize, into the fire, saying that they were lovers of truth and justice, not robbers and thieves. It is said that some of the rebels entered the wine cellar at the Savoy, and several drank so much sweet wine that they were incapable of leaving. They sang, joked and amused themselves in a tipsy fashion until the door was blocked by fire and stones. And so they died, for even if they had been sober they would have found themselves deprived of any exit. For the following seven days the trapped men were heard shouting and lamenting the enormity of their wickedness by the many people who visited the spot; but no one helped or consoled them in their trouble. And so those drunken men who came to consume wine perished in wine – to the number (so it was later said) of thirty-two or thereabouts.

When they had committed these and other injuries, the rebels returned to the New Temple which belonged to the prior of Clerkenwell and threw down many houses there. They broke the chests they found in the church or the apprentices' rooms; and also tore up with their axes all the church books, charters and records discovered in the apprentices' chests and then burnt them. The insurgents also overthrew the houses of the jurors in the city; even when old and senile, the rebels climbed with extraordinary agility as though they were rats or carried aloft by some spirit. This is certainly credible for the malign spirit which they followed

and served undoubtedly directed their steps. On that same day
the commons marched to Clerkenwell where, apart from the
church, they left little of the prior's mansion undestroyed. They
also completely destroyed the manor of Highbury two leagues
out of London which the said Robert de Hales prior had recently
and skilfully rebuilt like another paradise. The rebels killed at
once all the jurors of the city and apprentices in law they found.
If a particular rebel had a special enemy or opponent, the latter
would be sought for and beheaded immediately. When their
masters had been executed, many of the apprentices of the city
went off with the rebels; the latter never killed anyone except
by beheading him. They dragged Richard Lyons, a notable
burgess, out of his house and executed him in the street. Lyons
had been convicted in one of Edward III's parliaments for serious
fraud towards the king and queen as well as other lords and ladies
of the kingdom in his dealings with precious stones and other
jewels. Accordingly parliament had sentenced him to perpetual
imprisonment, with a daily stipend of twelve pence granted to
him by the king's grace; afterwards he was freed by favour but
now he was killed.[1]

The rebels committed these and many other enormities without
sparing any grade or order – in churches and cemeteries, in roads
and streets as well as in houses and fields. Neither fearing God nor
revering the honour of mother church, they pursued and executed
all those against whom they raised their noisy cry. After a whole
day spent in such detestable actions, they were at last exhausted
by their labours and the drinking of so much more wine than
usual; thus in the evening you could see them lying scattered about
on the streets and under the walls, sleeping like slaughtered pigs.
That night many of the rebels, emboldened by drink, secretly
killed those of their colleagues whom they previously hated; and
so there was much slaughter at the hands of one another rather
than by others.

On the following day, namely Saturday, they made their way
into Smithfield where they were met in the morning by the king,

[1] See above, no. 9.

wise and prudent despite his youth. He was approached by the rebels' leader, properly called Watte Tyler but now known by the different name of Jakke Strawe. Tyler stayed close to the king and spoke on behalf of the other rebels. He had drawn his knife, commonly called a dagger, and kept throwing it from hand to hand like a boy playing a game. It was believed that he would take the opportunity to stab the king suddenly if the latter refused what he demanded; those who stood near the king certainly feared what would happen. The rebels petitioned the king that all preserves of water, parks and woods should be made common to all: so that throughout the kingdom the poor as well as the rich should be free to take game in water, fish ponds, woods and forests as well as to hunt hares in the fields – and to do these and many other things without impediment. When the king paused to consider these demands, Jakke Strawe approached the king and spoke threateningly to him, seizing the bridle of the king's horse with unparalleled audacity. When John [recte William] de Walworth, burgher of London, noticed this, he feared the king was about to be killed and knocked Jakke Straw into the gutter with his baselard. Thereupon another esquire called Ralph Standish pierced his side with another baselard. And so he fell on his back and perished while his hands and feet quivered for some time. Thereupon an enormous wailing broke out, 'Our leader is dead'.

When Tyler was dead, he was dragged by his hands and feet like a vile thing into the nearby church of St Bartholomew. Many of the rebels then withdrew and about ten thousand, it is believed, suddenly fled and disappeared. The king repaid John de Walworth and Ralph de Standish for their services by raising them to the knighthood together with four other burgesses of the city, namely John Philpot, Nicholas de Brembre, John Launde and Nicholas Twyford. The king ordered these new knights to tell the remainder of the criminal crowd to depart and assemble in a field where he could negotiate a peaceful settlement with them. As they gathered there, behold a multitude of armed men arrived from the city, led by lord Robert Knolles and other knights. They surrounded the wretched band of rebels in the field, now like deserted sheep without their shepherd. Then the king, pious in all things, was moved by mercy and did not have the wretches killed. Sparing this foolish mob, he ordered each man to return to his own home; but many suffered death after the king had departed. There were twenty thousand men in this miserable crowd, their leaders being Thomas Baker, the first mover and later the chief leader, Jakke Strawe, Jakke Mylner, Jakke Carter, Jakke Trewman. [*Continued by no. 71B below, p. 381.*]

28 The Rebels in London according to Froissart

Froissart, trans. Berners, ed. G. C. Macaulay, pp. 255–61: continued from no. 22 above. Cf. Froissart, *Chroniques*, x 107–14, 116–24

Froissart's dramatic account of events in London after the entry of the rebels into the city is deservedly famous. Less detailed than the *Anonimalle Chronicle* and less impassioned than Walsingham, he is more entertaining than either. Froissart's descriptions of historical episodes were usually based on the facts provided by interviews with those who had been present at the time; and it is consequently true that the reliability of his narrative depends absolutely on the character and quality of his informants. In the case of the Peasants' Revolt in London, Froissart probably derived information from two French lords, Robert de Namur and Perducas d'Albret, both mentioned in the course of his story. The general level of accuracy is (for Froissart) impressively high although many of his details are clearly untrustworthy. It is hardly likely, for example, that Richard II's meeting with the rebels at Smithfield was accidental. As usual, Froissart's knowledge of English geography is seriously inadequate and most of the speeches he assigns to historical characters must be fictitious.

And when these people saw that [Richard II's return from Rotherhithe to the Tower by barge] they were inflamed with ire and returned to the hill where the great band was, and there shewed them what answer they had and how the king was returned to the Tower of London. Then they cried all with one voice, 'Let us go to London', and so they took their way thither; and in their going they beat down abbeys and houses of advocates and of men of the court, and so came into the suburbs of London, which were great and fair, and there beat down divers fair houses, and specially they brake up the king's prisons, as the Marshalsea and other, and delivered out all the prisoners that were within: and there they did much hurt, and at the bridge foot they threat them of London because the gates of the bridge were closed, saying how they would bren [burn] all the suburbs and so conquer London by force, and to slay and bren all the commons of the city. There were many [commons] within the city of their accord, and so they drew together and said: 'Why do we not let these good people enter into the city? they are our fellows, and that that they do is for us.' So therewith the gates were opened, and then these people entered into the city and went into houses and sat down to eat and drink. They desired nothing but it was incontinent brought to them, for every man was ready to make them good cheer and to give them meat and drink to appease them.

Then the captains, as John Ball, Jack Straw and Wat Tyler, went throughout London and a twenty [thirty] thousand with them, and so came to the Savoy in the way to Westminster, which was a goodly house [by the Thames] and it pertained to the duke of Lancaster. And when they entered, they slew the keepers thereof and robbed and pilled the house, and when they had so done, then they set fire on it and clean destroyed and brent it. And when they had done that outrage, they left not therewith, but went straight to the fair hospital of the Rhodes called Saint John's, and there they brent house, hospital, minster and all. Then they went from street to street and slew all the Flemings that they could find in church or in any other place, there was none

respited from death.[1] And they brake up divers houses of the
Lombards and robbed them and took their goods at their pleasure,
for there was none that durst say them nay. And they slew in the
city a rich merchant called Richard Lyon, to whom before that
time Wat Tyler had done service in France; and on a time this
Richard Lyon had beaten him, while he was his varlet, the which
Wat Tyler then remembered, and so came to his house and
strake off his head and caused it to be borne on a spear-point
before him all about the city.[2] Thus these ungracious people
demeaned themselves like people enraged and wood [i.e. mad],
and so that day they did much sorrow in London.

And so against night they went to lodge at Saint Katherine's
before the Tower of London, saying how they would never
depart thence till they had the king at their pleasure and till he
had accorded to them all [they would ask, and] that they would
ask accounts of the chancellor of England, to know where all the
good was become that he had levied through the realm [during
the last five years], and without he made a good account to them
thereof, it should not be for his profit. And so when they had
done all these evils to the strangers all the day, at night they
lodged before the Tower.

Ye may well know and believe that it was great pity for the
danger that the king and such as were with him were in. For some
time these unhappy people shouted and cried so loud, as though
all the devils of hell had been among them. In this evening the
king was counselled by his brethren and lords and by sir Nicholas
[recte William] Walworth, mayor of London, and divers other
notable and rich burgesses, that in the night time [at midnight]
they should issue out of the Tower [by four London streets] and
enter into the city, and so to slay all these unhappy people, while
they were at their rest and asleep; for it was thought that many of
them were drunken, whereby they should be slain like flies;

---

[1] According to the city account of the rebellion (below, no. 31), the Flemings
were killed on Friday 14 June.

[2] For Lyons, beheaded on 14 June, see above, pp. 86, 185. Froissart's story that
Tyler was his varlet is confirmed by no other source.

also of twenty of them there was scant one in harness. And surely the good men of London might well have done this at their ease, for they had in their houses secretly their friends and servants ready in harness, and also sir Robert Knolles was in his lodging keeping his treasure with more than a sixscore ready at his commandment; in like wise was sir Perducas d'Albret, who was as then in London, insomuch that there might well (have) assembled together an eight thousand men ready in harness. Howbeit, there was nothing done, for the residue of the commons of the city were sore doubted, lest they should rise also, and the commons before were a threescore thousand or more. Then the earl of Salisbury and the wise men about the king said: 'Sir, if ye can appease them with fairness, it were best and most profitable, and to grant them everything that they desire, for if we should begin a thing the which we could not achieve, we should never recover it again, but we and our heirs ever to be disherited.' So this counsel was taken and the mayor countermanded, and so commanded that he should not stir; and he did as he was commanded, as reason was. And in the city with the mayor there were twelve aldermen, whereof nine of them held with the king and the other three took part with these ungracious people, as it was after well known, the which they full dearly bought.[1]

And on the Friday in the morning [14 June] the people, being at Saint Katherine's near to the Tower, began to apparel themselves and to cry and shout, and said, without the king would come out and speak with them, they would assail the Tower and take it by force, and slay all them that were within. Then the king doubted these words and so was counselled that he should issue out to speak with them: and then the king sent to them that they should all draw to a fair plain place called Mile-end, whereas the people of the city did sport them in the summer season, and there the king to grant them that they desired; and there it was [the mayor of London] cried in the king's name, that whosoever would speak with the king let him go to the said place, and there he should not fail to find the king. Then the people began to

---

[1] See below, no. 32.

depart, specially the commons of the villages, and went to the same place: but all went not thither, for they were not all of one condition; for there were some that desired nothing but riches and the utter destruction of the noblemen and to have London robbed and pilled; that was the principal matter of their beginning, the which they well shewed; for as soon as the Tower gate opened and that the king was issued out with his two brethren and the earl of Salisbury, the earl of Warwick, the earl of Oxford, sir Robert of Namur, the lord of Vertaing, the lord Gommegnies and divers other, then Wat Tyler, Jack Straw and John Ball and more than four hundred entered into the Tower and brake up chamber after chamber, and at last found the archbishop of Canterbury, called Simon, a valiant man and a wise, and chief chancellor of England, and a little before he had said mass before the king. These gluttons took him and strake off his head, and also they beheaded the lord [grand prior] of Saint John's and a friar minor, master in medicine, pertaining to the duke of Lancaster, they slew him in despite of his master, and a serjeant at arms called John Leg; and these four heads were set on four long spears and they made them to be borne before them through the streets of London and at last set them a-high on London bridge, as though they had been traitors to the king and to the realm. Also these gluttons entered into the princess's chamber and brake her bed, whereby she was so sore affrayed that she swooned; and there she was taken up [by her servants] and borne to the water side and put into a barge and covered and so conveyed to [the Royal and] a place called Queen's Wardrobe; and there she was all that day and night like a woman half dead, til she was comforted with the king her son, as ye shall hear after.

When the king came to the said place of Mile-end without London, he put out of his company his two brethren, the earl of Kent and sir John Holland, and the lord of Gommegnies, for they

1 The 'Tower Royal' or 'La Reol' (so-called because it stood in the city street of that name) had been the wardrobe of Edward III's wife, Queen Philippa, between 1330 and 1369. In 1381 it was the London residence of Richard II's mother, the Princess of Wales, whose whereabouts at the time of the Mile End meeting are, however, a matter for debate: see below, p. 209.

durst not appear before the people: and when the king and his other lords were there, he found there a threescore thousand men of divers villages and of sundry countries in England; so the king entered in among them and said to them sweetly: 'Ah, ye good people, I am your king: what lack ye? what will ye say?' Then such as understood him said: 'We will that ye make us free for ever, ourselves, our heirs and our lands, and that we be called no more bond [*serf*] nor so reputed'. 'Sirs', said the king, 'I am well agreed thereto. Withdraw you home into your own houses and into such villages as ye came from, and leave behind you of every village two or three, and I shall cause writings to be made and seal them with my seal, the which they shall have with them, containing everything that ye demand; and to the intent that ye shall be the better assured, I shall cause my banners to be delivered into every bailiwick, shire and countries.'

These words appeased well the common people, such as were simple and good plain men, that were come thither and wist not why. They said, 'It was well said, we desire no better'. Thus these people began to be appeased and began to withdraw them into the city of London. And the king also said a word, the which greatly contented them. He said: 'Sirs, among you good men of Kent ye shall have one of my banners with you, and ye of Essex another, and ye of Sussex, of Bedford, of Cambridge, of Yarmouth, of Stafford and of Lynn, each of you one; and also I pardon everything that ye have done hitherto, so that ye follow my banners and return home to your houses'. They all answered how they would so do: thus these people departed and went into London. Then the king ordained more than thirty clerks the same Friday, to write with all diligence letter patents and sealed with the king's seal, and delivered them to these people; and when they had received the writing, they departed and returned into their own countries: but the great venom remained still behind, for Wat Tyler, Jack Straw and John Ball said, for all that these people were thus appeased, yet they would not depart so, and they had of their accord more than thirty thousand. So they abode still and made no press to have the king's writing nor seal, for all their intents was to put the city to trouble in such wise as to slay all the rich and honest persons and to rob and pill their houses. They of London were in great fear of this, wherefore they kept their houses privily with their friends and such servants as they had, every man according to his puissance. And when these said people were this Friday thus somewhat appeased, and that they should depart as soon as they had their writings, every man home into his own country, then king Richard came into the Royal, where the queen his mother was, right sore affrayed: so he comforted her as well as he could and tarried there with her all that night. . . .

Now let us return [*after the digression concerning Sir Robert Salle; see below, no. 42*] to the king. The Saturday [morning] the king departed from the [Queen's] Wardrobe in the Royal and went to Westminster and heard mass in the church there, and all his lords with him. And beside [within] the church there was a little chapel with an image of our Lady, which did great miracles and in whom the kings of England had ever great trust and confidence. The king made his orisons before this image and did there his offering; and then he leapt on his horse, and all his lords, and so [at about the hour of Tierce] the king rode toward London; and when he had ridden a little way, on the left hand there was a way to pass without London [which he took so that no one knew where he intended to go].

The same proper morning Wat Tyler, Jack Straw and John Ball had assembled their company to common [i.e. commune] together in a place called Smithfield, whereas every Friday there is a market of horses; and there were together all of affinity more than twenty thousand, and yet there were many still in the town, drinking and making merry in the taverns [at the expense of the Lombards] and paid nothing, for they were happy that made them best cheer. And these people in Smithfield had with them the king's banners, the which were delivered them the day before, and all these gluttons were in mind to overrun and to rob London the same day; for their captains said how they had done nothing as yet. 'These liberties that the king hath given us is to us but a small profit: therefore let us be all of one accord and let us overrun this rich and puissant city, or they of Essex, of Sussex, of Cambridge, of Bedford, of Arundel, of Warwick, of Reading, [of Berkshire], of Oxford, of Guildford, [of Coventry], of Lynn, of Stafford, of Yarmouth, of Lincoln, of York and of Durham do come hither. For all these will come hither; Baker[1] and Lister will bring them hither; and if we be first lords of London and have the possession of the riches that is therein, we shall not repent us; for if we leave it, they that come after will have it from us'.

To this counsel they all agreed; and therewith the king came the same way unaware of them, for he had thought to have passed that way without London, and with him a forty [sixty] horse. And when he came before the abbey of Saint Bartholomew and beheld all these people, then the king rested and said how he would go no farther till he knew what these people ailed, saying, if they were in trouble, how would he rappease them again. The lords that were with him tarried also, as reason was when they saw the king tarry. And when Wat Tyler saw the king tarry, he said to his people: 'Sirs, yonder is the king: I will go and speak with him. Stir not from hence, without I make you a sign; and when I make you that sign, come on and slay all them except the king; but do the king no hurt, he is young, we shall do with him as we list and shall lead him with us all about England, and so shall we be lords of all the realm without doubt'. And there was a doublet-maker of London called John Tycle, and he had brought to these gluttons a sixty doublets, the which they [Tyler and others] ware: then he demanded of these captains who should pay him for his doublets; he demanded thirty marks. Wat Tyler answered him and said: 'Friend, appease yourself, thou shalt be well paid or this day be ended. Keep thee near me; I shall be thy creditor [you have no need to fear].' And therewith he spurred his horse and departed from his company and came to the king, so near him that his horse head touched the croup of the king's horse, and the first word that he said was this: 'Sir king, seest thou

---

[1] Probably a mistake for Roger Bacon, a knight who led the rebel assault on Great Yarmouth on 18 June (see below p. 257), and not the Thomas Baker of Fobbing mentioned by Knighton (above, pp. 136, 187).

all yonder people?' 'Yea truly', said the king, 'wherefore sayest
thou?' 'Because', said he, 'they be all at my commandment and
have sworn to me faith and truth, to do all that I will have them'.
'In a good time', said the king, 'I will well it be so'. Then Wat
Tyler said, as he that nothing demanded but riot: 'What believest
thou, king, that these people and as many more as be in
London at my commandment, that they will depart from thee
thus without having thy letters?' 'No', said the king, 'ye shall
have them: they be ordained for you and shall be delivered every
one each after other. Wherefore, good fellows, withdraw fair
and easily to your people and cause them to depart out of
London; for it is our intent that each of you by villages and
townships shall have letters patents, as I have promised you.'

With those words Wat Tyler cast his eyen on a squire that
was there with the king bearing the king's sword, and Wat
Tyler hated greatly the same squire, for the same squire had
displeased him before for words between them. 'What', said
Tyler, 'art thou there? Give me thy dagger'. 'Nay', said the squire,
'that will I not do: wherefore should I give it thee?' The king
beheld the squire and said: 'Give it him; let him have it'. And so
the squire took it him sore against his will. And when this Wat
Tyler had it, he began to play therewith and turned it in his
hand, and said again to the squire: 'Give me also that sword'.
'Nay', said the squire, 'it is the king's sword: thou art not worthy
to have it, for thou art but a knave; and if there were no more
here but thou and I, thou durst not speak those words for as
much gold in quantity as all yonder abbey [St Paul's]'. 'By my
faith', said Wat Tyler, 'I shall never eat meat till I have thy head':
and with those words the mayor of London came to the king
with a twelve horses well armed under their coats, and so he
brake the press and saw and heard how Wat Tyler demeaned
himself, and said to him: 'Ha, thou knave, how art thou so
hardy in the king's presence to speak such words? It is too much
for thee so to do'. Then the king began to chafe and said to the
mayor: 'Set hands on him'. And while the king said so, Tyler
said to the mayor: 'A God's name what have I said to displease

thee?' 'Yes truly', quoth the mayor, 'thou false stinking knave, shalt thou speak thus in the presence of the king my natural lord? I commit never to live, without thou shalt dearly abye it'. And with those words the mayor drew out his sword [*baselaire*] and strake Tyler so great a stroke on the head, that he fell down at the feet of his horse, and as soon as he was fallen, they environed him all about, whereby he was not seen of his company. Then a squire of the king's alighted, called John Standish, and he drew out his sword and put it into Wat Tyler's belly, and so he died.[1]

Then the ungracious people there assembled, perceiving their captain slain, began to murmur among themselves and said: 'Ah, our captain is slain, let us go and slay them all': and therewith they arranged themselves on the place in manner of battle, and their bows before them. Thus the king began a great outrage [bravery]; howbeit, all turned to the best: for as soon as Tyler was on the earth, the king departed from all his company and all alone he rode to these people, and said to his own men: 'Sirs, none of you follow me; let me alone'. And so when he came before these ungracious people, who put themselves in ordinance to revenge their captain, then the king said to them: 'Sirs, what aileth you? Ye shall have no captain but me: I am your king: be all in rest and peace'. And so the most part of the people that heard the king speak and saw him among them, were shamefast and began to wax peaceable and to depart; but some, such as were malicious and evil, would not depart, but made semblant as though they would do somewhat.

Then the king returned to his own company and demanded of them what was best to be done. Then he was counselled to draw into the field, for to fly away was no boot [use]. Then said the mayor: 'It is good that we do so, for I think surely we shall have shortly some comfort of them of London and of such good men as be of our part, who are purveyed and have their friends and men ready armed in their houses'. And in the mean time voice and bruit ran through London how these unhappy people were

---

[1] According to Knighton (above, p. 186), Tyler's death-blow was delivered by Ralph Standish.

likely to slay the king and the mayor in Smithfield; through the
which noise all manner of good men of the king's party issued
out of their houses and lodgings well armed, and so came all to
Smithfield and to the field where the king was, and they were
anon to the number of seven or eight thousand men well armed.
And first thither came sir Robert Knolles and sir Perducas
d'Albret, well accompanied, and divers of the aldermen of
London, and with them a six hundred men in harness, and a
puissant man of the city, who was the king's draper [retainer],
called Nicholas Bramber, and he brought with him a great company; and ever as they came, they ranged them afoot in order of
battle: and on the other part these unhappy people were ready
ranged, making semblance to give battle, and they had with them
divers of the king's banners. There the king made three knights,
the one the mayor of London sir Nicholas [William] Walworth,
sir John Standish and sir Nicholas Bramber.[1] Then the lords said
among themselves: 'What shall we do? We see here our enemies,
who would gladly slay us, if they might have the better hand of
us'. Sir Robert Knolles counselled to go and fight with them and
slay them all; yet the king would not consent thereto, but said:
'Nay, I will not so: I will send to them commanding them to
send me again my banners, and thereby we shall see what they
will do. Howbeit, other by fairness or otherwise, I will have them'.
'That is well said, sir', quoth the earl of Salisbury. Then these
new knights were sent to them, and these knights made token to
them not to shoot at them, and when they came so near them
that their speech might be heard, they said: 'Sirs, the king
commandeth you to send to him again his banners, and we think
he will have mercy of you'. And incontinent they delivered again
the banners and sent them to the king. Also they were commanded on pain of their heads, that all such as had letters of the
king to bring them forth and to send them again to the king;
and so many of them delivered their letters, but not all. Then
the king made them to be all to-torn in their presence; and as soon

---

[1] Froissart is almost certainly incorrect in thinking that the knighting took
place before all danger from the rebels had ended. But see Knighton, above, p. 186.

as the king's banners were delivered again, these unhappy people kept none array, but the most part of them did cast down their bows, and so brake their array and returned into London. Sir Robert Knolles was sore displeased in that he might not go to slay them all: but the king would not consent thereto, but said he would be revenged of them well enough; and so he was after.

Thus these foolish people departed, some one way and some another; and the king and his lords and all his company right ordinately entered into London with great joy. And the first journey that the king made he went to the lady princess his mother, who was in a castle in the Royal called the Queen's Wardrobe, and there she had tarried two days and two nights right sore abashed, as she had good reason; and when she saw the king her son, she was greatly rejoiced and said: 'Ah, fair son, what pain and great sorrow that I have suffered for you this day'. Then the king answered and said: 'Certainly, madam, I know it well; but now rejoice yourself and thank God, for now it is time. I have this day recovered mine heritage and the realm of England, the which I had near lost.' Thus the king tarried that day with his mother, and every lord went peaceably to their own lodgings. Then there was a cry made in every street in the king's name, that all manner of men, not being of the city of London and having not dwelt there the space of one year, to depart; and if any such be found there the Sunday by the sun-rising, that they should be taken as traitors to the king and to lose their heads. This cry thus made, there was none that durst brake it, and so all manner of people departed and sparkled abroad every man to their own places. John Ball and Jack Straw were found in an old house hidden, thinking to have stolen away, but they could not, for they were accused by their own men. Of the taking of them the king and his lords were glad, and then strake off their heads and Wat Tyler's also, and they were set on London bridge, and the valiant men's heads taken down that they had set on the Thursday before. These tidings anon spread abroad, so that the people of the strange countries, which were coming towards London, returned back again to their own houses and durst come no farther.

29 The Peasants' Revolt according to the 'monk of Westminster'

Higden, *Polychronicon*, IX 1–6

The chronicle from which the following description of the revolt is translated forms one of the many continuations of Ranulf Higden's extremely popular 'world history' or *Polychronicon*. The solitary surviving manuscript (Corpus Christi College, Cambridge, MS. 197) narrates the political history of England from 1381 to 1394 in considerable detail. References within the text prove that the author was a monk of Westminster Abbey writing not long after the events he describes. Westminster was of course well placed to receive reliable information about events in London and this chronicle is one of the most trustworthy sources for the history of the insurrection. It adds several significant details, and even more significant dates and times, to the other authorities and naturally gives much emphasis to Richard's appearance at the abbey on the morning of Saturday 15 June. In general and despite some omissions, notably the exact identity of the rebel leader, the 'monk of Westminster' confirms the authenticity of the account of the rebellion in the *Anonimalle Chronicle*.

On 12 June in that year [1381] a large multitude of country people assembled from the counties of Essex and Kent. Those who had arrived from or through various parts of Kent ran wild like the most rabid dogs. They completely destroyed the houses and manors of many and beheaded others. They also compelled those people not belonging to their company whom they met to take an oath to join them in the defence of King Richard; for they pretended that they were protecting the king and the welfare of his realm against traitors to him. As their company grew larger they raged far and wide, asserting that Master Simon de Sudbury, then both archbishop and Chancellor of England, was a traitor and deserved to die. Accordingly they made their way to his manor of Lambeth and burnt the books, vestments, clothes and many other things found there. They broke open the casks of wine they found, drank some and poured what was left on the ground. They smashed all the kitchen utensils by breaking them together. Then they congratulated themselves as if they had done a praiseworthy deed and cried out, 'A Revell, A Revell'. These things were done on 12 June, the feast of Saints Basilides and Cyrinus, that is the eve of Corpus Christi Day. Meanwhile the archbishop, afraid that he would be captured by those who sought him, fled to the royal palace [presumably at Westminster] and then to the king in the Tower of London.

On the following day [13 June] the company of rustics, incited to a wild fury, invaded the duke's hospice called 'the Savoy' at about the fourth hour after noon. They broke down all barriers and spared nothing of value which they might burn or throw to sink in the river Thames. You could then perceive something unknown to our age. While they were seeking, gathering and collecting these most precious objects, the rustics did not dare to steal anything of value secretly; because if anyone had been caught in the act of stealing some object he would have been dragged off to death by execution without trial or judgment. Nor were the rebels' passions assuaged by these deeds; for they started fires at several points and reduced that beautiful place and famous hospice to ashes. Afterwards, during the following evening, the rebels went onwards to the house of St John's, Clerkenwell. They killed all those who opposed them and burnt all the houses there as well as the manor of Highbury, which Robert Hales (at that time prior of St John's and Treasurer of England) had recently built. And they destroyed by fire other manors also.

When they saw these deeds, both the archbishop and the Treasurer of England anticipated even worse ends from such beginnings. Fearing for their lives, they hid themselves in the Tower of London with the king. When the turbulent and disorderly crowd of rustics at length realised this, they asked the king to come to them so that they could hold a discussion with him and achieve their aims through his agency. But the archbishop and the Treasurer feared the dangers that would fall on the king and kingdom if the furious mob obtained what it demanded;

and they did not allow the king to go and meet the rebels. Consequently the latter, excited to an even greater fury, rushed towards the Tower of London and threatened to destroy it unless the king would meet them to satisfy their demands. The king took note of their insulting and disloyal audacity, assented to their petition and went to a place which is called in English 'Mile ende'. There the crowd of rustics assembled and most vehemently asked the king to give them all manner of liberty as well as a pardon for any offences committed during the course of the present disturbances or otherwise until that time. The king feared the harm that might result from the fury of the mob if he failed to accede to their demands; so he agreed to what they requested and gave them liberty and a pardon for their offences.

Meanwhile, as these negotiations were in progress, a wicked group of the company of villeins approached the Tower of London. They seized the archbishop, the Treasurer and a friar minor who was surgeon to the lord duke of Lancaster. The victims were then led to Tower Hill where they were beheaded together with John Leg, a royal serjeant, and one other person.[1] These executions took place at the eleventh hour on 14 June. Then the rebels fixed the heads of the archbishop and the others on stakes and carried them through the streets of London as if they were celebrating a famous victory. They placed the heads on London Bridge, putting the archbishop's head in the centre and at a higher level. And in order to distinguish his head from those of the others, they fixed a red mitre to the top of it with a nail.

But even these evils did not assuage the rebels' passion for slaughter and they went on to the banks of the river Thames where the majority of the Flemings lived; and they beheaded all the Flemings they found without judgment and without cause. For you could see heaps of dead bodies and corpses lying in the squares and other places. And so they spent the day, thinking only of the massacre of Flemings. [*Marginal note in MS.* Notice

[1] The author of the *Anonimalle Chronicle* (see above, p. 162) agrees that five men were beheaded on Tower Hill. Knighton (above, p. 183) raises the total number to seven.

that on this day they strove to plunder the treasury of the king at Westminster.] Meanwhile the king grieved at the situation, but wise counsel was almost completely lacking at this time of crisis; for the whole city of London was so disordered and, as many thought, divided within itself that it could not decide what to do. The city unwillingly endured the tumults and invasion of the mob of rustics as they killed citizens, consumed victuals without payment and destroyed buildings. For although the citizens wished to resist the aggression of the rustics, they lacked the force and courage to do so; for they feared that if they resisted the serfs at this time of their growing power, the commons [of the city] would rise with the serfs and as their accomplices against the rest of the citizens. And so the whole city was lost by its own divisions. Therefore the citizens remained quiet, fearful for their safety and waiting in anxiety for the outcome of events.

On the following day, a Saturday [15 June], the aforementioned mob carefully hunted out, in its usual way, all those persons whom it hated in order to seize and behead them. Among these men was a certain Richard Imworth, steward of the Marshalsea, who had fled to the church of Westminster for safety and was embracing the pillars of the shrine there. The rebels dragged him violently from this sacred place and then beheaded him, without any form of judicial process, in the middle of Cheap. But Saint Edward most rapidly avenged the injury committed against him – to the exaltation of his own sanctity and the consolation of the kingdom.[1] For, after the ninth hour of the same day, and amid all this upheaval, the king rode to Westminster in the company of lords, knights and many citizens to pray; the king had come to King Edward's sacred shrine to entreat for his help at a time when all human counsel was completely lacking. As the king approached the doors of the monastery, the convent went out to meet him in procession. Thereupon the king descended from his horse and knelt to kiss amid his tears the cross which had been carried before the monks. He then progressed to the shrine of

[1] King Edward the Confessor (1003–66) was the restorer of Westminster Abbey, whose relics had been translated to his shrine behind the high altar in 1269.

the glorious King Edward where he spent some time in prayer. Then you could see lords, knights, esquires and many others strive among themselves in pious devotion as to who should make the first offerings to the relics of the saints resting there and who should shed the most tears while they prayed. God's protection, thanks to the merits of Saint Edward, was not witheld from those who made these devout prayers; as they rose from their devotions, all received hope and reassurance of a good outcome. Encouraged in this way, they rode to the city and went on to the place which is called 'Plain Field' where they were to have a discussion with the leader of the band of villeins. This leader, with an innumerable crowd of rustics, awaited the king's arrival there in order to obtain from him an amended charter concerning their liberty; for the charter previously granted to them by the king displeased them.

On the arrival of the king and his company, which included the mayor of London, William Walworth, a discussion was held with John the tiler, leader of the said multitude, concerning the remission of servitude. But this impious leader, while they talked at length on the subject of the liberty of rustics, did not show due honour to his royal majesty. Rather he addressed the most audacious words to the king's person with his head covered and with a threatening expression. The mayor, noticing the shameful temerity of his speech and especially resenting the lack of reverence due to a king from his subject, addressed John in these words: 'Why do you show no reverence to your king?' The rebel leader indignantly replied, 'No honour will be shown the king by me'. To which the mayor responded, 'Then I arrest you'. The tiler drew his knife and tried to strike the mayor. The mayor then rushed on him and wounded him with his sword, while another esquire who was present seized the head of the iniquitous leader and threw him from his horse to the ground. And so fell the courage, hope and trust of the rustics. When the whole servile mob shouted out, 'Our chief is killed', the king replied, 'Be still: I am your king, your leader and your chief, and those of you who are loyal to me should go immediately into the field'.

Meanwhile this vigorous mayor rode at the greatest speed into the town, ordering everyone to take what arms they could and proceed as rapidly as possible into the fields to protect the king. The worthy community of the city immediately obeyed their mayor's commands. Rushing to arms, they poured out of one gate and another, running as quickly as they could to the field and to defend the king. They surrounded the crowd of rustics on all sides and threatened to kill them. But when the latter saw themselves surrounded everywhere by armed men and in imminent danger of death, they threw down their weapons, staffs, bows and arrows and other means of defence. They all sank to the ground beseeching the king's mercy and asking him not to punish them according to their deserts but rather to bestow his mercy on the undeserving. The king, because of his abhorrence for the shedding of civil blood, finally granted his pardon to these unworthy men; and he ordered each of the rebels to return to his home that night, threatening that anyone found within the walls of the town would suffer the extreme penalty. On receiving such grace from the king, the crowd gradually melted away as its members all returned to their homes.

30 The Peasants' Revolt according to the Continuator of the 'Eulogium Historiarum'

Eulogium Historiarum, Rolls Series (1858), III 351–4

The following brief but lively account of the Peasants' Revolt was written as part of a continuation of the world history or *Eulogium Historiarum sive Temporis* compiled by a Malmesbury monk from Higden's *Polychronicon* in the late fourteenth century. It survives in only one manuscript, possibly written by a Canterbury monk or by John Trevor, bishop of St Asaph, who died in 1410. Although the author was probably writing several years after 1381 he was quite well-informed and introduced several details not found elsewhere. Many of the latter are at variance with the facts as related by the author of the *Anonimalle Chronicle* and Thomas Walsingham and are perhaps the product of an over-vivid imagination. Others seem reasonably plausible and lend some slight weight to the theory (originally and most forcefully expressed by Kriehn) that Tyler's death at Smithfield may have been the result of a plot previously concocted by Richard and his advisers.

In this year [1381] two esquires were sitting in one of the London taverns and remarked that the total number of shillings collected that year was less than the total of groats received in the previous year; and so they went across to the Chancellor of England asking for justices in Kent and Essex to enquire about the collection of this money. And they offered the king a sum of gold to collect the rest. In Kent the reply was that after the payment of the groats many people of both sexes had died. But in Essex a judge held his session with others and summoned a certain baker, the collector of that place. The baker said to his fellows, 'What has been collected does not satisfy them, and now they come to collect a new tax; if I have help, I will oppose them'. Immediately all took up their tools and went to the spot ready to fight; on which the justice and his men fled forthwith. 'Behold', said the baker, 'it is clear that they did come for a new tax'. Then the people of that township crossed to a neighbouring one and caused it to rise, and then both did the same to a third. And so they passed through the whole county and that of Hertford; and afterwards they passed through Erith to Maidstone in Kent and then to Waltham and Canterbury. They raised the whole country and forced the people to follow, breaking into homes, consuming all the food, killing men, spoiling and destroying houses. And when they were asked who their captain was, they mockingly replied that they did not have one.

Jak Straw and Thomas Melro found their way back to the field called Blackheath and called the bishop of Rochester to their presence. And when the bishop asked who their chief was who could speak to him, there came forward a tiler from Essex who was extremely eloquent. He told the bishop of the simple people's many grievances because of taxes and the oppression of the great and asked him to relate these to the king. And they intended, so he [the tiler] said, to go home if proper amendment were made.

The king and archbishop arrived by water but when they saw the rebels the archbishop would not allow the king to go up to talk with them. 'Because', he said, 'they surround you, and with you could do all that they pleased'. The mayor and burgesses of London asked the citizens if they wished to lock up the city. The latter replied that they would not do this in the face of their neighbours and friends. The London burgesses sent men from the city to inform the band of rebels that they would stop them from disturbing the king in his apartments, and to declare that the city was armed against them. In fact the said messengers said, 'Come to us, we have been sent for you'. And before the rebels reached London, the men of London had burnt the Savoy, a manor of the duke of Lancaster. They threw all the jewels they found there into the Thames, declaring, 'We do not wish to be thieves'.

One good man, a herald of arms, stated that he had seen a hundred thousand men with several devils among them; he then began to sicken and died shortly afterwards. The terrible multitude, decrepit old men and young men armed with rusty axes and arrows, bows and sticks, then entered the city on Corpus Christi day [13 June] and killed all those squires who had procured justices. They dragged one of these from the shrine of St Edward, and altogether, including others and Flemings, about four hundred perished. They opened up prisons, releasing the prisoners and then offering the iron chains of Newgate in the church of the Friars Minor as well as breaking open the Marshalsea. They broke into the houses of the city and ate, drank and robbed without hindrance. The king and the most worthy knights and burgesses of the city were so frightened that they dared neither resist them nor defend the Tower.

On the next day [14 June] they went to the Tower and told the king they wanted to kill traitors and his evil counsellors. Leading out the archbishop and Chancellor of England, they cut off his head, while he said, as the stroke fell, 'This is the hand of the Lord'. Similarly they beheaded the Master of the Hospitallers, Treasurer of England, and many others. They demanded from the king that he should make them all free of his kingdom; and the king delivered his general letters patent of liberty to them. But the king, who was seriously concerned, and the burgesses, fearing the spoliation of the city, took council with Sir Robert Knolles about the way by which they could eject the rebels. And on his advice, it was publicly proclaimed in four parts of the city on Saturday [15 June] that the duke of Lancaster was advancing against the king and the band of rebels with 20,000 Scots; accordingly, the band [of rebels] should meet in Smithfield where the king would come to them. While the rebels hurried into Smithfield, the mayor of London ordered the citizens to arm themselves and follow Sir Robert Knolles.

Meanwhile the king arrived at Smithfield where he was approached by Walter the tiler who failed to uncover his head. Tyler said he wished to amend the charter of liberty which the king had handed him. The mayor of London said to him: 'Why are you speaking to the king in that way? Beseech him properly and take off your cap'. Tyler replied, 'You are a traitor'. Immediately a royal esquire transfixed Tyler with a dagger followed by the mayor and another burgess; and so he died. Now the company of rebels cried, 'What is the king doing with our spokesman?' Others said, 'He is making him a knight'. And all shouted, 'Let us cross to St John's Field and let our new knight come to us'. But they had dragged the wretch into a house. At that point the city's forces arrived, splendidly armed, and surrounded all the people in the said field, who then lost heart and knew not what to do. And the king asked Robert Knolles, 'Should they not be

8

killed?' But he replied, 'No, lord, for many of the wretches are here unwillingly'. Then Robert said to the rebels, 'Fall to the ground, you wretches, cut your bow-strings and depart. No one shall remain in this city or region tonight, on penalty of execution'. And immediately they all fled. And those who returned to Canterbury had their own ordinances proclaimed and killed a burgess there who contradicted them. They burnt charters, records and writings in the house of justice. In Suffolk, the rebels beheaded the prior of Bury, a justice of the king. In Norfolk, Sussex and the diocese of Winchester many murders were committed.

The king crossed into Essex and Hertfordshire, the earl of Kent into Kent and others into other parts of the realm; and the malefactors were drawn, hanged and beheaded, some to be divided into four parts.

31 The Peasants' Revolt according to 'City of London Letter Book H'

Printed in translation from *London Letter Book H*, fo. CXXXIII, by H. T. Riley, *Memorials of London*, pp. 449–51; cf. *Calendar of London Letter Book H*, p. 166

This brief but circumstantial account of London's involvement in the Peasants' Revolt was written for the record in the city corporation's official letter book several months and possibly several years after the events it describes. As Miss Bird (*Turbulent London of Richard II*, p. 53) has noticed, 'it omits so much – and such significant matters – that it is impossible to believe that it was not censored with a purpose'. Fortunately this purpose is not difficult to appreciate. The allegations (see below, no. 32) that prominent London aldermen had been guilty of admitting the rebels into the city were too dangerous to leave unchecked; and in this account the 'perfidious commoners' of London are the only group admitted to have assisted the rebellious peasants, itself a significant revelation from such a source. The mayor and aldermen now put forward the view that their participation in the great revolt was a cause for self-congratulation. Walworth is said to have killed Tyler unaided; and only the loyal support of the citizens themselves protected Richard II from the gravest peril.

Among the most wondrous and hitherto unheard-of prodigies that have ever happened in the city of London, that which took place there on the Feast of Corpus Christi [13 June 1381] seems deserving to be committed to writing that it may be not unknown to those to come.

For on that day, while the king was holding his council in the Tower of London, countless companies of the commoners and persons of the lowest grade from Kent and Essex suddenly approached the said city, the one body coming to the town of Southwark and the other to the place called Mile End, without Aldgate. By the aid within the city of perfidious commoners of their own condition, who rose in countless numbers there, they suddenly entered the city together, and, passing straight through it, went to the duke of Lancaster's mansion, called the Savoy, and completely levelled the same with the ground and burnt it. From thence they turned to the church of the Hospital of St John of Jerusalem, without Smithfield, and burnt and levelled nearly all the houses there, the church excepted.

On the next morning all the men from Kent and Essex met at the said place called Mile End, together with some of the perfidious persons of the city aforesaid, whose numbers in all were past reckoning. And there the king came to them from the Tower, accompanied by many knights and esquires and citizens on horseback, the lady his mother also following him in a chariot.[1]

---

[1] It seems unlikely that both this account and that of the *Anonimalle Chronicle* (above, p. 161) should be in error here; but both Walsingham and Froissart (above, pp. 172, 191) appear to be in no doubt that Joan of Kent, Richard II's mother, was in the Tower at the time the rebels entered it.

There at the prayer of the infuriated rout, our lord the king granted that they might take those who were traitors against him and slay them, wheresoever they might be found. And from thence the king rode to his Wardrobe, which is situate near to Castle Baynard, while the whole of the infuriated rout took its way towards the Tower of London.[1] Entering it by force, they dragged forth Sir Simon, archbishop of Canterbury, chancellor of our lord the king, and Brother Robert Hales, prior of the said Hospital of St John of Jerusalem, the king's treasurer; and, together with them, Brother William Appeltone of the Order of Friars Minor, and John Leg, serjeant-at-arms to the king, and also one Richard Somenour of the parish of Stebenhithe.[2] All of these they beheaded in the place called Tower Hill without the said Tower, and then carrying their heads through the city upon lances, they set them up on London Bridge, fixing them there on stakes.

Upon the same day there was also no little slaughter within the city, as well of natives as of aliens. Richard Lyons, citizen and vintner of the said city, and many others were beheaded in Cheapside. In the Vintry also there was a very great massacre of Flemings, and in one heap there were lying about forty headless bodies of persons who had been dragged forth from the churches and from their houses; and hardly was there a street in the city in which there were not bodies lying of those who had been slain. Some of the houses also in the said city were pulled down, others in the suburbs destroyed, and others burnt.

Such tribulation as this, greater and more horrible than could be believed by those who had not seen it, lasted down to the hour of vespers on the following day, which was Saturday the fifteenth of June. On this day God sent remedy for the same and

[1] The King's Wardrobe lay in the south-west corner of the city between Black Friars and Castle Baynard. This report agrees with that of the *Anonimalle Chronicle* as against Froissart and the 'monk of Westminster' in stating that the murders on Tower Hill took place after – and possibly as a consequence of – Richard's speech at Mile End.

[2] Possibly the juror mentioned by the *Anonimalle Chronicle* (above, pp. 162, 201).

His own gracious aid, by the hand of the most renowned man Sir William Walworth, the then mayor, who in Smithfield in the presence of our lord the king and those standing by him, lords, knights, esquires, and citizens on horseback, on the one side, and the whole of this infuriated rout on the other, most manfully by himself rushed upon the captain of the said multitude, Walter Tyler by name, and, as he was altercating with the king and the nobles, first wounded him in the neck with his sword and then hurled him from his horse, mortally pierced in the breast. And further, by favour of divine grace, he so defended himself from those who had come with him, both on foot and on horseback, that he departed from thence unhurt and rode on with our lord the king and his people towards a field near to the spring that is called Whittewellebeche; in which place, while the whole of the infuriated multitude in warlike manner was making ready against our lord the king and his people, refusing to treat of peace except on condition that they should first have the head of the said mayor, the mayor himself, who had gone into the city at the instance of our lord the king, in the space of half an hour sent and led forth therefrom so great a force of citizen warriors in aid of his lord the king that the whole multitude of madmen was surrounded and hemmed in; and not one of them would have escaped, if our lord the king had not given orders to allow them to depart.

Therefore our lord the king returned into the city of London with the greatest of glory and honour, and the whole of this profane multitude in confusion fled forthwith for concealment in their affright.

For this same deed our lord the king, beneath his standard in the said field, with his own hands decorated with the order of knighthood the said mayor and Sir Nicholas Brembre and Sir John Philipot, who had already been mayors of the said city, as also Sir Robert Laund.

32 The Treachery of London Aldermen according to the London Sheriffs' Inquisitions

The jurors' returns to the two inquisitions held before the sheriffs of London in the autumn of 1381 are unquestionably the most famous and important legal records of the great revolt to survive. When the second of the two indictments (that of 20 November) was first published in 1898 it appeared to have solved one of the most crucial problems of the rebellion – the apparent ease with which the rebels of Kent and Essex secured admission into the city of London. According to the jurors, the city was betrayed by a small group of substantial aldermen – John Horn, Adam Karlile, Walter Sibil, William Tonge and John Fresh. But recent research has thrown grave doubts upon the accuracy of these charges. In 1940 Professor Wilkinson published the first indictment of 4 November, apparently enrolled after the second return of 20 November because the latter was intended to serve as the revised and authoritative version. A comparison of the two texts reveals important discrepancies; and Professor Wilkinson was able to argue convincingly that the record of the inquisition on 20 November was a deliberately edited version of the earlier return 'with the aim of making it a more convincing indictment of Horn, Sibil and Fresh'.[1] For that matter neither return is very reliable: and Miss Ruth Bird (*Turbulent London of Richard II*, pp. 58–61) agrees with Professor Wilkinson – though on different grounds – that all the aldermen accused, with the possible exception of John Horn, were probably innocent of the crimes with which they were accused. The inquisitions were in fact prepared by one John More, who first voiced the charges in the parliament of October 1382. John of Northampton, the radical mayor of London between October 1381 and October 1383, seems to have seized the opportunity of an investigation into the circumstances of the revolt to discredit the victuallers, his political opponents in the city. By the time that the five aldermen were brought before a new jury in

---

[1] Compare Wilkinson, 'Peasants Revolt', pp. 13–14, with the translations of the two inquisitions printed below; and cf. Powell and Trevelyan, *Peasants' Rising and the Lollards*, p. 30.

January 1384, Northampton's great rival, Nicholas Brembre, was mayor and the accused were declared innocent and acquitted. Although Horn then disappeared into oblivion, Fresh, Karlile, Tonge and Sibil all went on to prosperous careers as aldermen or royal counsellors. In the circumstances it no longer seems possible to believe that a handful of aldermen were responsible for admitting the rebels into London. Those in the city who actively supported Tyler and his company appear to have come from the poorer classes – with one major exception, Thomas Farndon or Faringdon. Although his father was a bastard, Farndon bore the surname of one of the most famous of medieval London families. The accusations made below are substantially confirmed by a separate indictment of 10 July 1381 in which he was alleged to have been present at the destruction of Cressing Temple on 10 June as well as the sacking of the Savoy, St John's Clerkenwell and Highbury later in the week.[1]

A. THE INQUISITION OF 20 NOVEMBER 1382

Coram Rege Roll, Easter 6 Richard II [KB. 27/488], Rex, memb. 6; partly printed in Réville, pp. 190–6 and reprinted in Oman, *Great Revolt*, pp. 206–12. The prefatory description of the inquisition and the names of the jurors are here translated from the original enrolment.

An Inquisition taken before John Sely and Adam Bamme sheriffs of London by virtue of a writ addressed to them from the king . . . now by the oaths of William Tyngewyk, Robert Fraunceys, Robert Pipot, John Bydyngham, John Wylby, John Wyllardby, John Marcham, John Cole, Thomas Depham, Thomas Kyngesbrugge, John Boche and John Dancastr' who declare under oath that at the time of the evil insurrection and rebellion of the commons of Kent and Essex, namely in the fourth year of King Richard II, William Walworth, then mayor of the city of London, determined to resist the rebels with all his power, to deny them entry into the city and preserve it in

---

[1] *Coram Rege* Roll, Easter 5 Richard II [KB. 27/484], Rex, memb. 3. Despite the frenzy with which Farndon had pursued his vendetta against Treasurer Hales he received letters of pardon on 8 March 1382.

peace. Therefore, with the advice of the common council of the said city, he appointed John Horn, Adam Carlyll and John Fresch, citizens and aldermen of London, messengers and envoys to go and meet the people assembled together in defiance of the fealty and loyalty they owed to their king; and the mayor specially commanded these messengers to treat with the malevolent people and to tell them (on behalf of the king and the entire city) not to approach the city to the alarm and disturbance of the king, other lords and ladies as well as the city itself, but rather to obey and reverence the king in all matters as they ought. But the said John, Adam and John did not convey the message with which they had been entrusted; and they (the jurors) say that the aforesaid John Horn, with the assent of Adam and notwithstanding the mayor's command, exceeded his instructions and conspired with the principal rebels. The crowd had been on the point of returning to their homes (*hospicia*) but John Horn persuaded them with sweet words to move onwards to the city, telling their criminal leaders that the whole of the city of London felt as they did and that they would be received in the city with the friendship that a father offers his son or a lover his loved one. As a result of this false and malicious news given them by John Horn, Adam Carlylle and John Fresch, the rebels and malefactors became jubilant and hardened to their evil purposes. Accordingly they immediately approached the boundaries of the city on the eve of Corpus Christi [12 June] and broke into the king's prison of the Marshalsea.

That same evening the aforesaid John Horn led several of the chief rebels and insurrectionary leaders (namely Thomas Hawke, William Newman, John Sterlyng and others who were later convicted of this and sentenced to death) into London with him and criminally and traitorously entertained them in his house all night. Moreover, on that very night, when John Horn told the (greatly alarmed) mayor that the insurgents were advancing on London, he declared and undertook (under penalty of his own execution) that they would do no damage to the city or its suburbs. But on the following morning John Horn went to a certain John Marchaunt, one of the city's clerks, and spoke the following, or similar, words: 'The mayor has commanded you to lend me a standard bearing the royal arms'. After a long examination the said clerk handed such a standard to John Horn although he had absolutely no knowledge of what the latter intended to do with it. John Horn, however, divided the standard into two equal parts of which he tied one to a lance and gave the other to his servant for safe-keeping. Displaying this banner, John Horn then rode to Blackheath, not because he had any official status as a city envoy that day but only in order to fulfil the promises he had already made to the malefactors and to provoke them into entering the city although he knew the alarm and injury this would cause the king, magnates and citizens of London. They [the jurors] add that as he was riding to Black-heath, John Horn met a certain John Blyton who had been sent by the king and his council to warn the rebels not to approach London. Blyton spoke the following, or similar, words to John Horn: 'Lord, I would like to know any message you may be conveying to those rebels on behalf of the city in the hope that the message I am carrying on behalf of the king may agree with yours'. Horn immediately turned on him in anger and replied: 'I have no wish to interfere with your message nor ought you to interfere with mine; I will speak to the rebels as I please and you should do the same'. After the king's envoy had ridden forward to deliver the royal message to the rebels, John Horn arrived and contradicted him. In contempt of the king, Horn uttered the following criminal, false and treasonable words: 'Come to London because all of us there are your friends and are ready to do what you propose; we will offer you our favour and help in all that you need'. Horn made this speech in the knowledge that it was contrary to the king's will and his mayor's commands. And so through the agency and encouragement of John Horn (himself counselled and confirmed in his conspiracy by Walter Sybyle), the aforesaid malefactors and rebels together with Walter Tyler, Alan Thredre, William Hawk and John Stakpull, the principal leaders and traitors, came to London where they ran through the streets of the city shouting: 'To the Savoye, to the Savoye!' Consequently John Horn and Walter Sybyle were responsible for introducing the said criminals and traitors into the city – with the result that they broke into the king's prison of Newgate, burnt various tenements, destroyed houses, executed the archbishop and others as well as perpetrating many other evil and unparalleled atrocities.

And the jurors declare that as John Horn was walking through the streets of the city with the troops of malefactors, he asked if there was anyone who wished to declare before him any injury he had suffered, and promised that if so he and his men would do speedy justice in the case. Accordingly a certain Matilda Toky came before John Horn and complained that Richard Toky, grocer, had unjustly withheld her due inheritance. Matilda then conducted John Horn, in the company of a great crowd of ribalds and insurgents, to a certain tenement held by Richard Toky in Lombard Street; when they arrived there, John Horn assumed royal authority and gave open judgment that Matilda should have the aforesaid tenement and also adjudged that she should have all the goods and chattels found there as damages; and so Horn disseized and feloniously deprived Richard Toky of his property against the peace and law of the lord king, to the prejudice of the crown, the annulment of the royal dignity, the law of the land and the king's peace and the manifest destruction of the kingdom. They [the jurors] also state that John Horn, in the company of the aforesaid evil bands and sons of iniquity, compelled many inhabitants of London to ransom themselves from threats to their life and limbs; thus he criminally forced a certain Robert Nortoun, tailor, to pay a fine and ransom of £10 sterling to John Pecche, fishmonger. Nortoun put several jewels in pledge that he would pay this sum; for if he had not done so, John Horn swore that he would hand him over to the rebel bands for execution. Consequently John Horn was one of the principal rebels against the king and the chief counsellor of their evil deeds in that it was through the felonious and treasonable encouragement and agency of Walter Sybyle and himself that the malefactors were persuaded to come to London. Moreover, Sybyle and Horn treasonably brought the rebels into London, as a result of which all the said evil deeds were committed within the city and all its suburbs – notwithstanding that Sybyle and Horn were specially bound by their oaths as aldermen to keep the king's peace in London.

Item, the aforesaid jurors declare on oath that William Walworth, mayor, after deliberation with the common council of the city, ordered all the aldermen of London and their fellow citizens to arm themselves in order to keep the city, resist the said malefactors, deny them access to the city and defend both its gates and other entrances; and on the said Thursday Walter Sybyle, then an alderman, stationed himself on London Bridge. Although Sybyle knew and saw the evil deeds previously and then being committed by the angry and malevolent mob in Southwark, he asked for little or no assistance. Indeed he repulsed the many who wished to aid him in resisting the mob and altogether refused their help in culpable and contumacious language, openly saying: 'These Kentishmen are friends to us and the king'. And so he criminally allowed the said traitors and their bands free entry and exit into the city although he ought to have prevented them from entering and could have done so easily. When Walter Sybyle was notified that the said traitors and rebels had broken into the royal prison, executed several men and overturned a certain tenement near London Bridge, he belittled all these iniquities with the words: 'What of it? that tenement has deserved destruction for the last twenty years'.[1]

And the jurors allege that on that same Thursday, Thomas Cornewayles arrived with a large band of armed men and offered to assist Sybyle to defend the entrance to the bridge and resist the traitors there; the latter, incurring all possible forfeiture of his goods, criminally and treasonably refused their help and would not allow them to oppose the rebels but left the gates of the city open and without a guard. Consequently, because of the

[1] Presumably an allusion to the brothel mentioned by the *Anonimalle Chronicle*, above, p. 156.

malevolence of Walter Sybyle and his fraudulent conspiracy
with John Horn, other gates of the city were left open and
unlocked; the aforesaid and other malefactors were therefore
able to have free entry and exit through the gates with their
bands. This action was false, criminal and treacherous as well as,
at the worst, one from which the king, the entire city and kingdom faced the clear danger of final destruction.

Item, the said jurors declare that when, at Smithfield on Saturday 15 June, our lord the king and the mayor of the city were
surrounded by bands of malefactors and at their point of greatest
peril, the said Walter Sybyle suddenly left them and rode into
the city through Aldersgate and Westchepe, openly shouting
'Close your gates and defend your walls, for all is now lost'.
And the jurors say that Walter Sybyle and John Horn caused
Aldersgate to be criminally and treacherously locked; and that,
as far as they could, they prevented men from going to help
the lord king and the mayor although they knew that the latter
were in such danger. Sybyle and Horn therefore acted contrary
to the loyalty and fealty they owed the lord king, whom they
ought to have followed, helped and defended with all their might
and to the exclusion of all other considerations. Moreover, if
the citizens of London had not acted more quickly on their own
account, help would have reached the lord king and the mayor too
late just because of the words and deeds of the said Walter
Sybyle and John Horn.

Item, the jurors declare under oath that a certain Thomas
Farndon, at the time of the principal insurrection criminally
and on his own volition approached the malefactors from the
county of Essex; and he complained to them that he had been
unjustly expelled from his rightful inheritance by that reverend
knight, the prior of the Hospital of St John of Jerusalem. Consequently the said rebels conceived such great indignation and
rancour against the said prior that they caused great damage and
destruction to his places and tenements in the county of Essex.
On the Thursday of Corpus Christi [13 June] Thomas Farndon
came into London with the said rebels as one of their captains;

and he criminally and treasonably led a large band to one of the said prior's tenements called the Temple, in Fleet Street. Farndon signalled to his followers to throw down the Temple forthwith and then went on with them to the manor of Savoy where he stayed until it was completely destroyed and burnt. Farndon then called to his companions and led them to the priory of Clerkenwell which he looted, spoiled and put to flames. He and his bands of rebels then entered the city of London and spent the night there. During the night Farndon entertained many of the principal insurgents, namely Robert de la Warde and others, and entered into a conspiracy with them: he outlined the names of those citizens (written down on a certain schedule) whom he wished to be executed and whose tenements he wanted to destroy. On the following Friday morning [14 June] the said Thomas Farndon went with his many accomplices to Highbury and there completely destroyed by fire the noble manor of the prior of St John's. Then he went with the evil malefactors to 'le Milende' where he met our lord the king. Farndon criminally, treasonably and irreverently grabbed the reins of the king's horse and as he detained the king, spoke the following or similar words: 'Revenge me on that false traitor the prior, for he has falsely and fraudulently seized my tenements; do right justice in my case and deign to restore my tenements to me; otherwise, know that I am strong enough to do justice on my own account and to secure my possession and entry into those tenements'. The king immediately told Farndon: 'You shall have what is just'. But Farndon continued his obduracy and went on to the Tower of London which he criminally and treasonably entered, not wishing to leave until both the archbishop and the said prior had been executed. Farndon then progressed through the city seeking those whom he could force to ransom themselves under threat to their life and limbs and others whose tenements he wished to destroy. But while Farndon was busy throwing down the tenement of John Knot in Stanynglane he was captured and taken to prison. Now Farndon stood first among all the chief rebels of the county of Essex; and they [the jurors] say that from Monday in

Whitsuntide week [3 June] until the day of his capture, he sustained his malevolence in collecting and assembling the said rebels and planning the death of the said prior. He did these things both criminally and treasonably, contrary to his faith and loyalty, and to the destruction of the king's position and the overturning of the king and kingdom.

The said jurors also declare that after William Walworth, then mayor, closed the gate of Aldgate by night on the eve of Corpus Christi [12 June], lest the malefactors from Essex should enter thereby, a certain William Tonge evilly opened the gate and allowed the commons to enter against the mayor's will.

Item, the jurors declare that Adam atte Welle and Roger Harry, butchers, encouraged and incited the rebels from Essex to come to London for fourteen days before they arrived in the city. Adam and Roger had promised the insurgents many things; and afterwards, on the Thursday of Corpus Christi [13 June], they treasonably led the said rebels into the city and on that day conducted a great crowd to the manor of the lord duke of Lancaster called Savoy. Adam and Roger, acting as the principal leaders and counsellors of the rebels, provoked the crowd to burn and loot the said manor; and they carried off many jewels and other goods to the value of £20. Moreover, on the following Friday [14 June], the said Adam criminally forced a certain Nicholas Wyght at the shambles in the parish of St Nicholas to ransom his head for twenty shillings.

In testimony of which things both the said sheriffs and the jurors have placed their seals alternately to this indenture and inquisition. Dated at London, 20 November [1382].

B. THE INQUISITION OF 4 NOVEMBER 1382

Coram Rege Roll, Easter 6 Richard II [KB. 27/488], Rex, memb. 6; printed by B. Wilkinson, 'The Peasants' Revolt of 1381', *Speculum*, xv (1940) 32–5; partly printed in Réville, pp. 196–8

Another inquisition taken before the aforesaid sheriffs follows in these words: –

An inquisition taken before John Sely and Adam Bamme, sheriffs of London, on 4 November in the sixth year of King Richard II on the oaths of Robert Yorke, Thomas Bristowe, William Whecerpele, Robert Lindesey, William Randolfe, Edward Yernemouth, Stephen atte Frith, John Trentemarz, Thomas Brehill, Stephen Hamme, William Sherewode and John Beauchamp in accordance with a certain royal writ addressed to the said sheriffs. This writ directed them to inquire through whose agency the commons of Kent and Essex (recently assembled in several large bands against the fealty and allegiance they owed to the lord king) had been incited to enter the city of London and its suburbs bearing standards displaying the royal arms and where they committed acts of treason, murders, killings, executions, the burning and destruction of houses as well as other intolerable and hitherto unheard-of evils; and [also to inquire] who, and under what circumstances, prevented William Walworth, then mayor of the said city, and others from closing the city gates and raising the city bridge so that they were unable to resist the said commons and deny them entry into the city; and also who, and under what circumstances, knowingly and with malice aforethought, nevertheless iniquitously and maliciously allowed them access to the city and the suburbs.

The jurors declare under oath that in the fourth year of the present king at about the end of Trinity[1] certain great and fearful rumours reached the ears of the then mayor, William Walworth, and almost all the citizens of London. They heard that many liegemen of our lord the king in the counties of Kent and Essex had laid aside the loyalty which they owed to the king and had risen against his peace to the manifest disturbance of all his realm. In order to achieve more easily the evil aims they had long planned they assembled in several large bands. Accordingly, and in order to avoid the dangers which seemed likely to beset the king and the city, the said mayor (with the consent of the aldermen and the community of the city) sent into Kent on the Wednesday after Trinity [12 June] certain aldermen, appointed

1 Trinity Sunday fell on 9 June in 1381.

in his presence within the city, namely John Horn, fishmonger, Adam Carlel, grocer, and John Fressh, mercer. The mayor especially commanded them on behalf of the whole city that as soon as they met the rebel people they should carefully reconnoitre their bands and battle-order. Moreover, these aldermen were ordered to negotiate sensibly with the said multitude or at least with the chief leaders and persuade them not to disturb our lord the king at all but behave well, loyally and reverently towards him in all things as they ought. The envoys were asked to inform the rebels that our lord the king was then within the city and so they should not approach the city or its suburbs nor molest either the goods or the persons of the Londoners or those who were staying in the city.

Accordingly the said John Horn, Adam and John Fressh met that malicious band at or near Blackheath and conveyed the gist of the message with which they had been entrusted. But the jurors declare that at the same time the said John Horn left Adam and John Fressh and went on by himself to the place where the rebels were most thickly assembled; and against the purpose of his mission he negotiated and conspired deceitfully and treacherously with the chief leaders of the malefactors, comforting them maliciously and promising them the friendship and assistance of the entire city: he said that the rebels would have all the food and other things they needed if they decided to enter London. And so Horn disloyally and treacherously persuaded and incited the rebels to come to London against the peace of the lord king and the city. For which reason on the same Wednesday those same evildoers came to Southwark and broke open the royal prison of Marshalsea.

The jurors also declare under their oath that on the following day, Thursday 13 June, the same John Horn rode again to the said malefactors and handed over to them a certain standard bearing the arms of the lord king which he had brought with him from the city. With this standard openly displayed on a long lance carried before them, he treacherously brought Walter Tylere, Robert de la Warde, Thomas Hauk, Alan Thredere and many of the other principal leaders of the rebels (who were afterwards convicted for their offences and adjudged to death by the law of the realm) with their bands of innumerable fellows into the city. Horn's fellow-conspirator and principal colleague was a certain Walter Sybyle, stockfishmonger, then an alderman, who acted as his chief helper and assistant in introducing the malicious mob into the city.

The jurors also declare on their oath that the same Walter Sybyle maliciously opened the gates of the city, closed against the said evildoers by Mayor Walworth, in connivance with the said John Horn. Similarly, Walter Sybyle prevented many men of the city who wished to close the gates, defend them against the malefactors and draw up the bridge, from doing so. In the following, or similar, arrogant and insulting fashion, Sybyle told them, 'You do this; return to keep your own Wards or houses for no one is to interfere in my Ward except myself and my own fellows who are well able to do all that is necessary without further help'. He did this notwithstanding the fact that the royal prison of the Marshalsea in Southwark had (as has been said) been broken into by the said malefactors on the previous Wednesday and all the prisoners led out by the rebels, and that on that very Thursday a tenement near the end of the bridge had been pulled to the ground and many other enormities committed by the rebels. When all these matters were mentioned to Walter Sybyle, he nevertheless spoke to all the bystanders who could hear him above the tumult of the people, in the following or similar terms about the said malefactors: 'These Kentishmen are good men and our friends; God forbid that the gates should be closed or any resistance be offered to them'. Because of these words, many of the citizens then present, defensively armed and ready and probably able to prevent the entry of the rebels, departed and did not return to resist the rebels any further. And so this same Walter Sybyle maliciously and treacherously allowed the malefactors to enter, and offered them free entry at their pleasure – against the peace of the king and city and his own liegance when, as an alderman, he ought and could have

prevented them if he had wished. From this crime there followed
the horrible evils and iniquities committed by the said malefactors
in London and its suburbs on that Wednesday [sic] and the following three days, namely, the breaking open of royal prisons, the
beheading of prelates and others faithful to our lord the king,
the violation of churches, and the burning, destruction and looting
of the houses of the Savoy, the hospital of St John the Baptist
next to Smithfield and many others, all the horrible result of the
previous counsel and help given to Walter Tylere and his fellows
by the said John Horn and Walter Sybyle.

The jurors also declare under their oath that on the Friday
[14 June] immediately following the introduction of the said
evildoers into London by John Horn and Walter Sybyle as has
been said, the same John Horn led with him a large band of the
said armed malefactors, whose numbers at that time no one
could easily diminish. With the standard already mentioned, or
one similar to it, openly displayed and carried before him,
Horn went up to the tenement of a certain Richard Toky
situated in Lombard Street, London. He expelled Richard and
his tenants from the property and placed a certain woman called
Matilda Toky there instead. Taking royal power on himself,
he adjudged that all the goods then found in Richard Toky's
tenements should go to Matilda as her damages; and he ordered
that these goods should be delivered to her, notwithstanding that
by virtue of his aldermanic office he ought to have especially preserved the peace of the king and city, particularly within the city itself.

Item, the jurors declare under oath that on the Saturday after
Trinity [15 June] when Walter Tylere, the principal leader of the
said malefactors, had by the grace of God been killed in Smithfield and our lord king with his retinue was there in much
difficulty and in great danger of losing his life, Walter Sybyle
with the connivance of the said John Horn left Smithfield where
he had been present. Entering the city, Sybyle deceitfully and
treacherously closed Aldersgate and prevented many men of the
city from passing through this gate to go to the help of the king.
In a loud voice, Sybyle cried, 'Close the gates of the city quickly,

guard them and stay within the walls for our king and mayor have died in Smithfield,' although he knew the contrary to be the truth. Because of these deceitful words many and indeed almost all then gave up their attempt to aid the king; and if it had not been for the rapid arrival, thanks to God, of the mayor himself, who informed the people that Walter Sybyle's news was false and urged them to rescue the lord king bravely and without any delay, the king would have remained almost alone among his enemies, in great danger to himself and his whole realm, without the assistance of the city.

Item, the jurors state under oath that a certain William Tonge, then an alderman, on the said Wednesday [12 June] opened the gate of Aldgate at night and allowed the bands to enter thereby; although this gate had been closed by the said mayor in order to keep out enemies, namely the mobs from the county of Essex who had risen against the king's peace with the connivance of the Kentishmen. Immediately they had entered the city, the rebels from Essex joined forces with the said malefactors from Kent and together with their adherents perpetrated all the said ills. But they [the jurors] do not at present know whether William Tonge had Aldgate opened because of his own malice, because he was in league with John Horn and Walter Sybyle, or because he was frightened by the threats of the malefactors from Kent who were already within the city.[1]

Item, the jurors declare under their oath that a certain Adam atte Welle, then a butcher at the shambles of St Nicholas, London, and now a provider of victuals to the lord duke of Lancaster, travelled into Essex fourteen days before the arrival of the rebels from that county in the city of London; there Adam incited and encouraged the rebels of Essex to come to London and promised them many things if they did so. Afterwards, on Thursday 13 June, Adam brought the Essex men into London and led them in a great crowd to the manor of the said duke, the Savoy, where (as their chief leader and councillor) he

---

[1] But the jurors had already declared (p. 222) that the men of Kent entered the city on 13 June. See also the next paragraph.

provoked them to burn and plunder the manor. Adam himself criminally carried off many jewels and other things from the Savoy valued at more than twenty pounds sterling. Later, and on the next day, Adam made a certain Nicholas Wyghte, a tailor living near the aforesaid shambles, ransom his life for twenty shillings sterling.

And the jurors declare under oath that at present they do not know the names of many men who were chiefly responsible for inciting the said malefactors to enter the city, for bringing them within and allowing them to enter out of malice – except for those who for this reason received the just judgment of death by the law of the realm, and others who besought charters of remission from the king concerning such misdeeds before the date of this inquisition.

In testimony of which things, the said sheriffs and inquisitors have alternately applied their seals to this indenture and inquisition. Dated at London on 4 November [1382].

33 The Indictment of Walter atte Keye, Brewer, of Wood Street, London

Coram Rege Roll, Michaelmas 5 Richard II [KB. 27/482], Rex, memb. 43; partly printed in Réville, p. 206

In addition to the sheriffs' inquisitions of November 1382, legal records survive for the trials of more than a dozen Londoners. Perhaps the most intriguing is the indictment made against an obscure brewer, Walter atte Keye. According to the jurors, Walter and his companions planned to burn down the London Guildhall on Friday 14 June – one of the very few pieces of evidence to indicate the existence of a group of rebels prepared to challenge the authority of the civic hierarchy as well as that of royal officials and agents. It is impossible to do more than speculate as to the reasons for Walter atte Keye's frenzied search for the 'Jubilee Book' as the exact nature of this controversial volume remains a mystery. It was revised in 1384 during the mayoralty of Nicholas Brembre and was finally burnt on the orders of the mayor and council in March 1387.[1]

The lord king sent to his beloved and faithful William Walworth his letters close in these words: 'Richard, by the grace of God, king of England and France and lord of Ireland, to his beloved and faithful William Walworth, greetings. Wishing for various reasons (on a matter touching the indictments made before you and your colleagues, appointed as our justices to hear and determine various treasons, felonies, transgressions and injuries committed in our city of London and elsewhere) to determine before ourselves and not elsewhere the case of Walter atte Keye, brewer, of Wood Street, indicted for various treasons etc.; we order you to send openly and clearly the relevant indictments with all pertaining to them together with this writ – so that we should receive them by next Saturday wherever we are in the kingdom. We will then be able to act lawfully as the law and custom of the realm demands. Witnessed by myself at Westminster, 20 November [1381]'.

The indictments of which mention is made in this writ are as follows: – The jurors state that Walter atte Keye, leading a company of other malefactors, came to the house of Andrew Vernoun, brewer, at Paul's Wharf, London, on the said Friday [14 June]. Walter criminally and treasonably forced his way into the said house and threatened to kill Andrew and destroy his house unless the latter paid a fine to him. In face of these threats, and in fear of his life, Andrew paid a fine of 3s 4d which Walter received despite its criminal and treasonable form. Accordingly Walter was a common malefactor to take such fines, as he did with many men in the said city of London.

Item, the jurors state that Walter atte Keye, brewer of Wood Street, was one of the principal malefactors in that, together with

[1] *Calendar of London Letter Book L*, pp. 235, 303.

many other rebels unknown to the jurors, he came to the London Guild Hall (in the parish of St Laurence, Old Jewry) on the Friday after Corpus Christi [14 June]. Walter criminally and treasonably brought fire with him in order to burn the Guild Hall and a certain book called 'le Jubyle'. Moreover, on that same Friday, Walter was present with the said malefactors when the king's Compter in Milk Street was broken into and despoiled; and he performed many other illegal actions against the peace and, for this reason, he later fled.

Item, the jurors state that Walter atte Keye, brewer of Wood Street, was one of the rebels, etc., and led many other insurgents to the king's Compter in Milk Street on Friday after Corpus Christi [14 June]. While there, Walter was one of the chief malefactors in breaking into and despoiling the Compter and the chests therein: he was looking for a book concerning the constitutions of the city of London (called 'le Jubyle') in order to burn it if he could find it. Walter did other evil things there and for that reason he later fled. He has no chattels to confiscate.

34 Royal Letters of Pardon to Paul Salesbury of London

Patent Roll, 5 Richard II, part I [C. 66/311], memb. 31; partly printed in Réville, pp. 207–9. Cf. *C.P.R.*, *1381–5*, pp. 30–1

Although usually much less informative than the records of jurors' presentments, several of the letters of pardon granted by Richard II to individuals charged with offences during the rebellion preserve interesting circumstantial detail. The pardon conceded to Paul Salesbury late in July 1381 is one example: it reveals the way in which many Londoners took the opportunity of the turmoil in the city –

especially on Friday 14 June, the most turbulent day – to foreclose on city property which they believed, rightly or wrongly, to be legally theirs. Less typical of the rebels was Salesbury himself, the son of Sir Thomas Salesbury, knight. His two victims, William Baret and Hugh Fastolf, were both grocers and aldermen, prominent members of the civic oligarchy of the period.

The king to all bailiffs and faithful men to whom, etc. We have learnt that Paul Salesbury is indicted as one of the rebels who rose against us and our liegance. In that tumultuous time, namely on Friday 14 June last, Paul assembled his servant Thomas[1] and many other hired malefactors whose names are unknown but who rose against us; and he is reputed to have gone to the house of William Baret, alderman of London, situated in the parish of St Mary Bothawe. Paul and the said malefactors, armed with swords and staffs, criminally entered William's house and forcibly seized it to his own use. He then expelled William from the said house as well as his wife and all his servants, who were compelled to leave for fear of their death and were forced to stand in the high street outside their door. Paul then compelled William's wife to kneel before him for a long time; both she and her husband had to thank him for their long habitation of the said house as well as for their lives. Paul is also indicted because he and the said malefactors made William deliver to him there and under fear for his life two indentures (which contained matter relating to William's title to the said hospice as leased to him by Paul's father) as well as a schedule concerning a bond for £200 made by the latter in our chancery. Paul also made William deliver up to him all his title to the said house and forced him, on fear of death, to transfer it by a penny to himself as his lord; and at the same time he made William take an oath before the malefactors that he would release him [Paul] from the said bond at some later time when it pleased him.

[1] Unlike his master, Thomas was not pardoned at this time; and he appears on the list of those specifically excluded from the general pardon enacted at the parliament of November 1381 (*Rot. Parl.*, III 113).

Similarly, the said Paul is charged because on the said Friday and in the same way, he came with the aforementioned malefactors to the house of Hugh Fastolf in the parish of St Dunstan in the East and near the Tower of London, in Thames Street and adjoining the Thames. Paul treasonably entered the said house, claiming it as his own, and (with the armed help of the said traitors) made an assault on other tenements annexed to it and on the person of Joan, the wife of Hugh Fastolf. He made her deliver up to him the following: an indenture by which Thomas de Salesbury, knight, leased the said tenements to Hugh for the term of his life; a written statement of the annual rent of £20 to be received by Hugh for the term of his life from the lands and tenements of the said Thomas in London, its suburbs and the county of Essex; an indentured deed concerning the conditions by which this annual rent might be released; a deed by which the said Thomas granted the said tenements to the late Reginald Love for a term of years; and a box in which these writings were kept. And Paul and his companions are charged with treasonably taking and carrying off a sword valued at forty shillings and a pair of iron gauntlets worth ten shillings; and with drinking and wasting six casks of ale and a pipe of wine, valued at one hundred shillings, belonging to the said Hugh and found there. They also made threats against the said Hugh, declaring that he would have been beheaded if they had found him there. And Paul is also charged with making the said Joan transfer the title of that property to Paul, forcing her to pay a penny as a sign of seisin of the said tenements.

However we of our special grace have pardoned the said Paul from the suit of peace which belongs to us for all the treasons, felonies and transgressions of which he stands indicted, charged and appealed; and we also pardon him of any outlawries which he may have incurred because of the said offences, and grant him our firm peace: provided that he makes due answer in our court if either or both the said William and Hugh wish to implead him for these offences. In testimony, etc. Witnessed by the king at Berkhampstead, 22 July (1381).

PART IV

The Rising in the Eastern Counties

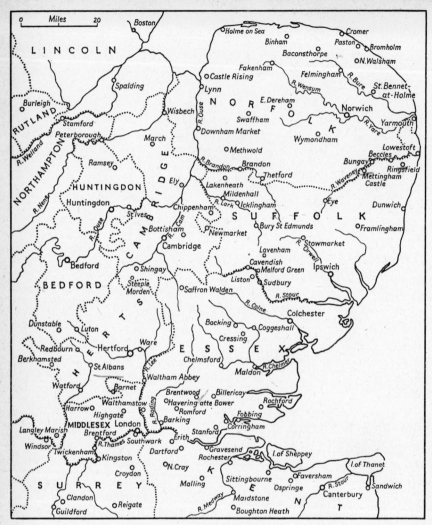

Eastern England in 1381

Inevitably overshadowed by the high drama of events in London, the riots and risings in the eastern counties of England are nevertheless an astonishing phenomenon in their own right. For periods of between a weekend and a fortnight much of East Anglia was plunged into a state of near anarchy: in many areas the forces of law and order collapsed in a way not to be paralleled until the days of Kett's rebellion in 1549. Although it would be an exaggeration to claim that the whole of eastern England was affected by the risings, it does seem to be the case that in June 1381 Norfolk, Suffolk and even Cambridgeshire were on the verge of experiencing a general revolution. Our knowledge of the activities of the rebels in these counties largely derives from the numerous if scattered legal records produced during the subsequent repression of the revolt. Some of the more violent and news-worthy incidents of the rebellion in eastern England did attract the brief attention of the chroniclers of the year (see below, nos. 35, 36, 38, 41, 42); but unfortunately there exists no sustained and comprehensive narrative of the revolt written by an author with first-hand experience of conditions in East Anglia.

As it is, the surviving evidence suggests that the eastern risings were highly local in character – a fact which obviously makes it impossible to generalise with confidence. Edgar Powell's view that these revolts were 'the matured result of a comprehensive plan, carried out by means of a more or less perfect organisation, extending throughout the Eastern Counties'[1] is hard to reconcile with the results of his own researches. Although Powell exaggerated the role and significance of the mysterious 'great society' occasionally mentioned in indictments (see below, no. 40), East Anglian burgesses and peasants were of course aware of the precedents set by the men of Kent and Essex. No record survives of serious rioting in the eastern counties until after Tyler and his company had begun their march on London. Without the stimulus provided by the risings farther south it seems unlikely that East Anglia would have

[1] Powell, *Rising in East Anglia*, p. 57.

suffered from a series of general revolts. The informal contacts between the rebels in London and those in eastern England were however influential without necessarily dictating the form that the rebellion took in Norfolk, Suffolk and Cambridgeshire. Particularly complex, for example, were developments in the towns of Cambridge and Bury St Edmunds (nos. 37 and 38), where the burgesses' attacks on great ecclesiastical corporations were in part promoted and in part prejudiced by an uneasy alliance with neighbouring bands of country rebels. Here as elsewhere the emergence of a successful leader seems to have been the decisive factor in determining whether or not the rebels would retain sufficient cohesion to present a sustained threat to the political and social order. The 'imfamous priest' John Wrawe seems to have imposed his authority on the insurgents in western Suffolk because of his audacity as well as other less admirable qualities (nos. 38, 39). More attractive and potentially more formidable was the 'idol Northfolkorum', Geoffrey Litster, who led a group of rebels drawn from widely different social backgrounds in a 'backwoods' provincial revolt against the English government (no. 41).

35 The Risings in the Eastern Counties according to the 'Anonimalle Chronicle'

Anonimalle Chronicle, pp. 150–1: continued from no. 25 above. Cf. Oman, *Great Revolt*, pp. 203–5

The following short account of outbreaks of revolt in the Eastern Counties was added by the author of the *Anonimalle Chronicle* to his much longer and more detailed description of events in London during the week ending on Saturday, 15 June. Despite its brevity, it serves as an excellent introduction to the confused story of the many riots in eastern England during the summer of 1381. The author is clearly much less concerned and well-informed about the disturbances in the provinces than those in the capital. But he correctly identifies the towns of Ramsey and Bury St Edmunds and also the county of Norfolk as the centres of exceptionally dangerous risings. The *Anonimalle Chronicle*'s account of the resistance to the rebels offered by the town of Huntingdon can be confirmed from other sources, notably the preamble to a royal charter of 12 December 1381 which thanked the borough for its loyalty during the previous summer. Huntingdon therefore presents an apparently unique case of a town in eastern England prepared to repel the rebels by armed force.

Meanwhile a party of the commons took their way towards Huntingdon in order to pass towards the north, where in their malice and villainy they intended to ravage the land and destroy good men; but they were turned back and could not pass the bridge of that town because William Wightman, spigurnel of Chancery,[1] Walter of Rudham and other good men of the town of Huntingdon and the neighbouring country met them at the bridge and gave them battle, killing two or three of the commons.

[1] i.e. a sealer of Chancery writs. On 22 May 1382 William Wightman was granted a royal pension of 6d daily for his services in repelling the commons at Huntingdon (*C.P.R., 1381–5*, p. 120).

Therefore the rest were glad to fly and went to Ramsey in order
to pass that way. They took shelter in the town there and sent to
the abbey [of Ramsey] for victuals to comfort and refresh them.
The abbot accordingly sent them bread, wine, ale and other
victuals in large quantities for he dared not do otherwise. The
rebels ate and drank to satiety, and afterwards slept late into the
morning, to their own confusion. For meanwhile the men of
Huntingdon rose, combined with others from the countryside
and suddenly fell on the commons at Ramsey, killing twenty-
four of them.[1] The others fled without delay; and many were
killed as they passed through the countryside and their heads
placed on high trees to serve as an example to others.

At the same time a great number of commons rose in Suffolk
and had as their chieftain a Suffolk chaplain, lord John Wraw by
name, who led with him more than ten thousand men. They
robbed many good men and threw their houses to the ground and
put them to fire and the said John sought to have gold and silver
for his own needs. He and his men came to Cambridge[2] where
they did great damage by burning houses; and then they went to
Bury, where they found in the town a justice of the law, Sir John
de Cavendish, Chief [Justice] of the King's Bench. They led him
to the pillory, cut off his head and set it on the said pillory. Afterwards they dragged out of the abbey [of Bury St Edmunds] its
prior, a good, wise man and an excellent singer, as well as
another monk, and cut off their heads at the pillory. The rebels
put their heads on poles above the pillory so that all who passed
along the street could see them; but the said John [Wraw], their
chieftain, was later taken as a traitor and led to London, where he
was condemned to death and drawn, disembowelled, hanged
and beheaded.

At this time a great number of men rose in Norfolk and did
great harm throughout the countryside. For which reason, the

[1] The *Anonimalle Chronicle* is probably confused here. It was Bishop Henry
Despenser of Norwich who dispersed the rebel band which was blackmailing
the abbot of Ramsey – at a skirmish which took place on 18 June.

[2] Probably a mistake for Cavendish on the river Stour where Sir John Cavendish
stored his valuables in the church tower (see below, no. 39).

bishop of Norwich, lord Henry Lespenser [Despenser] sent letters to the said commons instructing them to cease their malice and return to their own houses without doing any more harm or mischief.[1] But they would not do so and went through the land, destroying and wasting many towns and the houses of various people. During this period they met a brave and vigorous knight, Sir Robert Salle by name; but he was a great fighter and robber and they cut off his head. Therefore the said bishop collected many men-at-arms and archers and he attacked the rebels in several places wherever he could find them; and he captured many of them. The said bishop made them confess and then had them beheaded for their evil deeds. And so the said commons wandered throughout the countryside because of their crimes and mischiefs as well as their fear of the king and the lords; and they took to flight like beasts that run to earth. [*Continued by no. 52 below, p. 305.*]

36 The Risings in the Eastern Counties according to Henry Knighton

Chronicon Henrici Knighton, II 140–1

Henry Knighton is the primary authority for the existence of a general rising against the abbot of Peterborough. This revolt, presumably inspired by the disturbances in the neighbouring counties of Cambridge and Huntingdon, apparently occurred on Monday 17 June and was crushed by Bishop Henry Despenser of Norwich on the following day. The bishop then moved onwards to suppress the revolts in Cambridge and Norfolk (see below, no. 41).

[1] A study of Bishop Despenser's rapid movements during June 1381 shows that, if he did send letters to the Norfolk rebels, he can hardly have waited for an answer.

In Essex, Suffolk and Norfolk, the commons likewise rose in large numbers at various places, did many wrongs and beheaded many worthy men. What is more they employed the same method of murder everywhere. They beheaded John de Cavendish, chief justice of the king, and also executed lord Robert Salle, a knight famed for his valour in battle. And so enormous and unparalleled ills befell not only one area but much of the country.

Likewise at Peterborough the neighbours and tenants of the abbot rose against him and proposed to kill him – which they would have done without redress had God not laid his restraining hand upon them at the last moment. For help came in the shape of lord Henry le Spenser, bishop of Norwich, who, through the agency of divine mercy, arrived with a strong armed force. He prevented the malefactors from carrying out their aims and scattered the mob, paying them back as they deserved. Sparing no one, he sent some to death and others to prison. Several of the rebels fled to the church for protection but fell into the pit of perdition they had dug themselves: for those who had not feared to destroy the ramparts of the church did not deserve its immunity. Some were struck down with swords and spears near the altar and others at the church walls, both inside and outside the building. Just as they had spared no one from their own furious vengeance, so the bishop's eye now spared none of them – he repaid them in like kind and measure for measure. Because they had come to destroy the church and churchmen I dare to say that they deserved to perish at the hands of an ecclesiastic. For the bishop gladly stretched his avenging hand over them and did not scruple to give them final absolution for their sins with his sword. So was fulfilled the saying of the prophet: 'You will rule them with iron rods, and break them like a potter's vessel' [Ps. ii, 9]. This vigorous bishop took similar measures at various places in the counties of Cambridge and Huntingdon: wherever he heard of rebels, he immediately went to meet and disperse them, crushing their arrogance at its root. [*Continued by no. 44 below, p. 277.*]

37 The Rising in Cambridge according to the Rolls of Parliament

Rot. Parl., III 108

Although murder seems to have been relatively uncommon during the Cambridgeshire riots of 1381, the county was a centre of exceptional if short-lived upheaval during the week-end between Thursday 13 and Monday 17 June. Legal records for the risings in this county survive in considerable number and the course of events there has been described several times in varying degrees of detail.[1] Two distinct revolts in the north-east and south-west of the shire appear to have been motivated by hatred of the poll tax commissioners and other royal officials. In the Isle of Ely, on the other hand, the grievances of the rebels were largely economic in character and led to scenes of greater violence. Even more interesting is the rising in the town of Cambridge itself where the disturbances took the unique form of an attempt by the burgesses to exploit the situation in the interests of paying off old grudges against the university in general and two wealthy ecclesiastical corporations in particular – Corpus Christi College and the neighbouring priory of Barnwell. As the following extracts from the parliament roll suggest, the Cambridge burgesses began their campaign of terror on Saturday 15 June when they joined a confederation of county rebels, led by two substantial landowners, John Hanchach and Geoffrey Cobbe, in an attack on the manors of Thomas Haselden, fifteen miles south-west of the town. The risings in both borough and county came to an abrupt end (as did Hanchach's life) in the middle of the next week when Bishop Despenser arrived in Cambridge fresh from his triumph at Ramsey (see above, no. 35).

... a bill concerning certain articles maintained in parliament against the mayor and burgesses [of Cambridge], in the following form:

[1] Powell, *Rising in East Anglia*, pp. 41–56; Réville, pp. 241–50; *V.C.H. Cambridge*, II 398–402, a particularly illuminating analysis by H. C. Darby and E. Miller. For the rising in Cambridge itself see *V.C.H. Cambridge*, III 8–12.

9

54. Be it remembered that on Saturday 15 June the bailiffs and commonalty of burgesses of the town of Cambridge, on the advice and common assent of themselves and their mayor, assembled together and rode to the hospital of Shingay and the house of Thomas Haselden, six leagues and more outside the said town of Cambridge.[1] There they met many traitors and enemies of the king who had risen against him and his crown in the county of Cambridge; and they conspired together to commit the damages mentioned below.

Item, on the same day and after their return to the town hall (*l'Ostiel*), the mayor, bailiffs, burgesses and commonalty of the said town made a solemn proclamation and cry; and with one assent, they went up to the Tollbooth of the town and there elected Jakes of Grantchester as their captain, making him swear, under threat of his death, to be their loyal captain and governor.

Item, immediately afterwards the mayor, bailiffs, burgesses and commonalty of the said town with one accord and assent made the said Jakes and his brother Thomas free burgesses of the said town of Cambridge.

Item, the mayor, bailiffs, burgesses and commonalty of the said town assembled at the Tollbooth at about ten of the clock on the following night. There they took council and made a proclamation that everyone should go and break down the house of William Bedell[2] of the said town. And if anyone were to meet or find the said William they should cut off his head. Accordingly, the said mayor, bailiffs, burgesses and the commonalty went and destroyed William Bedell's house, where they seized and carried off his very valuable goods and chattels.

Item, the mayor, bailiffs, burgesses and the commonalty aforesaid went to Corpus Christi College, of the foundation of our

---

[1] Haselden was controller of John of Gaunt's household, which may account for the savage attack on his manors at Steeple Morden and Gilden Morden. The hospital of Shingay, one of the Knights Hospitallers' houses, was two miles nearer Cambridge.

[2] i.e. bedel of the university, whose Chancellor in 1381 was the hated John Cavendish, murdered on 14 June.

most excellent lord of Lancaster; then they broke into the enclo-
sure of the college and the dwellings of its scholars. They seized and
carried off their charters, writings, books and other muniments
as well as other goods and chattels of great value.

Item, on the following Sunday the said burgesses and commonalty assembled in great bands and rode out of the said town to
meet the traitors and king's enemies in the county of Cambridge.
They led them into the town, which the rebels would not have
dared approach without the assent of the said burgesses and
commonalty.

Item, on the same day the mayor, bailiffs, burgesses and commonalty of the said town compelled the masters and scholars of
the said university, under pain of death and destruction of their
houses, to renounce all kind of franchises and privileges granted
to them by all kings of England since the beginning of the
world; and they also made the said masters and scholars submit
to the rules and governances of the said burgesses for all time.

Item, the said mayor, bailiffs, burgesses and commonalty
compelled the said masters and scholars under threat of their
deaths to enter into bonds by which large sums of money might
be paid to the aforesaid burgesses. Their purpose was to release
each burgess of the town, before the king or anyone else, from
any recognition or bond resulting from any previous dispute or
strife between the masters and the scholars on the one side and
the burgesses of the town on the other. Under this duress, the
master and scholars were compelled to issue a general acquittance
from all kinds of action, real and personal. This acquittance,
together with the aforementioned bonds, was delivered to the
mayor, bailiffs and commonalty and placed in their treasury for
safe-keeping.

Item, the mayor, bailiffs, burgesses and commonalty compelled
the said masters and scholars under threat of death to deliver and
hand over to them their charters and privileges as well as the
letters patent sealed under the present king's seal and granted to
the university. They then burnt these documents in the market
place of the said town and completely obliterated the seals of the

said charters and letters patent with knives, sticks and other weapons, to the contempt of our lord the king.

Item, after the king's letters patent had been sent to the town of Cambridge where it was consequently proclaimed that every man (under penalty of losing life and limb and all things that could be forfeited) should remain in peace and aloof from any assemblies or conventicles or any other type of affray, the said mayor, bailiffs, burgesses and commonalty gathered to themselves a large number of other traitors and enemies to the king and made a proclamation in a meadow called Grenecroft near the town of Cambridge. Afterwards, with one accord and assent, they went to the priory of Barnwell and broke down the close there in a warlike manner. They cut down and carried off large numbers of trees growing there and committed other serious breaches of the peace.

Item, the said mayor, bailiffs, burgesses and commonalty, after the above-mentioned proclamation of the royal letters patent, seized and burnt the statutes, ordinances and many other evidences of the said university, to the contempt of the king and against the said letters patent.

[The mayor and bailiffs answered these charges in parliament; and argued that the disturbances in their town were due to the 'traitors and malefactors of the counties of Essex, Hertford and Kent' together with 'a certain small number of malefactors and rioters of their town' – an excuse which the government quite rightly refused to accept. The liberties of the borough were (at least in theory) seized into the king's hands before the burgesses were eventually pardoned in the autumn parliament of 1381].

38 John Wrawe and the Burgesses of Bury St Edmunds according to Thomas Walsingham

Walsingham, *Historia Anglicana*, II 1–4; cf. *Chronicon Angliae*, pp. 301–4

With the exception of the violent scenes in London between 13 and 15 June, no series of episodes during the Peasants' Revolt is better documented than those which took place in western Suffolk during the same week. After the murder of John Cavendish, Chief Justice of the King's Bench, on Friday 14 June, the disturbances came to centre on the town of Bury St Edmunds and, more especially, on its long and stormy relationship with the great Benedictine monastery there. This abbey suffered more severely at the hands of the rebels of 1381 than any other religious house in England – partly because of the vicious character of the local leader, John Wrawe, a poor clerk with few redeeming features (see below, no. 39). Walsingham, whose account of the rising is translated here, was probably informed about events there by a fellow Benedictine monk from the abbey of Bury St Edmunds who convinced him that the monastery's real enemies were the burgesses or 'villeins' of Bury. Although the townspeople gradually became aware of the need to disassociate themselves from the more violent actions of the unscrupulous Wrawe, their guilt was generally admitted. Bury was the single English town excluded from the royal amnesty proclaimed in December 1381; and its inhabitants only finished paying off a heavy fine of 2000 marks in January 1386.

A confused series of events happening simultaneously in many places necessitates a disordered way of writing history: hardly any logical order of composition can be maintained when so many crimes were committed in so many different areas at the same time. For, behold! while writing of the great and extraordinary atrocities which took place in London on Friday and Saturday [14 and 15 June], I am scarcely able to expound the tragedy of these events before it is necessary to write of the similar scenes at St Albans during the same days, as described above [see below, no. 43]. Nor can I enlarge upon the misery experienced at St Albans before other equally or even more shameful and notable examples of iniquity have to be considered.

On that same Saturday,[1] so general seemed to be the prevailing tempest, God showed the anger of his displeasure in the areas of Suffolk and Norfolk. There He sent as His harbingers of suffering certain wicked angels, namely some of the most dangerous men from the perfidious inhabitants of Essex; they were angels of Satan who incited a peaceful and innocent people to disturbances similar to their own, and turned the hearts of the serfs against their lords. Proving more active than farsighted, and led by a most scandalous priest called John Wraw who had been in London on the previous day and had been instructed by the aforementioned ruffian, Walter Tyler,[2] they immediately and easily assembled a mob, whose number is said to have exceeded fifty thousand people. This mob, like that which had run wild in London, stormed everywhere, destroying the houses and estates of the great men and lawyers and killing apprentices of the law. They captured Lord John Cavendish, Chief Justice of the kingdom, beheaded him and shamefully placed his head on the pillory in the market-place of Bury St Edmunds.[3] They suddenly captured the prior of Bury St Edmunds while he was striving to escape from them and cruelly put him to death by execution: lord John de Cambridge, this prior, was a worthy and artistic man, surpassing in the sweetness of his voice and his musical skill the Thracian Orpheus, the Roman Nero and the British Belga-

[1] It was on Wednesday 12 June, not three days later, that John Wrawe began to lead a serious rebellion centred on Sudbury (see below, no. 39); but Walsingham's view that the outbreak in western Suffolk owed much to the stimulus of the earlier rising in Essex has been confirmed by other sources.

[2] Réville (pp. 60-2) proved that the chronology of the risings in London and Suffolk made it impossible for Wrawe to have been in contact with Tyler on the day suggested by Walsingham. It seems highly improbable that the two men ever met.

[3] Sir John Cavendish was murdered at Lakenheath, near the edge of the Fens, on 14 June: see below, p. 255.

bred.[1] The cause of the prior's death was well known. As he was a circumspect and prudent man, he took care to protect the rights of his monastery; and because he had faithfully fought for his monastery's rights against the villeins of Bury, he was (as we have said) killed near the town of Mildenhall, which is known to belong to the jurisdiction of the abbey: but he was condemned to death not by the villeins of the said town of Bury, his adversaries, but by the decision and judgment of his own serfs and villeins. His body was stripped to his shirt and drawers; and he lay unburied in an open field for five days as no one dared to carry him away or deal with the body in the proper way for fear of the fury of the rustics.

After this horrible sin had been committed, John Wraw and his band, the leaders of the perfidious people, went on their way to the town of Bury. As no one opposed them, they entered the town and marched around as if in a procession, carrying the said prior's head high on a lance in full view of the townsmen until they reached the pillory. Then, in recognition of the previous friendship between the prior and John Cavendish and to pour scorn on both, they held together the two heads on the tops of the lances as if they were talking or kissing each other – an absurdly improper action. Later, when they were tired of such jests, they placed both heads above the pillory again. Soon afterwards, in hatred of the prior, they destroyed a house which he had built and had constructed anew from its foundations. After this, they entered the cloister of the monastery [of Bury St Edmunds] and demanded that lord John de Lakenheath, the keeper of the abbey's barony, be handed over to them under the threat of burning down the monastery if this was not done. But when Lakenheath stood before them, marvellous to relate, there was not one of the rebels who knew him. For all these crimes were committed at the instigation of the [Bury] villeins who had persuaded the rebels to act (as will easily be proved by what

1 King Belgabred of Britain, 'the god of minstrels', figures briefly in Geoffrey of Monmouth's *History of the Kings of Britain*. Prior Cambridge was beheaded at Mildenhall on the morning of 15 June.

follows) while themselves remaining aloof from the mob so as to seem innocent of such scandalous behaviour. Therefore the said John, wishing to save his monastery from danger, replied that he was the man they sought and asked what the commons requested. To which they replied, 'We seek your instant death, traitor; for you cannot prolong your life any longer'. John Lakenheath replied, 'I am prepared for death and will willingly embrace it; but on the condition that this monastery should not suffer any harm because of me'. And then he was dragged away by the rebels amid great shouts that they had found a false monk and were leading a traitor to justice; he was then beheaded in the market place after it had taken eight strokes to separate his head from his body. The rebels then placed Lakenheath's head above the pillory by the side of that of his prior. Not content with this, they sought to send another monk, namely Walter Todyngtone, to a similar death; but as he hid himself most carefully, they could not find him and he escaped with his life.

Afterwards, having called together all the monks, the rebels told them that for a long time they had oppressed by their power their own fellows, the burgesses of Bury. Therefore they willed that, in full view of the commons, the monks should return the bonds by which the burgesses were bound to the king and the monastery if they attempted any action against the abbey; and also return the charters of liberties of the town which Cnut, the founder of the monastery, had once granted, and which his successors as kings to the present day had conceded for the security of the abbey. Now the monks, fearing for themselves and their house if they did not obey the will of the commons, brought forward in the market place everything which was requested, whether it helped or injured the cause of the villeins; and they swore that they could not find any more charters, which might be of use to the villeins, in their possession. But the commons scarcely put any trust in what the monks said; and having summoned the villeins of the town (who pretended to be sad about these matters as though what was being done displeased them) they ordered them to undertake a careful inspection of the said bonds and charters. And if the old liberties which they used to enjoy did not emerge from a reading of these documents, they were to declare it. And the rebels proposed to release as abbot [of Bury St Edmunds] Edmund Brounfeld, who lay in prison at Nottingham,[1] in time to celebrate divine services in his monastery on the following feast of St John the Baptist [24 June]; and forty days after his arrival, Brounfeld would attach his seal to a charter they had drawn up, the convent agreeing to do the same with their common seal.

The monks were so frightened and under such pressure from the commons that they assented to these demands and all was done as the rebels asked. The greatest jewels of the monastery, a golden cross and a valuable chalice of yellow metal as well as other precious goods brought out of the abbey (whose value exceeded £1,000), were handed over to the villeins in pledge: on the condition that if Edmund Brounfeld was delivered from prison (as mentioned above) he should enjoy the honour of being abbot at Bury, and should with common consent attach his own seal and the common seal of the convent to the villeins' liberties within the prescribed time. If this condition was not observed, the said valuables were to remain in the villeins' possession for ever. And so it happened at Bury, wonderful to say, that the commons sought for the villeins [of the abbey] advantages which were of no relevance to themselves at all. But the commons would not have known about these issues or have acted as they did except on the information and by the instigation of the villeins. For who can believe that the commons would have sought the death of any monk unknown and unrecognised by them and innocent from their point of view, a monk, moreover, whom they did not recognise when he stood before them, unless they had been led on by others? Why should the commons seek liberties for the villeins when they did not even live in the town?

[1] Edmund Brounfeld had been appointed abbot of Bury by the pope in 1379 against the wishes of the convent. Although Brounfeld enjoyed much local support from the burgesses of Bury he had been ejected from the abbey and imprisoned on the grounds of his contravention of the Statute of Provisors.

And why, if all these crimes displeased the villeins [of Bury], did they delay in restoring what had been taken away from the abbey when the commons had left and peace had returned? Their behaviour seems absolutely inexcusable to me, as will appear more clearly from what follows.

[At this point Walsingham's account of the disturbances at Bury St Edmunds breaks off and he moves on to describe the course of events in Norfolk (see below, no. 41). The interesting account of the rebellion at Bury written by John Gosford, almoner of the monastery, (Powell, *Rising in East Anglia*, p. 25) mentions that the repression of disturbances in western Suffolk was entrusted by the king to William de Ufford, earl of Suffolk. He arrived at Bury with 500 lances on 23 June and seems to have met no serious opposition. The best modern account of the rising at Bury is that by M. D. Lobel, *Borough of Bury St Edmunds*, pp. 150-5.]

39 The Depositions of John Wrawe

Coram Rege Roll, Easter 5 Richard II [KB. 27/484], Rex, memb. 26; partly printed in Réville, pp. 175–82

After the collapse of the rebellion in western Suffolk, its leader John Wrawe (once a vicar of Ringsfield near Beccles) tried to escape punishment by flight. But he was soon captured and brought to London for a lengthy and elaborate trial during the course of which he turned king's evidence and drew up the following series of charges against his accomplices. Testimony from such a source is naturally somewhat suspect – especially as several of the rebels accused by Wrawe (notably Sir Thomas Cornuerd) were soon acquitted or pardoned. However Wrawe's revelations provide reliable evidence of the way in which the risings in Suffolk spread northwards from Liston on the Essex border towards Bury St Edmunds. Even more illuminating is Wrawe's description of the methods by which he and his associates organised plundering expeditions whose primary objective was the levying of blackmail and protection money from the surrounding localities. Wrawe's confessions confirm Réville's judgment that he was a bandit chief 'ambitieux sans idées et cupide sans scrupules'. The qualities, not readily discernible, by which Wrawe had achieved his marked ascendancy over his fellow rebels failed to save him from execution. His fate is described by Walsingham (*Historia Anglicana*, II 63) in these words: 'About the feast of St John before the Latin Gate [6 May 1382] all the important men in the kingdom were called to a parliament ... in which, by the petition of the knights of the shires, John Wraw, priest, the leader of the insurgents at Bury and Mildenhall, was sentenced to drawing and hanging – although many had thought he would be saved by the payment of money'.

The Appeal mentioned in the aforesaid writ [witnessed by Chief Justice Robert Tresilian at Westminster on 22 May 1382 and ordering the sheriffs and coroner of London to dispatch Wrawe's appeal to the King's Bench on the following day] follows in these words:

On the Wednesday after the feast of the Translation of St Thomas Martyr [10 July 1381] John Wrawe of Sudbury came before William Knyghtcote and Walter Doget, sheriffs of London, as well as John Charneye, coroner of that city, and confessed that he was a felon and a traitor to the lord king; because, on Wednesday 12 June 1381, he had gone to Liston near Melford in the county of Suffolk and there treasonably rebelled against the king in the company of many malefactors and rebels assembled there from the counties of Essex, Hertford, Suffolk and Norfolk. On that day and while at Liston, John Wrawe remained in the company of the said malefactors and agreed to go with them and do what they wished, although he could easily have left them and escaped if he had so wished. Instead John Wrawe immediately sent a message to the town of Sudbury summoning all the men of that town to come to him and his fellowship at Liston. Not long afterwards, and on that same day, the said malefactors set out together (by their own unanimous decision) for a certain manor held by Richard Lyons of London in that same vill of Liston. Then they criminally and treasonably broke down the doors, windows and walls of the buildings in Lyons's manor, smashed the tiles and did much other damage.

Item, John Wrawe also confessed that in the company of the said band of malefactors he continued his crimes and felonies on Thursday 13 June. On that day he went from the town of Sudbury to that of Bury, in the said county of Suffolk; Wrawe then raised a cry for all the men of Bury to go forthwith to the South Gate of the town where they were to meet the said crowd of malefactors and go with them and do as they did. Anyone who opposed this summons was threatened with execution.

Item, John Wrawe confessed that on Saturday 15 June he, together with Thomas Halesworth, esquire, and Geoffrey Denham, esquire, servants of the prior of the monastery of Bury St Edmunds, as well as Robert Westbroun of Bury and many other malefactors of his company went to Mildenhall Heath, near Mildenhall, in the county of Suffolk. There they were present at the killing of the prior of Bury, criminally and treasonably murdered by various evildoers of his company who were abetted and prompted by the said Thomas Halesworth, Geoffrey Denham and Robert Westbroun. John Wrawe expressly says that if Thomas, Geoffrey and Robert had not been present to procure the prior's death, then he would not have been killed. Accordingly John Wrawe became an approver and appealed the said Thomas, Geoffrey and Robert of the said murder.

Item, John Wrawe, as approver, appealed Thomas Langham of Bury on the grounds that he, in the company of Wrawe and of many other malefactors unknown to Wrawe but of the aforementioned fellowship, treasonably and criminally killed John de Lakenheath, monk of St Edmunds, on Saturday 15 June in the town of Bury (with the help and advice of Wrawe and the said malefactors).

On Thursday 11 July, John Wrawe, as approver, appealed Robert Tavell of Lavenham in the county of Suffolk and John Talmache, esquire, on the grounds that together (and in the company of Wrawe and many other malefactors unknown to Wrawe) they criminally and treasonably broke down – on Friday 14 June – a certain tenement and the adjacent buildings situated in the town of Bury and belonging to the prior of St Edmunds. Moreover, they criminally and treasonably seized and carried off various goods and chattels (of whose value Wrawe is completely ignorant) belonging to the prior and found in the said tenement. Similarly, in Bury on that same Friday, they broke into and entered a mansion belonging to John de Cavendish, lately royal justice. Various goods and chattels belonging to John de Cavendish and discovered in the said mansion were seized and carried away: among these, John Talmache received from a servant of Wrawe a sword decorated with silver, gilt and jewels which was worth 100 marks.

On Friday 12 July, John Wrawe, as approver, appealed the said John Talmache, squire, on the grounds that he, with Wrawe's assent and consent, criminally entered the abbey of Bury St Edmunds on Saturday 15 June in the company of several other malefactors unknown to Wrawe and in Wrawe's own presence. Talmache then stole a bay horse worth 20 marks which belonged to the said prior. Talmache kept this horse for himself and Wrawe had no part in it.

Item, the same John Wrawe, as approver, appealed Ralph Somerton of Bury, dyer [and seventeen other named men], on the grounds that they, together with himself and many other malefactors unknown to him but of the same company, came to the parish church of the town of Cavendish in Suffolk on Thursday 13 June 1381; and they broke open the said church criminally and treasonably and then entered it. There they took and carried off various goods and chattels belonging to John de Cavendish, recently justice of the king, namely two silver vessels, a piece of silver plate and a silver candlestick, priced at seven pounds, two pairs of knives and a jack of velvet, priced at 26s 8d, all belonging to the said John de Cavendish and found in the tower of the church. The said evildoers, by common assent, made Wrawe share these goods and chattels among themselves on that same Thursday.

The said malefactors and the approver then went that day to Melford Green in Suffolk where together they drank a pipe of red wine, valued at seven marks three shillings and four pence, for which sum Wrawe and the malefactors left the above-mentioned goods in pledge to Enewene the taverner. Wrawe later paid the said seven marks three shillings and four pence to the taverner from his own money and carried off the goods with him and left them in his room at Sudbury at the time of his capture. Immediately after his capture, these goods were arrested there for the king's needs. And so Wrawe appealed them of felony and treason.

Item, the same John Wrawe, as approver, appealed William Hook of Hecham in Suffolk on the grounds that he knew himself and was in his company and that of the other aforementioned malefactors when the goods of the said John de Cavendish were criminally and treasonably stolen at the parish church of Cavendish on Thursday 13 June; and also because Hook carried off six silver dishes (whose value the said approver does not know) from Cavendish's goods. When Hook asked Wrawe what he should do with the said dishes, he was told to keep them safely for the use of them both until they had time to share them between themselves. And so the said dishes still remain in the possession of William Hook, wherefore Wrawe appealed him.

Item, the same John Wrawe, as approver, appealed the said Ralph Somerton of Sudbury, dyer, on the grounds that on the same Thursday 13 June he treasonably and criminally took the keys to the doors of the church of Cavendish, opened them and led Wrawe and the other malefactors into the church tower where the goods of John Cavendish were concealed. He helped and assented to the seizing and carrying away of the said goods; and in the company of Wrawe and the others he drank his share of the wine at Melford, for which Cavendish's goods were put in pledge. Ralph also treasonably took and stole other goods for himself, wherefore Wrawe appealed him.

Item, the same John Wrawe, as approver, appealed Geoffrey Parfeye, vicar of All Saints Church, Sudbury, as well as Thomas,

Geoffrey's chaplain (whose surname Wrawe does not know), Adam Bray of the said parish in Sudbury and Thomas Munchesy, junior, squire of Edwardeston, on the grounds that they, in Wrawe's absence, went to the town of Thetford, in Norfolk, on Friday 14 June. There they criminally and treasonably took and carried off from the mayor and chief burgesses of Thetford twenty marks of gold paid to save the town. The accused threatened the mayor and burgesses that unless they handed over the said sum, John Wrawe would arrive with his band that same Friday to destroy and popress the mayor and chief burgesses and to burn down the town. Of these twenty marks recieved from the mayor and burgesses, Geoffrey Parfeye gave twenty shillings to Adam Bray. He kept forty shillings for himself and his chaplain Thomas; but afterwards delivered the remainder, i.e. fourteen marks, to John Wrawe at Sudbury. Geoffrey then told Wrawe how he and his companions had taken the said gold. John Wrawe therefore received the said fourteen marks at Sudbury knowing that they had been taken treasonably and criminally, and so consented to these crimes. Accordingly Wrawe appealed Geoffrey and the others, etc.

Item, the same John Wrawe, as approver, appealed Thomas of Cornuerd, knight, on the grounds that (without Wrawe's knowledge) he went on Friday 14 June to John Rokwode of Stanfield in Suffolk and criminally received from him either at Stanfield or at Bury the sum of ten marks. He threatened John Rokwode that unless he handed over the said sum, John Wrawe would come that Friday with many of the malefactors in his band to kill Rokwode and destroy and burn his tenements. Later that Friday the said Thomas Cornuerd came before Wrawe and told him that he had received eight marks, and not more, from John Rokwode. Cornuerd offered the said eight marks to Wrawe but asked that he should have something for his labour; and accordingly Wrawe took five marks and gave Cornuerd forty shillings for his labour. Thomas Cornuerd kept for himself the two marks whose receipt he had not acknowledged to Wrawe as well as the forty shillings which Wrawe gave him for his labour; and so

Cornuerd criminally and treasonably stole the said two marks, wherefore Wrawe appealed him.

And so the appeal of John Wrawe, approver, was completed. And he had no chattels either within or without the liberty of the city of London, as he declared under oath, etc.

40 Two Suffolk Rebels and the 'Great Society'

Printed from Ancient Indictments [KB. 9/128] in Powell, *Rising in East Anglia*, pp. 126-7

Although sporadic rioting and house-breaking continued to occur in Suffolk until very nearly the end of June, the most serious outbreaks of organised rebellion in the county were apparently over by 20 June. On 23 June the earl of Suffolk arrived in Bury St Edmunds with instructions to put down the revolt and punish the insurgents. He can have met little serious resistance to his work of pacifying the county for, as the following indictments prove, he was fully immersed in the business of hearing pleas during the next week. The accusations made against John Poter relate to Sir John Cavendish's murder at Laken-heath; but George de Donnesby, more interestingly, was charged with being an emissary of the 'great society'. This allegation, and a few other references to the *magna societas* made in trial records from East Anglia and Kent, have sometimes been interpreted as evidence of a vast conspiratorial organisation underlying the revolts of 1381. But the phrase is very unlikely to have any very specific or technical meaning. While there is no reason to doubt that several attempts were made by the leaders of rebel bands to procure allies in other areas, the contacts between one company and another would seem to have been occasional and irregular rather than the result of any centrally planned national organisation.

Pleas of the Crown at Mildenhall before William de Ufford, earl of Suffolk, Roger Skales, Thomas de Morieux, William de Elmham, John de Bourgh and William de Wyngefeld on Thursday 27 June 1381.

John Poter of Somerton, fuller, is impeached before the said justices by John de Pole, recently chamberlain of lord John de Cavendish, late Chief Justice of the lord king, on the grounds that he was present at Lakenheath on Friday 14 June 1381 and there rose against the king and the dignity of the crown with a great force and in a warlike manner. On the same day the said John Poter treasonably and feloniously abetted and encouraged other traitors and enemies of the lord king to kill the said John de Cavendish. For this reason John Poter was seized and is now led by the sheriff before the said justices to be asked how he wishes to acquit himself of the said treasons and felonies. He says that he is not guilty of any such offence and thereupon places himself on [the judgment of a jury of] the country. Accordingly a jury was formed of jurors who were elected and sworn for the purpose with the consent of the said John Poter. The jurors declare under oath that John Poter of Somerton, fuller, is guilty of the felonies and treasons charged against him. Therefore it is adjudged that the said John Poter should be beheaded and that his head should be fixed on the pillory. Let an enquiry be made of his lands and chattels.

Pleas of the Crown at the town of St Edmund before the said justices on Saturday 29 July 1381.

George de Donnesby of the county of Lincoln is impeached by John Osbern alderman of the said town [i.e. Bury St Edmunds] and by many trustworthy men of the same on the grounds that on that same day [14 June 1381] he came to St Edmunds and there persuaded various men of the town to rise against the lord king and his faithful lieges. He ordered and strictly enjoined them to

rise under pain of losing their lives and limbs. Moreover he said
that he was a messenger of the great society and had been sent
to the town of St Edmunds to make the commons of that town
rise. On these grounds he was seized and led before the said
justices by the sheriff and was forthwith asked how he wished to
acquit himself from the said treasons and felonies. The said
George freely and without force confessed and openly admitted
all the felonies and treasons charged against him. So it was
adjudged that the said George de Donnesby should be beheaded
and that his head should be fixed on the pillory, etc. And so let
an enquiry be made of his land and chattels.[1]

41 The Revolt in Norfolk according to Thomas Walsingham

Walsingham, *Historia Anglicana*, II 5-8: continued from no.
38. Cf. *Chronicon Angliae*, pp. 304-8

As late as the evening of Thursday 13 June it seemed possible that
Norfolk might escape serious involvement in the Peasants' Revolt.
But on the following day the arrival within the county of several gangs
of blackmailers (including the band led by Geoffrey Parfeye from
Sudbury to Thetford – see above, p. 253) provoked the first of an
astonishingly large number of outbreaks of mob violence. For at least a
week western Norfolk was overrun by a series of rebel 'companies' intent on plunder and ransom. In this region the risings were characterised
by 'village ruffianism', to use Oman's phrase, rather than any attempt
to express common political and social grievances. In eastern Norfolk
the position was very different. Here there emerged as 'king of the

---

[1] It may not be coincidental that the area near the village of Donnesby (now
Dunsby) in southern Lincolnshire was apparently the scene of one of the few
recorded risings in that county, a protest against labour services by tenants of the
Knights Hospitallers (Réville, p. 251).

commons' a Felmingham dyer, Geoffrey Litster, a rebel both able and willing to play Tyler to the men of Norfolk. An ambitious and articulate leader, Litster had already won mass support by 17 June when he made his triumphal entry into Norwich and established his headquarters in the castle there. As Walsingham makes clear, Litster deliberately tried to involve members of the Norfolk gentry in his rebellion: his most important ally was Sir Roger Bacon of Baconsthorpe who broke into Great Yarmouth on 18 June. Even at this early date Litster and his associates were in a dangerously isolated position. Hopes that Richard II might grant the Norfolk rebels charters of the sort he had previously conceded at the Mile End meeting were dashed when Bishop Despenser marched into the county. The bishop's bloody victory near North Walsham (where local tradition long preserved the memory that an 'a'mazin' lot of men are buried in that pightle'[1]) led to Litster's death and the effective end of militant opposition to the English government.

Having noted what happened at Bury St Edmunds, let us omit the crimes committed in the city and county of Cambridge as well as the Isle of Ely for these were completely similar, both as regards the slaughter of men and the demolition of houses, to the disgraceful evils perpetrated elsewhere. We will now consider events in Norfolk.

There a great crowd of commons assembled under the leadership of a Norwich dyer called 'John Littestere'. They began to act exactly like the commons in other areas; and were even more presumptuous in that they started to plunder. Therefore virtually no place could be safe from commons who had unanimously conspired to pursue their evil aims. And since it seemed to the rebels that their own authority was too slight to justify such evil actions, they determined to secure the support of the earl of Suffolk, Lord William Ufford, to the mob of commons: if the lesser men were later charged for their transgressions, they could then point out that they had been acting under the shadow and with the connivance of a greater man and a peer. But the earl

<hr>

[1] Quoted by Réville, p. 139.

was warned of the approach of the rebels and immediately rose from the table at which he was having his meal: always avoiding the crowds of commons, he made his way circuitously and through lonely areas to St Albans. And so he reached the king, disguising himself as a groom of Lord Roger de Boys and carrying a knapsack on his back. In their frustration, the commons suddenly took possession of the houses of various other knights. They compelled the knights found there to swear to assist them and ride with them around the country for the sake of greater security. If the knights had refused to swear, they would have immediately been put to a most shameful death. The names of the knights who were compelled to follow the commons were the lord of Scales, lord William de Morlee, lord John de Brewes, lord Stephen de Hales and lord Robert de Salle. The latter did not keep his life for long amidst the rebels for he did not know how to dissimulate like the rest and began to deplore and condemn their actions publicly. For which reason he was knocked on the head by a rustic who was one of his own serfs and soon died. This was a knight who would have terrified a thousand of the commons on his own if they had been fighting him on an open battlefield. The other knights realised they had either to disguise their true feelings or die a horrible death, and learnt their lesson from Salle's fate: they praised all that the rebels praised and cursed everything the rebels disliked. Thus in order to retain the favour of that ruffian, John Littestere, who called himself 'King of the Commons', they deigned to be tasters of his food and drink and knelt to him in deference as he sat at meals. As lord Stephen de Hales was an honourable knight, Littestere chose him to cut up and taste his food before he ate it himself; and he gave the rest of the knights other duties.

After many days had passed the commons began to grow weary. They took counsel and decided to send two of the knights, lords William de Morlee and John de Brewes, together with three members of the commons whom they trusted, to the king, either at London or wherever he could be found, to secure from him a charter of manumission and pardon. As this charter was to be

more distinctive than those granted previously or later to other
counties, the rebels handed to the said envoys a large sum of
money which they had taken from the citizens of Norwich on
the pretext of saving the town from slaughter, fire and plunder.
They hoped to buy with money that peace and liberty which
they certainly did not deserve.

The Wrath of the Bishop of Norwich

And so the knights, together with their companions from the
band of commons, set out to fulfil their instructions. But when
they came to the town of Icklingham, not far from another town
called Newmarket, they unexpectedly encountered the bishop
of Norwich, Lord Henry le Spencer: the latter was a man ideally
suited for fighting and had arrived armed to the teeth. For he
had heard the rumour of the uprising of the men of Norfolk
when he had been staying in his manor of Burleigh near the royal
castle of Oakham close to Stamford. He decided to go to Norfolk
to see whether the agitation would lead to action or had already
done so. The bishop had in his company not more than eight
lances and a tiny number of archers. When he met the knights
from Norfolk with their companions from the commons, he
ordered the former to declare on their loyalty if there were any
traitors to the king present with them. But the knights, exposed
to the fear of the rustics for so long, gave a false reply; for they
thought that the bishop, a young and daring man, had not asked
them the question seriously and would be unable to help them if
they betrayed the traitors. The bishop realised the truth of the
matter and exhorted the knights to act confidently and deliver
up any traitors who were present. The knights then took courage,
abandoned their deceit and replied that two of the greatest leaders
of sedition were in their company while a third had gone elsewhere to get food for their meal. Moreover, they told the
bishop the whole story of their mission. Thereupon the bishop
immediately had the two rebels beheaded and determined to hunt
out the third, in order that his sheep which had perished by
renouncing its faith to the king should suffer execution by his

episcopal decree. Once he had fixed up the heads of these traitors at Newmarket, the bishop hurried towards Norfolk with the knights, moving to North Walsham, the place the commons had chosen to wait for the king's reply and the return of their colleagues. As the bishop crossed through the country, the number of his forces increased. The knights and gentlemen of the area who had previously lain low for fear of the commons joined the bishop's side when they saw him dressed as a knight, wearing an iron helm and a solid hauberk impregnable to arrows as he wielded a real two-edged sword.

When the bishop, now attended by an adequate company, reached North Walsham he discovered that the rustics had surrounded their place of assembly with a ditch in military fashion. To help their defence they had fixed tables, shutters and gates together with stakes above the ditch. The bishop saw that they had placed their carts and carriages behind them although they had no intention of running away. Without delay the warrior bishop, ready to fight in open battle and indignant at the audacity of the ruffians, ordered his trumpeters and buglers to sound. He himself seized a lance in his right hand, sharply spurred his horse and threw himself on the rebels with such force and courage that he reached the ditch like a whirlwind and more quickly than the arrows of his men. There was no work for the archers as a hand-to-hand battle began straightaway. The warlike priest, like a wild boar gnashing its teeth, spared neither himself nor his enemies. He chose to fight where the danger was greatest, stabbing one man, knocking down another and wounding a third. Nor did he cease his violent struggles until the whole crowd which fell on him when he reached the ditch were ready to fly. Therefore the bishop's men fought more fiercely than the commons until, as is usual, a poor conscience deterred the unjust party and took away their resolution to be brave and willingness to die. Nothing is more unfortunate than to fight a war with a guilty conscience for it spreads fear and confusion and never leads to victory. So the fearful people fled and as the only avenues of escape open to them were the carts and carriages stationed behind them as we have said, they strove to leap up on to these. But the bishop, surveying everything like a general, frustrated those who made the attempt. He prevented those who thought of escaping by striking them down until he achieved total victory. By then the chief instigators of the mob had been captured, including their king, John Littestere: the bishop determined that so many of the commons should be killed and others kept alive.

The End of John Littestere, King of Norfolk

The bishop then sentenced the said John, the idol of the men of Norfolk, to drawing, hanging and execution. The bishop himself, having heard and absolved his confession by virtue of his office, accompanied Littestere to the gallows, thereby performing despite his victory a work of mercy and piety. He held up the rebel's head to prevent it knocking on the ground while he was being dragged to the place of his hanging. After this, the bishop still did not relax until he had searched the whole country for malefactors and done justice on them. And so the warrior bishop brought peace to the region and indescribable profit to the whole kingdom thanks to his commendable probity and bravery. [*Continued by no. 68 below, p. 363.*]

42 The Death of Sir Robert Salle according to Froissart

Froissart, trans. Berners, ed. G. C. Macaulay, pp. 257–8; cf. Froissart, *Chroniques*, X 114–16

Froissart inserted the *aventure* of Sir Robert Salle's dramatic death into the middle of his account of the activities of the rebels in London (see above, p. 193). As a comparison with Walsingham's chronicle (p. 258) soon reveals, Froissart's narrative fairly bristles with demonstrable errors: on the central fact of Salle's execution at the hands of the Norfolk rebels he has proceeded to construct an imaginative romance. Sir Robert Salle was not captain of Norwich, was not offered a quarter of the kingdom and apparently met his death after some form of 'trial' and not in the midst of an exciting hand-to-hand combat. But the story deserves attention as a *locus classicus* of Froissart's tendency to convert the history of his own times into 'honourable and noble adventures of feats of arms' as well as of Berners's skill as a translator. It is also significant that Salle's death made such a great impression on contemporary opinion – an indirect confirmation of the fact that the execution of county knights, as opposed to royal and ecclesiastical officials, was extremely uncommon in 1381.

Yet I shall shew you of an adventure that fell by these ungracious people before the city of Norwich, by a captain among them called Guilliam Lister of Stafford [*Stanfort*].[1] The same day of Corpus Christi [13 June] that these people entered into London and brent the duke of Lancaster's house, called the Savoy, and the hospital of Saint John's and brake up the king's prisons of Newgate and did all this hurt, as ye have heard before, the same time there assembled together they of Stafford, of Lynn, of Cambridge, of Bedford and of Yarmouth; and as they were coming towards London, they had a captain among them called Lister. And as they came, they rested them before Norwich, and in their coming they caused every man to rise with them, so that they left no villains behind them. The cause why they rested before Norwich I shall shew you.

There was a knight, captain of the town, called sir Robert Sale. He was no gentleman born, but he had the grace to be reputed sage and valiant in arms, and for his valiantness king Edward made him knight. He was of his body one of the biggest knights in all England. Lister and his company thought to have had this knight with them and to make him their chief captain, to the

---

[1] A characteristic mistake by Froissart: the rebel leader at Norwich was Geoffrey Litster (see above, pp. 256–7).

intent to be the more feared and beloved: so they sent to him
that he should come and speak with them in the field, or else they
would bren the town. The knight considered that it was better
for him to go and speak with them rather than they should do
that outrage to the town: then he mounted on his horse and issued
out of the town all alone, and so came to speak with them. And
when they saw him, they made him great cheer and honoured him
much, desiring him to alight off his horse and to speak with them,
and so he did: wherein he did great folly; for when he was
alighted, they came round about him and began to speak fair to
him and said: 'Sir Robert, ye are a knight and a man greatly
beloved in this country and renowned a valiant man; and though
ye be thus, yet we know you well, ye be no gentleman born, but
son to a villein [and a mason] such as we be. Therefore come you
with us and be our master, and we shall make you so great a
lord, that one quarter of England shall be under your obeisance.'
When the knight heard them speak thus, it was greatly contrarious
to his mind, for he thought never to make any such bargain, and
answered them with a felonous regard: 'Fly away, ye ungracious
people, false and evil traitors that ye be: would you that I should
forsake my natural lord for such a company of knaves as ye be,
to my dishonour for ever? I had rather ye were all hanged, as ye
shall be; for that shall be your end.' And with those words he
had thought to have leapt again upon his horse, but he failed of
the stirrup and the horse started away. Then they cried all at him
and said: 'Slay him without mercy.' When he heard those words,
he let his horse go and drew out a good [Bordeaux] sword and
began to scrimmish with them, and made a great place about him,
that it was pleasure to behold him. There was none that durst
approach near him: there were some that approached near him,
but at every stroke that he gave he cut off other leg, head or arm:
there was none so hardy but that they feared him: he did there
such deeds of arms that it was marvel to regard. But there were
more than forty thousand of these unhappy people: they shot
and cast at him, and he was unarmed: to say truth, if he had
been of iron or steel, yet he must needs have been slain; but yet,

or he died, he slew twelve out of hand, beside them that he hurt. Finally he was stricken to the earth, and they cut off his arms and legs and then strake his body all to pieces. This was the end of sir Robert Sale, which was great damage; for which deed afterward all the knights and squires of England were angry and sore displeased when they heard therof. [*Continued by no. 28 above, p.* 193]

PART V

Elsewhere in England

Although contemporary chroniclers rightly believed that Kent, Essex and the three East Anglian counties were the centres of the most extreme and violent risings in 1381, they were under no illusion that the Peasants' Revolt was confined to south-eastern England. But only with the publication of numerous legal records in the appendix of Réville's Le Soulèvement des Travailleurs *was the exact geographical extent of the revolt fully realised. A thorough reinvestigation of the record evidence would probably even now add several more instances of disorder to those collected by Réville. But, as it is, we already know that every English county to the south and east of the line formed by the rivers Trent and Severn was affected to a greater or lesser extent by the prevailing temper of rebellion against lord and master. The risings in the Home Counties were particularly frequent and are usually not too difficult to explain. Many of the inhabitants of Middlesex, Hertfordshire and northern Surrey were in direct contact with the peasants from Kent and Essex and themselves provided a remarkably large number of recruits to the companies of Wat Tyler and Jack Straw. In these areas peasant economic grievances and hopes for enfranchisement often found direct expression in the burning of manorial records and a series of armed assaults on ecclesiastical and other landlords. The monasteries of Grace, Dunstable and Redbourne all suffered at the hands of such rebels, as did the much more famous abbey of St Albans where the long and intricate story of the struggle between monks and townspeople was told by Thomas Walsingham (see below, no. 43). In midland, western and northern England, disorder was much less common and when riots occur they usually prove much more difficult to interpret. In the absence of any commentary by a local chronicler, it is, for example, almost impossible to know whether the unrest displayed by the tenants of the monasteries of Chester and Worcester (nos. 49, 50) was as dangerous as the authorities believed. The riots at Bridgwater in Somerset on 19 June (no. 45) certainly prove, if proof were needed, that* news of the rebellion in London rapidly spread throughout the country; and it is undeniable that the example set by the Kent and Essex rebels incited many of the king's subjects who lived hundreds of miles away to similar acts of defiance. In most cases however disturbances took the form of an acceleration or intensification of existing quarrels rather than the appearance of radically new social movements. The interesting if mysterious trio of urban riots at York, Scarborough and Beverley (nos. 46–8) are explicable only in terms of the political and economic balance of power within those towns and certainly not in the phrases of John Ball's sermons. More significant still is the fact that in the largest county of England the 'Peasants' Revolt' provoked not peasant but burgess risings.

43 The Rebels at St Albans according to Thomas Walsingham

Walsingham, *Historia Anglicana*, I 467–73; II 27. Cf. *Chronicon Angliae*, pp. 299–301

Thomas Walsingham was himself a cloister monk of St Albans in 1381 and his lengthy description of the rebellion against the great Benedictine abbey is inevitably that of a partisan as well as an eye-witness. Nowhere is the monastic chronicler's incomprehension of the movement and lack of sympathy with its aims more obvious than in Walsingham's denunciation of the misdeeds of St Albans' own tenants. But almost in spite of the author, the following extracts from his record of events at St Albans are of exceptional value to the historian of 1381.[1] Not only is the reader made aware that the rising (like that at Bury St Edmunds) was only an exceptionally stormy episode in the long and bitter struggle between monks, tenants and local townspeople. He is likely to be impressed by the restraint with which the rebels pursued their quest for 'a little liberty'. Under the leadership of the talented and attractive William Grindcobbe, the men of St Albans put forward their specific objectives in an articulate, moderate and constitutional form. No monk lost his life at the hands of the rebels; but several of the insurgents, including Grindcobbe himself, were executed during the subsequent repression of the revolt by Robert Tresilian, Chief Justice of the King's Bench.

As we have already mentioned[2] the villeins of St Albans and the servants of the abbey reached the manor of Highbury on Friday

---

[1] Even more valuable is the circumstantial and well-documented narrative of the revolt of the St Albans tenants provided by *Gesta Abbatum Monasterii Sancti Albani*, III (Rolls Series, 1869) 285–372 – a source upon which this summary is heavily reliant. Unfortunately far too long and detailed to be translated here, this narrative makes it possible to analyse villein grievances and objectives at St Albans (as nowhere else) at 'grass-roots' level.

[2] See above, p. 171.

14 June and then went onwards to London. There the said villeins soon abandoned the abbey servants and turned to works of iniquity. For they went to the church of St Mary Arches in the city and began to discuss their subservience to the monastery and the methods by which they could achieve the aims they had long secretly desired: namely, to have newly defined boundaries around their town within which they might pasture their animals freely; to enjoy fishing rights in various places without dispute; to possess hunting and fowling rights in certain places; and to be able to erect hand-mills where they pleased and as they wished. They demanded that the bailiff of the liberty [of St Albans] should not intervene within the boundaries of the town; and that there should be returned to them the bonds which their parents had once made to Abbot Richard of Wallingford of blessed memory as well as other charters prejudicial to themselves.[1] To be brief about it, they asked for all records in the abbey which might be of help to them or to the detriment of the monastery.

In order to obtain what they desired more quickly, certain of the villeins recommended that they should receive power from Walter Tyler, then leader of the ruffians and rustics from Kent; for they believed that there would in future be no more important man than Tyler within the kingdom and that the laws of the land would be henceforward invalid - because most of the lawyers had already been destroyed and they expected the remainder to perish soon. They then proposed to return to the monastery and demand what they wanted under strict conditions; for if the abbot should think of denying them what they sought, they would threaten the abbey with fire and the monks with death, even to the extent of completely destroying the entire monastery where they would leave not one stone standing upon another.

Other villeins declared that it would be safer to go to the king's presence, then denied to no one, and ask him for a letter under

---

[1] An allusion to Abbot Wallingford's success in depriving the St Albans townspeople of the liberties they had won in the revolutionary year of 1327. For the causes of the discontent at St Albans in 1381 see A. E. Levett, *Studies in Manorial History*, pp. 79–81, 203–5.

his privy seal to be sent to the abbot, directing him to restore to them the liberties and rights held by their fathers and ancestors in the days of King Henry.[1] Both recommendations were approved and they approached the king for a letter to be sent to the abbot; and also asked Walter Tyler to send some of his ruffians, if it proved necessary, to help them and destroy the monastery.

The chief agent of this business before the king was William Grindcobbe, a man who owed much to the monastery because he had been educated, nourished and maintained there, and because of his relationship to those monks who had been and still were his kinsmen. He obtained the said letters after he had knelt to the king six times in the presence of the mob.[2] Grindcobbe was also the chief spokesman for the villeins in their business before the said Walter, idol of the rustics. But there were many other workers of malice who came before Walter Tyler to slander the abbot and prior as well as several other monks for their unjust lordship over their rustics and for oppressing the commons and withholding the stipends of poor men and labourers. And so they persuaded Walter, although he had not planned to leave London or to send any of his followers away from himself, to promise to arrive with 20,000 men to shave the beards of the abbot, prior and other monks (that is, to behead them) if it proved necessary or if the villeins sent for him. Walter's condition was that the villeins [of St Albans] should obey all his orders and omit to do nothing that he commanded. And he instructed them, in the same way as he had ordered all men who had left or were to leave his presence, that soon after their return home they should swear under oath to observe absolutely all his commands and instructions, as we will describe them later. On receiving this assurance, the villeins prepared to return home. However one of the abbey servants, riding at great speed, arrived before they did

[1] See below, p. 275. In 1381 the burgesses of Dunstable similarly appealed against the priory there to a supposed charter of liberties conceded by Henry I to their ancestors.

[2] It seems likely that Grindcobbe made his request to Richard II at the Mile End conference on 14 June. The King's letters were delivered to the St Albans rebels early on the following day (see below, p. 274).

10

and announced the deaths of the archbishop, Treasurer and many others as well as the news that the commons lacked all mercy or compassion and were killing those they hated without pity. And so the prior would be beheaded and other monks suffer great danger if they waited for the arrival of the commons.

Therefore the prior and four other monks fled together with several servants of the monastery; after a long and very dangerous journey, some on foot and some on horseback, the frightened monks arrived at Tynemouth.[1] Not long after the prior's departure, the villeins returned to St Albans. First to arrive were William Grindcobbe and William Cadyndon, a baker, who had hurried ahead to show themselves well at work before the arrival of their fellows. For these two men desired to be held specially responsible for what was done in order to be treated as great men thereafter. And so, on their arrival, they announced that all had gone well, that henceforward they would be no longer serfs but lords and that great and wonderful matters against the abbey had been accomplished.

Accordingly and in order to defy the abbot they first had the folds erected by him in Falcon Wood and other woods broken down and the gates of Eywood and other woods destroyed that same night. They also decided to destroy completely the sub-cellarer's house, which stood opposite the street where fish are sold, because it seemed to hinder the outlook of the burghers and slighted the nobility of the citizens (for such they now called themselves). Without delay these fools, agreeing to the suggestions of other fools, proved themselves completely mad by spending the whole night before they went to rest in breaking down folds, destroying gates and overturning the said house. These deeds were perpetrated at St Albans on the said Friday and were the beginning of subsequent evils, which I will partly describe in the next chapter; they must be distinguished from those of the Saturday to make what happened later more intelligible.

[1] In Northumberland: the site of St Albans' most important daughter-house or cell.

And so on the Saturday morning the inhabitants of the town of St Albans rose to discuss the actions already taken; and the villeins went out to Falcon Wood in great splendour. Beforehand a proclamation was made that no one capable of bearing arms should remain at home; but that everyone should follow immediately with the arms and tools by which they could best defend themselves, under penalty of execution and the destruction of their houses (if they had their own) and the loss of all the goods found there. This serious threat compelled both those who favoured the abbey and those who did not to go forth and follow those authors of iniquity, William Grindcobbe (whose name we have already mentioned) and William Cadyndon as well as others whom I will refrain from listing.

A large mob assembled at the appointed place, where counsel was taken as to what they should seek, do and threaten. First, they decided to destroy immediately any folds in woods, or gates into woods, which still remained intact, so that they could never be applied to other uses thereafter. This wicked advice was put into effect by the work of malicious men.

Then the mob returned to the town, where their arrival was awaited by the rustics and commons of the neighbouring vills and monastic demesne who had assembled there, not unwillingly, to the number of two thousand or more ruffians. For the men of the vills of the liberty of St Albans had been ordered to assemble together, leaving aside all excuses and under the aforesaid penalties, in order to demand and enjoy the liberties which the villeins had determined to request. These men were also ordered not to allow any gentleman to stay at home but to lead everyone with them to the aid of the villeins. They were commanded to behead and destroy or burn the houses of all those who would not proceed with them or promise fealty to them; for this was a lesson they had been taught by Walter Tyler, their lord and master.

And when the villeins saw the crowd which had assembled at their orders, they thought themselves great men and were much reassured and elated. Joining their right hands they promised to be faithful to one another. Then they marched forward in great pride to the gates of the monastery in order to display the great power they had acquired from the said Walter. When they reached the gates, which were left open for them, with unspeakable arrogance they ordered the porter to open the prison to them. The porter, not unaware of what they proposed to do (for the abbot had been secretly informed of all these matters by several of the villeins whose hearts God had touched, and had instructed the porter how to act), immediately unlocked the doors of the prison. The villeins entered and brought out all the prisoners, ordering them to go freely provided only that they should henceforward be loyal and favourable to the community and adhere inseparably to the commons. Making themselves judges and butchers they condemned one of the released prisoners as a man who deserved death and beheaded him on the large piece of land before the abbey gates. With a devilish shouting which they had learnt in London at the time of the archbishop's execution, they carried off his head and fixed it to the top of the pillory so that it would appear openly to all that they were able to enjoy new laws and were supported by new privileges. Not long afterwards the villeins of Barnet, who were in league with the St Albans villeins, arrived to reinforce the number of miscreants. They too came to oppose the abbey.

At about the third hour of the day [i.e. *c.* 9.0 A.M.] there arrived Richard of Wallingford who had ridden from London at great speed. He was the most important of the St Albans villeins and had remained in London to carry the letter for which (as we have related above) William Grindcobbe had been a suppliant to the king so many times. He bore before him a displayed banner or pennant with the arms of St George in the manner of those who committed so many atrocities in London. When they learnt of his arrival, the villeins [of the town] together with the mob of commons and rustics from the country they had summoned to assemble, ran to meet him in the square before the abbey. After he had dismounted, Richard fixed his standard and ordered everyone to close on it as if on the battlefield. After a short interval which he spent in debate and discussion with the villeins concerning future negotiations with the abbot, Richard ordered the common people to stand by the standard and wait for his return there. They were to remain present until they received definite news as to how the abbot would respond to the petitions addressed to him on behalf of the people. Richard and many of the greatest rebels then entered the church and sent for the abbot to come and answer the commons. For at that time they gloried in such a name and believed no name was more honourable than the name of 'community'; according to their foolish minds there would be no lords thereafter but only king and commons. Now the abbot had already decided that it was better to die in order to preserve the liberty of the monastery rather than to do anything which would prejudice his church; but he was swayed by the prayers, warnings and advice of his monks who said his death for this cause would be of no advantage to the monastery. Although he had decided to die when the senseless people had declared their firm intention of either obtaining what they sought or killing him and his monks as well as burning the monastery, the abbot was nevertheless finally won over and went down to meet them. When he appeared in the church, Richard of Wallingford greeted him briefly and held out the royal writ which (as we have said) William Grindcobbe had lately extorted rather than obtained from the king. The tenor of the letter was as follows:–

The King's Letter to the Abbot concerning the Royal Charters
'Very dear in God – At the petition of our beloved lieges of the town of St Albans, we will and command that (as law and right demands) you cause to be delivered to the said burgesses and good men of the town certain charters in your custody which were made by our ancestor, King Henry, to the said burgesses and good men concerning common, pasture, fishing rights and several other commodities mentioned in the said charters; so that they may have no reason to complain hereafter to us for this reason. Given under our signet at London, 15 June, in the fourth year of our reign [1381].'

The lord abbot received this letter with due reverence and read it through. He then tried to inform and remind the rebels that all these issues had been terminated in the time of their fathers and a record of the judgments was written in the royal rolls at Westminster. Therefore according to the long established laws of the realm, the abbot asserted that the rebels had no right or legal claim to any of those things which they sought. Richard of Wallingford, spokesman for them all, replied that the commons now ruled over the laws, which therefore no longer had any effect. They neither expected nor would accept such an argument. . . .

It seems most appropriate to end this extract from Walsingham's narrative at the point when the long and intricate negotiations between Abbot Thomas de la Mare and the rebels began. Thanks to their possession of Richard II's letter, the St Albans burgesses were temporarily successful in their demands for the surrender of several royal charters – the most objectionable of which they then proceeded to burn in the market-place. Although their primary objective, an imaginary charter of King Offa conferring liberties on the inhabitants of the town, could not be discovered, the rebels remained comparatively calm. The abbot too kept a cool head and his readiness to negotiate was successful in persuading the townsmen to continue the debate rather than resort to violence. When the news of Tyler's death reached St Albans the rebels became much more cautious and composed a comparatively moderate charter for presentation to the abbey. The eventual suppression of the revolt was also an unusually long and tortuous although peaceful process. The townspeople finally surrendered their charters and bound themselves to pay £200 in compensation for damage done to monastic property. Richard II's arrival at St Albans on 12 July and his subsequent taking of the fealty of the men of Hertfordshire marked the effective end of the disorders. Eighty or so persons were arrested in the county and tried before Robert Tresilian in October; but (according to Walsingham) only fifteen of the insurgents were executed. Of these, the most important was William Grindcobbe whose alleged speech while on bail from prison in Hertford provides the most moving epitaph on the revolt at St Albans: –

'Fellow citizens, for whom a little liberty has now relieved the long years of oppression, stand firm while you can and do not be afraid because of my persecution. For if it should happen that I die in the cause of seeking to acquire liberty, I will count myself happy to end my life as such a martyr. Act therefore now as you would have acted if I had been beheaded at Hertford yesterday. For nothing could have saved my life if the abbot had not called back his esquires in time. They had accused me of many things and had a judge partial to themselves and eager to shed my blood.'

44 Panic in Leicester according to Henry Knighton

Chronicon Henrici Knighton, II 141-3: continued from no. 36 above

As a canon of the abbey of Leicester Henry Knighton was well placed to provide a vividly dramatic sketch of the near-hysteria which gripped his local borough – as it probably affected most English provincial towns after the news of the rebels' entry into London. At Leicester the mayor proved less timid than the abbot; but the future was to show that neither need have been seriously alarmed. The insurgents never reached the town and the midland counties in general escaped the worst excesses of the summer of 1381.

At St Albans the commons of the town and many others from the neighbouring area rose and (forgetful of good things) rushed to the abbey where they forced the abbot and convent, to their great cost and inconvenience, to assent to their petitions and concede many liberties. The abbot's tenants proposed that they should hold these in perpetuity. But the king arrived shortly afterwards and had the charter quashed and the malefactors punished. Similarly in many places the tenants began to rise against their lords, for as it is written, 'No one is more violent than the humble when he rises himself on high'. They were besides themselves, failed to appreciate their condition and had not considered what the end would be. They were like fools who leap before they look. By their crimes was fulfilled what is written of the holy Apostles, 'Their sound went out in all lands, etc.' [Ps. xix, 4]. The hearts of all men in every part of the realm, however remote, trembled with fear of the rebels; and everywhere it was fearfully believed that the rebels were about to arrive in person and without warning.

In Leicester one evening a messenger came to the mayor of the town and said that the rebels were approaching and had reached Harborough. He said that a detachment from the impious mob in London would arrive at the town of Leicester on the following morning at the first hour of the day: they had come to destroy the duke of Lancaster's manor there and to tear up, throw down and burn all his goods they found there. The duke kept certain of his practical necessities in this manor for he often entertained his family there; but at the time of this crisis he was on the March negotiating the kingdom's affairs with the Scots. What more can I say? The mayor was most disturbed and alarmed and in a quandary as to what action he should take in so difficult a situation. If he decided to resist the rebels, perhaps he might fail and so be killed with his men. If he received the rebels in peace, he would afterwards be adjudged their accomplice. Needing sensible advice he called his neighbours, jurors and other shrewd men; and, by their counsel, on the same evening he made a proclamation under the king's name at the high cross and four gates of the town – that in the morning everyone should be ready to defend himself and his neighbours. Likewise, under threat of penalties from the king, everyone in the town, rich and poor, master and servant, was instructed to arm himself in the best way he could and, without excuses, assemble with his weapons in the morning on a hill called Galtrehill outside the town. They would then oppose, if they could by means of God's grace and support from the neighbourhood, these enemies who had arrived before them so suddenly. When the men from Leicester had assembled on the hill they totalled about 1200, some good and others less so.

On a second day, they did likewise, appearing on the same spot and waiting in great fear for what might happen. They sent out scouts to investigate the rebels' actions and whereabouts, when they would approach Leicester and whether they would come peacefully or under arms: but not one of these scouts returned to bring either good news or bad. Accordingly they were even more afraid. Meanwhile the keeper of the lord duke's wardrobe returned from London[1] also fearing that the rebels would arrive to destroy what they could discover in the duke's castle of Leicester. As rapidly as possible, he had all he could find in the castle loaded into carts and drawn to the abbey of Leicester for safe keeping from the said enemies. And when the carts arrived there on the following Tuesday at about noon, the abbot was terrified like the others in the kingdom and dared not receive them into his hospice in case this should lead to the complete destruction of the abbey. For during this crisis the commons held the peaceful duke of Lancaster as their most hated enemy of all mortal men and would certainly have destroyed him immediately if they had found him. Accordingly the loaded carts left as they had come and the duke's goods were deposited in the yard of the church of St Mary of the Castle to await divine providence, without whose support nothing survives.

45 The Bridgwater Rising

Bridgwater, in northern Somerset, was one of the six towns originally singled out by the Commons for exclusion from the general amnesty

[1] See above, p. 184.

proclaimed in the parliament of November–December 1381. In the absence of any chronicler's account of the rising there and the survival of only a few of its records, the exact nature and extent of the revolt remains somewhat obscure. But it is reasonably clear that (as at St Albans and Bury St Edmunds) the struggle took the form of a contest between the townspeople and the most important religious house in their borough, the Augustinian Hospital of St John.[1] An earlier quarrel concerning the advowson of Bridgwater's parish church was revived by its vicar, Nicholas Frompton. The latter was reported to have been encouraged to adopt strong-arm methods by the example of the disorders which he had himself witnessed at London. Frompton seems to have met with no difficulty in finding allies among members of the gentry families of the Bridgwater area, one of whom, Thomas Engilby, was prepared to use murder to pay off his private grudges. Both Frompton (on 16 February 1382[2]) and Engilby were later pardoned; and the Bridgwater rising was certainly not a peasant revolt. But it deserved the attention it received as the most serious recorded case of lawlessness in south-west England as well as an outbreak directly promoted by the example of the collapse of governmental authority in London.

A. ACCORDING TO THE PARDON OF THOMAS ENGILBY

Patent Roll, 6 Richard II, part 3 [C. 66/315], memb. 12; partly printed in Réville, pp. 283–4. Cf. *C.P.R.*, *1381–5*, p. 270

The king to all his bailiffs and faithful men who read these letters, greetings. Know that Thomas Engilby is indicted, as we understand, because on Wednesday 19 June [1381] he together with Adam Brugge and others treasonably came to the hospital of St John of Bridgwater displaying our banners. He broke into the buildings of the hospital and threatened both its master, William Cammell, and the convent with the burning of their houses and the mutilation of their bodies. Thomas seized the said master

---

[1] Both Petit-Dutaillis (Réville, p. CIX) and Oman (*Great Revolt*, p. 139) misrepresent the Bridgwater rising by their erroneous belief that the townsmen attacked the hospital because it belonged to the Knights Hospitallers.

[2] *C.P.R.*, *1381–5*, p. 95; cf. Réville, p. 293.

and held him in custody until he had handed over various written bonds imposing certain conditions in an agreement between William Cammell and the men of Bridgwater. The same master also had to release all his rights and profits to the rector [*recte* vicar] of the church of Bridgwater, Nicholas Frompton, except for the corn and hay tithes pertaining to the church. The master of the hospital also had to make a fine of 200 marks with Engilby and the others, in order to secure his release, save his life and preserve his convent.

Moreover, Thomas threw to the ground houses belonging to John Sydenham of Bridgwater at Sydenham and removed John's goods and chattels which he found there, to the value of £100. Thomas also went to another house (in the same town) belonging to John Sydenham when John was staying there; and he treasonably took and burnt certain documents and records relevant to his own inheritance as well as court rolls of James Daudelegh, knight, and John Cole which had been kept there in the custody of the said John Sydenham. He tore to pieces and removed the seals attached to these records.

On the same day, Thomas Engilby treasonably threw down and burnt a tenement in the same town belonging to Thomas Duffeld and worth £20. On the same day he went to the house of Walter Baron, worth 100s, at East Chilton and burnt it as well as other goods and chattels in the form of corn and other things, valued at £10. While there he treasonably caused the said Walter to be beheaded.

On the following Friday [21 June] Thomas Engilby went to Ilchester. On his journey to the town he forced John Bursy, then living in his house at Long Sutton, to go with him against his will. Thomas treasonably broke into our gaol and seized Hugh Lavenham who was lodged there as a man indicted of felony. In contempt of ourselves and our crown, Thomas forced John Bursy against his will to behead the same Hugh and carry his head on a lance to Bridgwater. Thomas placed Hugh's head together with that of Walter Baron on lances over the bridge at Bridgwater, to the contempt of ourselves and our crown.

Nevertheless, we by our special grace and because of this present feast of Easter, and on the condition that he behaves well to us and our people henceforward, have pardoned Thomas; and we give him the form of peace that pertains to us for all the treasons, transgressions and felonies mentioned above (as well as all others whatsoever perpetrated by him during the risings of certain communities of our realm of England against ourselves and our crown) of which he is indicted, charged or accused. We also pardon him of any sentences of outlawry which may have been brought against him for these offences, and give him our firm peace, notwithstanding that he was, as one of the chief rebels, excluded from all grace in our various parliaments – provided that he duly answers any suit of peace in our court if anyone wishes to implead him for the aforesaid misdeeds. In testimony, etc. Witnessed by the king at Westminster, 28 March [1383]. By a writ of privy seal.

B. ACCORDING TO THE ACCUSATIONS AGAINST SIR WILLIAM COGGAN (brought by Richard de Clyvedon in the November–December parliament of 1381)
Rot. Parl., III 105–6

43. Item, Richard de Clyvedon, esquire, put before parliament a bill in the following form:

To our very sovereign and gracious lord the king, Richard Clyvedon declares that there was a dispute between the commons of the town of Bridgwater and the master of the hospital of St John in the same town on the subject of a vicarage in the said place; but the two parties came to an agreement on the matter, partly by legal process and partly by other means. Afterwards they understood that there was a great disturbance in London, to the serious harm of the king and kingdom. Present at the time were Nicholas Frompton, chaplain and provisor of the said vicarage, and other men of Bridgwater, who left London soon after the said disturbance. And on their arrival at Bridgwater, they took counsel together; and they summoned William Coggan, knight, who came and deliberated with them. Afterwards William, in the company of other men of Bridgwater, went to the aforementioned hospital and asked, in the name of the commons of the town, the master and brothers to submit to them and alter things previously done, under threat of a future penalty if they did not.

William gave the master until ten o'clock on the next day to reply, and then he departed to lodge at Huntspill. On the following day he returned to the commons at Bridgwater to accomplish the business he had undertaken with the master. When they had spoken together, William went to the hospital, followed by the commons with a raised banner. His negotiations with the master ended in the latter paying a fine of £200 sterling and handing over a bond of £100 and other muniments to save the brethren's lives and goods.

And if the said William Coggan denies this bill, Richard Clyvedon will prove it with his body before our redoubtable king and his most wise council in the way that the law of arms requires. . . . This bill was read in parliament, after which Richard by word of mouth offered to prove it by his body according to the law of arms or in another way that the court might ask of him, but not by the verdict of jurors. For he said that Sir William Coggan was a rich man and he was poor; and therefore he would not be able to prevail by inquest although his cause was as true as there is God in heaven above.

45. To this the said Sir William Coggan, there present, affirmed that he was a layman and not sufficiently knowledgeable of the law or other matters to reply in so high a place; and so he asked to have counsel so as to be able to answer according to the law. The serjeants of the king told him that the contents of the said bill raised the question of treason; and in such a case he had, by the law of the land, to make his reply in person and not by counsel. Then Sir William deliberated a little with his friends and allies; and in person made a protestation that in time to come he

would amend and correct, etc. He declared that he was guilty of none of the charges brought against him by the said Richard in the bill – as to which he would put himself for good and all on the verdict of the country. Accordingly at the end of this parliament the case between the two parties was adjourned before the justices of the common law as far as it pertained to the law.

46 The Riots at York

For Sir Charles Oman, the rising in York was a 'squalid and obscure municipal quarrel, which had obviously no relation to the general causes of the rebellion of 1381' (*Great Revolt*, p. 146). The last point is clearly valid and it is one of the major paradoxes of the Peasants' Revolt that it should have helped to incite urban factions to violence within a city whose status was generally recognised by contemporaries as second only to that of London. But however squalid the riots in York may or may not have been, they resulted in no loss of life within the city. Moreover, the York disturbances seem to reflect, however obliquely, one of the major themes in the constitutional history of the late medieval town – the attempt of the *communitas* to challenge the oligarchic power of the urban merchant aristocracy. In York itself the news of rebellion in southern England was almost certain to provoke disorder because of the prevailing tension within the city. During the previous November there had been a forceful and temporarily successful attempt to oust John de Gisburne from the mayor's office in the interests of his rival Simon de Quixlay. As the first extract reveals, news of this civil strife reached Northampton shortly before the termination of the parliament which conceded the third poll tax. Although Quixlay, who seems to have attracted political support from the lesser craftsmen of the city, was duly elected mayor in February 1381, the situation remained explosive. When the report of the 'devilish insurrection' in Kent and Essex reached York (apparently on Monday, 17 June) there followed a general assault on several religious houses within the city which can hardly have been condoned by the leaders of either city faction. Less than a fortnight later, on 1 July, the ex-mayor Gisburne and his followers attacked Bootham Bar and formed a liveried association, apparently in the hope of recapturing political power. Under Quixlay's prejudiced eye two of Gisburne's henchmen, Robert de Harom and Richard de Kendale, were accused of a variety of crimes, including a murder of as long ago as 1372. Like the modern student of the revolt, the English government seems to have found itself unable to discover the truth amid the series of charges and counter-charges brought by the two parties. In November 1382 the city was required to pay 1,000 marks for a general pardon.[1]

A. ACCORDING TO A PARLIAMENTARY PETITION, NOVEMBER–DECEMBER 1380

Rot. Parl., III, 96–7

50. Item, the commons pray to the king their lord concerning a great and notorious report in this present parliament of the horrible deed recently performed by various malefactors belonging to the commons of the city of York – who assumed royal power to themselves by a false alliance and confederacy. According to the liberties and customs of the said city, their mayor should be elected on the day after the feast of the Purification [3 February] to serve for a year. Accordingly the citizens elected, on 3 February 1380, John de Gysburn to be their mayor for this present year. Gysburn held the said office peacefully until the Monday after the feast of St Katherine [26 November] when the said malefactors rose in force and chased their mayor out of the city. They then forcibly broke down by means of their axes and other arms the doors and windows of their Guildhall, entered it and made a certain Simon de Quixlay swear to be their mayor – against his will and that of the good men of the city. They compelled all the

---

1 Réville, pp. 271–4; and see *V.C.H. Yorkshire, City of York* (1961), pp. 80–2, for a short but very valuable account of the York risings.

good men then in the city to swear [loyalty] to their new mayor, for fear of death and against their will. The malefactors also made a new ordinance declaring that whenever the bells on the Bridge sounded 'aukeward', whether by day or night, all the commons of the city should rise together and have proclaimed various ordinances newly composed by them in opposition to the law and the established good customs of the city. And so they continue, pursuing their spiteful and horrible actions from one day to another, to the destruction of the city and the great danger of the realm unless a speedy and forceful punishment is now decreed. Let it please you, with the good advice of the lords and the other wise men assembled in this present parliament, to provide a remedy that will correct all other malefactors in the kingdom by punishing those of York.

The king wills, with the assent of the lords and commons in parliament, first that a commission should be sent in haste to the earl of Northumberland and other lords, knights and esquires of the country to enquire about the said malefactors – by means of good and worthy men who live near the city or by other methods as seems best to them. The commissioners are to discover the real truth and return a list of the names of those found blameworthy to the royal council without delay; so that they can be punished as an example to all other rioters and malefactors in time to come. Writs should also be made and sent to York by two serjeants-of-arms to summon before the king and his council without delay twenty-four of the most notorious leaders and abettors of the said rioters and malefactors, their names to be sent to the Chancellor of England. When they have arrived, let them be ordered into custody and not delivered by mainprise until the said earl and his fellow justices of the said commission have certified what they have discovered about them.

Item, another writ should be sent to Simon de Quixlay, sworn mayor of the said conspirators, ordering him to abandon that office which he holds to the detriment of royal power and against the Crown; the same writ is to order him to come before the king and his council on a fixed day to account for his action, etc.

Item, another writ should be sent to John de Gysburn, mayor of the said city in that he was elected by means of a free and common election, ordering him to occupy and serve in his office of mayor until the day after the next feast of the Purification [3 February 1381] – according to the liberties and customs of the city.

Item, another writ should be sent to the bailiffs, good men and all the commonalty of the said city, commanding them to respect the said John, their mayor, as the person who represents the state of our lord king in the said city, under penalty of forfeiting their goods, chattels and everything else. And the king wills that a proclamation to this effect should be made within the city so that no one can excuse himself by ignorance, etc.

B. ACCORDING TO THE YORK 'MEMORANDUM BOOK'

York Memorandum Book, ed. M. Sellers (Surtees Society, 1912–15), II 69–70

Memorandum that on 24 November 1381 all the charters of the convent of Friars Preachers at York were confirmed by the king, and these confirmations enrolled on the king's roll. On Monday 17 June in the same year the earthen walls against the city walls were destroyed and lowered to the ground and the great gates, both towards the Ouse and towards kynges toftes, were carried off by the rebellious commons of the city. And during the following Lent, Simon de Quixlay, then mayor of the city, was compelled by the king's council in chancery to renovate and repair these walls and gates at the expense of the city. Simon entered into an obligation in the royal chancery to complete these repairs before the following 24 June under penalty of 5000 marks. Under the same penalty he undertook that men of the city would not henceforward use violence against the abode of the Friars Preachers. All these things were obtained and procured, at his own expense, by the reverend friar John Paris.

C. ACCORDING TO THE YORK JURORS' PRESENTMENTS, AUGUST 1381

Coram Rege Roll, Michaelmas 5 Richard II [KB. 27/482], Rex, memb. 11; briefly and slightly inaccurately summarised in Réville, p. 272 (the same roll, memb. 35, contains the indictments, made on the same day by the same York jurors, against the late mayor, John de Gisburne and three more of his associates)

The indictments mentioned in the abovementioned writ [by which, on 12 September 1381 Richard II had ordered Simon de Quixlay and his fellow justices to dispatch the said indictments to the royal chancery] follow in these words: –

Presentments and indictments taken at York before Simon de Quixlay, Thomas Gra, John Berden and Thomas Thurkill, keepers of the peace and royal justices appointed to hear and determine various transgressions and other misdeeds committed in the city of York, on Thursday 29 August [1381] at York. The twelve jurors of the city of York [whose names are recorded] declare on their oath that Robert de Harom, mercer, Richard de Kendale and several other malefactors and disturbers of the king's peace came to York on Monday 1 July [1381] in a warlike manner and arrayed with armed force. Armed in hauberks, with pieces of iron and other weapons they assaulted at Bootham Bar in the suburbs of York William de Hornby, Thomas de Santon, Adam de Wyghale, John de Stodeleye and others of the king's people in the city; and there the accused threatened to injure and kill them if they managed to meet them. And so the accused besieged the city of York outside Bootham Bar on that day; and threatened to kill and wound the said persons. And they rode in armour and array to the disturbance of the king's and the people's peace; and they had sworn and allied themselves at York to do these things on that day.

And [the jurors] say that Robert de Harom, mercer and Richard de Kendale had come to York in a warlike manner and armed in hauberks, with pieces of iron, swords, bows and arrows and other arms on Wednesday 29 January [1376]; and there they had assaulted John de Blaktoft, skinner, Peter de Heselyngton, skinner, William de Betelwang, skinner, and Alan de Bradelay, and proceeded to strike, wound, maltreat and otherwise persecute them – to the grave injury of the said victims and against the king's peace.

And [the jurors] say that the same Robert de Harom and Richard de Kendale are common malefactors and disturbers of the king's peace because they maintained and sustained the aforesaid transgressions and misdeeds against William de Hornby, Thomas de Santon, Adam de Wyghale and others of the king's people of the city of York. The same Robert de Harom and Richard de Kendale attempted to assemble various conventicles in York on the two occasions mentioned above. And at York on Thursday 1 August [1381] they gave caps and other liveries of one colour to various members of their confederacy and to maintain their said schemes – against the form of the ordinance and statutes of the lord king on this matter – namely to Thomas Hudson, Thomas Raper, John Carter and Richard de Assheby. This was done to the disturbance of the king's subjects and his peace.

And [the jurors] declare on oath that Richard de Kendale, late servant of John of Gysburn of York, feloniously murdered and killed William de Dalton, webster, out of malice aforethought at Bootham Bar in York on Monday 16 August [1372].

47 The Riots at Scarborough

Coram Rege Roll, Easter 9 Richard II [KB. 27/500], Rex, membs. 12, 12v; partly printed in Réville, pp. 253–6

Of all the towns of northern England the relatively small port of Scarborough would seem to have been one of the least likely to succumb to the epidemic of lawlessness which swept the country in June 1381. Yet if, as seems likely, the following inquisitions can be believed, the news of rebellion further south provoked at least 500 inhabitants of Scarborough into violent demonstration. Robert Galoun and his colleagues were clearly intent on paying off old grudges; but in the absence of the background detail available for York and Beverley it is difficult to speculate on the general aims and grievances of the Scarborough rioters. Scarborough was a borough much less privileged than York or Beverley and it is therefore not surprising that the chief targets of hostility in the coastal town were royal bailiffs and officials drawn (like the unpopular Acclom dynasty) from an exclusive native urban oligarchy. There is little evidence of genuine class antagonism at Scarborough in 1381: the rebel leader, Robert Galoun, was wealthy enough to have undertaken the foundation of a perpetual chantry in the parish church during the previous year.[1] News of the upheavals at Scarborough reached the royal government in the summer of 1381 and Henry Percy, earl of Northumberland, was charged with the duty of trying the rebels immediately. In his presence, the twelve jurors of Scarborough itself, of the wapentakes of Dickering and Buckrose and of the liberty of Pickering, made their different presentments. Galoun, Hunter, Symson and Lovell were eventually pardoned by letters close of 10 May 1386; and the town itself escaped with a fine of 400 marks.

The jurors [of Scarborough] declare under oath that Robert Galoun, William Marche, Robert Hunter, John Cant, Thomas Symmeson senior, John Broun and many other malefactors whose names are unknown heard and knew that the risings and assemblies in the southern parts [of England] were the work of rebels and the king's enemies and desired to do likewise; and so they raised hostile fellowships, groups and assemblies at Scarborough and acted as the king's enemies also. On the preceding eve of the Nativity of St John the Baptist [23 June 1381] they gathered together at least five hundred men, allied with one another by means of an oath and the livery of many hoods. That same night, the accused (in the company of the said groups and fellowships)

---

[1] *Fasti Parochiales III* (Yorkshire Archaeological Society, Record Series, 1967), pp. 110–11.

crossed through the town of Scarborough in a hostile manner and as the king's enemies; and they besieged many liegemen of the king, namely Robert de Aclom, John de Aclom, William de Shropham, Alan Waldyfe, John de Stokwyth and several others, in their own houses within the town. Later they led the said liegemen to prison and kept them there until they swore that they would be faithful to the said accused and the commons of all England – to the prejudice of the crown, without royal authority and notwithstanding the royal mandate already sent to them forbidding them to rebel. Moreover, they feloniously took and carried off various possessions of the said liegemen, namely £10 belonging to John Stokwyth and a hauberk worth forty shillings from John de Aclom.

Item, another inquisition taken before the said earl and others at Scarborough on the same day, by the oath of twelve jurors of the wapentakes of Dickering and Buckrose, namely, etc. The jurors declare on oath that at Scarborough on Sunday 23 June Robert Galoun, William de Marche, Robert Huntere, John Cant, shoemaker, Thomas Symson, basket-maker (*panyarman*), John Broun, John Lovell and others formed a mutual confederacy and bound themselves by oath (as enemies and traitors to the king) to destroy and rise against any people with whom they had, or wished to have, any grievance. The accused unanimously swore to maintain each of their individual complaints in common; and, as enemies and rebels to the lord king, they rose in various fellowships and bands against the king and his liegemen, making and wearing a livery of hoods for that purpose. On their own authority the accused also deposed and moved from their offices Robert de Aclom, one of the bailiffs of Scarborough, as well as all the other royal officials in the town; and they assumed royal power to appoint other men at their will to these offices, to the prejudice of the king and his crown. Item, [the jurors] declare that on 7 August William del Marche, a sworn member of the said league designed to proceed against those with whom any individual member had a grievance, came to the house of William Bann-burgh at Scarborough with the consent of all the others and wearing one of the said hoods; and, as a rebel and enemy to the king, he criminally extorted eight marks of gold and silver from him.

Item, another inquisition taken before the said earl and others at Scarborough on the same day, by the oath of twelve jurors of the liberty of Pickering, namely William del Halle of Aslakby and others. These jurors declare under oath that Robert Galoun, William Marche, Robert Hunter, John Broun, Thomas Symson, basket-maker (*panyarman*), and John Lovell rose criminally and treasonably against the king and his liegemen in various armed fellowships and bands at Scarborough on the eve of the Nativity of St John the Baptist [23 June]. The accused removed Robert de Aclom, one of the bailiffs of the town of Scarborough, from his office; and they besieged in their houses not only Robert de Aclom but also many other liegemen of the king, namely Robert Pad, John Stokwyth, William Scot, William Semer, William Person, William Manby, John Bonde, Henry Bannburgh, John Cartere and several others whose names are unknown. Later the accused dragged these victims, whom they would otherwise have wished to kill or burn in their houses, to prison; and they detained them there until they had paid fines and ransoms at the will of the accused. Item, the jurors declare that William Marche and Robert Hunter, together with many other malefactors of their conspiracy, feloniously and treasonably came on the same 23 June to the house of John Stokwyth of Scarborough (where he was living at the time) together with a great crowd of men called *rowtes*. Marche and Hunter dragged the said John out of his house and led him from street to street in Scarborough with a great shout called *hountays* until they reached the prison where they detained him until the following day. They took ten pounds of gold and silver from Stokwyth which they kept and still keep. On the next day, they had Stokwyth brought before them in the place where they were assembled; and some of the rebels declared that he should be beheaded and others that he should be hanged. Afterwards they made Stokwyth, together with other worthy men, enter into a written bond of £100 that he would await the judgment of the said malefactors on the following Saturday [29 June]. Notwithstanding this bond, they led Stokwyth back to prison and held him there for three or four days until a certain Henry de Rooston junior (who had married Stokwyth's daughter) made a general proclamation throughout the town that if anyone wished to lay a complaint against his father-in-law he should come and Henry would make amends at their will even though he might have to sell his lands, tenements, goods and chattels. Thus Henry saved John Stokwyth's life by pacifying the claimants with the sum of at least three pounds. Item, [the jurors] declare that William Marche was the chief of the said malefactors; but when John Stokwyth came before him (on the date and in the place mentioned above) beseeching him to spare his life for the love of God and the sake of charity, Marche spoke on behalf of himself and his fellows assembled in bands and refused to grant his request unless Stokwyth would give forty shillings; which sum Stokwyth paid to Marche to save his life and to fulfil Marche's will. Item, [the jurors] state that William del Marche, draper, Robert Galoun, Robert Huntere, John Cant, shoemaker, and all the commons of Scarborough criminally and treasonably besieged – on the Sunday after the feast of St Peter [30 June] – John Lascy of Ffolketon in the house of Robert de Aclom for a quarter of a day; so that the said John Lascy scarcely escaped from the town with his life and has never dared to re-enter Scarborough since that time. Item, [the jurors] declare that at Scarborough on the Nativity of St John the Baptist [24 June] William del Marche and Robert Hunter together with many others criminally and treasonably came to the house of William de Manby of Scarborough; allied and leagued together in a sworn confederacy, they rose against the latter, broke down his house and its doors and windows and took him away and imprisoned him for four days because he refused to go with them to chastise and wound the men in the cemetery of St Mary's church and to break down the gates and doors of the Friars Minor in order to apprehend Robert de Aclom and many others. After four days, the accused brought William de Manby out of prison and led him to a certain place where they threatened to behead him unless he would give them twenty marks; and the said William, for fear of his death, bound himself to give them as much as they asked for, according to the discretion of the earl of Northumberland. Item, [the jurors] declare that Robert Galoun, William Marche and Robert Huntere were the first and the leaders of those who rebelled within the town of Scarborough on the said date.

48 The Riots at Beverley

Ancient Petitions [SC.8], no. 11205; printed by C. T. Flower, 'The Beverley Town Riots', *Trans. Royal Hist. Soc.*, new series, XIX (1905) 94–5

The disturbances at Beverley in 1381 and 1382 were not only more violent but also presented a much greater challenge to traditional civic authority than those in York and Scarborough. Despite the formal nature of the original evidence, it is possible to establish the existence of a genuine class-conflict in late fourteenth-century Beverley – a struggle between a relatively small merchant oligarchy (the *probi homines* of the royal writs) and a group of lesser burgesses, usually craftsmen of the town, who were described by royal chancery clerks as the *communitas* of Beverley or, more accurately, as the *viri mediocres* and 'less sufficient men of the community of the town'. The course of this long contest is too devious and complex to be outlined here; but it needs to be noticed that the leaders of the *viri mediocres*, Richard de Midelton, Henry de Newark and Thomas White, were already wielding power as alderman and chamberlains of Beverley for several months before the outbreak of revolt in southern England. It was apparently the news from the south which encouraged

Midelton, Newark and White to carry out a policy of terror against the great Beverley patrician families of Coppendale, Beverley, Gerveys and Dudhill. Between 8 June 1381 and the end of the month, Midelton and his colleagues forced their way into the houses of their enemies and compelled them – in a manner characteristic of so many rebels during the year – to enter into written bonds with the insurgents.

When, in the late summer of 1381, the *probi homines* began to launch their counter-revolution with the government's assistance, the cancellation of these bonds and their defeasances was their primary objective. The letter printed below is representative of what Flower described as 'the steady and persistent flow of royal writs' which then descended on all those in office at Beverley. The attempts by Thomas de Manby and his two chamberlains, themselves apparently members of the *viri mediocres*, to postpone the day of reckoning met with little success. A compromise solution to the conflict was eventually achieved in the summer of 1382 and the bonds, still among the Chancery records, were presumably cancelled. The royal government showed its displeasure at the recent feuds by laying a heavy collective fine of 1,100 marks on the town in October 1382. As in London, York and several other English towns of the late fourteenth century, the ascendancy of a small mercantile oligarchy had been challenged but not displaced.

Richard, by the grace of God, king of England, France and lord of Ireland, to his beloved Thomas de Manby, alderman, Simon Cartwryght and William Ithoun, chamberlains, of the town of Beverley, greetings. A complaint has been made to us in our parliament that many malefactors and disturbers of our peace from the community of the said town, forgetful of its prosperity, have recently risen in bands against our peace; in the said town they went up to the houses of several of our lieges in armed force, and threatened to kill them and throw down or burn their dwellings. Moreover, by threats of force and fear of death, they compelled Adam Coppendale, Thomas de Beverley, John Gerveys, William Dudhill and other worthy men of the same town to make and then deliver to Richard de Midelton, late alderman, Thomas White, tiler, and Henry de Newark, late chamberlains, various bonds requiring large sums of money to be paid at a specified time and under certain forms and conditions. And we are requested to provide a remedy for this. We, desiring what is just to all of our subjects and with the assent and counsel of the peers and magnates assisting us in the said parliament, order you as strictly as we may to send the said bonds – which it is said are now in your keeping – safely and securely to us in our chancery at the next quinzaine of St Hilary wherever it should then be; and you are to command the said late alderman and chamberlains on your behalf (and under forfeit of the sums mentioned in the said bonds) to be there in person to show if they have or know any reason why the said bonds ought not to be cancelled and annulled as documents made under duress and compulsion against the law of our kingdom of England. And you are to make the said late alderman and chamberlains appear before us there; so that, having heard their reasons and inspected and carefully examined the said bonds, we will be able to proceed further in this matter and do what is just and reasonable. And you are to have there this writ, informing us clearly and openly of what you have done as a consequence of these letters. Witnessed by myself at Westminster, 10 December [1381].

(ENDORSEMENT) The Reply of Thomas de Manby, alderman, and the chamberlains of the town of Beverley. As regards sending certain bonds mentioned in this writ, no such documents are held by us or ever came into our custody; and so we cannot send these bonds on the day referred to in the writ. Moreover, they declare that Richard de Midelton, late alderman, Thomas White, tiler, and Henry de Newark, late chamberlains, were not to be found within the liberty of Beverley after the receipt of this writ: on account of which we cannot execute the intentions of this writ in the said matters.

49 Rising of the Villeins of the Abbot of Chester

Powell and Trevelyan, *Peasants' Rising and the Lollards*, pp. 14-16; transcribed from Chester Indictment Roll [Chester 25], no. 8, memb. 57

The following record of an insurrection by the *nativi* of the abbot of Chester was first discovered by Powell and Trevelyan at the end of the nineteenth century. This isolated reference to a peasants' revolt in the remote north-western county of Cheshire is of obvious significance in suggesting that the upheavals of 1381 spread very far indeed. However the Wirral was a notoriously lawless part of an often turbulent medieval county; and it is not absolutely certain that the rebels there were stirred to revolt by the example of events in Kent and Essex. The conspiracies in the Wirral took place as late as the end of July, that is after the justices, chamberlains and other notables of Chester had already received Richard II's letters patent (of 18 June 1381) ordering them to suppress all suspect risings and confederations. After reciting the contents of these letters patent, the Chester indictment roll continues as follows:—

By virtue of these letters a proclamation was made in the full county court of Chester on Tuesday 23 July 1381 according to the tenor and intention of the said letters. Similarly and in order to maintain the king's peace more surely, the bailiffs of the hundred of Wirral were given instructions in these words: –

'Richard, by the grace of God, king of England and of France, lord of Ireland, to the bailiffs and sheriffs of the hundred of Wirral, greetings. From the evidence of trustworthy men we have learnt that several of the villeins (*nativi*) of our beloved in Christ the abbot of Chester have made certain assemblies within the area of your jurisdiction; and they have gathered in secret confederacies within the woods and other hidden places in the said hundred. They have held certain secret counsels there

contrary to our recent proclamation on the subject; and they have
contributed to certain levies of pence which they then granted
to various men of your hundred – in order to have their help and
maintenance in the matter of several complaints and articles
illegally brought against the abbot by the said villeins. Therefore
we firmly command you to have it publicly proclaimed in those
places within your area of jurisdiction which seem most expedient
to you that everyone residing in your said hundred, of whatsoever
estate or condition, should absolutely refrain from such assemblies
and remain in peace. No one is to grant or concede taxes, levies
or financial contributions to any of our people in order to maintain such illegal complaints and articles – under penalty of losing
life, limbs and all that can be forfeited to us; the same penalties
apply to anyone who presumes to receive such subsidies, goods
or rewards for their services in maintaining such actions. And you
are to inform us how you have executed this order in our exchequer of Chester next Saturday, when you must return this
writ. You are not to omit to do this under penalty of paying £40
to us. Given at Chester 1 September [1381].'

Afterwards, on Wednesday 25 September 1381, before John
de la Pole, justiciar of Chester, twelve named jurors swore under
oath that in the full county court held at Chester on Tuesday 23
July 1381, and within the city of Chester on the Saturday then
following, and again at the parish church of Eastham on the next
Sunday, the aforesaid royal letters were read and a public proclamation made in the said places exactly in accordance with the
tenor of the king's mandates. And the jurors say that on the
following Monday Hugh Hervy [and fifteen other named men],
villeins of the abbot of Chester by right of his church of St
Werburgh of Chester, together with other villeins of the abbot
rose in arms. They assembled at the lee near Backford in the
hundred of Wirral, contrary to the said proclamation and royal
letters – to the contempt of the lord king, the breaking and
manifest disturbance of the peace, the terror of the king's people
in the city and the entire county of Chester, as well as to the
annihilation and destruction of the said abbot and convent and

the goods and chattels of their monastery and church. So they were seized, etc. And afterwards the said Hugh Hervy and the others were committed to the constable of Chester Castle. [The villeins were later allowed to leave prison under surety and the case was adjourned to the next county court.]

50 Rising of the Tenants of the Priory of Worcester

Documents illustrating the activities of the General and Provincial Chapters of the English Black Monks, ed. W. A. Pantin [Camden Third Series, 1931–7], III 204–5

Abbots and priors of English Benedictine monasteries were often less than candid in the excuses they gave for their inability to attend the general chapters of their Order in person. But there is no good reason to reject the substantial accuracy of the prior of Worcester's comments in his letters of proxy of July 1381. The prior, like most substantial English landlords during that summer, was fearful of impending calamity at the hands of his rebellious peasants; but his nervousness is of particular significance in that it was experienced in an area of England, the west country, where there is no direct documentary evidence for serious peasant unrest.

Let it be known to all that we, Walter [de Leigh], prior of the cathedral church of Worcester, make, ordain and constitute our beloved brother in Christ John Grene, fellow of our convent and doctor of theology, our proctor, representative, excuser and special envoy; and he is to appear on our behalf and in our name at the chapter general of the Black Monks to be held in St Andrew's monastery, Northampton, Lincoln diocese, on the next Monday after the feast of the Translation of St Thomas Martyr [8 July] and the following days. We give and grant to the said our proctor both general power and special instructions to offer excuses for our necessary and genuine absence; and to declare and state the reason for our inability to appear personally before the lords presiding at and others celebrating the chapter there, namely the great turbulence of our and our church's tenants, both free men and serfs as well as others who support them in their cause. These tenants, on the pretext of their claim to have a certain manumission, have risen in pride and impudence; and they openly and expressly refuse to do and perform the services they owe us, services on which a large part of our and our chapter's sustenance relies. On these grounds they are preparing to rebel against us and our church in violence and with all their strength. It is therefore necessary that we and our men should remain watchful and vigilant by night and day in order to suppress the malice of these tenants; and, in the meantime, we dare not absent ourselves lest the irreparable harm publicly threatened to us and our church should befall us. . . . In testimony of which things we have caused our seal to be affixed to these letters. Given at our priory of Worcester, 5 July [1381].

PART VI

Suppression and Survival

Nothing, according to Swift, renders a movement more popular than 'some degree of persecution'. Certainly the killing of Wat Tyler and the subsequent execution of the most notorious rebel leaders (Jack Straw, John Ball, Geoffrey Litster and William Grindcobbe among them) has done more to win posthumous sympathy for their cause than anything they said or did while alive. The chroniclers of the great revolt (nos. 52–5) all suggest that the suppression of the insurrection in south-eastern England after Smithfield and Billericay was pursued in the same vengeful and often vicious spirit that characterised the role played by Bishop Despenser of Norwich in East Anglia (see above, nos. 36, 41). Those who had taken up the sword of rebellion died by the avenging sword of retributive justice; and only Richard II's personal inclinations towards clemency stood between the commons and a veritable blood-bath. But at no point in the history of the revolt is the evidence of these chroniclers more untrustworthy and more at odds with the less melodramatic picture presented by legal records and charters of pardon (nos. 57, 58; and see above, nos. 23, 24, 32–4, 40, 45). Seventy years ago Charles Petit-Dutaillis was able to demonstrate, on the basis of Réville's transcripts from the Coram Rege Rolls and Ancient Indictments, that relatively few of the insurgents can be proved to have lost their lives or even their liberty as a consequence of their implication in the rebellion. More remarkable still were the pardons often rapidly conceded to various important rebel leaders (e.g., Thomas Farndon and John Horn of London, Sir Roger Bacon of Baconsthorpe in Norfolk, Robert Cave of Kent, Thomas Sampson of Suffolk and Sir William Coggan of Bridgwater), whose personal responsibility for crimes of violence and sometimes murder can be in no serious doubt. Presumably in this case, as in so many others, the poor found it more difficult than the rich to escape the inequitable workings of a corrupt and partial system of justice. But it seems clear that England as a whole experienced no 'reign of terror' in late 1381 and 1382; nothing, it might be said, became the English government more than the moderation with which it repressed a revolt it had helped to cause and failed to prevent.

An episode as shattering and cataclysmic as the great revolt inevitably left in its wake a series of minor riots and conspiracies during succeeding years (nos. 59, 61). But not one of these threatened to provoke another major upheaval – itself an indirect tribute to the king's and council's wisdom in treating the defeated rebels with a sensible combination of firmness and caution. The commons who assembled at the Westminster parliament during the first week of November 1381 showed a similar and, in the circumstances, commendable circumspection (no. 60); more realistic than the chroniclers, they blamed the errors of the government rather than the sins of the peasants for the late catastrophe. The immediate abandonment of the poll tax and the gradual decay of the more humiliating and irksome aspects of villein status (no. 63) removed at least some of the grievances which caused the explosion of 1381. Many grievances of course survived – to find different expression in various fifteenth-century rebellions, most notably that of Jack Cade in 1450 (no. 62). But severe agrarian distress and discontent can persist without necessarily inducing agrarian revolution; and the revolutionary transformation of the English social, economic and religious scene during the Tudor period was accompanied by several risings but by no real equivalent of the German Peasants' War of 1524–6 (no. 64) – a movement which seems to throw more retrospective light on the issues of 1381 than does, for example, the Norfolk rebellion led by Robert Kett in 1549. If Kett was the heir of Geoffrey Litster, so was Thomas Muntzer the spiritual descendant of John Ball as well as of John Wycliffe.

51 'The Ax was Scharp'

Robbins, *Historical Poems*, p. 54; cf. Wright, *Political Poems*, I 278; Sisam, *Fourteenth Century Verse and Prose*, p. 161

The following quatrain survives on an otherwise blank leaf near the end of Cambridge University MS. Dd. 14. 2. A better-known version of the last two lines ascribes the persecution to the year 1391:—

> 'The ax was sharpe, the stokke was harde,
>   In the xiiii yere of Kyng Richarde.'

But Robbins argues very plausibly that the poem originally referred to the repression following the Peasants' Revolt.

> Man be ware and be no fool:
> Thenke apon the ax, and of the stool!
> The stool was hard, the ax was scharp,
> The iiii yere of kyng Richard.

(stool: *executioner's block*)

52 The Suppression of the Revolt according to the 'Anonimalle Chronicle'

Anonimalle Chronicle, p. 151: continued from no. 35 above. Cf. Oman, *Great Revolt*, p. 205

The *Anonimalle Chronicle* closes its account of the Peasants' Revolt with the following very general description of the repressive measures taken by Richard II after Smithfield. The view that the government began by executing many rebels but then showed clemency in return for cash seems the correct one; but it is somewhat opposed to that of Walsingham, as seen in the next extract (no. 53).

Afterwards the king sent his messengers to various parts of the country in order to capture the malefactors and put them to death. Many were taken and hanged in London and elsewhere, numerous gallows being erected around the city of London and other cities and towns of the south country. Finally, as it pleased God, the king saw that too many of his liege subjects would be undone and much blood shed; so he took pity in his heart and with the advice and assent of his council ordained that they should receive his grace and pardon for their misdeeds – on condition that they should never rise again, under penalty of losing life and limbs. Everyone was to have his charter of pardon and pay the king as fee for his seal twenty shillings, to make him rich. And so finished this evil war.

53 The Suppression of the Revolt according to Thomas Walsingham

Walsingham, *Historia Anglicana*, II 13–15, 16–22; cf. *Chronicon Angliae*, pp. 312–17. Continued from no. 68 below

Walsingham's report of the repression of the rebellion in the counties of Kent and Essex is both longer and more entertaining than that provided by any other chronicler. Despite some obvious errors (e.g. the size of Richard's army), documentary evidence confirms the general reliability of his narrative and account of the king's movements in the weeks after Smithfield. Moreover Walsingham himself took pains to insert authentic copies of two important royal proclamations at the appropriate points in his story. The rebels from Kent apparently made no attempt to organise concerted resistance to the government after Tyler's death and in that county the work of pacification could be safely entrusted to small groups of local levies. In Essex the royalist counter-attack met with some opposition but this was rapidly swept aside at a skirmish in the woods near Billericay on 28 June, two or three days after the collapse of the Norfolk rising at North Walsham. Walsingham makes no attempt to hide either his glee at the rebels' final humiliations or his approval of the harsh sentences pronounced by the new Chief Justice of the King's Bench, Sir Robert Tresilian.

We have now written, not without labour, and for the attention and instruction of posterity, the tragic history of the lordship of the rustics, the debauchery of the commons and the madness of the villeins (*nativorum*). It now seems fitting to relate what rewards their actions brought them once the king and nobles could breathe like lords again.

On the death, already mentioned, of that most arrogant rascal Walter Tylere, the hope and trust of the rustics collapsed. But as the king and his counsellors were yet in doubt as to whether the people were still disposed to evil, they granted charters of manumission and pardon to them, as we have said, and allowed them to depart.

After this, the king assembled an army of Londoners and sent messengers into the country asking all those who loved him and honoured the realm to hurry to him in London, well-armed and on horse-back: no one was to come weaponless and no one on foot and those who lacked either arms or horses were to stay at home. And so it happened that within three days 40,000 properly armed horsemen had gathered around the king. Each day the king himself went out to Blackheath to review the number of new arrivals, riding first among his armed men on a great war-horse. His standard was carried before him and he enjoyed being seen in his army and recognised as their lord by his men. After this great force had been assembled, larger than any ever seen in England before, the king heard that the Kentishmen were conspiring again and had assembled another wicked confederacy to the ruin of the whole kingdom. What more need I say? The king was outraged and his army furious. They set out immediately for Kent, having decided to remove the entire race of Kentishmen and Jutes from the land of the living. But the king was pacified by the intervention of the magnates and notables of Kent who were with him and stood surety for the commons and told him of the evils that such persecution would inflict upon all members of an ignorant people. Therefore justices were first sent to sit and inquire about the malefactors and especially those who had been the authors, inciters and leaders of sedition among the mobs in Kent. And the land grew silent at the sight of the justices; and the people trembled.

Then the mayor of London, sitting in his judicial capacity, within the liberty of the city, began to try not only the malefactors of his own city but also all those who could be caught from Kent, Essex, Sussex, Norfolk, Suffolk and other counties where there were commons. They were boldly brought to public justice and the mayor had all those whom he found to be involved in the said infamies beheaded. [*Cf. nos. 56–8 below.*]

The beheading of the leaders of the Commons at London
Then John Straw, John Kyrkeby and Alan Tredere, leaders of the commons, were beheaded – as was John Starlyng of Essex who boasted that he had executed the archbishop.[1] The latter, soon after that atrocious crime, was seized by the devil and became insane. Returning home, he hung a naked sword from his neck and before his chest and an unsheathed knife (which we call a 'daggere') at his back. Then like a madman he wandered through the roads and streets, shouting and protesting that he had been one of those who killed the archbishop. And after he had stayed in his house for several days he returned to London

---

[1] Possibly to be identified with John Sterlyng, the rebel leader entertained by Alderman Horn in London on the night of 12–13 June: see above, p. 214.

declaring that he had come to accept the reward for his deed. As he continued to state that he had beheaded the archbishop, he received for his reward a sentence of capital punishment. And let it be known that all the men of Kent and Essex who had laid their guilty hands on the archbishop confessed in a similar way, however unwillingly; and in the end all these guilty men came forward of their own accord and were, for the most part, beheaded in London. . . .

Meanwhile the king stayed (in the company of a large crowd) either in London or Waltham,[1] considering what should be done for the peace and advantage of the common realm. At last the king's council decided to send out the following letters throughout the country:–

Royal Commission to resist the disturbers of the peace of the Realm
'Richard, by the grace of God, king of England and France and lord of Ireland, to all and each of the sheriffs, mayors, bailiffs and our other faithful men of the county of N., greetings. Because we understand that various of our subjects have risen in various counties of England, against our peace and to the disturbance of the people, and have formed various gatherings and assemblies in order to commit many injuries against our faithful subjects, and because they affirm and inform our people that they have made the said assemblies and risings by our will and with our authority; we hereby notify you that these risings, assemblies and injuries did not and ought not to derive from our will or authority, but that they displease us immensely as a source of shame to us, of prejudice to the crown and of damage and commotion to our entire kingdom. Wherefore we command and order you to have this publicly proclaimed, in the places where it seems to you this can be best and most quickly done to preserve the peace and resist the said insurgents against our peace; you are to do this to the limit of your ability and with force, if necessary, so that for lack of such proclamations and resistance, damages and ills

1 Richard II had reached Waltham by Sunday 23 June (Réville, p. 286).

shall not continue to be perpetrated by the said assemblies or risings. And you are to omit nothing, under pain of complete forfeiture of your goods; and you must command all and each of our liege-men and subjects to desist completely from such assemblies, risings and injuries and return to their homes to live there in peace, under penalty of losing life and limb and all their goods. Witnessed by myself at London, 18 June [1381].'

This commission much comforted those faithful to the king and kingdom but alarmed, quite deservedly, the wicked. Those who had previously enjoyed the centre of the stage were now forced to seek hiding-places, while the lawyers who had fled from the fury of the mob now dared to return from their caves. The former now waited in silence, fearing the judgment and justice to be enforced upon them; the latter lost their fear and joyfully prepared to avenge their injuries. However the rustics were not yet reduced to such fear in every part of the country. In Essex, where the madness had its original roots, the rustics again assem-bled a great crowd at Billericay (a vill near the town called Hatfield Peverel). Trusting too much to their own strength and deceived by their own pride they determined either to enjoy the liberty they sought by violence or to die in fighting for it.

Messengers are sent by the Rustics to the King from Essex, demanding liberty

The men from Essex therefore sent messengers to the king, then staying at Waltham, to discover whether he planned to allow them to enjoy the aforesaid liberty. They also requested that they should be equal in liberty to the lords and should not be compelled to attend courts, with the one exception of the view of frank-pledge twice a year. But the king and his attendant council marvelled greatly at the temerity of the rustics. For a time they hesitated as to what reply to give, until the king himself made the following answer: 'O!', he said, 'you wretched men, detestable on land and sea, you who seek equality with lords are not worthy to live. You would certainly have been punished by the most shameful death if we had not determined to observe the laws

concerning [the safe-conduct of] envoys. But as you have come
here in the guise of envoys, you will not die now but may keep
your lives until you have accurately informed your fellows of
our reply. So give this message to your colleagues from the king.
Rustics you were and rustics you are still; you will remain in
bondage, not as before but incomparably harsher. For as long as
we live and, by God's grace, rule over the realm, we will strive
with mind, strength and goods to suppress you so that the rigour
of your servitude will be an example to posterity. Both now and
in the future people like yourselves will always have your misery
as an example before their eyes; they will find you a subject for
curses and will fear to do the sort of things you have done. But
as for you, who have come here as envoys, once you have carried
out our command and the duties of your embassy, you may keep
your lives if you decide to return to us and remain faithful and
loyal. Choose now what you judge the best course, for you must
return to your fellows and fulfil our commands.'

Immediately after these messengers had departed, Lord Thomas
Woodstock, earl of Buckingham, and Lord Thomas Percy,
brother of the earl of Northumberland, were sent into Essex to
crush the pride of the aforementioned rustics. These villeins
fortified their position in the same way as we have described the
men of Norfolk doing: they used ditches, stakes and carts besides
enjoying the more secure protection of woods and forests. But
although there were a great number of them, they were easily
dispersed by only ten lances (to use the common term) who had
gone ahead of the said lords.

The Slaughter of the Rustics

So when these two lords arrived and discovered that the rebels
had fled, they surrounded the woods in case any of them should
escape, for it would have been dangerous to pursue them into the
forest. Eventually five hundred of the rustics were killed here and
there by the lords' men while the rest were protected and saved
by the cover of the woods. The rebels abandoned to the soldiers
eight hundred horses which they had brought with them to draw

and carry their loads. But even after this victory the malice of the rascals did not come to an end. For those who had managed to escape the slaughter again began to agitate and grow malicious. Those rebels who had been scattered, reassembled once more and went to Colchester where they began to incite the townsmen by means of urgent entreaties, threats and arguments to yet new disturbances and madness. But after failing to do this, they moved on to Sudbury. For they knew that Lords FitzWalter and John Harleston were following their route with an armed force. Suddenly, when the rebels were making their usual proclamations on behalf of the commons, this force rushed upon them unexpectedly, killing as many as it wished. The remainder were allowed to live or sent to prison.

The King proceeds to Havering in Essex

While these events were taking place in Essex and Suffolk, the lord king, wishing to do justice on Essex in his own person, went to an estate of his called 'Haveryng atte Bour' near the town of Chelmsford.[1] There he appointed Lord Robert Tresilian as justice to sit and investigate the malefactors and disturbers of the country as well as to punish the guilty according to the customs of the realm. Now when the Essex men realised their bad fortune and approaching fate, more than five hundred of them, with bare feet and their heads uncovered, came before the king in supplication, seeking his grace and mercy. Such mercy was granted to them on condition that they revealed the names of the more important malefactors and inciters of the previous disturbance and handed them over to the king. So it was done and many were delivered into custody. To decide whether or not they should be killed, the justice obliged twenty-four men to swear on their consciences that they would speak truthfully as to their actions and conduct – no one was to be spared by favour or to be persecuted because of private hatred. The result was that many, say a dozen, perished by drawing and hanging, while another nineteen were hanged from a gallows.

[1] Richard II was at Havering-atte-Bower on 7 July (Réville, p. cxv).

Previously, the judges who sat in Essex, Kent and London had beheaded many rustics because of the multitude of people to be executed – until it seemed that this type of capital punishment no longer corresponded to the crimes committed. Such a penalty was too mild a punishment for the cases in question. Wherefore it was later decreed, according to the customs of the realm, that all those discovered to be criminals should, as we have said, be punished by drawing and hanging; and this was the method employed in Essex. [Walsingham concludes his description of the repression of the revolt in Essex by inserting in his narrative a copy of Richard II's proclamation, dated at Chelmsford on 2 July, formally revoking all the charters of amnesty and enfranchisement he had granted at Mile End on 14 June: also printed in Rymer's *Foedera*, vol. III, pt III (Hague, 1740), p. 124.]

54 The Suppression of the Revolt according to Henry Knighton

Chronicon Henrici Knighton, II 150–1

In comparison with Walsingham, Henry Knighton offers little information on the repression of the great revolt: he probably knew nothing of the measures taken by the government in and around London after 15 June. But Tresilian's 'bloody assize' afforded an obvious topic of general interest; and as a loyal adherent of the house of Lancaster, Knighton gave John of Gaunt some of the credit for Richard II's later clemency to the defeated rebels. It is doubtful whether the additional influence of Richard's new queen, Anne of Bohemia, was more than nominal; but a considerable number of the individual pardons conceded in 1382 and 1383 were in fact said to have been granted at her request.

After these events [the reconciliation of John of Gaunt and Richard II at the council of Reading in August 1381] and a return to tranquillity, the time came for the king to punish the delinquents. Lord Robert Tresilian, justice, was therefore sent by the king's command to investigate and punish those who had risen against the peace. He was active everywhere and spared no one, so causing a great slaughter. And because the malefactors had attacked and put to death all the justices whom they could find, including John de Cavendish, and had spared the lives of none of the lawyers of the realm whom they could apprehend, so Tresilian now spared no one but repaid like for like. For whoever was accused before him on the grounds of rebellion, whether justly or out of hate, immediately suffered the sentence of death. He condemned (according to the nature of their crimes) some to beheading, some to hanging, some to drawing through the cities and then hanging in four parts of the cities and some to disembowelling, followed by the burning of their entrails before them while the victims were still alive, and then their execution and the division of their corpses into quarters to be hanged in four parts of the cities. Lord John Ball was himself captured at Coventry and brought to St Albans where, by royal command, he was drawn, hanged and quartered so that the four parts of his body should be sent to hang in four different places.

In the same year [actually 20 January 1382] King Richard married at Westminster, Anne, the daughter of the king of Bohemia and the sister of the Emperor. It is said that the king gave the Emperor £10,000 to marry her, not including the expense of seeking her out and leading her to England at his own cost.

In the following year, 1382, at the special request of Queen Anne and other magnates of the realm, especially the pious duke of Lancaster, the lord king gave a general pardon to all the aforesaid rebels and malefactors, their adherents, abettors and followers. He granted charters to this effect and through God's mercy the previous madness came to an end.

55 The Suppression of the Revolt according to Froissart

Froissart, trans. Berners, ed. G. C. Macaulay, pp. 261–2; cf. Froissart, *Chroniques*, X 129–31

Froissart's brief account of the vengeance taken by Richard II in the summer of 1381 concludes his long description of the Peasants' Revolt. In characteristic but unhistorical fashion, he simplified a complicated process and used his imagination to reconstruct an episode at Ospringe in Kent which might serve to symbolise Richard's attitude to the rebels. The story may indeed be completely fictitious. Richard II's well-established itinerary during the summer months of 1381 would seem to have left him with no time to visit all the towns mentioned by Froissart. There is certainly no doubt that the author's desire to praise 'noble and great lords' led him to exaggerate the extent of the young king's personal participation in the work of repression.

Now I shall shew you the vengeance that the king of England took of these ungracious people in the mean season, while the duke of Lancaster was in Scotland.[1]

When these people were reappeased and that [Thomas] Baker was executed to death [at St Albans], and Lister at Stafford (*Stafort*), Wat Tyler, Jack Straw, John Ball and divers other at London, then the king was counselled to go visit his realm, through every shire, bailiwick and village, to purge and punish all the said evil-doers, and to get again all such letters as by force he had given them in divers places, and so to bring again his realm in good order. Then the king sent secretly for a certain number of men of arms to come to him at a day appointed, and so they did to the number of a five hundred spears and as many archers; and when they were all come as the king had devised, the king

[1] John of Gaunt left Edinburgh on 10 July and met the king at Reading on 10 August (Armitage-Smith, *John of Gaunt*, pp. 251–4).

departed from London with his household-men all only and took the way into Kent, whereas first these ungracious people began to stir: and these foresaid men of war followed after the king and coasted [flanked] him, but they rode not in his company. The king entered into Kent and came to a village called Ospringe,[1] and called the mayor and all the men of the town before him. And when they were all come into a fair place, the king made to be shewed them by one of his council how they had erred against the king, and how they had near turned all England to tribulation and to loss. And because that the king knew well that this business was begun by some of them and not by all, wherefore it were better that some did bear the blame than all, therefore he commanded them that they should shew what they were that were culpable, on pain to be for ever in the king's indignation and to be reputed as traitors against him. And when they that were there assembled heard that request and saw well that such as were culpable should excuse all the other, then they beheld each other and at last said: 'Sir, behold him here by whom this town was first moved.' Incontinent he was taken and hanged, and so there were hanged to the number of seven; and the letters that the king had given them were demanded again, and so they were delivered again, and torn and broken before all the people. And it was said to them all: 'Sirs, ye that be here assembled, we command you in the king's name on pain of death every man to go home to his own house peaceably, and never to grudge nor rise against the king nor none of his officers; and this trespass that ye have done the king doth pardon you thereof.' Then they cried all with one voice: 'God thank the king's grace and all his council!'

In like manner as the king did at Ospringe, he did at Canterbury, at Sandwich, at Yarmouth, at Orwell and in other places: in like wise he did in all other places of his realm, whereas any rebellion had been; and there were hanged and beheaded more than fifteen hundred.

[1] A village immediately south-west of Faversham and one certainly involved in the recent disturbances.

56 Royal Commission to keep the Peace in the City of London, 15 June 1381

Printed by Réville, pp. 234–5, from Patent Roll, 4 Richard II, part 3, memb. 5; cf. *C.P.R.*, *1381–5*, p. 18

The first measures to suppress the Peasants' Revolt by due processes of law were undertaken by the government on the very day of Tyler's death. Although Richard and his councillors recognised that it was still impossible to rely on the loyalty of the sheriffs and other royal officials of the English counties, they rightly believed that London itself could and should now be safely secured. Late on Saturday 15 June and presumably not long after the young Richard's triumphal re-entry into the city from Clerkenwell Fields, five commissioners were appointed to safeguard London and punish the rebels. The men chosen to re-establish law and order were, significantly, the four London aldermen (William Walworth; Nicholas Brembre; John Philipot; Robert Launde) knighted by Richard II a little earlier in the day with the addition of Edward III's war captain, Sir Robert Knolles, who had led troops from the city to the king's rescue soon after Tyler's downfall. Another royal commission, issued at the same time but not translated here, gave Walworth, Brembre, Philipot, Launde and Knolles together with two distinguished lawyers, Robert Bealknap and William Cheyne, power to arrest and implead rebels from the counties of Essex, Kent, Surrey, Sussex and Middlesex. Because of these two commissions, the ensuing speedy prosecution of many English countrymen by a panel largely consisting of London merchants was legally valid although undoubtedly unusual.

'*Concerning certain persons appointed to safeguard the City of London*' The king to his beloved and faithful William Walworth, mayor of his city of London, Robert Knolles, John Philipot, Nicholas Brembre and Robert Launde, greetings. We desire with all our heart, especially at this time of disturbance, to duly protect, save and securely rule the city of London in the face of the invasion and assaults of those men who (as you know) have recently risen against our will in various parts of our realm of England and at present assemble in illegal groups to the greatest possible harm and prejudice of ourselves and our faithful liege subjects. [Therefore] we assign, appoint and ordain you, separately and together, to keep, defend, protect, rule and govern the said city, its suburbs and other places without, both by sea and by water, at our command but according to your own discretion, by the means which seem to you most safe and expedient; and also to resist any who wish to attack or assault the city, its suburbs or the parts without or to form assemblies or groups of the sort mentioned above with all your power and with that of those from London, its suburbs or elsewhere whom you can associate with you. And if, which God forbid, there are in the future any assemblies or disturbances in the city, its suburbs or elsewhere, you are to similarly settle and pacify them in the most fitting way you can; . . . and you are to punish everyone who makes or presumes to make riots, risings and assemblies against our peace, according to their deserts and our orders, either according to the law of our kingdom of England or by other ways and methods, by beheadings and the mutilation of limbs, as seems to you most expeditious and sensible. . . . And if men are likely to disturb the city and its suburbs by coming with supplies of victuals and other necessities for the sustenance and defence of London, then you are to go and meet them with a sufficient force at the places which seem most suitable to you. You are then to have these victuals and other goods taken and led into the city, either by land or water, provided only that those who possessed these commodities shall have reasonable satisfaction and payment. . . . We also command all and each of our sheriffs, aldermen, citizens, law-worthy men, commons and our other faithful liege subjects of the city, its suburbs and elsewhere that they shall obey you in the carrying out of these letters, serving and assisting you faithfully . . . according to the faith and loyalty which they owe to us and under penalty of forfeiting all their goods if they do not. . . . Witnessed by the king himself at London, 15 June.

57 The Trial and Pardon of John Awedyn of Essex

Coram Rege Roll, Easter 6 Richard II [KB. 27/488], Rex, memb. 23; partly summarised by Réville, p. 209

According to most of the chroniclers Walworth and his colleagues carried out their commission to punish the late rebels with harsh severity as well as speed. But the evidence of trial records suggests that the justices were less vindictive than even Froissart – who estimated that about 1500 rebels were hanged or beheaded – believed. Not many more than 100 persons can actually be proved to have been sentenced to capital punishment for their participation in the rising. But the question is a difficult one, partly because at least some of the more notorious rebels were executed summarily without a formal trial, and more especially because our knowledge of how Walworth and his fellow-justices conducted their indictments usually only emerges when a case was evoked to the king's court (cf. above, no. 33). The following is a representative example of the procedure followed in such cases, and has the added interest of involving one of the captains of the commons from Essex (who nevertheless secured a full pardon). The record also proves that Walworth's legal proceedings against the rebels, complete with juries of presentment, were under way by Monday 17 June, two days after Smithfield.

London. The lord king sent his letters close to his beloved and faithful William Walworth in these words: 'Richard, by the grace of God, king of England and France, and lord of Ireland, to his beloved and faithful William Walworth, greetings. For certain reasons the indictment made before you and your fellows, our late justices (appointed to chastise and punish certain rebels, who had risen against our peace and their allegiance in the city of London and elsewhere, for various treasons, felonies and other offences), whereby John Awedyn was indicted should be determined, it is said, before us and not elsewhere. Therefore we order you to send us the said indictment and all which pertains to it openly and clearly under your seal together with this writ; so that we shall have it next Thursday wherever in England we happen to be and can proceed further in the matter according to the law and custom of the kingdom. Witnessed by myself at Westminster on 20 April in the sixth year of my reign [1383].'

The indictment mentioned in the said writ follows in these words: An indictment made before William Walworth, mayor of the city of London, and his colleagues, justices of the lord king, appointed to commence, hear and determine cases of various felonies and treasons committed by several malefactors who recently in the city of London, its suburbs and several other counties criminally and treasonably rose against the lord king and assembled in illicit bands, committing murders, treasons and felonies in the king's own presence, to the harm of the king and his faithful liegemen, at the Guildhall in London on 17 June 1381, by virtue of the royal letters patent addressed to the said justices, etc.

The sworn jurors of Candelwykstrete in London, namely . . . [twelve names follow] . . . present that John Awedyn of the county of Essex was on Friday after the feast of Corpus Christi [14 June 1381] one of the rebels against the lord king in the city of London; and that on the same day, he, as a captain of the said rebellious malefactors, came with others, and displaying a banner, to the house of Nicholas Hawtot in the parish of St Swithun's London, and there took possession of the said tenements and forthwith expelled the same Nicholas and all his family and made him deliver all the said tenements to himself. [The remainder of the entry on the Coram Rege roll recites the outcome of the trial. Although excluded from the general amnesty of late 1381, Awedyn had received letters of pardon from the king on 16 March 1383 at the request of the earl of Oxford. Accordingly when he appeared at the King's Bench on 29 April 1383, he presented this pardon as well as letters *de non molestando* (protecting him against further proceedings for the same offence by royal officials) of the same date and was allowed to go free.]

58 A Tall Story: Oxfordshire Rebels as French Agents

Coram Rege Roll, Hilary 5 Richard II [KB. 27/483], Rex, memb. 27; partly printed by Petit-Dutaillis in introduction to Réville, p. LVIII

This second example of trial proceedings conducted in London during the week after Smithfield throws a vivid light on the hysteria which accompanied the great revolt and testifies indirectly to the continued fear of a French invasion (cf. above, nos. 11, 13). Jean de Vienne, the famous French admiral mentioned in Robert Benet's confession, had helped to organise earlier raids on the south coast and was later to lead a substantial expeditionary force to Scotland in 1385. But Benet's revelations and charges against his two companions were clearly – in Sir Charles Oman's words – 'all wild invention'; and it is strange that Petit-Dutaillis, who apparently believed the story, should have proved more credulous than the contemporary justices. Not even Jean de Vienne is likely to have been able to afford such large bribes; and the episode is essentially a tribute to Benet's impressive powers of implausible invention. Even these were not impressive enough; and Benet was later condemned to death for his role as leader of rebellion in Middlesex and his participation in the burning of the Savoy (Réville, p. 201).

Robert Benet of Barford St John in the county of Oxford was taken and brought before William Walworth, mayor of the city of London, in the London Guildhall on Wednesday 19 June [1381] on the grounds that he, together with other malefactors, recently rose as enemies against the lord king, his lieges, various magnates and other loyal and faithful men of the kingdom. Benet was present when the king's prison at Newgate, London, was broken into and the prisoners detained there were carried off. On the following Thursday [20 June] the said Robert Benet appeared in the Guildhall again to answer these charges before

William Knyghtcote and Walter Doget, sheriffs of London, as well as John Charneye, coroner of the city. And he confessed that he, together with Richard Kemmes, who lived either in the town of Barton or that of Bodycote, Oxfordshire, and John Hardy of the same county, criminally and treasonably took 100 pounds of gold on Friday 14 June from lord John Vyane of France at the hands of one of the latter's esquires at Portsmouth in the county of Southampton. This was as the result of an agreement made between Richard Kemmes, John Hardy and John Vyane at Portsmouth. Kemmes, Hardy and the said Robert Benet, approver, ought to have received another 100 pounds of gold from John Vyane at Rye, Sussex, within the following two weeks: on condition that they withdrew themselves and as many others from England as they could, permitting the enemies of France to lay terror to parts of England with their 'balingers' and there to burn, kill and destroy. Richard Kemmes and John Hardy retained the 100 pounds received from this source but Robert Benet kept nothing himself. Wherefore Benet appeals his two fellows. [This appeal was later adjudged to be untrustworthy evidence and both Richard Kemmes and John Hardy were released.]

59 A New Conspiracy in Kent, September 1381: John Cote's Confession

Translated in W. E. Flaherty, 'Sequel to the Great Rebellion in Kent of 1381', *Archaeologia Cantiana*, IV (1861) 75–6, from record in *Coram Rege* Roll, Michaelmas 5 Richard II [KB. 27/482], Rex, memb. 1 (cf. ibid., memb. 30)

The Peasants' Revolt has no fixed terminal date. The great rebellion of June 1381 had emerged from a background of obscure riots in

south-eastern England and was in its turn to be succeeded by a series
of similar local disturbances. But none of the risings of the late summer
and autumn of 1381 had any serious chance of success in the face of a
now more confident and vigilant government. The wild conspiracy
organised by a group of Kentish artisans and craftsmen to the south of
Maidstone is a case in point. Under the leadership of a mason, Thomas
Hardyng, the rebels assembled in arms at Boughton Heath (midway
between the two disaffected villages of Loose and Linton) on the night
of 30 September. The plot was almost immediately betrayed to the
sheriff of Kent and the insurgents were brought to prison at Deptford
on 8 October. Their immediate aims had been the death of the sheriff
and other gentlemen of Kent and the capture of Maidstone itself.
Especially interesting is the evidence of a Loose mason, John Cote,
who turned king's evidence. Although Cote's charges against his
former associates were later dismissed as a 'false appeal', his testimony
provides an extraordinary instance of the self-contradictory rumours
prevalent in 1381. On the mistaken report from Canterbury pilgrims
that John of Gaunt had enfranchised all his villeins, the rebels were
alleged to have planned the deposition of Richard II and his replacement as king by the duke of Lancaster. Here the wheel had turned full
circle; and the almost universal object of peasant hostility in June
had superseded the young Richard in the role of 'saviour of the
commons' by October.

On Monday the seventh day of October, in the fifth year of
King Richard II [1381], John Cote, mason, of Loose in the parish
of Maidstone, in the county of Kent, came before John Hende
and John Rote, sheriffs of London, and John Charneye, coroner of
the said city, and confessed that he, together with Thomas
Hardyng, mason, William de Delton [and twenty-four other
named persons, mostly of Loose, Maidstone and the parish of
Hunton] and many other malefactors, in like manner congre-
gated from the county of Kent (of whose number and names the
foresaid John Cote is utterly ignorant), by night on Monday, the
last day of the month of September [30 September 1381], at
Boughton Heath, near Melkhouse in the county of Kent, of the
connivance (*coniva*) made between them, by the instigation and

procurement of the foresaid Thomas Hardyng, did willingly of their own malice together make insurrection against our foresaid lord the king, by duress (*per duriciam*), to grant and confirm to the said malefactors all their liberties and pardons which they lately, at the time of the foresaid insurrection, with fury demanded of our foresaid lord the king, against his peace, at 'le Mylende', near London, in the county of Middlesex. And, in case that our said lord the king, their said liberties and pardons to them, at their will, were unwilling gratuitously to grant and confirm, the forenamed malefactors and others (whom they, one and all, had then wished to congregate and associate with them), our said lord the king and all the magnates of his kingdom, and other faithful lieges of the said king, imagining their death, intended feloniously and traitorously to have slain, and the laws and statutes of the said king and his foresaid kingdom, willed in all things to have destroyed and annulled.

And also the said John Cote confessed that pilgrims who had come out of the north country to the town of Canterbury, related in the said county of Kent that John, duke of Lancaster, had made all his natives free, in the different counties of England; whereupon, the foresaid malefactors wished to have sent messengers to the foresaid duke, if it were so or not: and if it were so, then the said malefactors consented one and all, to have sent to the said duke, and him, by their own real power (*per realem potestatem suam*) to have made their lord and king of England, and to have held with the said duke in all things to live and die, against our said lord King Richard and his people aforesaid. And so the said John Cote became approver, and appeals the foresaid malefactors of the foresaid felony and treason, and had two days further assigned him according to law, viz. Tuesday and Wednesday next following, on which days the same approver said as above, and no more. He has no chattels within the liberty of the foresaid city.

60 Post-mortem and Pardon: the Westminster Parliament of November-December 1381

Rot. Parl., III 98–103

Throughout the summer and autumn of 1381 reports of riots and isolated acts of violence helped to preserve an atmosphere of alarm and crisis. For several months the English lords and prelates could not be absolutely confident that the danger of another general insurrection was over. It was probably for this reason that the parliament originally called (by writs of 16 July) for assembly on 16 September was postponed until the first week of November, five months after the outbreak of the great revolt. Its first session – in which all the following proceedings occurred – lasted until 13 December when it was adjourned, to meet again between 27 January and 25 February 1382. The surviving records of the parliament, official though these are, show that lords and commons discussed the situation in a spirit of reasonable moderation. The popular demand for emancipation from villein status was inevitably rejected out of hand by the commons; but through their Speaker, Sir Richard Waldegrave, they developed one of their more familiar arguments and blamed the corruption of royal officials rather than the inherent sins of the peasantry for the revolt (cf. no. 67 below). No attempt was made to inaugurate a period of savage persecution. In the end only one town, Bury St Edmunds, and 287 named persons (of whom 151 were Londoners) were excluded from the general amnesty available to those who sued for charters of pardon before the following Whitsuntide. In general the commons endorsed the policy of moderate repression practised by the government during the previous four months; but the way in which they did so provides an excellent and comparatively little known example of the important role already played by parliament in English public life.

Let it be remembered that as All Souls Day [2 November] this year fell on a Saturday and as the next day was a Sunday, this parliament did not begin until the Monday, 4 November. On which Monday there arrived the lord king with a great number of prelates and lords of the realm. But as some of the sheriffs had not yet returned their writs of parliament and as many of the prelates and lords of the realm who had received summonses to parliament had still not arrived, the king had this parliament adjourned until the next day. On which day, the Tuesday, our lord the king and the lords and prelates who had come to Westminster entered the Painted Chamber; and the knights, citizens and burgesses were called within by their names. As many were lacking, parliament was again adjourned by royal command to the following Wednesday. On which Wednesday a great debate broke out between the duke of Lancaster and the earl of Northumberland, causing complaint to be made to the king and much rumour among the people, because of the great force of armed men and archers arrayed in warlike manner who had come to parliament for one or other of the parties; and the king, council and lords of the realm were fully occupied in arranging a good and easy settlement. Therefore the king once again adjourned the parliament until the following Saturday; and so it was done. And the king commanded all those who had been summoned to parliament by himself to return to the said place on Saturday to hear the reasons for which the king had summoned this parliament; so that in the meantime he could hear the case between the duke and the earl and, with Our Lord's help, put an end to their debate.

2. Item, on Saturday [9 November] when the king was in parliament and the commons had all been called by their names, the reverend father in God, William de Courtenay, late bishop of London, archbishop-elect of Canterbury and Chancellor of England[1], said, at our lord king's command, 'Lords and Sirs, our lord king here present, whom God protect, has ordered me to expound before you some of the causes of the summoning of this parliament'. And he spoke on the text, *The King makes his council meet* (Acts xv)[2], making a good sermon in English, applying

---

[1] William Courtenay had been appointed Chancellor on 10 August 1381 at about the time he was translated from the see of London to that of Canterbury.

[2] *Sic*: but this supposed Biblical text cannot be exactly identified.

all his matter to the good and virtuous government of the king and kingdom. He affirmed in this speech that a kingdom could not long endure or survive at all if its inhabitants were vicious. . . . [The appointment of the receivers and triers of petitions then follows]

8. Item, on the following Wednesday [13 November], the commons were called again by their names into the White Chamber; and there, in the presence of our lord the king, Sir Hugh Segrave, Treasurer of England, speaking on behalf of the king, said to them: 'Lords and Sirs, you are aware how the honourable father in God, the lord William, archbishop-elect of Canterbury and Chancellor of England, lately explained to you on behalf of the lord our king the causes of the summoning of this parliament in general, telling you at that time and among other things that the same causes would be more openly declared to you afterwards in particular. For this reason, our lord the king here present, whom God save, has commanded me to make the following declaration unto you. First, our lord the king, desiring above all that the liberty of Holy Church should be entirely preserved without blemish, and that the estate, peace and good government of his kingdom should be maintained and preserved as best it was in the time of any of his noble progenitors, the kings of England, wills that if any default can be found anywhere, this should be amended by the advice of the prelates and lords in this parliament.

'And the king especially wishes to make a good ordinance providing for the return of the king and his realm to peace and quiet after the great turmoil and rumour lately moved in certain parts of the said realm because of the rising and insurrection of certain mean commons and others, and their horrible and contemptuous misdeeds against God, the peace of the land, the king's regality, estate, dignity and crown. Although these same commons coloured their misdeeds in another manner by saying that they wished to have no king except our lord king Richard. The king wishes to provide against another rising (which God forbid) of the same sort and to seek and discover the ways by which the malefactors may be punished and the said rumours completely removed and eradicated; and to investigate and search for the causes and principal reasons for the said risings, so that when these have been discovered and known, and completely removed, people will have confidence in the remedy now to be ordained, should the commons again wish or prepare in malice to do evil in the same way.

'Item, it is not unknown to you how our lord the king, during the said troubles, was constrained to make and grant letters of liberty, franchise and manumission under his great seal to the villeins (neifs) of his kingdom and others, then well aware that he could not do this in good faith and according to the law of the land; but he did this for the best, to put an end to their clamour and malice, for he did not then enjoy his rightful power as king. But as soon as God by his grace had restored him to his power and former state as king and when the said mischief had partly ceased, our lord king, with the advice of his council then present, had the said grants revoked and repealed, for they had been made under compulsion, against reason, law and good faith – to the disinheritance of the prelates and lords of his realm. But now the king would like to know the wishes of you, my lords prelates, lords and commons here present, and if it seems to you that he did well by this repeal and to your pleasure or not. For he says that if you desire to enfranchise and make free the said villeins with your common assent – as it has been reported to him that some of you wish – the king will assent to your request.'

After this, the said Treasurer asked the commons on behalf of the king to withdraw to their place in the abbey of Westminster, to consider these matters well and diligently as well as the remedies which seemed to them should be ordained. And if it happened that they came to agree on a definite purpose in this matter, they were to inform our lord the king and the lords of parliament. . . .

9. Item, on the following Monday, 18 November, in the third week of parliament, the commons returned into parliament; and there Sir Richard de Waldegrave,[1] who had the words for the

---

[1] Waldegrave, a Suffolk knight, had been one of the commissioners appointed in March 1381 to investigate the evasions of the poll tax in Essex.

commons, strove to excuse himself from this office of Speaker (*Vant-parlour*). But the king charged him to perform it by his allegiance, since he had been elected to this office by his companions.

10. The said Sir Richard then made his protestation to the effect that if he said anything other or more or less than had been previously assented and agreed to by his companions then he could amend it by the advice of his said fellows; and he said:

11. 'My liege lord, my companions here present and I have talked together about the charges lately laid upon us by your royal majesty; but we are in part at variance amongst ourselves, concerning the same charge. Therefore, if it please you, we will have the same charge rehearsed before you here; or, if it pleases your royal majesty, may you have it rehearsed another time before us, so that we can understand it clearly and be able to come to one accord among ourselves about it.'

12. And the king commanded Sir Richard le Scrope, knight, recently created Chancellor of England,[1] to rehearse the said charge, touching on the points mentioned. This he did clearly, with especial reference to the recent repeal of the grant of franchise and manumission of the bondsmen (*neifs*) and villeins of the land. And all present in full parliament there were again asked directly whether this repeal pleased them or not.

13. To which the prelates and temporal lords as well as the knights, citizens and burgesses replied with one voice that this repeal was well done. They added that such a manumission and enfranchisement of the villeins could not be made without their assent, who had the greatest interest in the matter. And they had never agreed to it, either voluntarily or not, nor would they ever do so, even if it were their dying day. They (that is to say, the prelates, lords and said commons) prayed humbly to our lord the king that as these letters of manumission and enfranchisement had been made and granted through coercion, to the disinheritance of themselves and the destruction of the realm, they should be

[1] Scrope replaced Archbishop Courtenay as Chancellor on 4 December while parliament was in session. He had already held the office between 1378 and 1380 (see above, p. 111).

wiped out and annulled by authority of this parliament, the said
repeal to be confirmed because it had been well and justly done.
And this was agreed and assented to unanimously there. . . .

17. Item, the said commons returned into parliament another
time, making their protestation as before, and saying that on the
charges laid before them they had diligently communed with the
prelates and lords given to them for this purpose; and it seemed
to them that if the government of the realm was not shortly to
be amended, the very kingdom itself would be completely lost
and destroyed for all time and, as a result, our lord the king and
all the lords and commons, which God, in his mercy, forfend.
For it is true that there are many faults in the said government,
about the king's person, and in his household and because of the
outrageous number of servants (*familiers*) in the latter, as well as
in the king's courts, that is to say in the Chancery, King's Bench,
Common Bench and the Exchequer. And there are grievous
oppressions throughout the country because of the outrageous
multitude of embracers of quarrels and maintainers, who act like
kings in the country, so that justice and law are scarcely ad-
ministered to anybody. And the poor commons are from time
to time despoiled and destroyed in these ways, both by the
purveyors of the said royal household and others who pay nothing to the commons for the victuals and carriage taken from
them, and by the subsidies and tallages levied upon them to their
great distress, and by other grievous and outrageous oppressions
done to them by various servants of our lord the king and other
lords of the realm – and especially by the said maintainers. For
these reasons the said commons are brought to great wretched-
ness and misery, more than they ever were before.

One might also add that although great treasure is continually
granted and levied from the commons for the defence of the
realm, they are nevertheless no better defended and succoured
against the kingdom's enemies, as far as they know. For, from
year to year, the said enemies burn, rob and pillage by land and
sea with their barges, galleys and other vessels; for which no
remedy has been, nor is yet, provided. Which mischiefs the said

poor commons, who once used to live in all honour and prosperity, can no longer endure in any way. And to speak the truth,
the said outrages as well as others which have lately been done to
the poor commons, more generally than ever before, made the
said poor commons feel so hardly oppressed that they caused
the said mean commons (*menues communes*) to rise and commit the
mischief they did in the said riot. And greater mischiefs are to be
feared if good and proper remedy is not provided in time for the
above-mentioned outrageous oppressions and mischiefs.

Therefore, may it please our lord the king and the noble lords
of the realm now assembled in this parliament, for the mercy of
Jesus Christ, to apply such remedy and amendment to all parts of
the said government that especially the state and dignity of our
lord the king and the noble estates of the lords of the realm
should be entirely preserved, as the commons desire and always
have desired; and also that the commons can be restored to quiet
and peace by removing whenever they are known evil officers
and counsellors and putting better and more virtuous and more
sufficient ones in their place, as well as removing all the evil
circumstances from which the late disturbance and the other mischiefs befell the realm, as said above. Otherwise, all men think
that this realm cannot survive for long without greater mischief
than has ever befallen it before, which God forbid. And so that
God may not be forgotten, by all means let the person of
the king and his council be surrounded with the most sufficient
and discreet lords and bachelors to be found within the
kingdom.

30. *Request of the Commons for the having of graces and pardons, etc.*
Item, the commons returned into parliament another time,
showing a schedule containing in three articles the three types of
grace and pardon to be now made, if it pleased our lord the king,
to his commons of his realm. The first grace was for the lords,
gentlemen (*gentils*) and others who killed certain persons without
due process of law while resisting the rioters and traitors. The
second was to pardon the evil people who had risen during the

said disturbance of the treason and felony they had then committed. The third was the grace to be awarded to good men who remained peaceful and did not rise. They prayed that they might wait for the king's gracious reply about these graces, for the quiet and common profit of the realm; provided in all cases that certain people who were the principal inciters and beginners of the said troubles, whose names are known and will later be delivered in parliament, should have not the least part in the said graces. On this, the king our lord, by the advice of his lords, justices and others of his council, had the manner and form of the said pardons prescribed, in the form which follows:

31. *Grace for the lords, gentlemen, etc. . . .*

32. *Grace for the rebels*

Item, our lord the king has considered how the lieges and subjects of his kingdom bore themselves well and governed themselves peaceably all the time from his coronation until the said insurrections and risings, and showed themselves benevolent and of good will towards him in all his business and necessities. And although many of them during the said risings committed such treason and felony towards him, the crown and the laws of the land that they have forfeited their bodies, lands and goods to him, nevertheless for reverence of God and his sweet mother St Mary and at the special request of the noble lady, Lady Anne, daughter of the noble Prince Charles, lately Emperor of Rome, and soon to arrive, if God pleases, as queen of England; and also so that the said subjects should have greater courage to remain faithful and loyal in the future, as they did before the said rising; by his special grace, he has pardoned the said commons and each individual member of them not belonging to the towns of Canterbury, Bury St Edmunds, Beverley, Scarborough, Bridgwater and Cambridge.[1] Also specially excluded are the persons whose names are written hereafter, their names being put forward in parliament as those who are arrested and accused for being

---

[1] At the king's suggestion, Bury alone was finally refused pardon (*Rot. Parl.*, III 118).

chiefs, leaders, inciters and principals of the said risings and misdeeds by the commons of their country in this parliament. Also excluded are all approvers and those appealed of the said treasons and felonies, as well as those who killed Simon, archbishop of Canterbury, recently Chancellor, the Prior of St John, then Treasurer, and John de Cavendish, Chief Justice of our said lord. Also excluded are those who have escaped or left prison, and who have not yet returned or been returned there. Which persons the king does not at present wish to have any part of the said grace as regards all manner of treasons and felonies made and perpetrated by them in the said insurrections between 1 May last and the feast of All Saints following, for which they have been indicted, charged or accused and to which outlawries, etc. And it is not the king's intention that parties injured in the said risings shall be prevented by means of this grace from recovering their damages and losses suffered in the said risings by using various legal actions which stop short of a judgment of death. And it is agreed that he who wishes to enjoy this grace should take pains to have his individual charter between now and next Whit Sunday.
33. *Grace for the good and loyal commons, etc.* . . .

61 The Persistence of Revolt

Few problems present the historian of any age with greater difficulties than the exact measurement and analysis of social disorder. It is certainly impossible to prove that acts of lawlessness and disaffection were either more frequent or more severe in the years following the great revolt than they had been in the preceding period. What is certain is that neither the conflict between landlord and tenant nor the strife of civic faction were brought to an end by the repressive policies pursued after Smithfield. For several years the memory of the great deeds of 1381 continued to act as a stimulus to discontent and dissidence. Such was evidently the case in the first two disturbances described below; while in 1384 another Norfolk band was specifically accused of planning 'to fulfil the proposals of the traitors and male-factors who in 1381 feloniously rose against their allegiance' (Réville, p. CXXXIV). Concerted action by peasants of particular villages to withdraw their services from the local landlord or destroy his manorial records was a common feature of the English social scene after 1381; but only rarely (as in Cheshire and West Yorkshire in 1392–3) were there signs of a widespread series of simultaneous risings as in 1381. In London and many of the provincial towns, there is evidence that dis-order and rioting persisted during the 1380s but tended to diminish during subsequent decades. Minor acts of plunder and vandalism of course continued and are represented here by the account of 'a company of trewe men' of London in 1412 – who had at their disposal a means of propaganda (the anonymous bill written in English) apparently not exploited by the rebels of 1381 but relatively common in fifteenth-century disturbances.

A. A CONSPIRACY IN NORFOLK, 1382

Walsingham, *Historia Anglicana*, II 70; cf. *Chronicon Angliae*, p. 354

About the feast of Michaelmas [29 September 1382] certain people in Norfolk were so stirred by the devil that they were undeterred and unchecked by the dangers, deaths and torments that had befallen others. They made a conspiracy and assembled in iniquity with the firm intention, if fortune favoured them, of capturing and killing the bishop of Norwich[1] and all the great men of the country unexpectedly. In order to increase their power, they determined to go secretly to Saint Faith's fair and force all the people gathered there either to swear to support them or to suffer immediate slaughter. If successful, they planned to occupy the abbey of St Benet of Hulme secretly[2]; for this

[1] Henry Despenser, bishop of Norwich 1370–1406, for whose activities in suppressing the 1381 Norfolk revolt see above, nos. 35, 41.

[2] This famous Benedictine abbey, significantly close to the main area of Norfolk rebellion in June 1381, was admirably sited (near the centre of the Broads) for defensive purposes.

abbey struck these perfidious men as a powerful stronghold if they were to encounter any dangers in the future.

But all these plans were revealed before they could be brought into effect, for one of the sworn conspirators betrayed the counsels of the others. And so it came about that the conspirators were captured without warning and then beheaded at Norwich, a fitting penalty for their malice.

B. AN ABORTIVE RISING IN KENT, 1390

Polychronicon, IX 220; cf. Walsingham, *Historia Anglicana*, II 196, who identifies these rebels as Kentishmen.

Item, on 13 January [1390] sixteen men, skilled in various mechanical arts, were captured at Croydon and imprisoned in the Marshalsea. Some of them were workmen who wished to rise against churchmen as well as other lay neighbours of theirs in order to kill them. They planned to promote another rising, worse than the others already mentioned; but their schemes were too quickly revealed. And so three of these men were drawn and hanged at the gallows in February.

C. AN ATTACK UPON PROPERTY IN LONDON, 1412

Translated in J. H. Flemming, *England under the Lancastrians* (1921), pp. 266–7, from London Plea and Memoranda Roll, A. 42, memb. 2

We, Robert Chichele, mayor of the city of London, Walter Cotton and John Reynewell, sheriffs, by authority of the king, of the same city, certify you, that before the receipt of the writ of the lord the king [of 6 April 1412 demanding cause of imprisonment] attached to this bill, William, clerk, and John Leek, *tawere* [i.e. leather-dresser], named in the said writ, were taken in the said city and committed to the prison of the said lord the king, and there detained because, on 24 January [1412], a certain wall of earth enclosing a certain garden in the parish of All Hallows', Barking, in the ward of Tower Street, in London aforesaid, was broken down about midnight by a band of unknown men; and we have information that the said William wrote a certain bill on paper in English, and that the said John Leek fixed the bill with wax on to the door of the said garden, a copy of which bill follows in these words.

'Here hath ben this nyght a company of trewe men by comen assent of alle this worshipfull citee to warne you with a litel stroke or more harme come to gader up your erbys and trees or elles it shall be distroied ryght as ye see, for we wole have our grounde whos evyr be groucche it for we have geven a stroke and more is for to come, but yf ye with your owne goode wylle amende it your selfe, for this is not don of on or two but of many one and mo wel come of al the craftes of alle this worshipfull citee, and therfor thanke god that ye have no more harm at this tyme.'

62 The Complaints and Requests of the Commons of Kent, 1450

John Stow, *Annales*, ed. E. Howes (London, 1631), pp. 388–390

The preceding examples, in combination with the many others which could easily be added, leave no doubt that outbreaks of lawlessness and rebellion were genuinely characteristic of English public life for many decades after 1381. And even the more obviously 'political' rebellions of the Lancastrian period usually reflect some of the grievances expressed by Tyler and his fellows. Thus the rebels headed by Archbishop Scrope of York in 1405 attacked – admittedly in the interests of the northern magnates – governmental corruption and 'excessive and intolerable taxes and subsidies'; and in 1430 Jack Sharpe echoed the views of John Ball as well as John Wycliffe when he proposed 'that alle the temporaltes of chyrches thus apropred ageyns

Crystes lore be turned to Godde, and to the prosperyte of the reme'.[1]
But for an extensive national rising at least superficially similar to that
of Wat Tyler, the historian is inevitably compelled to turn his attention
to Jack Cade's revolt of 1450. In its very different way, Cade's rebellion
remains as enigmatic and mysterious as that of 1381. At first sight, the
resemblances between the two movements seem significantly close.
Both revolts began in the late spring and followed a period of English
military humiliation at the hands of the French monarchy: both
were centred in south-eastern England and both can be interpreted
in terms of a disgruntled popular reaction to excessive war taxation.
As their 'complaint' shows, the rebels of 1450, like those of 1381, were
careful to distinguish between their loyalty towards the person of the
king and their hatred of the real 'traitors' to his kingdom – the government's central and local officials. It is no coincidence that, in both
risings, the Treasurer of England lost his head. Above all, the two rebellions reveal the curious fragility of the late medieval English state and
its extreme vulnerability in the face of a sudden popular movement.

But perhaps the differences between the risings of 1381 and 1450
are more interesting than their similarities. The royal court lost its
confidence on both occasions; but the contrast between Richard's
precocious sang-froid and the timidity displayed by Henry VI (who
retreated to Kenilworth on the approach of the Kentishmen) speaks
volumes for the difference in their respective attitudes to the conduct
of kingship. The identity of the one or two Jack Cades, like that of
the several Walter or Wat Tylers, is among the most baffling problems
of English medieval history; but it is at least clear that Cade was a
politically conscious and devious rebel leader in a way that Tyler failed
to be. Their 'complaint' similarly suggests that the rebels of 1450 were
capable, as those of 1381 apparently were not, of expressing their aims
in the form of a coherent written programme. No doubt this difference
was partly the result of the more purely 'political' ambitions of the men
who joined or led Cade's revolt. Nevertheless several of the peasant
grievances only incidentally revealed by the chroniclers of 1381
certainly recur sixty-nine years later: the corruption of royal ministers,
extortionate taxation, the forest laws and even the statutes of labourers
were still among the burning issues of the day. Cade's rebels, like
Tyler's, were the spokesmen for social as well as political discontent;

[1] *Annales Henrici Quarti* (Rolls Series, 1866), p. 403; *Annales a Johanne
Amundesham* (Rolls Series, 1870–1), I 456.

and it is tempting to believe that the former's 'complaints' were at one level the consequence of the extension of literacy in late medieval England. Perhaps Tyler and Ball would have written as well as preached their gospel if they had been in a position to do so. As it was, no later English revolutionary movement could ever be quite so inarticulate as that of 1381.

In the meane time the King sent notable men to the said Captaine and his fellowship, to know the purpose and the cause of their insurrection: unto whom the Captaine answered, that hee and his company were assembled there [at Blackheath in mid-June 1450] to redresse and reforme the wrongs that were done in the Realme, and to withstand the malice of them that were destroiers of the common weale, and to amend the defaults of them that were chiefe Counsellers to the King, and shewed unto them the Articles of complaints touching the misgovernement of the Realme, wherein was nothing contained but seemed reasonable, whereof a copie was sent to the parliament holden that time at Westminster, with also one other Bill of requestes by them made, of things to be reformed, and to have answere thereof againe, but hee had none. The bill of Articles they intituled.

The complaint of the commons of Kent, and causes of the assembly on the Blackheath.

1. Inprimis, it is openly noysed that Kent should be destroyed with a royall power, and made a wilde Forest, for the death of the Duke of Suffolke, of which the commons of Kent were never guiltie.[1]
2. Item, the king is stirred to live onely on his commons, and other men to have the revenewes of the crowne, the which hath caused poverty in his excellency, and great payments of the people, now late to the king granted in his Parliament.
3. Item, that the Lords of his royall bloud have bin put from his

---

[1] This unpopular Lancastrian lord had been intercepted and murdered (on 2 May 1450) off the Kentish coast as he was sailing into exile. R. L. Storey, *The End of the House of Lancaster* (London, 1966), pp. 43–68, provides valuable new insight into Cade's rebellion.

daily presence, and other meane persons of lower nature exalted and made chiefe of his privy counsell, the which stoppeth matters of wrongs done in the realme from his excellent audience, and may not be redressed as law will, but if bribes and gifts be messengers to the hands of the said counsell.

4. Item, the people of his realme be not paid of debts owing for stuffe and purveiance taken to the use of the king's houshold, in undoeing of the saide people, and the poore commons of this Realme.

5. Item, the kings meniall servants of houshould, and other persons, asked daily goods and lands, of [those] empeached or indited of treason the which the king graunteth anon, ere they so endaungered, be convict. The which causeth the receivers thereof to enforge labours and meanes applied to the death of such people so appeached, or indited, by subtile meanes, for covetise of the said grants: and the people so impeaced or indited, though it be untrue, may not be committed to the law for their deliverance, but held still in prison to their uttermost undoeing and destruction for covetise of goods.

6. Item, though divers of the poore people and commons of the Realme, have never so great right, truth and perfect Title to their Land, yet by untrue claime of ineffment, made unto divers states, gentiles, and the Kings meniall servants in maintenances against the right, the true owners dare not hold claime, nor pursue their right.

7. Item, it is noysed by common voyces, that the Kings Lands in France have beene aliened and put away from the Crowne, and his Lords and people there destroyed with untrue meanes of treason, of which it is desire, enquiries through all the Realme to be made, how, and by whom, and if such traytours may be found guilty, them to have execution of Law, without any pardon, in example of other.[1]

8. Item, Collectors of the 15 peny in Kent, be greatly vexed and hurt in paying great summes of money in the exchequer, to sue out a writ, called *Quorum Nomina*, for allowance of the Barons

[1] An allusion to the French success in expelling the English from Normandy during the weeks that followed the battle of Formigny (15 April 1450).

of the [Cinque] ports, which now is desired that heereafter in the lieue of the Collectors, the Barons aforesaid may sue it out for their ease, at their owne costs.

9. Item, the Shrieves, and under-shrieve, let to ferme their offices and Bayliwikes, taking great surety therefore, the which causeth extortion done by them and by their Bayliffes to the people.

10. Item, simple and poore people that use not hunting, be greatly oppressed by inditements fained and done by the said Sherifes, under-sherifes, bayliffes and other of their assent, to cause their increase for paying of their said ferme.

11. Item, they returne in names of Enquests in writing into divers courts of the Kings, not summoned nor warned, where through the people daily lose great summes of money, well nye to the uttermost of their undoing: and make levy of amercements, called the *Greene Waxe*, more in summes of money, than can be found due of record in the Kings bookes.[1]

12. Item, the Ministers of the court of Dover in Kent, vex and arrest divers people through all the Shire, out of Castle Ward, passing their bands and liberty used of old time, by divers subtile and untrue meanes and actions falsely fained, taking great fee at their lust in great hurt of the people in all the Shire of Kent.

13. Item, the people of the said shire of Kent, may not have their fre election in the choosing [of the] Knights of the Shire, but letters have beene sent from divers estates to the great rulers of all the Countrey, the which enforceth their tenants and other people by force to choose other persons then the common will is.

14. Item, whereas Knights of the Shire should choose the Kings Collectors indiferently, without any bribe taking: they have sent now late to divers persons notifying them to be Collectours, whereupon gifs and bribes be taken, and so the Collectours office is bought and sold extortionously at the Knights lust.

15. Item, the people be sore vexed in costs, and labour, called to the Sessions of peace in the said Shire, appearing from the farthest, and uttermost parts of the West into the East, the which causeth

---

[1] A seal in green wax, used by the Treasurer's Remembrancer, was attached to royal summonses demanding the repayment of new debts to the Exchequer.

to some men five daies journey, whereupon they desire the said appearance to be divided into two parts, the which one part to appeare in one place, another part in another place, in relieving of the grievance and intollerable labors and vexations of the said people.

The requests by the Captaine of the great assembly in Kent
In primis, desireth the Captaine of the Commons, the welfare of our Soveraigne Lord, the King, and all his true Lords, spirituall and temporall, desiring of our said soveraigne Lord, and of all the true Lords of his Councell, he to take in all his demaines, that he may raigne like a King royall, according as he is borne our true Christian King anoynted, and who so wil say the contrary, we all wil live and dye in the quarrell as his true liege man.
2. Item, desireth the said Captaine, that hee will avoyde all the false progeny and affinity of the Duke of Suffolke, the which hath been openly knowne, and they to be punished after the custome and Law of this Land, and to take about his Noble person, the true Lords of his royall blood of this his Realme, that is to say, the High and mighty Prince, the Duke of Yorke, late exiled from our said soveraigne Lords presence[1] (by the motion and stirring of the traiterous and false disposed the Duke of Suffolke and his affinitie) and the mightie Princes and Dukes of Excester, Buckingham and Norfolke, and all the Earles and Barons of this land: and then shall hee bee the richest King Christian.
3. Item, desireth the captaine and commons punnishment upon the false traitors, the which contrived and imagined the death of the high and mightfull excellent Prince the Duke of Glocester, the which is too much to rehearse, the which Duke was proclaymed as traitour.[2] Upon the which quarrell, wee purpose all to live and die upon that it is false.

---

[1] Richard, duke of York, had been appointed King's Lieutenant in Ireland in July 1448; and Cade's revolt was, whether or not with the duke's approval, a 'Yorkist' movement.

[2] Humphrey, duke of Gloucester, died in mysterious circumstances soon after his arrest in February 1447.

4. Item, the Duke of Excester, our holy father the Cardinall, the Noble Prince Duke of Warwike, and also the Realme of France, the Dutchy of Normandy, Gascoine, and Guien, Anioy and Maine, were delivered and lost, by the meanes of the said traitors, and our true Lords, Knights and Esquiers, and many a good yeoman lost and solde ere they went, the which is great pitie to heare, of the great and grievous losse to our soveraigne Lord and his Realme. 5. Item, desireth the said Captaine and commons, that all the extortions used daily among the common people, might be layed downe, that is to say, the greene Wax the which is falsely used, to the perpetuall destruction of the kings true commons of Kent, Also the kings bench, the which is too greefefull to the shire of Kent without provision of our soveraigne Lord and his true Counsell. And also in taking of wheat and other graines, beefe, mutton, and all other victuall, the which is importable to the said commons, without the breefe provision of our said soveraigne Lord, and his true Councell, they may no longer beare it. And also unto the statute of labourers and the great extortioners, which is to say, the false trators, Sleg, Crowmer, Isle and Robert Est.

63 The Disappearance of English Villeinage

The demand for the general abolition of villeinage in England lies near the heart of the otherwise often incoherent programme of the rebels of June 1381. Almost all the chroniclers of the revolt emphasise, if only to deplore, the peasants' claim 'that no one in the future should be a serf'. At the height of the crisis, Richard II had been compelled to issue general charters of manumission relieving all the villeins within particular counties of the obligations of their servile status (see above, pp. 180–1). But as early as 2 July 1381 the king annulled these charters, and in the parliament of the following November the commons vehemently resisted the implication that English villeins could ever be enfranchised by statute [nos. 53, 60]. But although serfdom was never legally abolished in late medieval and Tudor England, by the early sixteenth century it had already been reduced to a relatively minor and anomalous feature of the English social order. The causes and exact chronology of this decisive trend towards the 'withering away' of legal villeinage remain extremely mysterious and elusive. Most curious of all perhaps is the absence of any substantial body of contemporary comment on the reasons for the decline of serfdom in England. Copies of particular charters of manumission (of which two examples are translated below) survive in great number among the records of ecclesiastical – although not lay – landlords; but such individual acts of enfranchisement were too common a feature of west European life throughout several centuries to throw much light on the general trend towards emancipation. In any case the real key to the problem clearly lies in the effect of long-term economic forces on popular social attitudes to villein tenure. Villeinage and 'serfdom' died when the words themselves became socially valueless. In his recent survey of the problem Professor Hilton has shown how villeinage was 'withering away' long before the revolt of 1381.[1] The effect of the great rebellion on this process was, in any case, possibly minimal and certainly very difficult to assess. The last two passages translated here demonstrate that for both the London aldermen and the parliamentary commons after 1381, the maintenance of distinctive villein status was as desirable as had been its abolition in the eyes of the peasants themselves. However difficult a condition it was and is to define, villeinage and the desire for *libertas* clearly aroused stronger feelings in the late fourteenth-century Englishman than his modern historian has sometimes acknowledged.

A. ROYAL MANUMISSIONS IN YORKSHIRE, 1338

Rymer's *Foedera*, vol. II, pt IV (Hague, 1740), p. 20

The king to all to whom, etc., greetings. Know that because of the fine which John Simondson, our bondsman (*nativus*) of our

---

[1] R. H. Hilton, *The Decline of Serfdom in Medieval England* (London, 1969), where these issues are debated.

manor of Brustwyk, has made before our faithful John de Molyns, Nicholas de Bokeland and Hugh de Berewyk, whom we have assigned for the purpose of receiving such fines for the manumissions of our bondsmen in those parts, we have manumitted the aforesaid John Simondson and his entire issue, and exonerated and pardoned them from all servile work towards us; willing and granting for ourselves and our heirs that the same John Simondson and his entire issue aforesaid shall be free and of free condition for ever, so that neither we nor our said heirs shall be able to require or claim anything in future from the said John Simondson or his issue by reason of his villeinage (*villenagii*). Witnessed by the king at the Tower of London, 16 May [1338].

Similar letters of manumission were directed to two other bondsmen of the same manor on that day.

B. MANUMISSION BY THE BISHOP OF HEREFORD, 1419

Registrum Edmundi Lacy, Canterbury and York Society, XXII (1918) 62–3

To all, etc. Edmund, etc. Since from the beginning nature created all men free and of free condition, and afterwards the *jus gentium* imposed upon some the yoke of servitude, we believe this to be truly an act of piety and justly deserving a reward from God, to restore those whose merits require this to their pristine freedom. For which considerations, we have manumitted and have freed from every servile yoke by these present letters, John del Wode, legitimate son of William del Wode, our bondsman (*nativus*), a servant in our kitchen and a bondsman belonging to our lordship of Colewalle, with all his offspring now or later begotten, and with his goods and chattels, so that he and they shall be free in whatever part of the world it shall please him or them to go, without any right of reclaim by us or our successors. In testimony of which etc. Dated at Whiteborne, 4 April [1419].

C. BONDSMEN NOT TO ENJOY THE LIBERTIES OF THE CITY OF LONDON, 1387

Liber Albus in vol. I of *Munimenta Gildhallae Londoniensis* (Rolls Series, 1859), p. 452: cf. pp. 33-4. Calendared in *Calendar of London Letter Book H*, p. 309

Be it remembered that on 18 July [1387], it was ordained – to avoid shame and scandal to the city of London – by Nicholas Exton, mayor, and the aldermen, with the assent of the common council of the city, that henceforward no foreigner should be enrolled as an apprentice nor received into the city's liberty by the way of apprenticeship, unless he first swears that he is a free man (*liber homo*) and not a bondsman (*nativus*). And anyone who is in future received into the city's liberty whether by purchase or some other method than apprenticeship, shall take the same oath; and he shall find six worthy citizens of the city to stand surety for him as was the ancient custom.

And if it should happen that a bondsman is admitted to the city's liberty through false information and in the ignorance of the chamberlain, then immediately after it is publicly established before the mayor and aldermen that he is a bondsman, let him lose the liberty of the city and pay a fine for his deception according to the discretion of the mayor and aldermen – always saving the freedom which pertains to the said city's franchise.

Item, if it should happen henceforward, which God forbid, that such a bondsman (i.e. a man whose father was a bondsman at the date of his birth) is elected to a judicial office in the city, such as that of alderman, sheriff or mayor, he shall pay £100 to the chamberlain for the needs of the city unless he notifies the mayor and aldermen of his servile condition before he accepts the office. And nevertheless he shall lose his liberty as laid down above.

D. PARLIAMENTARY PETITION TO ENFORCE VILLEIN DISABILITIES, 1391

Rot. Parl., III 294

Item the commons pray for an ordinance by which no bondsman or villein (*neif ou vileyn*) belonging to an archbishop, bishop, abbot, prior or any other religious within your kingdom of England shall be allowed to purchase lands or tenements in fee – under penalty of forfeiting all such purchases to our lord the king. The reason is that such purchases pass for all time from the hands of temporal lords to those of spiritual lords, to the great destruction of the lay fee of this kingdom.

And let it also be ordained and ordered that no bondsman or villein should henceforward place his children in schools in order to advance them into the clergy; such an order would maintain and protect the honour of all free men (*frankes*) of the kingdom.

The king refuses (*s'avisera*).

64 The Twelve Articles of Memmingen, 1525

Translated by B. J. Kidd, ed., *Documents illustrative of the Continental Reformation* (Oxford, 1911), pp. 174–9, from H. Böhmer, *Urkunden zur Geschichte des Bauernkrieges* (Lietzmann, Kleine Texte, nos. 50–1, 1910). The translation by H. J. Hillerbrand, *The Reformation in its own Words* (London, 1964), pp. 389–91, has also been used

The original evidence for the English Peasants' Revolt of 1381 is itself so voluminous that considerations of space alone would have made it impossible to include within this collection documents illustrative of the many analogous peasant or urban rebellions in late medieval Europe. To this somewhat reluctant policy of self-denial, it seems both pardonable and important to make one exception. The Twelve Articles of Memmingen, a crucial document for the historian of the sixteenth-century Protestant Reformation, is most famous for its revelation of the remarkable impact made by Luther's teaching on the German peasantry. But it is even more interesting for the manner in which it summarises and recapitulates so many of the social grievances and aspirations experienced throughout western Europe in the preceding two centuries. The Swabian peasents' emphasis on the role of their freely elected local minister certainly strikes a novel and radical note; but the majority of the Twelve Articles merely clothe long-familiar objectives in the language of the Bible and the German Reformation. The English peasants of 1381 would have appreciated and shared the determination to resist both new taxes and extortionate labour services. The argument advanced for individual liberty in the Third Article places the sentiments of John Ball's sermon in a new context – not surprisingly when one remembers that translated versions of the famous couplet, 'When Adam delved and Eve span/Who was then the gentleman?', long circulated throughout central Europe. The Twelve Articles were probably drafted by Sebastian Lotzer, a Swabian tanner from the town of Memmingen south of Ulm, in early 1525 – that is during an early and remarkably moderate phase of the great German Peasants' War of 1524–6, itself merely the most dangerous of a long series of peasant movements in south-western Germany. Like their predecessors, the *Bundschuh*, and like the English rebels of 1381, the German revolutionaries of the mid-1520s shook, but failed to transform, the social structure of their communities. They can hardly be said to have achieved victory in either the long or the short term; for it is arguable that neither the English nor the German peasantry ever influenced political events so much again as they did in 1381 and 1525.

To the Christian Reader, Peace and the Grace of God through Christ
There are many Antichrists who on account of the assembling of the peasants, cast scorn upon the Gospel, and say: Is this the fruit of the new teaching, that no one obeys but all everywhere rise in revolt, and rush together to reform, extinguish, indeed destroy the temporal and spiritual authorities? The following articles will answer these godless and blaspheming fault-finders. Firstly, they will remove any reproach from the Word of God and secondly

give a Christian excuse for the disobedience or even the revolt of the entire peasantry.... Therefore, Christian reader, read the following articles with care, and then judge. Here follow the Articles:

The First Article: – First, it is our humble petition and desire, indeed our will and resolution, that in the future we shall have power and authority so that each community should choose and appoint a minister, and that we should have the right to depose him should he conduct himself improperly. The minister thus chosen should teach us the holy Gospel purely and simply, without any human addition, doctrine or ordinance. For to teach us continually the true faith will lead us to pray God that through his grace his faith may increase within us and become a part of us. For if his grace is not within us, we will always remain flesh and blood, which avails nothing; since the Scripture clearly teaches that only through true faith can we come to God. Only through his mercy can we become holy. Therefore such a guide and minister is necessary and justified by the Scriptures.

The Second Article: – Since the right tithe is established by the Old Testament and fulfilled in the New, we are ready and willing to pay the fair tithe of grain. None the less it should be done properly. The Word of God plainly provides that it should be given to God and passed on to his own people. If it is to be given to a minister, we will in the future collect the tithe through our church elders, appointed by the congregation, and distribute from it, for the sufficient livelihood of the minister (elected by the entire congregation) and his family, according to the judgment of the whole congregation. The remainder shall be given to the poor of the place, as the circumstances and the general opinion demand....

The Third Article: – It has been the custom hitherto for men to hold us as their own property, which is pitiable enough considering that Christ has redeemed and purchased us without exception, by the shedding of his precious blood, the lowly as well as the great. Accordingly, it is consistent with Scripture that we should be free and we wish to be so. Not that we want to be absolutely free and under no authority. God does not teach us that we should lead a disorderly life according to the lusts of the flesh, but that we should live by the commandments, love the Lord our God and our neighbour. . . . We therefore assume that you will release us from serfdom, as true Christians, unless we can be shown from the Gospel that we are serfs.

The Fourth Article: – In the fourth place it has been the custom hitherto that no poor man was allowed to catch venison or wild fowl, or fish in flowing water, which seems to us quite unseemly and unbrotherly, as well as selfish and not according to the Word of God. . . . Accordingly, it is our desire if a man holds possession of waters that he should prove from satisfactory documents that his right has been wittingly acquired by purchase. We do not wish to take it from him by force, but his rights should be exercised in a Christian and brotherly fashion. But whoever cannot produce such evidence should willingly surrender his claim.

The Fifth Article: – In the fifth place we are aggrieved in the question of wood-cutting, for our noble folk have appropriated all the woods to themselves alone. . . . It should be free to every member of the community to help himself to such firewood as he needs in his home. Also, if a man requires wood for carpenter's purposes he should have it free, but with the approval of a person appointed by the community for that purpose. . . .

The Sixth Article: – Our sixth complaint is in regard to the excessive services demanded of us, which are increased from day to day. We ask that this matter be properly looked into, so that we shall not continue to be oppressed in this way, and that some gracious consideration may be given us, since our forefathers were required to serve only according to the Word of God.

The Seventh Article: – Seventh, we will not hereafter allow ourselves to be further oppressed by our lords. What the lords possess is to be held according to the agreement between the lord and the peasant. . . . The peasant should help the lord when necessary and at proper times – when it suits the peasant, and for a proper payment.

The Eighth Article: – In the eighth place, we are greatly burdened by holdings which cannot support the rent exacted from them. The peasants suffer loss in this way and are ruined. We ask that the lords may appoint honourable persons to inspect these holdings and fix a rent in accordance with justice, so that the peasant shall not work for nothing, since the labourer is worthy of his hire.

The Ninth Article: – In the ninth place, we are burdened with a great evil in the constant making of new laws. We are not judged according to the offence, but sometimes with great ill will, and sometimes much too leniently. In our opinion we should be judged according to the old written law, so that the case should be decided according to its merits, and not with favours.

The Tenth Article: – In the tenth place, we are aggrieved that certain individuals have appropriated meadows and fields which at one time belonged to the community. These we will take again into our own hands unless they were rightfully purchased. . . .

The Eleventh Article: – In the eleventh place we will entirely abolish the custom called *Todfall* (i.e. heriot), and will no longer endure it, nor allow widows and orphans to be thus shamefully robbed against God's will, and in violation of justice and right, as has been done in many places, and by those who should shield and protect them. . . .

Conclusion: – In the twelfth place it is our conclusion and final resolution, that if any one or more of these articles should not be in agreement with the Word of God, as we think they are, we will willingly abandon such an article when it is proved to be against the Word of God by a clear explanation of the Scripture. . . . For this we shall pray to God, since He can grant all this and He alone. The peace of Christ abide with us all.

PART VII

Interpretations of the Peasants' Revolt

No sooner had the immediate dangers of the great revolt receded than contemporaries began to speculate on its causes and its significance both for the immediate future and sub specie æternitatis. The common belief that medieval chroniclers and other writers had no sense of historical causation and little interest in explaining the reasons for the events they related can hardly survive a study of the commentators on 1381. Indeed writers of the late fourteenth century usually generalised about the causes of the insurrection with a confidence sadly lacking in modern historians. Needless to say, much of this early comment was highly rhetorical and excessively moralistic in tone (nos. 65, 66, 73). It was generally and immediately assumed that the revolt was the direct result of man's sinfulness and God's consequent displeasure. For those who cared to probe more deeply, the gravity and extent of the rebellion tended to seem inexplicable except in terms of some vast conspiratorial thesis. However, the evidence for the existence of a large and well-organised peasant 'underground' movement was, as it still is, extremely slender and ambiguous. Walsingham and Knighton hardly strengthened their case by introducing into their chronicles copies of mysterious allegorical letters, alleged to have been written by John Ball and other rebels. These famous 'dark sayings' throw more light on the religious attitudes than the political objectives of the English commons: by the standards of the slightly later 'protest' literature with which they ought to be compared, the letters of John Ball, Jack Mylner, Jack Carter and Jack Trewman are a curiously equivocal and muted clarion-call to riot and revolution (no. 71). The same ambiguity surrounds the historical role played by John Ball, the 'foolish priest' almost universally chosen to serve as symbol of the commons' misguided aspirations. For Froissart, Ball was the Mazzini of the Peasants' Revolt, the preacher whose inflammatory sermons called the rebels to arms (no. 69). According to Walsingham and, more especially, Henry Knighton, John Ball was doubly dangerous as the purveyor of religious as well as of political sedition (no. 70). By the end of Richard II's reign (despite some dis-agreement as to who had laid the eggs and who had hatched them), the legend of an unholy alliance between John Ball and John Wycliffe had emerged to give concrete expression to the fears and anxieties of estab-lished authorities in both church and state.

During the course of the fifteenth century it became apparent that although it might be possible to discredit the Peasants' Revolt by tarring it with Wycliffe's brush, conservative publicists found it more imperative and persuasive to use the opposite argument – that unchecked religious dissent and heresy would eventually cause the collapse of the social order and bring about the fulfilment of the dreadful portents of 1381. The history of England in the sixteenth century was in fact to reveal that the two dangers were not identical, that radical religious reform did not necessarily imply social revolution. Opposition to popular sedition and rebellion proved more obsessive and deeply rooted than resistance to doctrinal change: John Wycliffe was lauded as a hero for centuries before John Ball was rescued from the limbo to which Walsingham had confined him. After the Reformation, as before, the Peasants' Revolt survived in folk-memory as the classic example of the fate that would befall a society where the natural principles of subordination collapsed and chaos displaced order. From the late fourteenth to the late eighteenth centuries the question of the grievances, real or imagined, of Tyler and his fellows was immaterial compared with the central issue – made explicit by Chancellor de la Pole as early as 1383 (no. 67) – of dis-obedience to the prince and the prince's servants. 'O Lord, how horrible a thing is division in a realm' is the theme of both the early Elizabethan A Mirror for Magistrates and the late Elizabethan drama, The Life and Death of Jacke Strawe (no. 74). Nor did the establishment of an English republic in the mid-seventeenth century lessen the abhorrence with which the rebels of 1381 were regarded by the politically conscious. That 'the world cannot subsist without Order and Subjection, men cannot be freed from Lawes' were the words actually put into Richard II's own mouth by John Cleveland, author of The Rustick Rampant, the first detailed history of the great revolt.[1] Cleveland was admittedly a cavalier poet; but even the greatest of the Levellers, 'Free-born John' Lilburne, looked on Jack Straw and Wat Tyler (like other 'famous men mentioned with a black pen in our Histories') as extreme 'contemners of Authority' rather than as men who belonged to his own extremely revolutionary tradition.[2] Only after the outbreak of the French Revolution in 1789 did Wat Tyler and John Ball begin to enjoy their posthumous careers as spokesmen for the eternal poor and apostles of popular liberty. The fact that they figured in the famous debate between Edmund Burke and Thomas Paine was in itself enough to ensure that the rebels of 1381 would be enlisted to serve as founding-fathers of the 'good old cause' and the new English radical movement (nos. 75, 76). A sense of fellow-feeling with the medieval English commons led to the brief appearance of such phenomena as the Chartist 'Wat Tyler Brigade'. But the legacy of the Peasants' Revolt to the nineteenth-century working class was rarely relevant and often ambiguous. Since the publication of Engels's masterly The Peasant War in Germany, (no. 78), English socialists as well as Marxists have wisely adopted an ambivalent and often mistrustful attitude to medieval peasant risings. At a less sophisticated and more popular level, the egalitarian and romantic ideals of the nineteenth century can be said to have done their work (nos. 77, 79). If tears are still shed for the victims of 'the hurlyng time', they are more likely to fall for John Ball and Wat Tyler than for Simon de Sudbury and Robert Hales.

[1] J. Cleveland, The Rustick Rampant (London, 1658), p. 65.
[2] The Leveller Tracts, 1647–1653 ed. W. Haller and G. Davies (New York, 1944), p. 427.

65 A 'Warnyng to Be Ware'

Robbins, *Historical Poems*, pp. 57–60

The author of these English verses draws the obvious religious moral from the three catastrophes of the early 1380s – the great rising of 1381, the earthquake of May 1381 and a new outbreak of bubonic plague or 'Pestilens'. The work was apparently written by a clerk soon after the events to which he alludes and should be compared with no. 10 above. Only five of the poem's eleven stanzas are copied here:

> Yit is God a Curteis lord,
>   And Mekeliche con schewe his miht;
> Fayn he wolde bringe til a-cord
>   Monkuynde, to live in treuthe ariht.
> Allas! whi set we that lord so liht,
>   And al to foule with him we fare?
> In world is non so wys no wiht,
>   That thei ne have warnyng to be ware.
>
> Whon the Comuynes bi-gan to ryse,
>   Was non so gret lord, as I gesse,
> That thei in herte bi-gon to gryse,
>   And leide heore Iolyte in presse.
> Wher was thenne heore worthinesse,
>   Whon thei made lordes droupe and dare?
> Of alle wyse men I take witnesse,
>   This was a warnyng to be ware.
>
> Bi-fore, if men hedde haad a graas,
>   Lordes mihte wondur weel
> Han let the rysing that ther was,
>   But that god thoughte it sumdel
> That lordes schulde his lordschup feel,
>   And of heore lordschipe make hem bare.
> Trust ther-to as trewe as steel,
>   This was a warnyng to be ware.

The Rysing of the comuynes in londe,
    The Pestilens, and the eorthe-quake –
Theose threo thinges, I understonde,
    Beo-tokenes the grete vengaunce and wrake
That schulde falle for synnes sake,
    As this Clerkes conne de-clare.
Nou may we chese to leve or take,
    For warnyng have we to ben ware.

Be war, for I con sey no more,
    Be war for vengauns of trespas,
Be war and thenk uppon this lore!
    Be war of this sodeyn cas;
And yit Be war while we have spas,
    And thonke that child that Marie bare,
Of his gret godnesse and his gras,
    Send us such warnyng to be ware.

Glossary

mekeliche, *powerfully*; foule, *outrageously*; gryse, *feel terror*; in presse, *aside*; dare,
be dismayed; graas, *grace*; let, *put down*; sumdel, *to some extent*; bare, *stripped*.

66 'Tax has tenet us alle'

Wright, *Political Poems*, I 224–6; a variant version is printed
in Robbins, *Historical Poems*, pp. 55–7

Although they strike the same characteristically sombre note as the
previous poem, the following verses, presumably written soon after
1381, are an interesting if crude attempt to provide a verse narrative
rather than interpretation of the great revolt. The author's decision
to write alternate lines in English and Latin and to adopt a very

restrictive rhyming scheme was certainly over-ambitious; and artistic-
ally the final result is not very far removed from doggerel. However
the main outlines of the story of the rebellion are expounded with a
surprising degree of accuracy – even if the writer falls into the common
error of confusing Jack Straw with Wat Tyler. The whole of the poem
(with translations of the Latin lines) runs as follows:

> Tax has tenet us alle,
> > *probat hoc mors tot validorum,*[1]
> The kyng therof hade smalle,
> > *fuit in manibus cupidorum;*[2]
> Hit hade harde honsall
> > *dans causam fine dolorum;*[3]
> Revrawnce nede most falle,
> > *propter peccata malorum.*[4]
>
> In Kent this kare began,
> > *mox infestando potentes,*[5]
> In rowte the rybawdus ran,
> > *sua pompis arma ferentes;*[6]
> Folus dred no mon,
> > *regni regem neque gentes,*[7]
> Churles were hor chevetan,
> > *vulgo pure dominantes.*[8]
>
> Thus hor wayes thay wente,
> > *pravis pravos æmulantes,*[9]
> To London fro Kent
> > *sunt predia depopulantes;*[10]
> Ther was an uvel covent,
> > *australi parte vagantes*[11]
> Sythenne they sone were schent,
> > *qui tunc fuerant superantes.*[12]
>
> Bondus they blwun bost,
> > *nolentes lege domari,*[13]
> Nede they fre be most,
> > *vel nollent pacificari;*[14]

Charters were endost,
   hos libertate morari;[15]
Ther hor fredam thay lost,
   digni pro cæde negari.[16]

Laddus loude thay lowght,
   clamantes voce sonora,[17]
The bisschop wen thay slowght,
   et corpora plura decora;[18]
Maners down thay drowghte,
   in regno non meliora;[19]
Harme thay dud inowghte,
   habuerunt libera lora.[20]

Iak Strawe made yt stowte
   cum profusa comitiva,[21]
And seyd all schuld hem lowte
   Anglorum corpora viva,[22]
Sadly can they schowte,
   pulsant pietatis oliva,[23]
The wycche were wont to lowte,
   aratrum traducere stiva.[24]

Hales, that dowghty knyght,
   quo splenduit Anglia tota,[25]
dolefully he was dyght,
   cum stultis pace remota,[26]
There he myght not fyght,
   nec Christo solvere vota.[27]

Savoy semely sette,
   heu! funditus igne cadebat,[28]
Arcan don there they bett,
   et eos virtute premebat,[29]
Deth was ther dewe dett,
   qui captum quisque ferebat.[30]

Oure kyng myght have no rest,
   alii latuere caverna,[31]
To ride he was ful prest,
   recolendo gesta paterna;[32]
Iak Straw down they cast,
   Smethefeld virtute superna.[33]
Lord, as thou may best,
   regem defende, guberna.[34]

[1] the death of so many worthy men proves this.
[2] it passed into the hands of the greedy.
[3] giving cause for sorrow in the end.
[4] on account of the sins of the evil.
[5] soon to disturb the powerful.
[6] bearing their arms on display.
[7] neither the king nor the people of the kingdom.
[8] completely lording it over the people.
[9] the wicked copying the wicked.
[10] emptying the land of people.
[11] wandering through the south of the land.
[12] who had previously been supreme.
[13] refusing to be subdued by the law.
[14] or they would not be pacified.
[15] allowing them to remain in freedom.
[16] deservedly denied them because of their slaughter.
[17] crying with loud voices.
[18] and many other fine persons.
[19] none better in the kingdom.
[20] they enjoyed free rein.
[21] with a large company.
[22] the living bodies of Englishmen.
[23] they pulled down the branch of piety.
[24] drawing the plough along the furrows.
[25] in whom all England gloried.
[26] when peace was removed by fools.
[27] nor fulfil his vows to Christ.
[28] alas! completely fell by fire.
[29] and he overcame them by his virtue.
[30] by whoever took them captive.
[31] others lay hidden in caves.
[32] recalling his father's deeds.
[33] by heavenly grace at Smithfield.
[34] govern and defend the king.

tenet, *ruined*; honsall, *omen*; chevetan, *captains*; uvel, *evil*; schent, *destroyed*; blwun bost, *bragged boastfully*; lowght, *reverenced*; bisschop, *Simon Sudbury, archbishop of Canterbury*; Maners, *manor-houses*; drowghte, *threw down*; made yt stowte, *swaggered*; lowte, (i) *reverence*, (ii) *lurk*; Arcan . . . bett, *they beat Achan, who offended against the law of Joshua by stealing valuables from the city of Jericho (Joshua 7).*

67 The Causes of the Revolt according to Sir Michael de la Pole, 1383

Rot. Parl., III 150

The following extract from the opening speech of Michael de la Pole, the new Chancellor of England, to the parliament which met at Westminster in late October 1383 is as significant as it is brief. Two years after the great revolt, Richard II's most powerful minister drew an obvious and authoritarian lesson – that disobedience to the king's local agents might finally result in rebellion against the person of the monarch himself. As if to prove the point, de la Pole's compliments to the *gentils* of parliament failed to prevent either his own parliamentary impeachment (in 1386) or his king's quasi-parliamentary deposition (in 1399).

6. 'Item, another reason for the summoning of the present parliament is as follows: that is to say, to ordain that the keeping of peace within the kingdom and the obedience due to our lord the king from all his subjects be performed better than has been the case hitherto. For the acts of disobedience and rebellion which men have recently committed and which continue from one day to another towards the lesser servants of the king, such as the sheriffs, escheators, collectors of the subsidies and others of the same type, were the source and chief cause of the treasonable

insurrection recently made by the commune of England within this realm. This insurrection, as you well know, was firstly a rebellion against the said lesser servants, than against the great officers of the kingdom and finally against the king himself. And therefore just as rebellion of this sort was and is the source and commencement of mischief and trouble within the realm, so (on the other hand) is true obedience to the king and his servants the foundation of all peace and quiet in the realm itself – as appears clearly from the obedience which the gentlemen (*gentils*) showed to the king during the said insurrection.'

68 The Causes of the Revolt according to Thomas Walsingham: Jack Straw's Confession

Walsingham, *Historia Anglicana*, II 8–13; cf. *Chronicon Angliae*, pp. 308–12. Continued from no. 41 above

According to one of his greatest admirers, the sixteenth-century polemicist John Bale, Thomas Walsingham wrote 'many the most choice passages of affairs and actions, such as no other hath met with'. Walsingham's final random remarks on the Peasants' Revolt certainly show him at his inimitable best and worst. No other medieval chronicler, one feels, would have had the effrontery to place the ultimate blame for the great revolt on the shoulders of such unlikely candidates as the mendicant friars. At this point of his chronicle Walsingham gladly relieves himself of the need to adhere to the facts and gives free rein to his powerful imagination. Perhaps, although it is by no means certain, Walsingham's personal prejudices and obsessive sense of national sin were characteristic of his fellow monks at St Albans and elsewhere. Equally problematical and much more interesting to the historian of the insurrection is the veracity of Jack Straw's supposed 'confession'. No doubt modern critics have been wise to reject the story; but, on the other hand, it is unlikely to be a mere figment of Walsingham's imaginative powers. At the least, it seems not too implausible that some of the more audacious rebel leaders hoped to secure their ends by capturing the person of the king. Similarly the known facts of Wat Tyler's and Geoffrey Litster's careers lend some credence to Walsingham's belief that the rebels aimed at the destruction of central government in the interests of the revival of a 'backwoods' provincialism to be based on the unit of the English county or shire.

Chapter proving how the rebels conspired to destroy the Church, the Christian Faith and the King

Now that I have related a few of the incidents which took place in Norfolk, I will forbear from describing the other evils committed in that county and the heavy losses suffered by other shires at the hands of devilish men – to the uproar of the whole kingdom. For unless they had been possessed by devils, the rebels would never have conspired to destroy Holy Church and the Christian religion as well as to overthrow the kingdom. These intentions are proved by their deeds and also by the confessions of several rebels who were captured later, as we will narrate in the proper place. These men are to be judged by their works, in that they killed the father of all the clergy and the head of the English church, the archbishop of Canterbury. What other damage did they do to the faith? They compelled the masters of grammar schools to swear that they would henceforward never instruct their young pupils in religious matters. What else did they do? They strove to burn all old records; and they butchered anyone who might know or be able to commit to memory the contents of old or new documents. It was dangerous enough to be known as a clerk, but especially dangerous if an ink-pot should be found at one's elbow: such men scarcely or ever escaped from the hands of the rebels.

How the insurgents planned to destroy the realm is proved by the confession of John Straw, the most important of their leaders after Walter Tylere. After Straw had been captured and sentenced to execution in London by the mayor, the latter spoke to him publicly: 'Behold, John! you are certain to die soon and have no hope of saving your life. Therefore, to ease your passage from this world and for the health of your soul, tell us in all honesty what plans you rebels pursued and why you stirred up the crowd of commons.' After Straw had hesitated for some time and refrained from speaking, the mayor added: 'I promise you, John, that if you do what I ask, I will make arrangements for the sake of your soul and will have many masses celebrated for it during the next three years.' Many citizens who were present promised the same thing, one mass from each person. Straw was so moved by such fine promises that he began:

The Confession of John Straw

'It no longer serves me to lie, nor is it proper to speak falsehoods, especially as I know that my soul would be subjected to harsher torments if I did so. Moreover, I hope for two advantages in speaking the truth: first because what I say may profit the country; and also because, according to your promises, I will have the help of your prayers after my death. So I will speak without any attempt to deceive. At the time when we assembled at "le Blakehethe" in order to arrange to meet the king, our plan was to kill all the knights, esquires and other gentlemen who came with him. Then we would have taken the king around with us from place to place in the full sight of all; so that when everybody, and especially the common people, saw him, they would willingly have joined us and our band – for it would have seemed to them that the king was the author of our turbulence. And when we had assembled an enormous crowd of common people throughout the country, we would suddenly have murdered all those lords who could have opposed or resisted us. First, and above all, we would have proceeded to the destruction of the Hospitallers. Then we would have killed the king and driven out of the land all possessioners, bishops, monks, canons and rectors of churches. Only the Mendicants were to survive and they would have sufficed for the celebration of the sacraments and the conferment of orders throughout the land. Since there would be no one left who was senior, stronger or more knowledgeable than ourselves, we would have founded laws at our own pleasure by which all subjects would be ruled. Moreover, we would have created kings, Walter Tylere in Kent and one each in other counties, and appointed them. Because this design of ours was hindered by the archbishop, our greatest hatred was directed against him and we longed to kill him as quickly as possible. Moreover, on the evening of that day on which Walter Tylere was killed, we proposed, because the common and especially poorer people of London favoured us, to set fire to four parts of the city and burn it down and divide all the precious goods found there among ourselves.' And he added: 'These were our aims, as God will help me on the point of death'.

After he made this confession, he was executed and his head placed on London Bridge near the head of his colleague, Walter Tylere. And so we learn how the rebels conspired to destroy the realm. And if the evidence of this one confession should seem insufficient, many other captured rebels made confessions of a similar nature when they saw their death before their eyes.

The Names of the Leaders of the Rebels

If anyone would like to know the names of those who incited and led the commons, he will find them listed here. The first and chief leader was called 'Walter Tylere', or as some say, 'Walter Helyer'; the second, 'John Straw'; the third, 'John Kyrkeby'; the fourth, 'Alan Threder'; the fifth, 'Thomas Scot'; the sixth, 'Ralph Rugge'. Tylere invested many men with many possessions when he was their leader. These men, and many others, were the leaders of the men of Kent and Essex.

Of those rebels who went wild at Mildenhall and Bury St Edmunds, Robert Westbroun who made himself king was the most renowned after John Wrawe. As the latter was a priest, he did not wish, as we say, to place one crown above another; content with one crown, namely that of a priest which was quite enough for him, he left the royal title and crown, if it pleased him, to the said Robert. At North Walsham, as we have said, John Littestere exercised both the title and the power of a king.

Opinions as to why these evils occurred

All these evils befell the various regions of England at about the same time and almost on the same days, namely within the octave of Corpus Christi, despite the long distances that separated them. Many held the negligence of the archbishop and his provincial bishops responsible, for in their care lies the faith and stability of the Christian religion. Certainly they allowed their sons, John Wycliffe and his followers, to behave shamefully and to put forward the perverse and damned doctrine of Berengarius concerning the sacrament of the body and blood of Christ. They extended their preaching throughout the country to the pollution of the people and so that the notable men of the counties almost followed their error; for the Wycliffites knew that 'the giddy mob always changes with its prince' and that the lesser men would follow the example of the greater. Nor was there any mitred bishop who wished or dared to oppose such evils and correct his impious sons by due chastisement. Many believe that the Lord deliberately sent these sufferings at the time when the Holy Church was making a special issue of the transubstantiation of the Body of Christ. Some believe that the archbishop himself, although it is credible that he ended his life as a martyr, was punished by the horrid passion of his death because of the lukewarmness of his care in such matters. Thus he asked the Holy Spirit that he might be purged of this sin or any other small fault (for there is no life in this world without sin); and then, as in the words of Proverbs, [*Proverbs* xxiv 16] 'a just man falls down seven times in a day and rises up again', so he might be completely purified by his harsh and terrible passion in this life.

Others ascribed the cause of these evils to the sins of the lords, who proved faithless to God. For it is alleged that some of them believed there was no God, no sacrament of the altar and no resurrection after death: they thought that man's life, like that of

13

a beast of burden, came to an end with death. Moreover the lords were tyrants to their subjects, arrogant to their equals and suspected by both. They lived in debauchery, violated the marriage bond and destroyed churches.

Others attributed the disaster to the crimes of the common people and alleged that because they lived in peace they wasted the benefits of peace. They poured scorn on the actions of the lords and spent sleepless nights in drinking, revelling and evildoing. They lived without peace in a land of peace, brawling, struggling and disputing with their neighbours. They pursued fraud and falsehood continually, gave way to lust, wallowed in fornication and were polluted with adultery: 'every one neighed after his neighbour's wife' [Jeremiah v 8]. And besides all this, many of them wavered in their beliefs and the articles of the Faith. For which reasons it was supposed that God's anger had deservedly fallen on the children of unbelief.

Against the Mendicant Friars

But it seems to me that these evil times were attributable not only to the said crimes, but more generally to the sins of all the inhabitants of the earth, specifically including the Mendicant Orders who added notably to the other offences. These men, forgetful of their profession, also forgot for what reasons their Orders had been instituted. For their legislators, most holy men, had wished them to be poor and completely untied by material possessions – so that (to speak the truth) they should have held nothing which they feared to lose. But now their desire for possessions has led them to approve the crimes of the magnates and foster the errors of the common people while commending the sins of both. In order to acquire possessions which they had renounced and to collect money when they had sworn to persevere in poverty, they say that good is bad and bad is good – seducing princes with their flattery, the people with their lies and leading both into error with themselves. To such an extent have they polluted their profession of truth by perverse living that nowadays there is a saying which takes the shape of a logical argument valid in both form and content: 'This is a Friar, and therefore a liar', to be compared to the dictum, 'This is white, and therefore coloured'.

But lest it should seem that we have written these things out of spite, let us acknowledge that we are all to blame, and amend as best we can those sins which we have knowingly committed. And let us pray to God more zealously for peace and charity so that he will bring peace and truth in our time. [*Continued by no. 53 above, p. 306.*]

69 The Causes of the Revolt according to Froissart

Froissart, trans. Berners, ed. G. C. Macaulay, pp. 250–1; cf. Froissart, *Chroniques*, x 94–7

The few sentences with which Froissart introduced his account of the Peasants' Revolt comprise the most famous and influential commentary on the rebellion ever written. Froissart's habit of stating controversial half-truths as if they were of undeniable veracity has raised problems long discussed and still unresolved. With his allegation that the revolt was essentially attributable to 'the ease and riches that the common people were of' rather than their poverty and misery, Froissart stumbled into a curious anticipation of de Tocqueville's general theories of revolution. Similarly the argument that there were more 'serfs' in England than in any other country is unacceptable in itself but does raise the important point that the concomitants of villein status were probably more conspicuous in late fourteenth-century England than in those areas of Europe (the Low Countries and northern France) which Froissart knew best. Above all, the famous sermon which Froissart put into the mouth of John Ball has had an effect on his modern readers quite the opposite of what the author can have intended. As translated by Berners, Ball's sermon becomes the most moving plea for social equality in the history of the English language.

In the mean season while this treaty was,[1] there fell in England great mischief and rebellion of moving of the common people [*menu peuple*], by which deed England was at a point to have been lost without recovery. There was never realm nor country in so great adventure as it was in that time, and all because of the ease and riches that the common people were of, which moved them to this rebellion, as sometime they [*li Jacques Bonhomme*] did in France, the which did much hurt, for by such incidents the realm of France hath been greatly grieved.[2]

It was a marvellous thing and of poor foundation that this mischief began in England, and to give ensample to all manner of good people I will speak thereof as it was done, as I was informed, and of the incidents thereof. There was an usage in England, and yet is in divers countries, that the noblemen hath great franchise over the commons and keepeth them in servage, that is to say, their tenants ought by custom to labour the lords' lands, to gather and bring home their corns, and some to thresh and to fan, and by servage to make their hay and to hew their wood and bring it home. All these things they ought to do by servage, and there be more of these people in England than in any other realm. Thus the noblemen and prelates are served by them, and specially in the county of Kent, Essex, Sussex and Bedford. These unhappy people of these said countries began to stir, because they said they were kept in great servage [*servitude*], and in the beginning of the world, they said, there were no bondmen [*serfs*], wherefore they maintained that none ought to be bond, without he did treason to his lord, as Lucifer did to God; but they said they could have no such battle [were not of that nature] for they were neither angels nor spirits, but men formed to the similitude of their lords, saying why should they then be kept so under like beasts; the which they said they would no longer suffer, for they would be all one, and if they laboured or did anything for their lords, they would have wages therefor as well as other.

---

[1] John of Gaunt's negotiations on the Border aimed at renewing the truce between the kingdoms of England and Scotland.

[2] Froissart's allusion is to the French *Jacquerie* of 1358.

And of this imagination was a foolish priest in the country of Kent called John Ball, for the which foolish words he had been three times in the bishop of Canterbury's prison: for this priest used oftentimes on the Sundays after mass, when the people were going out of the minster, to go into the cloister and preach, and made the people to assemble about him, and would say thus: 'Ah, ye good people, the matters goeth not well to pass in England, nor shall do till everything be common, and that there be no villains nor gentlemen, but that we may be all united together [*tout-unis*], and that the lords be no greater masters than we be. What have we deserved, or why should we be kept thus in servage? We be all come from one father and one mother, Adam and Eve: whereby can they say or shew that they be greater lords than we be, saving by that they cause us to win and labour for that they dispend? They are clothed in velvet and camlet furred with grise, and we be vestured with poor cloth: they have their wines, spices and good bread, and we have the drawing out of the chaff and drink water: they dwell in fair houses, and we have the pain and travail, rain and wind in the fields; and by that that cometh of our labours they keep and maintain their estates: we be called their bondmen and without we do readily them service, we be beaten; and we have no sovereign to whom we may complain, nor that will hear us nor do us right. Let us go to the king, he is young, and shew him what servage we be in, and shew him how we will have it otherwise, or else we will provide us of some remedy; and if we go together, all manner of people that be now in any bondage will follow us to the intent to be made free; and when the king seeth us, we shall have some remedy, either by fairness or otherwise.'

Thus John Ball said on Sundays, when the people issued out of the churches in the villages; wherefore many of the mean people loved him, and such as intended to no goodness said how he said truth; and so they would murmur one with another in the fields and in the ways as they went together, affirming how John Ball said truth.

The archbishop of Canterbury, who was informed of the

saying of this John Ball, caused him to be taken and put in prison a two or three months to chastise him: howbeit, it had been much better at the beginning that he had been condemned to perpetual prison or else to have died, rather than to have suffered him to have been again delivered out of prison; but the bishop had conscience to let him die. And when this John Ball was out of prison, he returned again to his error, as he did before. [*Continued by no. 22 above, p. 137.*]

70 The Significance of John Ball

Few features of the early stream of commentary on the great revolt of 1381 are more impressive than the unanimity with which the chroniclers stress the importance of the role played by the 'foolish priest' of Kent. Froissart, Walsingham and Knighton, writers of very different temperaments and interests, all agreed in seeing John Ball as the *éminence grise* of the Peasants' Revolt. Although their search for a scapegoat no doubt led contemporaries to exaggerate Ball's significance and influence, it probably is the case that he was the only rebel leader to have won more than very local notoriety for himself before May 1381. Even so, remarkably little is known about his career. According to the letter ascribed to him by Walsingham (see below, no. 71a), he had once been 'Seynte Marie prest of York', i.e. probably a chantry priest in that city. As early as 1366 the unorthodox character of his sermons while in Essex had led to a formal prohibition of his preaching activities (Wilkins, *Concilia*, III 64); and in early 1381 his invectives against pope and prelates resulted in excommunication and imprisonment in Maidstone gaol – from which (according to Knighton) he was released by the Kentish rebels shortly before their march on London (above, p. 136).

For modern students of the revolt Ball's importance lies in the representative rather than exceptional nature of his career and teachings.[1]

---

[1] In a paper delivered to the Anglo-Soviet Conference of Historians (September 1969) Professor R. H. Hilton cites the case of the twelfth-century poet Wace who ascribed to the rebellious Norman peasants of 996 the sentiment, 'we are men like them . . . and can suffer like them'.

The crude egalitarianism of Ball's message is now recognised to have been something of a commonplace in fourteenth-century sermons; and it can be argued that Ball is most appropriately seen as an example of those numerous unbeneficed clerks of late medieval England who formed the most radical and 'lunatic fringe' element of both the rising and the contemporary social order. For the English chroniclers however, Ball's pernicious influence was more specific still. The belief (expressed by Walsingham and Knighton in the extracts which follow) that John Ball's activities furthered the cause of Lollardy was obviously very widely held; and from that point it was a short, natural and almost inevitable step to the view that Ball was himself a disciple of the great heresiarch. It will be seen that this argument was taken to its extreme conclusion by the author of the slender connecting narrative to be found in the remarkable *Fasciculi Zizaniorum*. According to the most recent study of this Carmelite history of the rise and fall of English Lollardy, the passage quoted below may have been written as early as the mid-1390s, a period when the conservative reaction was already in full progress. Ball's 'confession' is an obvious fabrication; and Wycliffe, fortunately for his sixteenth-century reputation, made clear his personal hostility towards the great revolt within a few months of Smithfield. Although less intransigent in his attitude to the peasants than was Luther in the analogous circumstances of 1525, Wycliffe condemned the insurrection in unequivocal terms. But the lesson he drew from the storms of 1381 was inevitably his own: 'Now it is said that secular lords can remove the temporalities from a delinquent church – which would, after all, be more sensible than that peasants (*rurales*) should take the life of the primate of that church'.[1]

A. JOHN BALL ACCORDING TO THOMAS WALSINGHAM

Walsingham, *Historia Anglicana*, II 32–3; cf. *Chronicon Angliae*, pp. 320–2

Moreover, on that day [Saturday 13 July] the same Robert [Tresilian] sentenced John Balle, priest, after hearing of his scandalous and confessed crimes, to drawing, hanging, beheading, disembowelling and – to use the common words – quartering:

[1] Wycliffe, *Tractatus de Blasphemia* (Wyclif Society, 1893), p. 190.

he had been taken by the men of Coventry and on the previous day brought to St Albans and into the presence of the king whose majesty he had insulted so gravely. His death was postponed until the following Monday [15 July] by the intervention of Lord William [Courtenay], bishop of London, who obtained a short deferment so that Balle could repent for the sake of his soul.

For twenty years and more Balle had been preaching continually in different places such things as he knew were pleasing to the people, speaking ill of both ecclesiastics and secular lords, and had rather won the goodwill of the common people than merit in the sight of God. For he instructed the people that tithes ought not to be paid to an incumbent unless he who should give them were richer than the rector or vicar who received them; and that tithes and offerings ought to be withheld if the parishioner were known to be a man of better life than his priest; and also that none were fit for the Kingdom of God who were not born in matrimony. He taught, moreover, the perverse doctrines of the perfidious John Wycliffe, and the insane opinions that he held, with many more that it would take long to recite. Therefore, being prohibited by the bishops from preaching in parishes and churches, he began to speak in streets and squares and in the open fields. Nor did he lack hearers among the common people, whom he always strove to entice to his sermons by pleasing words, and slander of the prelates. At last he was excommunicated as he would not desist and was thrown into prison, where he predicted that he would be set free by twenty thousand of his friends. This afterwards happened in the said disturbances, when the commons broke open all the prisons, and made the prisoners depart.

And when he had been delivered from prison, he followed them, egging them on to commit greater evils, and saying that such things must surely be done. And, to corrupt more people with his doctrine, at Blackheath, where two hundred thousand of the commons were gathered together, he began a sermon in this fashion:

> 'Whan Adam dalf, and Eve span,
> Wo was thanne a gentilman?'

And continuing his sermon, he tried to prove by the words of the proverb that he had taken for his text, that from the beginning all men were created equal by nature, and that servitude had been introduced by the unjust and evil oppression of men, against the will of God, who, if it had pleased Him to create serfs, surely in the beginning of the world would have appointed who should be a serf and who a lord. Let them consider, therefore, that He had now appointed the time wherein, laying aside the yoke of long servitude, they might, if they wished, enjoy their liberty so long desired. Wherefore they must be prudent, hastening to act after the manner of a good husbandman, tilling his field, and uprooting the tares that are accustomed to destroy the grain; first killing the great lords of the realm, then slaying the lawyers, justices and jurors, and finally rooting out everyone whom they knew to be harmful to the community in future. So at last they would obtain peace and security, if, when the great ones had been removed, they maintained among themselves equality of liberty and nobility, as well as of dignity and power.

And when he had preached these and many other ravings, he was in such high favour with the common people that they cried out that he should be archbishop and Chancellor of the kingdom, and that he alone was worthy of the office, for the present archbishop was a traitor to the realm and the commons, and should be beheaded wherever he could be found.

B. BALL AND WYCLIFFE ACCORDING TO HENRY KNIGHTON

Chronicon Henrici Knighton, II 151, 170

(A.D. 1382) At this time flourished master John Wycliffe, rector of the church of Lutterworth in the county of Leicestershire. He was a most eminent doctor of theology in those days, unrivalled in scholastic disciplines and held as second to none in philosophy. He especially strove to surpass the talents of others by the subtlety of his learning and the depth of his intelligence, and to produce opinions at variance with those of other men. He introduced many beliefs into the church which were condemned by the catholic doctors of the church, as will appear later. He had as his precursor John Balle, just as Christ's precursor was John the Baptist. Balle prepared the way for Wycliffe's opinions and, as is said, disturbed many with his own doctrines, as I have already mentioned. . . .

Now on his appearance Master John Wycliffe had John Balle to prepare the way for his pernicious findings. The latter was the real breaker of the unity of the church, the author of discord between the laity and clergy, the indefatigable sower of illicit doctrines and the disturber of the Christian church. . . .

C. BALL AND WYCLIFFE ACCORDING TO THE *FASCICULI ZIZANIORUM*

Fasciculi Zizaniorum, Rolls Series, 1858, pp. 272–4

Let us recognise the malice and iniquity of Master John Wycliffe both by means of his pestilential doctrines as well as the preaching of his followers and adherents who invariably sowed dissension and provoked the people to rebellion; so that hardly any of such men preached without inciting their listeners to fight among themselves and causing townships to be in a state of schism. Therefore, the knights and others who assembled in parliament on behalf of the realm required the archbishop [Courtenay] with his suffragans to make an end of such errors and heresies; and the king and his followers promised the bishops their lawful assistance.[1]

Accordingly, when parliament was ended, William [archbishop] of Canterbury, a firm pillar of the church, summoned his suffragan bishops together with other doctors of theology, canon and civil law and other worthy men, to deliberate on the subject of various heretical conclusions which Wycliffe and the sect which is called of the Lollards had preached. And they condemned certain conclusions set out below that year, namely

[1] The parliament in question met at Westminster in May 1382, several months after William Courtenay's promotion to the see of Canterbury.

in 1382, after lunch on St Dunstan's day [19 May], at the Friars Preachers in London.

However, on that day, at about the second hour after noon, there was an earthquake throughout all England. Therefore certain of the suffragans and others wanted to forego the whole business; but that strong man, zealous for the church of God, William of Canterbury, comforted them with the warning that they should not be slothful in the cause of the church. For the earthquake really portended the cleansing of the kingdom from heresies: just as infected air and spirits are enclosed within the bowels of the earth only to issue forth at a time of earthquake, thus purifying the earth at the cost of great violence, so in the past there had been many heresies locked in the hearts of the sinful by the condemnation of which the kingdom had been purified although not without great sickness and disturbance. Accordingly after certain conclusions of Master John Wycliffe had been carefully examined, the archbishop declared, determined and ordained several of these to be heretical and others to be erroneous[1] – as will appear in a letter directed to Brother Peter Stokys, doctor of divinity, of the order of Carmelites [quoted later in the text].

One matter is omitted above which is worthy of note, namely that so serious and extensive was the division and dissension within England produced by John Wycliffe and his accomplices that orthodox men feared that their preaching would provoke yet another insurrection against the lords and the church in the future. They believed this more especially because of a beloved follower of Wycliffe, a priest named John Balle, who was imprisoned by Simon, archbishop of Canterbury, and William, bishop of London, on account of the heresies that he preached. But during the insurrection, the commons delivered him from prison. And then Balle began to preach to them and taught them to kill Simon, archbishop of Canterbury, and others: these deeds and the turmoil

---

[1] Several of Wycliffe's theses condemned at this famous 'Earthquake Synod' of May 1382 had been censured at St Paul's five years earlier; in the interval Wycliffe had proved himself completely obdurate and retired to Lutterworth where he died in 1384.

in the country were achieved under his leadership. At last, after the kingdom had been pacified and while the king was staying in the town of St Albans to do justice on the traitors, the said John Balle was brought from Coventry to that town, where he was adjudged a traitor by Robert Tresilian and sentenced to drawing, hanging and quartering.

When Balle realised that he was doomed, he called to him William, bishop of London and later of Canterbury, as well as lords Walter Lee, knight, and John Profete, notary; and he confessed publicly to them that for two years he had been a disciple of Wycliffe and had learned from the latter the heresies which he had taught; from Wycliffe had arisen the heresy concerning the sacrament of the altar and Balle had openly preached this and other matters taught by him. Balle also declared that there was a certain company of the sect and doctrines of Wycliffe which conspired like a secret fraternity and arranged to travel around the whole of England preaching the beliefs taught by Wycliffe: in this way it was planned that all England would consent at the same time to his perverse doctrine. Balle named to them Wycliffe himself as the principal author, and also mentioned Nicholas Hereford, John Aston and Lawrence Bedenam, Masters of Arts. Balle added that if they had not encountered resistance to their plans, they would have destroyed the entire kingdom within two years.

This confession was drawn up in a certain form under a public instrument, as will appear later [the text of the *Fasciculi Zizaniorum* does not in fact revert to this topic and no copy of Ball's supposed 'confession' survives – if it had ever existed at an early date it is inconceivable that it would not have been exploited by contemporary churchmen and chroniclers].

To the general rule that we are constrained to see the peasants of 1381 through the hostile eyes of their opponents, there is only one major exception – a handful of obscure but moving vernacular letters making much use of internal rhyme and couched in the language of late fourteenth-century popular allegory. Six of these letters survive and all owe their preservation to the chance that Thomas Walsingham and Henry Knighton decided to insert copies into their narratives of the great revolt. Such letters were presumably circulating quite widely throughout parts of England in 1381; and it is just possible that the chroniclers may have been correct in seeing them as direct appeals for immediate revolutionary action. This is still the generally accepted view; and according to one recent writer, Ball's letters not only call 'for an armed rising of the people' but 'reveal the mind of a mature political thinker'![1] With all respect for the letters' undeniable fascination, it must be said that these 'dark sayings' (which Walsingham himself was evidently at a loss to understand in any precise terms) have created more problems than they have solved. On this occasion we are confronted with evidence that is intentionally obscure. All attempts to interpret the letters in literal terms have proved less than convincing; and it is, for example, unlikely that 'Hobbe the Robbere' should be identified, as is often done, with Treasurer Robert Hales rather than the common late medieval personification of robbery. It is conceivable that the common refrain, 'for now is tyme' (which occurs in four of the letters copied by Knighton), may – as argued by Professor Cohn[2] – point to a chiliastic element in the great revolt. On the other hand it should be noticed that the recipients of at least one of the letters were urged to 'seketh pees, and holde yow therinne'.

The most cursory reading of the letters proves that all six are textually inter-related and were presumably written either by a close-knit group of writers or (more probably) by one man. If one accepts Walsingham's evidence for the identification of 'John Schep' (or Shepherd, i.e. priest) with John Ball, then it probably does follow that the latter wrote all six letters under various pseudonyms. It is much more certain, despite

[1] R. H. Hilton and H. Fagan, *The English Rising of 1381*, p. 100.
[2] N. Cohn, *The Pursuit of the Millennium*, p. 216.

the chroniclers' suspicions to the contrary, that the names of the recipients of the letters are 'masonic' rather than genuine names of identifiable rebels. More generally, the correspondence reveals two essential characteristics of the author and his audience – a strong sense of personal identification with the ideal of a social brotherhood, and a deeply personal devotion to the most simple and literal truths of the Christian religion. As Professor Skeat suggested long ago, Langland's *Piers the Plowman* (of which the B-text was written about 1377) provides the key to both the precise meaning and the cultural milieu of Ball's correspondence. The latter's references and allusions to *Peres Ploughman* himself and to the visions of *Do-wel* and *Do-bettre* seem deliberate enough; and the letters can only be explained, if at all, when placed within the context of Langland's 'faire felde of folke'. According to Skeat himself, Ball perverted Langland's 'bold words . . . into watchwords of insurgency'.[1] Perhaps so: but it seems likely that Langland's own ideal of 'The kynge and the comune. and kynde witte the thridde/Shope lawe and lewte. eche man to knowe his owne.'[2] was not too far removed from that of the rebels of 1381. More explicitly provocative than the letters of that year are several political poems written during the subsequent period and printed here for purposes of comparison. A number of the themes of 1381 certainly recur. *Hobb* makes another appearance among the Yorkshire partisans of 1392; and their love of 'trewth' and hatred of 'traytors' forms a common bond between the Kentish rebels of 1381 and their successors in 1450 (cf. above, no. 62). Such letters and verses are fragile evidence from which to prove the existence of a powerful radical tradition in late medieval England; but at least they remind us that the king's low-born subjects were not always and inevitably inarticulate.

A. JOHN BALL'S LETTER TO THE ESSEX COMMONS

Walsingham, *Historia Anglicana*, II 33–4; cf. *Chronicon Angliae*, p. 322; Sisam, *Fourteenth Century Verse and Prose*, pp. 160–1 (for a preferable text of the letter itself)

Moreover, he had sent a certain letter, full of obscurities, to the leaders of the commons in Essex, encouraging them to finish

[1] Langland, *Piers the Plowman*, ed. W. W. Skeat (1923 edn.), p. xxx.
[2] Ibid., p. 5 (Prologue, lines 121–2).

what they had begun. Afterwards this letter was found in the tunic of a man who was to be hanged for his share in the disturbances, and it ran as follows: –

'Iohon Schep, som tyme Seynte Marie prest of York, and now of Colchestre, greteth wel Iohan Nameles, and Iohan the Mullere, and Iohon Cartere, and biddeth hem that thei bee war of gyle in borugh, and stondeth togidre in Godes name, and biddeth Peres Ploughman go to his werk, and chastise wel Hobbe the Robbere, and taketh with yow Iohan Trewman, and alle hiis felawes, and no mo, and loke schappe you to on heued, and no mo.

Iohan the Mullere hath ygrounde smal, smal, smal;
The Kynges sone of heuene schal paye for al.
Be war or ye be wo;
Knoweth your freend fro your foo;
Haueth ynow, and seith "Hoo";
And do wel and bettre, and fleth synne,
And seketh pees, and hold you therinne;
And so biddeth Iohan Trewman and alle his felawes.'

John Ball confessed that he had written this letter and sent it to the commons; and he admitted that he had written many others. Therefore, as we have said, he was hanged, drawn and beheaded at St Albans on 15 July in the king's presence; and the f. quarters of his corpse were sent to four cities in the kingdom.

B. THE LETTERS OF JAKKE MYLNER, JAKKE CARTER, JAKKE TREWMAN AND JOHN BALL

Chronicon Henrici Knighton, II 138–40: continued from no. 27 above. Cf. Stow, *Annales* (London, 1631), p. 294; Robbins, *Historical Poems*, p. 54

There were twenty thousand men in this miserable crowd, their leaders being Thomas Baker, the first mover and later the chief leader, Jakke Strawe, Jakke Mylner, Jakke Carter, Jakke Trewman. Jakke Mylner addressed his fellows in this way: –

Jakke Mylner asketh help to turne hys mylne aright. He hath grounden smal smal; the kings sone of heven he schal pay for alle.

Loke thy mylne go aright, with the foure sayles, and the post stande in stedfastnesse. With ryght and with myght, with skyl and with wylle, lat myght helpe ryght, and skyl go before wille and ryght before myght, than goth oure mylne aryght. And if myght go before ryght, and wylle before skylle; than is oure mylne mys adyght.

Jakke Carter

Jakke Carter prayes yowe alle that ye make a gode ende of that ye haue begunnen, and doth wele and ay bettur and bettur, for at the even men heryth the day. For if the ende be wele, than is alle wele. Lat Peres the Plowman my brother duelle at home and dyght us corne, and I will go with yowe and helpe that y may to dyghte youre mete and youre drynke, that ye none fayle; lokke that Hobbe robbyoure be wele chastysed for lesyng of youre grace for ye have gret nede to take God with yowe in alle youre dedes. For now is tyme to be war.

Jakke Trewman

Jakke Trewman doth yow to understande that falsnes and gyle havith regned to long, and trewthe hat bene sette under a lokke, and falsnes regneth in everylk flokke. No man may come trewthe to, bot he syng si dedero. Speke, spende and spede, quoth Jon f Bathon, and therefore synne fareth as wilde flode, trew love is away, that was so gode, and clerkus for welthe worche hem wo. God do bote, for nowye is tyme.

Exemplar of a Letter of John Balle

Jon Balle gretyth yow wele alle and doth yowe to understande, he hath rungen youre belle. Nowe ryght and myght, wylle and skylle. God spede every ydele. Nowe is tyme. Lady helpe to Ihesu thi sone, and thi sone to his fadur, to make a gode ende, in the name of the Trinite of that is begunne amen, amen, pur charite, amen.

First Letter of John Balle

John Balle seynte Marye prist gretes wele alle maner men and byddes hem in the name of the Trinite, Fadur, and Sone and Holy Gost stonde manlyche togedyr in trewthe, and helpez trewthe, and trewthe schal helpe yowe. Now regnith pride in pris, and covetys is hold wys, and leccherye withouten shame and glotonye withouten blame. Envye regnith with tresone, and slouthe is take in grete sesone. God do bote, for nowe is tyme amen.

C. THE SONG OF THE 'YORKSHIRE PARTISANS', 1392

> Powell and Trevelyan, *Peasants' Rising and the Lollards*, pp. 19–20; Robbins, *Historical Poems*, pp. 60–1; cf. Chambers and Daunt, *Book of London English*, p. 276

And the jurors declare that the said John Berwald junior of Cottingham and others composed a certain rhyme in English and had it publicly proclaimed at Beverley on Sunday 21 July, at Hull on the following Sunday [28 July] and at other times in various places within the county of York during the sixteenth year of King Richard II [1392–3]. This rhyme runs as follows:

> In the Countrey hard was wee,
> that in our soken shrewes should be
>   with all forto bake;
> Among the fryers it is so,
> and other orders many mo,
>   whether they slepe or wake.
>
> And yet will ilke-an hel up other
> and meynteyne him als his brother,
>   both in wrong and right;
> And also will we stand and stoure
> mayntayn our neighbour
>   with all our might.

Ilke man may com and goe
among us both to and fro,
   I say sikerly.
but hething will we suffer non-
neither of hobb nor of Jon,
   with what man he be.

For unkind we ware
If we sufferd lesse or mare
   any villan hething,
But it were quit double againe,
and accord, and be full fayne
   to byde our dressyng.

And on that purpose yet we stand:
who-so doth us any wrong
   In what place it fall,
yet he might als weele,
als haue I hap and sel,
   Doe againe us all.

Glossary

soken, *district*; bake, *support*; sikerly, *truly*; hething, *derision*; dressyng, *direction*.

D. A SONG OF FREEDOM, *c.* 1434

Robbins, *Historical Poems*, p. 62

For thou art comen of good blood,
or for art a riche man of good;
For thou art well loued of moo,
and for thou art a yong man al-soo.

Thin ffadere was a bond man,
thin moder curtesye non can.
Euery beste that leuyth now
Is of more fredam than thow!

If thou art pore, than art thou fre.
If thou be riche, than woo is the.
for but thou spendyte well ere thou goo,
thin song for euer is 'well-ay-woo'.

E. 'CRYSTE MAY SEND NOW SYCH A YERE', *c*. 1450

Robbins, *Historical Poems*, pp. 62–3

Anoder yere hit may betyde
This compeny to be ful wyde,
And neuer on-odyr to abyde;
    Criste may send now sych a yere.

Another yere hit may befall
The lest that is withyn this hall
To be more mastur then we all;
    Criste may send now sych a yere.

This lordis that ben wonder grete,
They threton powre men for to bete;
Hyt lendith lytull in hur threte;
    Cryste may send sich a yere.

F. SONG OF THE KENTISH REBELS, 1450

Robbins, *Historical Poems*, p. 63, cf. C. L. Kingsford, *English Historical Literature in the Fifteenth Century* (Oxford, 1913), p. 359, and above, no. 62

God be oure gyde, and then schull we spede.
Who-so-euur say nay, ffalse for ther money reuleth!
Trewth for his tales spolleth!
God seend vs a ffayre day!
a-wey traytours, a-wey!

72 Geoffrey Chaucer and the Peasants' Revolt

Nun's Priest's Tale, lines 4564–4587 of *The Canterbury Tales*, ed. A. W. Pollard in *Works of Geoffrey Chaucer* (London, 1898)

Despite its notoriety and great dramatic qualities, the story of the Peasants' Revolt has received curiously little attention from the more familiar figures in the history of English literature. Most surprisingly, Geoffrey Chaucer – in 1381 on the threshold of the most prolific part of his career as a poet – mentions the insurrection only once and then very indirectly. It is quite probable that Chaucer was living in London during the turbulent days of June 1381, possibly in the apartment over the gate of Aldgate which he leased from the city corporation between 1374 and 1386. Yet his only literary reference to this experience occurs by way of illustration to his 'murie tale of Chaunticleer'. As Chaucer probably wrote the following lines before the end of the decade, they are of some interest in suggesting that the confusion as to the identity of the captain of the rebels was already prevalent in courtly and literary circles at an early date. Like Henry Knighton, Chaucer seems to regard Jack Straw rather than Wat Tyler as the leader of the peasants.

> Now wol I torne to my tale agayn.
> This sely wydwe, and eek hir doghtres two,
> Herden thise hennes crie and maken wo,
> And out at dores stirten they anon,
> And syen the fox toward the grove gon,
> And bar upon his bak the cok away,
> And cryden, 'Out! harrow! and weyl-away!
> Ha! Ha! the fox!' and after hym they ran,
> And eek with staves many another man;
> Ran Colle, oure dogge, and Talbot, and Gerland
> And Malkyn, with a dystaf in hir hand;
> Ran cow and calf, and eek the verray hogges,
> So were they fered for berkynge of the dogges,
> And shoutyng of the men and wommen eek;

They ronne so hem thoughte hir herte breek.
They yolleden, as feendes doon in helle;
The dokes cryden, as men wolde hem quelle;
The gees, for feere, flowen over the trees;
Out of the hyve cam the swarm of bees;
So hydous was the noise, a *benedicitee*!
Certes, he Jakke Straw, and his meynee,
Ne made never shoutes half so shrille,
Whan that they wolden any Flemyng kille,
As thilke day was maad upon the fox.

73 John Gower and the Peasants' Revolt

Vox Clamantis, Book I, lines 880–936; translated by E. W. Stockton, *The Major Latin Works of John Gower* (Seattle, 1962), pp. 69–70

Nothing could stand in sharper contrast to Chaucer's off-hand and somewhat frivolous reference to 'Jakke Strawe and his meynee' than the attitude of his famous contemporary, John Gower. The latter's *Vox Clamantis*, written in highly derivative Latin elegiacs, was already inordinately long (in its final form it is about the length of the *Aeneid*) when Gower decided to add a new first book describing his personal experiences of the Peasants' Revolt. The following extract relates the entry of the peasant mob into London and is representative of the author's monotonous, heavy-handed and extremely pessimistic approach to his theme. 'New Troy' is a familiar name for London and alludes to the famous legend of the foundation of Britain by the Trojan Brutus. Here, as elsewhere, Gower borrows freely from Peter of Riga's versified text of the Bible, the *Aurora*, and from the works of Ovid; but the sustained note of apocalyptic gloom is almost entirely his own. John Gower and not – as Sir Charles Oman suggested – John Ball deserves the title of 'Jeremiah of late fourteenth-century England'.

On my right I then thought I saw New Troy, which was power-
less as a widow. Ordinarily surrounded by walls, it lay exposed
without any wall, and the city gate could not shut its bars. A
thousand wolves and bears approaching with the wolves determined to go out of the woods to the homes of the city. There
was no monstrous thing or species on earth whose fury could
hurt the land but that it came forth and multiplied. Like a shower
scattered by the east wind, some of their furor was at hand on
every side. Then the monsters which previously had lurked in
hiding went out into the open and were received by their companions. The fierce and mighty beast, which used to rage not so
much from fury as from hunger, came out of the woods and
marshes. But it raged more from fury against the wasted city,
which was stunned at the coming of such a strange calamity.
They swore with savage rage in the woods that they would
trample on justice in a mad frenzy by overthrowing all laws. So
great was the number of these slaves of perdition that scarcely any
wall could contain them.

Since madness prompted the goings-on, all restraint was gone,
and the madness plunged into any – and everything forbidden.
Wanting not at all to be held in check, they hurried on of their
own accord so that no one could block the course they had taken
up. Everything was surrendered. We unlocked our doors to the
enemy and faith was kept only in faithless treason. Just as a
spirited war horse snorts and leaps through the sounding air and
remains unaware of the perils closer by, so the fierce peasantry
started out heedless of their perils, and did not visualize their
ultimate death from them. The slavish band, which utter lunacy
possessed, tried to join the hand of victory with theirs. And so the
savage throngs approached the city like the waves of the sea and
entered it by violence. O what a tremendous affair and astonishing
surprise sprang up unexpectedly with the approach of this
calamity! The magnificent and palatial court in the city was
changed and transformed completely into the likeness of a hut.
And fate, which then became most faulty in its judgments,
suddenly turned the meanest huts into palaces.

Behold, it was Thursday, the Festival of Corpus Christi, when madness hemmed in every side of the city. Going ahead of the others, one peasant captain urged them all to follow him. Supported by his many men, he crushed the city, put the citizens to the sword, and burned down the houses. He did not sing out alone, but drew many thousands along with him, and involved them in his nefarious doings. His voice gathered the madmen together, and with a cruel eagerness for slaughter he shouted in the ears of the rabble, 'Burn! Kill!' What had been the Savoy burned fiercely in flames, so that Lancaster did not know which path to take. The Baptist's house, bereft of its master, fell to the sword and was soon ashes because of the flames.[1] Holy buildings burned in wicked fires, and shameless flame was thus mixed with a sacred flame. The astonished priests wept with trembling heart, and fear took away their body's strength.

74 'The Life and Death of Jacke Strawe', 1593

First edition printed by John Danter, London, 1593; *Old English Drama*, Students' Facsimile Edition, 1911, pp. 3-5

Although Shakespeare's *Richard II* makes no explicit reference to the Peasants' Revolt it is not difficult to guess what his attitude to the rebellion would have been. Shakespeare's vicious treatment of Jack Cade in *Henry VI, Part II* leaves no doubt that he would have used the careers of Tyler and his men to illustrate one of his more familiar themes – the fickleness and overweening arrogance of the English commons. A similar view is evident in the short four-act *Life and Death*

[1] An allusion to the destruction of the priory of St John of Jerusalem at Clerkenwell.

of Jacke Strawe, a play designed to demonstrate the dangers of popular
rebellion as well as to glorify William Walworth and hence the city
of London. This play, just possibly written by George Peele, the
dissipated London actor and playwright, has more historical than
literary merit: it was obviously based on a careful reading of the
sixteenth-century London chronicles compiled by Grafton, Holinshed
and then John Stow. But much its most interesting feature is the way
in which the rebels and their grievances are presented with a considerable
degree of sympathy. Like Froissart, and presumably more by accident
than design, the author gives the best lines in the play to John Ball,
whose 'sermon' from the first act is as follows:

Parson Ball

Neighbors, neighbors, the weakest now a dayes goes to the
　　wall,
But marke my words, and follow the counsell of *John Ball*,
England is growne to such a passe of late,
That rich men triumph to see the poore beg at their gate.
But I am able by good scripture before you to proue,
That God doth not this dealing allow nor loue,
But when *Adam* delued, and *Eue* span,
Who was then a Gentleman.
Brethren brethren, it were better to haue this communitie,
Then to haue this difference in degrees:
The landlord his rent, the lawyer his fees.
So quickly the poore mans substance is spent,
But merrily with the world it went,
When men eat berries of the hauthorne tree,
And thou helpe me, Ile helpe thee,
There was no place for surgerie,
And old men knew not vsurie:
Now tis come to a wofull passe,
The Widdow that hath but a pan of brasse,
And scarse a house to hide her head,
Sometimes no penny to buy her bread,
Must pay her Landlord many a groat,
Or twil be puld out of her throat:

Brethren mine so might I thriue,
As I wish not to be aliue,
To see such dealings with extremitie,
The Rich haue all, the poore liue in miserie:
But follow the counsell of *John Ball*,
I promise you I loue yee all:
And make diuision equally,
Of each mans goods indifferently,
And rightly may you follow Armes,
To rid you from these ciuill harmes.

Jacke Straw

Well said Parson so may it bee,
As wee purpose to preferre thee:
Wee will haue all the Rich men displaste,
And all the brauerie of them defaste,
And as rightly as I am *Jacke Straw*,
In spight of all the men of Law,
Make thee Archbishop of Caunterberie,
And Chauncellor of England or Ile die,
How saist thou *Wat*, shall it bee so?

Wat Tyler

I *Jacke Staw*, or else Ile bide many a fowle blow.
It shall be no other but hee,
That thus fauours the Communaltie,
Stay wee no longer prating here,
But let us roundly to this geare,
Tis more than time that we were gone,
Wele be Lords my Maisters euery one.

75 Edmund Burke and the Peasants' Revolt

An Appeal from the New to the Old Whigs; ed. in *Works of Edmund Burke*, Oxford, World's Classics, 1907, v 102–4

Since at least the age of the Elizabethan drama the Peasants' Revolt has never ceased to be a subject of popular entertainment; and the story of Wat Tyler at Smithfield would no doubt have always held its place among the more familiar vignettes of English history because of its inherent dramatic interest. But only in the last decade of the eighteenth century did Tyler begin a flourishing new posthumous career in the role of England's first popular revolutionary leader. Shortly after 1789 a controversy about the aims of Tyler and his fellows developed as a by-product of the great debate on the French Revolution, 'perhaps the most crucial ideological debate ever carried on in English'.[1] In this dispute the great protagonists were Edmund Burke and Thomas Paine, the first writers who attempted to show the relevance of Tyler and Ball to the modern world. It was hardly surprising that Burke should find interesting parallels between the anarchy of 1381 and the alarming activities of the revolutionaries across the Channel. But to be attacked by Burke in the years after 1789 was to ensure sympathy for oneself; and perhaps nothing contributed more to the Peasants' Revolt new *réclame* than Burke's heavy sarcasm at its expense.

When great multitudes act together, under that discipline of nature, I recognise the PEOPLE. I acknowledge something that perhaps equals, and ought always to guide the sovereignty of convention. In all things the voice of this grand chorus of national harmony ought to have a mighty and decisive influence. But when you disturb this harmony; when you break up this beautiful order, this array of truth and nature, as well as of habit and prejudice; when you separate the common sort of men from their proper chieftains so as to form them into an adverse army, I no longer know that venerable object called the people in such a disbanded race of deserters and vagabonds. For a while they may be terrible

[1] T. W. Copeland, *Edmund Burke: Six Essays* (London, 1950), p. 148.

indeed; but in such a manner as wild beasts are terrible. The mind owes to them no sort of submission. They are, as they have always been reputed, rebels. They may lawfully be fought with, and brought under, whenever an advantage offers. Those who attempt by outrage and violence to deprive men of any advantage which they hold under the laws, and to destroy the natural order of life, proclaim war against them.

We have read in history of that furious insurrection of the common people in France called the *Jacquerie*; for this is not the first time that the people have been enlightened into treason, murder and rapine. Its object was to extirpate the gentry. The *Captal de Buche*, a famous soldier of those days, dishonoured the name of a gentleman and of a man by taking, for their cruelties, a cruel vengeance on these deluded wretches: it was, however, his right and his duty to make war upon them, and afterwards in moderation, to bring them to punishment for their rebellion; though in the sense of the French revolution, and of some of our clubs, they were the *people*; and were truly so, if you will call by that appellation *any majority of men told by the head*.

At a time not very remote from the same period (for these humours never have affected one of the nations without some influence on the other) happened several risings of the lower commons in England. These insurgents were certainly the majority of the inhabitants of the counties in which they resided; and Cade, Ket, and Straw, at the head of their national guards, and fomented by certain traitors of high rank, did no more than exert, according to the doctrines of our and the Parisian societies, the sovereign power inherent in the majority.

We call the time of those events a dark age. Indeed we are too indulgent to our own proficiency. The Abbé John Ball understood the rights of man as well as the Abbé Grégoire. That reverend patriarch of sedition, and prototype of our modern preachers, was of opinion with the National Assembly, that all the evils which have fallen upon men had been caused by an ignorance of their 'having been born and continued equal as to their rights.' Had the populace been able to repeat that profound maxim all would have gone perfectly well with them. No tyranny, no vexation, no oppression, no care, no sorrow, could have existed in the world. This would have cured them like a charm for the toothache. But the lowest wretches, in their most ignorant state, were able at all times to talk such stuff; and yet at all times have they suffered many evils and many oppressions, both before and since the republication by the National Assembly of this spell of healing potency and virtue. The enlightened Dr Ball, when he wished to rekindle the lights and fires of his audience on this point, chose for the text the following couplet: –

> When Adam delved and Eve span,
> Who was then the gentleman?

Of this sapient maxim, however, I do not give him for the inventor. It seems to have been handed down by tradition, and had certainly become proverbial; but whether then composed, or only applied, this much must be admitted, that in learning, sense, energy, and comprehensiveness, it is fully equal to all the modern dissertations on the equality of mankind; and it has one advantage over them – that it is in rhyme.

76 Thomas Paine and the Peasants' Revolt

Thomas Paine, *The Rights of Man*, Pt 2, Everyman edition 1915, pp. 236–7

Burke's *Appeal from the New to the Old Whigs*, in which the first part of *The Rights of Man* was said to be scarcely worth 'any other refutation than that of criminal justice', was published in August 1791. Paine, absolutely predictably, accepted the challenge immediately and the second part of the *Rights* appeared as early as February 1792. Despite his sneer that 'I see nothing in Mr Burke's *Appeal* worth taking much notice of', Paine could not resist taking up his cudgel in defence of the rebels of 1381. In a short but influential footnote he overturned the accepted view of the revolt: the barons of Magna Carta are compared unfavourably to the peasants of 1381 and William Walworth, for long the official hero of the great revolt, becomes 'a cowardly assassin'. But a few months after writing these words, Paine had to leave England for ever: and Tyler is still without his monument at Smithfield.

Several of the Court newspapers have of late made frequent mention of Wat Tyler. That his memory should be traduced by Court sycophants and all those who live on the spoil of a public is not to be wondered at. He was, however, the means of checking the rage and injustice of taxation in his time, and the Nation owed much to his valour. The history is concisely this: – In the time of Richard II a poll tax was levied of one shilling per head upon every person, of whatever state or condition, on poor as well as rich, above the age of fifteen years. If any favour was shown in the law it was to the rich rather than to the poor, as no person could be charged more than twenty shillings for himself, family and servants, though ever so numerous, while all other families under the number of twenty were charged per head. Poll taxes have always been odious, but this being also oppressive and unjust, it excited, as it naturally must, universal detestation among the poor and middle classes. The person known by the name of Wat Tyler, whose proper name was Walter, and a tyler by trade, lived at Deptford. The gatherer of the poll tax, on coming to his house demanded tax for one of his daughters, whom Tyler declared was under the age of fifteen. The tax-gatherer insisted on satisfying himself and began an indecent examination of the girl, which, enraging the father, he struck him with a hammer that brought him to the ground, and was the cause of his death.[1]

This circumstance served to bring the discontent to an issue. The inhabitants of the neighbourhood espoused the cause of

[1] This explanation of the outbreak of the rising, derived from John Stow's story of the killing of a tax-collector by John Tyler of Dartford, formed a popular part of the myth of the Peasants' Revolt in the eighteenth century.

Tyler, who in a few days was joined, according to some histories, by upwards of fifty thousand men, and chosen their chief. With this force he marched to London to demand an abolition of the tax and a redress of other grievances. The Court, finding itself in a forlorn condition, and unable to make resistance, agreed, with Richard at its head, to hold a conference with Tyler in Smithfield, making many fair professions, courtier-like, of its dispositions to redress the oppressions. While Richard and Tyler were in conversation on these matters, each being on horseback, Walworth, then Mayor of London, and one of the creatures of the Court, watched an opportunity, and like a cowardly assassin, stabbed Tyler with a dagger, and two or three others falling upon him he was instantly sacrificed.

Tyler appears to have been an intrepid disinterested man with respect to himself. All his proposals made to Richard were on a more just and public ground than those which had been made to John by the Barons, and notwithstanding the sycophancy of historians and men like Mr Burke who seek to gloss over a base action of the Court by traducing Tyler, his fame will outlive their falsehood. If the Barons merited a monument to be erected in Runnymede, Tyler merits one in Smithfield.

77 Robert Southey's 'Wat Tyler'

Southey's *Wat Tyler: A Dramatic Poem*, published by W. T. Sherwin (London, 1817) pp. 14–15

One of Thomas Paine's early converts was the radical young Robert Southey, capable as late as 1795 of apostrophizing the author of *The Rights of Man* as 'hireless Priest of Liberty! unbought teacher of the poor!'[1] Under Paine's influence the twenty-year old Southey wrote his dramatic poem *Wat Tyler* at break-neck speed (he is said to have completed the work in three days) while at Oxford in the summer of 1794. Then in his most Jacobin phase and an ardent admirer of Robespierre, the young poet found the theme of the Peasants' Revolt irresistible – not least because he believed that Wat Tyler was one of his ancestors. Southey then put the work aside and it was only rescued from oblivion by his political opponents over twenty years later; a small group of radicals and dissenters published the poem in 1817 in a not unsuccessful attempt to embarrass the now staunchly conservative Poet Laureate. The Spa Fields riots of 1816 had revived interest in the seizure of London by the rebels of 1381; and several radicals and Chartists of the early nineteenth century were proud to evoke the names of their medieval predecessors, some even winning notoriety as the 'Wat Tyler Brigade'. After enjoying a short-lived but intense *succès de scandale*, Southey's *Wat Tyler* disappeared from view. But it deserves to be remembered as a work quite as revolutionary in its tone as the more famous political poems of Byron and Shelley. The following representative passage from the last scene of the play shows that no one has ever made John Ball seem a more dangerous preacher of sedition to the modern world than the young Southey.

Sir John Tresilian

Did you not tell the mob they were oppress'd,
And preach upon the equality of man;
With evil intent thereby to stir them up
To tumult and rebellion?

John Ball

That I told them
That all mankind are equal, is most true;
Ye came as helpless infants to the world:
Ye feel alike the infirmities of nature;
And at last moulder into common clay.

[1] G. Carnall, *Robert Southey and his Age* (Oxford, 1960), p. 45.

Why then these vain distinctions! – bears not the earth
Food in abundance? – must your granaries
O'erflow with plenty, while the poor man starves?
Sir Judge, why sit you there clad in your furs?
Why are your cellars stor'd with choicest wines?
Your larders hung with dainties, while your vassal,
As virtuous, and as able too by nature,
Tho' by your selfish tyranny depriv'd
Of mind's improvement, shivers in his rags,
And starves amid the plenty he creates.
I have said this is wrong, and I repeat it –
And there will be a time when this great truth
Shall be confess'd – be felt by all mankind.
The electric truth shall run from man to man,
And the blood-cemented pyramid of greatness
Shall fall before the flash! . . .

The truth, which all my life I have divulg'd
And am now doom'd in torment to expire for,
Shall still survive – the destin'd hour must come,
When it shall blaze with sun-surpassing splendor,
And the dark mists of prejudice and falsehood
Fade in its strong effulgence. Flattery's incense
No more shall shadow round the gore-dyed throne;
That altar of oppression, fed with rites,
More savage than the Priests of Moloch taught,
Shall be consumed amid the fire of Justice;
The ray of truth shall emanate around,
And the whole world be lighted!

78 Engels on the Peasant Risings of the Middle Ages

F. Engels, *The Peasant War in Germany*, Moscow, 1956, pp. 55–60

Engels wrote *The Peasant War in Germany* in the summer of 1850, during that period of his partnership with Marx when the two men – in the wake of the collapse of the revolutions of 1848 – were applying their discovery of economic motivation to the interpretation of the past rather than the present. Edmund Wilson's comment on Marx's own *The Eighteenth Brumaire* is equally applicable to Engels's literally sensational work: 'Nowhere perhaps in the history of thought is the reader so made to feel the excitement of a new intellectual discovery'.[1] The fact that Engels knew little, if any, medieval English history and that his knowledge of the German Peasants' War of 1524–6 was almost exclusively derived from the book published by Wilhelm Zimmermann in 1841 detracts not at all from the novelty of his interpretation. Engels's arguments are too densely packed and at times too self-contradictory to be analysed here; but the reader will soon appreciate that the problems he raised are the problems still. By a profound if puzzling paradox, the rebellious peasant of the middle ages was only capable of 'communism nurtured by fantasy'. He could point to the future but never reach it.

The revolutionary opposition to feudalism was alive all down the Middle Ages. It took the shape of mysticism, open heresy, or armed insurrection, all depending on the conditions of the time. As for mysticism, it is well known how much sixteenth-century reformers depended on it. Münzer himself was largely indebted to it. The heresies gave expression partly to the reaction of the patriarchal Alpine shepherds against the feudalism advancing upon them (Waldenses), partly to the opposition to feudalism of the towns that had outgrown it (the Albigenses, Arnold of Brescia, etc.), and partly to direct peasant insurrections (John Ball,

[1] E. Wilson, *To the Finland Station* (original English edition, n.d.), p. 201.

the Hungarian teacher in Picardy, etc.). We can here leave aside the patriarchal heresy of the Waldenses, and the Swiss insurrection, which was, in form and content, a reactionary, purely local attempt at stemming the tide of history. In the other two forms of medieval heresy we find the twelfth-century precursors of the great antithesis between the burgher and peasant-plebeian oppositions, which caused the defeat of the Peasant War. This antithesis is evident all down the later Middle Ages.

The town heresies – and those are the actual official heresies of the Middle Ages – were turned primarily against the clergy, whose wealth and political importance they attacked. Just as the present-day bourgeoisie demands a *gouvernement à bon marché* (cheap government), the medieval burghers chiefly demanded an *église à bon marché* (cheap church). Reactionary in form, like any heresy that sees only degeneration in the further development of church and dogma, the burgher heresy demanded the revival of the simple early Christian Church constitution and abolition of exclusive priesthood. This cheap arrangement would eliminate monks, prelates, and the Roman court, or, in short, everything in the Church that was expensive. The towns, republics themselves, albeit under the protection of monarchs, first enunciated in general terms through their attacks upon Papacy that a republic was the normal form of bourgeois rule. Their hostility to a number of dogmas and church laws is explained partly by the foregoing, and partly by their living conditions. Their bitter opposition to celibacy, for instance, has never been better explained than by Boccaccio. Arnold of Brescia in Italy and Germany, the Albigenses in Southern France, John Wycliffe in England, Hus and the Calixtines in Bohemia, were the principal representatives of this trend. The towns were then already a recognised Estate sufficiently capable of fighting lay feudalism and its privileges either by force of arms or in the Estate assemblies, and that explains quite simply why the opposition to feudalism appeared only as an opposition to *religious* feudalism.

We also find both in Southern France and in England and Bohemia, that most of the lesser nobility joined the towns in their struggle against the clergy, and in their heresies – a phenomenon explained by the dependence of the lesser nobility upon the towns, and by their community of interests as opposed to the princes and prelates. We shall encounter the same thing in the Peasant War.

The heresy that lent direct expression to peasant and plebeian demands, and was almost invariably bound up with an insurrection, was of a totally different nature. Though it shared all the demands of burgher heresy with regard to the clergy, the Papacy, and revival of the early Christian Church constitution, it also went infinitely further. It demanded the restoration of early Christian equality among members of the community, and the recognition of this equality as a prescript for the burgher world as well. It drew on the 'equality of the children of God' to conclude civil equality, and partly even equality of property. Equality of nobleman and peasant, of patrician and privileged burgher, and the plebeian, abolition of compulsory labour, ground rents, taxes, privileges, and at least the most crying differences in property – those were demands advanced with more or less determination as natural implications of the early Christian doctrine. At the time when feudalism was at its zenith there was little to choose between this peasant–plebeian heresy, among the Albigenses, for example, and the burgher opposition, but in the fourteenth and fifteenth centuries it developed into a clearly defined party opinion and usually took an independent stand alongside the heresy of the burghers. That was the case with John Ball, preacher of Wat Tyler's Rebellion in England, alongside the Wycliffe movement, and with the Taborites alongside the Calixtines in Bohemia. The Taborites even showed a republican trend under a theocratic cloak, a view further developed by representatives of the plebeians in Germany in the fifteenth and early sixteenth century.

The fanaticism of mystically-minded sects, of the Flagellants and Lollards, etc., which continued the revolutionary tradition in times of suppression, rallied round this form of heresy.

At that time the plebeians were the only class that stood outside the existing official society. They stood outside both the feudal,

and burgher associations. They had neither privileges nor property; they did not even have the kind of property the peasant
or petty burgher had, weighed down as it was with burdensome
taxes. They were unpropertied and rightless in every respect;
their living conditions never even brought them into direct contact with the existing institutions, which ignored them completely. They were a living symptom of the decay of the feudal
and guild–burgher society, and at the same time the first precursors of the modern bourgeois society.

This explains why the plebeian opposition even then could not
stop at fighting only feudalism and the privileged burghers; why,
in fantasy at least, it reached beyond the then scarcely dawning
modern bourgeois society; why, an absolutely propertyless faction, it questioned the institutions, views and conceptions common to all societies based on class antagonisms. In this respect, the
chiliastic dream-visions of early Christianity offered a very
convenient starting point. On the other hand, this sally beyond
both the present and even the future could be nothing but violent
and fantastic, and of necessity fell back into the narrow limits set
by the contemporary situation. The attack on private property,
the demand for common ownership was bound to resolve into a
primitive organisation of charity; vague Christian equality could
at best resolve into civic 'equality before the law'; elimination of
all authorities finally culminates in the establishment of republican
governments elected by the people. The anticipation of communism nurtured by fantasy became in reality an anticipation of
modern bourgeois conditions.

Morris, *Selected Works*, ed. G. D. H. Cole (Nonesuch Press, 1948), pp. 264–5

Despite the greater insight and accuracy of Engels's analysis of the medieval peasant revolt, it seems most appropriate to let the last words on the insurrection of 1381 be those of William Morris – an English idealist and socialist who was not an orthodox Marxist. *The Dream of John Ball*, first published in 1888, is deservedly less famous than the author's slightly later prose romance, *News form Nowhere*. But it preaches the same idiosyncratic and somewhat ambiguous message. Morris's 'dream' is that of an escapist as well as a visionary; and the work is marred by a common Victorian sentimentality of approach to the middle ages as well as an urgent personal desire to 'Forget six counties overhung with smoke'. For these reasons what Morris tells John Ball is more interesting (as in this extract) than what Ball says to Morris. And perhaps Morris voiced the aspirations of the rebels of 1381 more exactly than he knew himself; for they too were capable of believing that 'At the even men heryth the day'.

'Only this may I tell thee,' said I; 'to thee, when thou didst try to conceive of them, the ways of the days to come seemed follies scarce to be thought of; yet shall they come to be familiar things, and an order by which every man liveth, ill as he liveth, so that men shall deem of them, that thus it hath been since the beginning of the world, and that thus it shall be while the world endureth; and in this wise so shall they be thought of a long while; and the complaint of the poor the rich man shall heed, even as much and no more as he who lieth in pleasure under the lime-trees in the summer heedeth the murmur of his toiling bees. Yet in time shall this also grow old, and doubt shall creep in, because men shall scarce be able to live by that order, and the complaint of the poor shall be hearkened, no longer as a tale not utterly grievous, but as a threat of ruin, and a fear. Then shall these things, which to thee seem follies, and to the men between thee and me mere wisdom and the bond of stability, seem follies once again; yet, whereas men have so long lived by them, they shall cling to them yet from blindness and from fear; and those that see, and that have thus much conquered fear that they are furthering the real time that cometh and not the dream that faileth, these men shall the blind and the fearful mock and missay, and torment and murder: and great and grievous shall be the strife in those days, and many the failures of the wise, and too oft sore shall be the despair of the valiant; and back-sliding, and doubt, and contest between friends and fellows lacking time in the hubbub to understand each other, shall grieve many hearts and hinder the Host of the Fellowship: yet shall all bring about the end, till thy deeming of folly and ours shall be one, and thy hope and our hope; and then – the Day will have come.'

Select Bibliography

1 ORIGINAL SOURCES IN THE PUBLIC RECORD OFFICE CITED IN THE TEXT

C.54	—	Close Rolls
C.60	—	Fine Rolls
C.66	—	Patent Rolls
KB.9	—	King's Bench, Ancient Indictments
KB.27	—	King's Bench, *Coram Rege* Rolls
SC.8	—	Ancient Petitions
Chester 25	—	Chester Indictment Rolls

2 CHRONICLES AND LITERARY SOURCES

Anonimalle Chronicle, 1333 to 1381, ed. V. H. Galbraith (Manchester, 1927).

Brinton, *Bishop of Rochester (1373–89), The Sermons of Thomas*, ed. M. A. Devlin (Camden Third Series, 1954).

Eulogium Historiarum sive Temporis, ed. F. S. Haydon, 3 vols (Rolls Series, 1858–63).

Fasciculi Zizaniorum Magistri Johannis Wyclif cum tritico, ed. W. W. Shirley (Rolls Series, 1858).

Froissart, *Chroniques de J.*, x (1380–2), ed. G. Raynaud (Société de l'Histoire de France, Paris, 1897).

Froissart, *The Chronicles of*, translated Lord Berners, ed. G. C. Macaulay (London, 1895).

Froissart, *Chronicles*, selected, translated and ed. G. Brereton (Penguin ed., 1968).

Gower, *The Complete Works of John*, ed. G. C. Macaulay, 4 vols (Oxford, 1899–1902).

Gower, *John, The Major Latin Works of*, trans E. W. Stockton (Seattle, 1962).

Knighton, Henry, *Chronicon*, ed. J. R. Lumby, 2 vols (Rolls Series, 1889–95).

Langland, W., *The Vision of William concerning Piers the Plowman*, ed. W. W. Skeat, 2 vols (Oxford, 1886).

Meaux, *Chronicon monasterii de*, ed. E. A. Bond, 3 vols (Rolls Series, 1866–8).

Polychronicon Ranulphi Higden, ed. C. Babington and J. R. Lumby, 9 vols (Rolls Series, 1865–86). For the chronicle of the 'monk of Westminster', see vol. IX.

Robbins, R. H. ed., *Historical Poems of the XIVth and XVth Centuries* (New York, 1959).

Sisam, K., ed., *Fourteenth Century Verse and Prose* (Oxford, 1921).

Stow, John, *Annales*, ed. E. Howes (London, 1631).

Vita Ricardi Secundi, ed. T. Hearne (Oxford, 1729).

Walsingham, Thomas, *Chronicon Angliae*, ed. E. M. Thompson (Rolls Series, 1874).

——, *Gesta Abbatum*, ed. H. T. Riley, 3 vols (Rolls Series, 1867–9).

——, *Historia Anglicana*, ed. H. T. Riley, 2 vols (Rolls Series, 1863–4).

——, *Ypodigma Neustriae*, ed. H. T. Riley (Rolls Series, 1876).

Wright, T., ed., *Political Poems and Songs*, 2 vols (Rolls Series, 1859–61).

Wyclif, Iohannis, *Tractatus de Blasphemia*, ed. M. H. Dziewicki (Wyclif Society, 1893).

3 RECORD AND OTHER SOURCES

Calendar of Close Rolls, 1327–99 (Stationery Office, 1896–1927).

Calendar of Fine Rolls, 1307–99 (Stationery Office, 1912–29).

Calendar of Letter Books of the City of London (C. to H.) ed. R. R. Sharpe (London, 1901–7).

Calendar of Patent Rolls, 1327–99 (Stationery Office, 1891–1916).

Chaucer's World, compiled by E. Rickert (New York, 1948).

Documents Illustrating. . . . Chapters of the English Black Monks, 1215–1540 ed. W. A. Pantin, 3 vols (Camden Third Ser., 1931–7).

Flaherty, W. E., 'The Great Rebellion in Kent of 1381 illustrated from the Public Records', *Archaeologia Cantiana*, III (1860) 65–96.

——, 'Sequel to the Great Rebellion in Kent of 1381', *Archaeologia Cantiana*, IV (1861) 67–86.

Flemming, J. H., *England under the Lancastrians* (University of London Intermediate Source-Books, no. 3, 1921).

Flower, C. T., 'The Beverley Town Riots, 1381–2', *Transactions of Royal Historical Society*, NS, XIX (1905) 79–99.

Hughes, D., *Illustrations of Chaucer's England* (University of London Intermediate Source-Books, no. 1, 1918).

London English, A Book of, ed. R. W. Chambers and M. Daunt (Oxford, 1931).

Memorials of London and London Life, ed. H. T. Riley (London, 1868).

Munimenta Gildhallae Londoniensis, ed. H. T. Riley, 3 vols (Rolls Series, 1859–62).

Palmer, W. M., 'Records of the Villein Insurrection in Cambridgeshire', *The East Anglian*, NS, VI (1895–6).

Palmer, W. M. and Saunders, H. W., 'The Peasant Revolt of 1381 as it affected the Villages of Cambridgeshire', *Documents relating to Cambridgeshire Villages* (Cambridge 1926), pp. 17–36.

Powell, E. and Trevelyan, G. M., *The Peasants' Rising and the Lollards* (London, 1899).

Réville, A., *Le Soulèvement des Travailleurs d'Angleterre en 1381*, Appendices (Paris, 1898).

Rotuli Parliamentorum: Edward I–Henry VII, 6 vols (London, 1783).

Rymer's *Foedera* (3rd. edn, The Hague, 1737–45).

Some Sessions of the Peace in Lincolnshire, 1360–75, ed. R. Sillem (Lincoln Record Society, XXX, 1937).

Some Sessions of the Peace in Lincolnshire, 1381–96, ed. E. G. Kimball (Lincoln Record Society, XLIX, LVI; 1955, 1962).

Sparvil-Bayly, J. A., 'Essex in Insurrection, 1381', *Transactions of Essex Archaeological Society*, NS, I (Colchester, 1878) 205–19.

Statutes of the Realm, I (London 1810).

Wilkins, D., *Concilia Magnae Britanniae et Hiberniae*, 4 vols (London, 1737).

York Memorandum Book, ed. M. Sellers, 2 vols (Surtees Society, 1912–15).

4 SECONDARY WORKS RELATING TO 1381

Armitage-Smith, S., *John of Gaunt* (London, 1904).

Aston, M., *Thomas Arundel: a study of church life in the reign of Richard II* (Oxford, 1967).

Bird, R., *The Turbulent London of Richard II* (London, 1949).

Bird, W. H. B., 'The Peasant Rising of 1381; the King's Itinerary', *English Historical Review*, XXXI (1916) 124–6.

Clarke, M. V., 'Nephandus Culpeper de Cancia nominatus Jak Strawe', in *Fourteenth Century Studies* (Oxford, 1937) pp. 95–7.

Clayton, J., *Leaders of the People* (London, 1910).

Coulton, G. G., 'The Peasants' Revolt', in *Great Events in History*, ed. G. R. Stirling-Taylor (London, 1934), pp. 197–274.

Cox, J. C., *A Poll-Tax Roll of the East Riding with some account of the Peasant revolt of 1381* (privately printed at Hull, n.d.).

Dahmus, J., *The Prosecution of John Wycliff* (New Haven, 1952).

——, *William Courtenay, Archbishop of Canterbury, 1381–96* (Pennsylvania U.P., 1966).

Darby, H. C. and Miller, E., 'Political History', *Victoria County History of Cambridge*, II (1948) 377–419.

Galbraith, V. H., *The St Albans Chronicle 1406–1420* (Oxford, 1937).

——, 'Thomas Walsingham and the St Albans Chronicle', *English Historical Review*, XLVII (1932) 12–29.

——, 'The Chronicle of Henry Knighton', *Fritz Saxl Memorial Essays* (London, 1957), pp. 136–45.

Harvey, B. F., 'Draft Letters Patent of Manumission and Pardon for the men of Somerset in 1381', *English Historical Review*, LXXX (1965) 89–91.

Hilton, R. H. and Fagan, H., *The English Rising of 1381* (London, 1950).

Hilton, R. H., 'Peasant Movements in England before 1381', reprinted from *Economic History Review*, 2nd ser., II (1949) in *Essays in Economic History*, II (1962), ed. E. M. Carus-Wilson, pp. 73–90.

Honeybourne, M. B., *Sketch Map of London under Richard II* (London Topographical Society's Publications, no. 93, 1960).

Kriehn, George, 'Studies in the Sources of the Social Revolt in 1381', *American Historical Review*, VII (1901–2) 254–85, 458–84.

Lindsay, P. and Groves, R. *The Peasants' Revolt, 1381* (London, 1950).

Lipson, E., *The Economic History of England*, I (9th edn., London, 1947).

Lobel, M. D., *The Borough of Bury St Edmunds* (Oxford, 1935).

McKisack, M., *The Fourteenth Century, 1307–1399* (Oxford, 1959).

Maurice, C. E., *Lives of English Popular Leaders in the Middle Ages: No. 2 – Tyler, Ball and Oldcastle* (London, 1875).

Oman, C., *The Great Revolt of 1381* (Oxford, 1906; new edn., 1969).

Petit-Dutaillis, C., 'Causes and General Characteristics of the Rising of 1381', in *Studies and Notes supplementary to Stubbs' Constitutional History*, II (Manchester, 1915).

Petrushevsky, D., *Vozstanie Vota Tailera* [The Uprising of Wat Tyler] (Moscow, 1901):reviewed by A. Savine in *English Historical Review*, XVII (1902) 780–2.

Pollard, A. F., 'The Authorship and Value of the "Anonimalle" Chronicle', *English Historical Review*, LIII (1938) 577–605.

Powell, E., *The Rising in East Anglia in 1381* (Cambridge, 1896).

Putnam, B. H., *The Enforcement of the Statute of Labourers, 1349–1359* (New York, 1908).

Putnam, B. H., *Proceedings before the Justices of the Peace in the Fourteenth and Fifteenth Centuries* (Ames Foundation, 1938).

Ramsay, J., *The Genesis of Lancaster, 1307–99* (Oxford, 1913).

Réville, A., *Le Soulèvement des Travailleurs d'Angleterre en 1381* (Paris, 1898).

Round, J. H., (Survey of Essex rising) in *Victoria County History of Essex*, II (1907) 213–16.

Russell, P. E., *The English Intervention in Spain and Portugal in the time of Edward III and Richard II* (Oxford, 1955).

Steel, A., *Richard II* (Cambridge, 1941).

Stubbs, W., *The Constitutional History of England*, II (Oxford, 1875).

Tait, J., review of Oman's *Great Revolt of 1381*, *English Historical Review*, XXII (1907) 161–4.

Taylor, J., *The Universal Chronicle of Ranulf Higden* (Oxford, 1966).

Tout, T. F., *Chapters in the Administrative History of Mediaeval England*, III (Manchester, 1928).

Trevelyan, G. M., *England in the Age of Wycliffe* (new edn., London, 1909).

Wallon, H., *Richard II*, 2 vols (Paris, 1864).

Warren, W. L., 'The Peasants' Revolt of 1381', reprinted from *History Today*, XII–XIII (1962–3) in *English Society and Government in the Fifteenth Century*, ed. C. M. D. Crowder (Edinburgh, 1967), pp. 41–70.

Wilkinson, B., 'The Peasants' Revolt of 1381', *Speculum*, XV (1940) 12–35.

Workman, H. B., *John Wyclif*, 2 vols (Oxford, 1926).

5 THE PEASANTS' REVOLT IN LATER ENGLISH LITERATURE

Cleveland, John, *The Rustick Rampant, or rurall anarchy affronting monarchy; in the insurrection of Wat Tyler:* an edition of *The Idol of the Clownes* (London, 1658).

Jacke Strawe, The Life and Death of: a play in four acts, first printed at London by John Danter, 1593 (*Old English Drama*, Students' Facsimile Edition, 1911).

Just Reward of Rebels, The, or the life and death of Jacke Straw and Wat Tyler (London, 1642).

Morris, William, *A Dream of John Ball*: a romance first published in 1888 (Nonesuch Press ed., 1948).

Southey, Robert, *Wat Tyler, A Dramatic Poem: written in 1794* (printed by W. T. Sherwin, Fleet Street, London, 1817).

Wat Tyler and Jacke Straw, or the Mob Reformers: a dramatic entertainment: in three acts, in verse and prose (London, 1730).

Wat Tyler and Jacke Straw, The History of: a chap-book (London, 1750); and many later editions.

6 THE SOCIAL AND ECONOMIC BACKGROUND
(A short selection from a voluminous literature)

Aston, M. E., 'Lollardy and Sedition, 1381–1431', *Past and Present*, no. 17 (1960), pp. 1–44.

Bean, J. M. W., 'Plague, Population and Economic Decline in the Later Middle Ages', *Econ. Hist. Review*, 2nd ser., xv (1962–3) 423–37.

Beresford, M. W., *The Lost Villages of England* (Lutterworth, 1954).

Beresford, M. W. and St Joseph, J. K. S., *Medieval England: an Aerial Survey* (Cambridge, 1958).

Beresford, M. W., *Lay Subsidies and Poll Taxes* (Phillimores, 1963).

Bloch, M., *Les Caractères Originaux de l'histoire rurale française* (new ed., Paris, 1952).

Bridbury, A. R., *Economic Growth: England in the Later Middle Ages* (London, 1962).

Brooke, C. N. L., and Postan, M. M., eds, *Carte Nativorum: A Peterborough Abbey Cartulary of the Fourteenth Century* (Northants Record Society, xx, 1960).

Cambridge Economic History of Europe, i, *The Agrarian Life of the Middle Ages*, ed. M. M. Postan (2nd ed., Cambridge, 1966).

Carus-Wilson, E. M., *Medieval Merchant Venturers* (London, 1954).

Carus-Wilson, E. M., and Coleman, D., *England's Export Trade 1275–1547* (Oxford, 1963).

Cazelles, R., 'Les mouvements révolutionnaires du milieu du XIVe siècle et le cycle de l'action politique', *Revue Historique*, ccxxviii (1962) 279–312.

Cohn, N., *The Pursuit of the Millennium* (London, 1957).

Coulton, G. G., *The Medieval Village* (Cambridge, 1925).

Davenport, F. G., *The Economic Development of a Norfolk Manor 1086–1565* (Cambridge, 1906).

Dobb, M., *Studies in the Development of Capitalism* (London, 1946).

Du Boulay, F. R. H., *The Lordship of Canterbury* (London, 1966).

Duby, G., *L'Économie Rurale et la Vie des Campagnes dans l'Occident Médiéval*, 2 vols (Paris, 1962).

Dyer, C., 'A Redistribution of Incomes in Fifteenth-century England?', *Past and Present*, no. 39 (1968), pp. 11–33.

Fletcher, A., *Tudor Rebellions* (Seminar Studies in History; London, 1968).

Fourquin, G., *Les Campagnes de la Region Parisienne à la fin du Moyen Age* (Paris, 1964).

Franz, G., *Quellen zur Geschichte des Bauernkrieges* (Munich, 1963).

Graus, F., 'The Late Medieval Poor in Town and Countryside', reprinted in *Change in Medieval Society*, ed. S. Thrupp (New York, 1964) pp. 314–24.

——, 'Social Utopias in the Middle Ages', *Past and Present*, no. 38 (1967), pp. 3–19.

Harvey, B. F., 'The Population Trend in England between 1300 and 1348', *Trans. of Royal Hist Soc.*, 5th ser., XVI (1966) 23–42.

Heers, J., *L'Occident aux XIV et XV siècles* (Paris, 1963).

Hilton, R. H., *A Medieval Society: The West Midlands at the end of the Thirteenth Century* (London, 1966).

——, *The Economic Development of some Leicestershire Estates in the fourteenth and fifteenth centuries* (Oxford, 1947).

——, 'A Thirteenth-century Poem on Disputed Villein Services', *Eng. Hist. Rev.* LVI (1941) 90–97.

——, 'Freedom and Villeinage in England', *Past and Present* no. 31 (1965), pp. 3–19.

——, *The Decline of Serfdom in Medieval England* (Economic History Society, London, 1969).

Holmes, G. A., *The Estates of the Higher Nobility in Fourteenth Century England* (Cambridge, 1957).

Holt, J. C., 'The Origins and Audience of the Ballads of Robin Hood', *Past and Present* no. 18 (1960), pp. 89–110.

Homans, G. C., *English Villagers of the Thirteenth Century* (Boston, 1941).

Hoskins, W. G., *The Midland Peasant* (London, 1957).

——, *Provincial England* (London, 1963).

Jusserand, J. J., *English Wayfaring Life in the Middle Ages* (London, 1889).

Keen, M., *The Outlaws of Medieval Legend* (London, 1961).

Koenigsberger, H. G., 'The Reformation and Social Revolution', in *The Reformation Crisis*, ed. J. Hurstfield (London, 1965).

Kosminsky, E. A., *Studies in the Agrarian History of England in the Thirteenth Century* (Oxford, 1956).

——, 'The Evolution of Feudal Rent in England from the XIth to XVth Centuries', *Past and Present*, no. 7 (1955), pp. 12–36.

Levett, A. E., *Studies in Manorial History* (Oxford, 1938).

Maitland, F. W., 'The History of a Cambridgeshire Manor', *Collected Papers*, II (Cambridge, 1911) 366–402.

Miller, E., 'The English Economy in the Thirteenth Century', *Past and Present*, no. 28 (1964), pp. 21–40.

Morton, A. L., *The English Utopia* (London, 1952).

Oman, C. W. C., 'The German Peasant War of 1525', *English Historical Review*, V (1890) 65–94.

Owst, G. R., *Preaching in Medieval England* (Cambridge, 1926).

——, *Literature and Pulpit in Medieval England* (Cambridge, 1933).

Pantin, W. A., *The English Church in the Fourteenth Century* (Cambridge 1955).

Perroy, E., 'A l'Origine d'une Économie Contractée. Les crises du XIV siècle', *Annales, ESC*, IV (1949), pp. 167–82.

Pirenne, H., *Le Soulèvement de la Flandre Maritime de 1323–1328* (Brussels, 1900).

Postan, M. M., 'The Chronology of Labour Services', *Trans. Royal Hist. Soc.*, 4th ser. XX (1937) 169–93.

——, 'Some Economic Evidence of Declining Population in the later Middle Ages', *Econ. Hist. Rev.*, 2nd ser., II (1950) 221–46.

——, 'The Costs of the Hundred Years' War', *Past and Present*, no. 27 (1964), pp. 34–53.

Raftis, J. A., *Tenure and Mobility: Studies in the Social History of the Medieval English Village* (Toronto, 1964).

Ritchie (*née* Kenyon), N., 'Labour, Conditions in Essex in the reign of Richard II', reprinted from *Economic History Review*, IV (1934) in *Essays in Economic History*, II (1962), ed. E. M. Carus-Wilson, pp. 91–111.

Rosenkranz, A., *Der Bundschuh, 1493–1517*, 2 vols (Heidelberg, 1927).

Russell, J. C., *British Medieval Population* (Albuquerque, 1948).

——, 'Recent Advances in Medieval Demography', *Speculum*, XL (1965), pp. 84–101.

Saltmarsh, J., 'Plague and Economic Decline in England in the later Middle Ages', *Cambridge Historical Journal*, VII (1941–3) 23–41.

Slicher van Bath, B. H., *The Agrarian History of Western Europe*, trans O. Ordish (London, 1963).

Thirsk, J., 'The Common Fields', *Past and Present*, no. 29 (1964), pp. 3–25.

Thompson, A. H., 'The Pestilences of the Fourteenth Century in the Diocese of York', *Archaeological Journal*, LXXI (1914) 97–154.

Thrupp, S. L., *The Merchant Class of Medieval London* (Chicago, 1948).

Titow, J. Z., *English Rural Society 1200–1350* (London, 1969).

Turner, R. E., 'Economic Discontent in Medieval Western Europe', *Journal of Economic History*, supplement 8 (1948).

Vinogradoff, P., *Villainage in England* (Oxford, 1892).

Watts, D. G., 'A Model for the Early Fourteenth Century', *Econ. Hist. Rev.*, 2nd Ser., XX (1967) 543–7.

Ziegler, P., *The Black Death* (London, 1969).

Index